Walter Charles Metcalfe

A book of Knights banneret

Walter Charles Metcalfe

A book of Knights banneret

ISBN/EAN: 9783337279936

Printed in Europe, USA, Canada, Australia, Japan

Cover: Foto ©Andreas Hilbeck / pixelio.de

More available books at **www.hansebooks.com**

A Book

OF

Knights Banneret, Knights of the Bath, and Knights Bachelor

MADE

BETWEEN THE FOURTH YEAR OF KING HENRY VI.
AND THE RESTORATION OF KING CHARLES II.,

With the Arms given in Cotton MS. Claudius, from 1 King Henry VIII.
to 28 Queen Elizabeth,

AND

Knights made in Ireland

BETWEEN THE YEARS 1566 AND 1698,

TOGETHER WITH

An Index of Names.

BY

WALTER C. METCALFE, F.S.A.

LONDON:
MITCHELL AND HUGHES, 140 WARDOUR STREET, W.
1885.

Preface.

THIS is an attempt to give, in a convenient form, a Book of Reference to Knights made during the periods covered by the Titlepage.

It has been compiled from the most authentic Records available for the purpose, such as the Cotton, Harleian, and Lansdowne MSS.; Hall's Chronicle; Stow's Survey of London; Sir H. A. Nicolas's Orders of Knighthood; the printed books by Philipot and Walkley on the reigns of James I. and Charles I.; and other authorities referred to throughout the Work.

No attempt has been made to annotate further than by way of explaining discrepancies and correcting mistakes; my object has been rather to provide a book for present use, than to delay its production for possibly a lifetime, by the accumulation of genealogical and other notes, the extent of which no one could foresee. *Bis Dat Qui Citò Dat.*

I have endeavoured, by all the means in my power, to render the book complete and accurate, and hope it may prove of some service to those who consult its pages, especially with the aid of the carefully-prepared Index.

WALTER C. METCALFE.

10 LUPUS STREET, S.W.
1st May, 1885.

Table of Contents.

A Book of

Knights Banneret, Knights of the Bath, and Knights Bachelor made between the years 1426 and 1660.

Knights made between 4 King Henry VI., 1426, and the accession of King Henry VII., 1485.

(Cotton MS., Claudius, c. iii., fol. 61–67.)

1426.

After the battell of Vernoill in Perche, the Duke of Bedford came over into England, and on Whitsonday this same yere, Anno 4 Henry VI., at Leycester, he dubbed **Kinge Henry** Knight, and forthwith the sayd Kinge Henry the Sixt dubbed all these Knightes whose names follow, viz. :

Richard, Duke of York.
. . . . the sonne and heire to the **Duke of Norfolk.**
The Erle of Oxford.
The Erle of Westmerland.
Henry, sonne and heire to the **Erle of Northumberland.**
Henry, the sonne and heire to the **Erle of Ormond.**
The Lord Roos.
James Butler.
The Lord Maltravers.
Henry Grey of Tankervill.
Will'm Nevill, beinge Lord Faucon-berge.
George Nevill, Lord Latymer.
The Lord Welles.
The Lord Berkeley.   [Talbot.
The sonne and heire to the **Lord Rauf Grey of Werke.**
Robert Feere.

Richard Grey.
Edmond Hungerford.
Robert Wingfeld.
John Butler.
Reignold Cobham.
John Pasheley.
Thomas Tunstall.
John Chidioke.
Rauf Langford.
Will'm Drury.
Will'm ap Thomas.
Richard Carbonell.
Richard Wydevill.
John Shirdelowe.
Nicholas Blonket.
Rauf Radclif.
Edmond Trafford.
Will'm Cheyney.
Will'm Babington.
John June, and
Gilbert Beauchampe.

B

1460.

Knightes made at the battell of Northampton, the 9th day of July 1458, Anno 36 Henry VI. (*sic*):

Sʳ Henry Stafford.

Thomas Dymmoke.

Will'm Tyrell.

Will'm Tyrell of the Beche.

Thomas Stranley.

Will'm Norrys.

John of Asheton.

Henry Lewys.

Sʳ Thomas Thorpe.

Knightes made at the battell of Wakefeld, the same yere, 31 of December, Anno 39 Henry VI., by the handes of Henry, Duke of Somersett:

The Lord Clifford.

James Lutterell.

Robert Whittingham.

. . . . Latymer of Som'setshire.

And by the handes of the Erle of Northumberland:

Sʳ Richard Percy, his brother.

Sʳ Will'm Gascoigne.

Thomas Metham.

Will'm Bertram.

Richard Alborough.

Thomas Eldreton.

John Malev'er.

Will'm St Quyntin.

And by the handes of the Erle of Devonshire:

Sʳ John Courteney, his brother.

Thomas Fulforde.

Alexander Woody.

Richard Cary.

And by the handes of the Lord Clifford:

Sʳ Roger Clifford, his brother.

Sʳ Richard Tempest.

Sʳ Henry Bellingham.

And by the handes of the Lord Roos:

Sʳ Thomas Babthorpe.

1461.

And at the second battell of St. Albon's, the xixth of February 1461 (*sic*), Anno 39 Henry VI.:

Prince Edward, sonne to Kinge Henry the Sixt.

Sʳ John Done.

Sʳ Will'm Taylboys.

Sʳ Symond Hammys.

Knightes made by King Edward the Fourthe at the battell of Towton, Anno . . . . :

Sʳ Will'm Hastynges.

Sʳ Walter Devereux.

Sʳ Humfrey Stafford.

Sʳ Thomas Montgomery.

Sʳ John Howard.

Sʳ Thomas Walgrabe.

Sʳ Rauf Grey was a Knight of the Bathe as it appeereth by his disgradynge in Anno 4 Edward IV., but where and when he was made *inquiratur*.

Knightes of the Bathe made at the Tower of London before the coronation of Kinge Edward the Fourthe (1461):

George, Duke of Clarence, Richard, Duke of Gloucester, bretherne to the Kinge.

John Mowbray, sonne and heir to the **Duke of Norfolk.**

John Stafford, afterwards **Erle of Wilteshire.**

Lord Thomas Fitz Alane, sonne and heir to the **Erle of Arundell.**

. . . . **Lord Straunge.**

Sr John Markham.
Sr Robert Danby.
Sr Will'm Pelverton.
Sr John Wingefeld.
Sr Walter Blount.
Sr Robert Markham.
Sr Robert Clifton.
Sr Will'm Stanley.
Sr Nicholas Byron.
Sr Will'm Cantelowe.

Sr John Fogge and **Sr John Scott** were made Knightes of the Carpett, and wold not pay their fees to the Office of Armes, wherfore the Heraldes then wrote *Aug Was Vallough.*

1471.

Knightes made by Kinge Edward the Fourthe in the field of Grafton besydes Tewksbury, Anno 10, 1471, 3 Maii:

The Lord Cobham, John.
Sr George Nevill, sonne and heire to the **Lord of Abergavenny.**
Sr Thomas Wingefeld.
Sr Henry Wingfeld.
Sr Philippe Courteney.
Sr Henry Beaumont.
Sr Maurice Berkeley.
Sr Richard Hastinges, called by his wyfe **Lord Welles.**
Sr Rauf Hastinges.
Sr Robert Harrington.
Sr Thomas Grey.
Sr James Tyrell.
Sr Henry Ferrers.
Sr John Aparre.
Sr Henry Perpoynt.
Sr John Done.
Sr Roger Kingeston.
Sr Richard Crofte.
Sr John Pilkington.
Sr John Lyngeyne.
Sr John Harley.
Sr Will'm Botteller.

Sr Christopher Moresby.
Sr John Clay.
Sr Robert Greene.
Sr John Willoughby.
Sr Roger Reed.
Sr John Savage.
Sr Thomas Strickland.
Sr George Browne.
Sr Will'm Motton.
Sr John Croker.
S^r . . . . Skerne of Essex.
Sr James Crowmer.
Sr Will'm Sandes.
Sr John Devereux.
Sr Henry Grey.
Sr John Seyntloe.
Sr Edward Woodhouse.
Sr Will'm Brandon.
Sr Richard Beauchamp.
Sr Thomas Cornewall.
Sr Roger Corbett.
Sr Humfrey Blount.
S^r . . . . Poole.

At the Kinge's retourne to London, the 20 day of May 1471, from the feild of Tewkesbury, in the highway without Shordiche, he dubbed Knightes as followeth, Aldermen of the Citie, as he was then rydinge into Kent :

Sr John Stockton, Maior of London.

Sr Mathew Philippe, Maior Anno 3.

Sr Richard Lee, Maior Anno 9.

Sr Will'm Tayler, Maior Anno 8.

Sr Rauf Verney, Maior Anno 5.

Sr Will'm Hampton, afterward Maior Anno 12.

Sr Will'm Stocker, afterward Sherif Anno 13, and Maior Anno 2 R. III.

Sr George Ireland, Sherif Anno p'mo.

Sr Thomas Stalbroke, Sherif Anno 7.

Sr John Crosby, Sherif.

Sr Richard Horswyke.

Sr John Yonge, Maior Anno 6.

Sr Bartholmew James, afterward Maior Anno 19.

All the which liberally payd their fees to the Officers of Armes.

Bannerettes made in that voyage and late iourney, whose Pennons and Standardes (in the difference of Pennons) were rent by the Kinge's commaundement :

Sr Thomas Grey.

Sr Richard Hastinges, afterward Lord Wells.

Sr John Courteney.

Sr Nicholas Latymer.

Sr Rauf Hastinges.

Sr Roger Toketts.

Sr John Stanley.

Sr Symon Mountford.

Sr John Henningham.

Sr Will'm Stanley.

1475.

Knightes of the Bathe made with the Prince and his brother at Westm., in St. Edwarde's Chamber, Anno 1475, on Whitsonday :

All these on the right syde of the Chamber—

Prince Edward,

Richard, Duke of Yorke, bretherne.

The Erle of Lincoln, sonne and heire to the Duke of Suffolke.

George, Erle of Shrewsbury.

Edward, Erle of Wiltshire.

The Lord Nevill.

The sonne and heire to the Lord Awdeley.

Sr Richard Beauchamp of St Amand.

The sonne and heire to the Lord Stourton.

Sr Walter Herbert, brother to the Erle of Penbroke.

Sr Thomas Bryan, Justice.

Sr Tho. Lytleton, Justice.

Sr Henry Bodringan.

Sr Richard Charleton.

Sr .... Pilkington.

All these Knightes were on the lefte syde of the Chamber—

Lord Thomas Grey, made Marquise Dorcett the same day after dynner, and so dyned in his habitte.

Lord Richard Grey, his brother.

Sr Edward Wydevill.

The sonne and heire to the Lord Berkeley.

George, sonne and heire to the Lord Stanley.

Edward, sonne and heire to the Lord Hastinges.

The sonne and heire to the Lord Ferrers of Chartley.

Sr Thomas Vaughan.

Sr Bryan of Stapleton.

And in the Chamber end were these three, viz.—

Sr Will'm Knyvett. | Sr Richard Ludlowe. | Sr Richard Charlton.

1477.

Knightes made at the mariage of Richard, Duke of Yorke, to Lady Anne, daughter and heire of John, Duke of Norff., 17 vel 18 Januarii, Anno 17 Edward IV., Anno D'ni 1477.

The mariage was solemnized on the xv^th day of January. These Knightes wer elected on the 17 day, and dubbed on the 18 day of the same moneth :

1. Henry, sonne and heire to the Lord Bourghchier.
2. The Lord Latymer.
3. The Lord Barnes.
4. The Lord Morley.
5. The Lord Powys.
6. The Lord De la Warre.
7. The Lord Montjoy, John.
8. John, sonne and heir to the Lord Beauchamp.
9. Sr Thomas, son and heir to John, Lord Howard.
10. Sr Thomas Bourghchier.
11. Sr Thomas Seintleger.
12. Sr John Elrington, Threasoror of the Kinge's house.
13. Sr Henry Taylboys.
14. Sr Will'm Gascoigne.
15. Sr Gyles Dawbeney.
16. Sr Will'm Stonner.
17. Sr Richard De la Bere.
18. Sr Guy Fayrfax.
19. Sr Robert Broughton.
20. Sr Thomas Frowyke.
21. Sr Will'm Redman.
22. Sr Richard Wentworth.
23. Sr Richard Latyn.

1481.

Bannerettes and Knightes made by Richard, Duke of Gloucester, in Scotland, at Hoton feld besyde Berwyke, the 22 day of August Anno 20 Edward IV., Anno D'ni 1481.

Anno 1461 (sic), Berwyke was delyvered to the Scottes by Kinge Henry the Sixt, and now recovered.

Knightes :

Frauncys, Lord Lovell.

Lord Fitzhugh.

Lord Scroope of Masham.

George, Lord Lumley.

. . . . Greystoke.

Bannerettes :

Sr Thomas Pilkington. | Sr Robert Ryder.

Other Knightes and Bannerettes :

1. Sr Will'm Darcy.
2. Sr John Melton.
3. Sr John Savell.
4. Sr Rauf Bulmer.
5. Sr Rauf Bigod.
6. Sr Rauf Bowes.
7. Sr John Constable of Holdernes.
8. Sr James Strangways.
9. Sr Robert Middelton.
10. Sr Will'm Fitzwilliam.
11. Sr Thomas Fitzwilliam.
12. Sr Thomas Wortley.
13. Sr James Danby.
14. Sr Thomas Malyverer.
15. Sr Rauf Fitz Randoll.
16. Sr Charles Pilkington.
17. Sr Robert Waterton.
18. Sr John Nevill of Leversege.
19. Sr Richard Coigners of Cowton.
20. Sr Will'm Beckwithe.

Knightes dubbed by the Erle of Northumberland on the mayne of Sefford the same tyme, Anno 20 Edward IV. :

1. Sr Marmaduke Constable.
2. Sr Christopher Warde.
3. Sr Roger Heron.
4. Sr Thomas Grey.
5. Sr Will'm Malory.
6. Sr Piers Middelton.
7. Sr Stephen Hamerton.
8. Sr Robert Helyarde.
9. Sr Rauf Wodrington.
10. Sr Rauf Harbottell.
11. Sr John Everingham.
12. Sr John Aske.
13. Sr Rauf Babthorpe.
14. Sr Roger Thorneton.
15. Sr Christopher Curwen.
16. Sr John Salveyn of Dufflett.
17. Sr Thomas Grey of Horton.
18. Sr Thomas Tempest.

These two were dubbed after the Parliament was ended, Anno 20 Edward IV. :

Sr John Woode, Speaker of the Parliament.

Sr William Catesby, Justice.

1482.

Bannerettes made in Scotland the 24 day of July Anno D'ni 1482, Anno 22 Edward IV., by the Duke of Gloucester :

1. Sr Edward Wydevill.
2. Sr Walter Herbert.
3. Sr Herbert Crepstoke.
4. Sr John Elrington.
5. Sr Henry Percy.
6. Sr Will'm Gascoigne.
7. Sr Edmond Hastinges.
8. Sr James Tyrell.
9. Sr James Danby.
10. Sr Hugh Hastinges.
11. Sr Rauf Asheton.
12. Sr Will'm Redman.
13. Sr Richard Radclif.
14. Sr Thomas Malyverer.
15. Sr Bryan Stapleton.
16. Sr John Savage.
17. Sr Will'm Evers.
18. Sr Piers Middelton.
19. Sr Christopher Warde.
20. Sr Stephen Hamerton.

21. S⁏ Thomas Tempest.
22. S⁏ John Everingham.
23. S⁏ Robert Harrington.
24. S⁏ Thomas Broughton.
25. S⁏ John Aske.
26. S⁏ Thomas Grey of Warke.
27. S⁏ Rauf Woderington.

28. S⁏ Roger Thorneton.
29. S⁏ Thomas Molyneux.
30. S⁏ Alexander Houghton.
31. S⁏ Piers a Legh.
32. S⁏ Edward Stanley.
33. S⁏ John Grey of Wilton.
34. S⁏ Richard Hodleston.

Knightes made the same day by the sayd Duke :

1. S⁏ Will'm Nevill of Thorneton Bridge.
2. S⁏ Richard Hawte.
3. S⁏ John Woderington.
4. S⁏ Will'm Engleby.
5. S⁏ Thomas Gowre.
6. S⁏ Randolf Pygott.
7. S⁏ John Darell.

8. S⁏ Will'm Houghton.
9. S⁏ Will'm Parker of London.
10. S⁏ Roger Cotton.
11. S⁏ Thomas Bowles.
12. S⁏ Thomas Bridges.
13. S⁏ Alexander Baynham.
14. S⁏ Sandy Jarden, a Scott.

Knightes made the same day in the Englishemen's campe, by Alexander, Duke of Albany, the 24 of July 1482 :

1. S⁏ Adam Murrey.
2. S⁏ Thomas Lyndsey.

3. S⁏ John Coningham.
4. S⁏ John Rotherford.

Knightes made the same day by the Erle of Northumberland in Scotland :

1. S⁏ John Penyngton.
2. S⁏ Robert Plompton.

3. S⁏ Martyn of the Sea.

Knightes there made the same day by the Lord Stanley, Steward of the Kinge's House :

1. S⁏ Christopher Southworth.
2. S⁏ Richard Langton.
3. S⁏ Will'm Stanley.
4. S⁏ John Bowthe.
5. S⁏ George Holforde.
6. S⁏ Richard Bolde.
7. S⁏ Richard Townley.
8. S⁏ James Lawrence.

9. S⁏ Thomas Talbott.
10. S⁏ Henry Tarbocke.
11. S⁏ John Talbott.
12. S⁏ Alexander Standishe.
13. S⁏ Christopher Standishe.
14. S⁏ Will'm Farrington.
15. S⁏ Henry Kyghley.

Be it remembred that these fower, S⁏ Richard Lakyn, S⁏ Will'm Readman, S⁏ Thomas Frowyke, and S⁏ Henry Wentworth, dubbed Knightes at the mariage of Richard, Duke of York, second sonne to Kinge Edward the Fourthe, not counselled to their most worshippe, denyed part of the Duties belonginge unto the Officers at Armes, which beinge referred to the Lord Chamberleyne, who well understoode the auncyent customes of Chivalvry, he shewed it unto the Kinge's grace and to the high and mightie Prince the Duke of Gloucester, High Constable of England, who then was Judge of the Office of Armes. The sayd Constable went in his owne p'son and com'aunded Will'm Gryffyth, one of the Marshalles of the Kinge's hall, to charge every man of the said Company to pay the duties unto the Officers of Armes, vid'z, Every bacheler knight xx⁸, every Baronne xl⁸, and so double accordinge to their estates and degrees, which wer kept and observed by all except the Lord Barnes.

1483.

Knightes made by Kinge Richard the Third on the Sonday before his Coronation, 5 July 1483, after he had created certeyn Lordes, as the Lord Howard to be Duke of Norff., his son Thomas to be Erle of Surrey, the Viscount Berkley to be Erle of Nottingham, and the Lord Lisle to be Viscount Lysle:

1. Sᵣ Robert Dymmoke, his Champion.
2. Sᵣ Will'm Hopton.
3. Sᵣ Robert Persay.
4. Sᵣ Will'm Jenney, Justice.

Knightes of the Bathe made the same 5 day of July:

Lord Edmond, sonne and heire to John, Duke of Suff.
George, Lord Grey, sonne and heire to the Erle of Kent.
Sᵣ Will'm, Lord Zouche, or els sonne and heire to the Lord Zouch.
The Lord of Ormond, or els called Sᵣ Thomas Ormond.
Sᵣ George Nevill, sonne and heire to the Lord of Abergavenny.
Sᵣ Will'm Berkley of Beverston.
Sᵣ Christopher Willoughby.

Sᵣ Edmond Cornwall, Baron of Burford.
Sᵣ Will'm Berkley of Wyley.
Sᵣ Will'm Boullen.
Sᵣ Edmond Beningefeld.
Sᵣ Will'm Say.
Sᵣ Gervays Clifton.
Sᵣ Thomas Arundell.
Sᵣ Will'm Babington.
Sᵣ James Lewkenor.
Sᵣ Will'm Enbreby.
Sᵣ John Browne.

Sᵣ Richard Storkey, Baron of the Exchequer, was dubbed Knight of the Carpet after, on Saturday in the Tower.

Sᵣ James Tyrell, the murtherer, was dubbed in Anno p'mo Richard III., in the Kinge's journey towardes Gloucester, and was worthely beheadded in Anno . . Henry VII.

Knightes dubbed the 13 day of . . . . Anno secundo Richard III.:

The Lord Brighton or Brighton, a Scottishman, } before dynner.
Sᵣ Robert Brakynbery,
Sᵣ Thomas Byll, Mayor of London, after dynner.

Kinge Richard the 3 on Twelfday, when he had created the Viscount Lovell, he made Sᵣ Thomas Thwaytes Knighte.

𝕿𝖍𝖊 𝕹𝖆𝖒𝖊𝖘 𝖆𝖓𝖉 𝕬𝖗𝖒𝖊𝖘 𝖔𝖋 𝖘𝖚𝖈𝖍𝖊 𝖆𝖘 𝖍𝖆𝖇𝖊 𝖇𝖊𝖊𝖓 𝖆𝖉𝖇𝖆𝖓𝖈𝖊𝖉 𝖙𝖔 𝖙𝖍𝖊 𝖍𝖔𝖓𝖔𝖗𝖆𝖇𝖑𝖊 𝕺𝖗𝖉𝖗𝖊 𝖔𝖋 𝕶𝖓𝖎𝖌𝖍𝖙𝖍𝖔𝖔𝖉𝖊 𝖎𝖓 𝖙𝖍𝖊 𝖙𝖞𝖒𝖊 𝖔𝖋 𝖙𝖍𝖊 𝖕𝖗𝖚𝖉𝖊𝖓𝖙 𝖆𝖓𝖉 𝖕𝖗𝖔𝖘𝖕𝖊𝖗𝖔𝖚𝖘 𝖗𝖊𝖎𝖌𝖓𝖊 𝖔𝖋

𝕶𝖎𝖓𝖌𝖊 𝕳𝖊𝖓𝖗𝖞 𝖙𝖍𝖊 𝕾𝖊𝖇𝖊𝖓𝖙𝖍.

(Cotton MSS., Claudius, c. iii., fol. 1–60, by Robert Glover.)

Knightes made at the landinge of Kinge Henry the Seventh at Mylforde Haven:

𝕾ʳ 𝕰𝖉𝖜𝖆𝖗𝖉 𝕮𝖔𝖚𝖗𝖙𝖊𝖓𝖊𝖞, after created Erle of Devonshire at the Kinge's coronation. 𝖁𝖎𝖘𝖈𝖔𝖚𝖓𝖙 𝖂𝖊𝖑𝖑𝖊𝖘.

Or, three torteaux, a label of three points Azure. *Crest*—Out of a ducal coronet Or a plume of ostrich-feathers Argent.

Quarterly—1 and 4, Or, a lion rampant double queued Sable; 2 and 3, Gules, a fess dancettée between six cross-crosslets Or (BEAUCHAMP; the fess should be plain). *Crest*—An ostrich's head and wings Argent, ducally gorged Gules, in the beak a horse-shoe Azure.

𝕷𝖔𝖗𝖉𝖊 𝕾𝖈𝖍𝖆𝖓𝖉𝖊 𝖔𝖋 𝕾𝖆𝖇𝖔𝖞, after created Erle of Bathe.

𝕾ʳ 𝕵𝖔𝖍𝖓 𝕮𝖍𝖊𝖓𝖊𝖞.

Quarterly—1 and 4, Azure, six lioncels rampant Argent, a canton Ermine; 2 and 3, Ermine, a chief per pale indented Or and Gules, in the dexter side a rose of the last (SHOTISBROOKE); over all a crescent for difference. *Crest*—Two bulls' horns Argent, separated from the scalp, roots Or, "fixed to the mantels without torce."

𝕾ʳ 𝕽𝖎𝖈𝖍𝖆𝖗𝖉 𝕲𝖚𝖎𝖑𝖋𝖔𝖗𝖉.

Quarterly—1 and 4, Or, a saltire between four martlets Sable; 2 and 3, Argent, a chief Sable; over all a bend engrailed Gules. *Crest*—On a chapeau Sable turned up Ermine and charged with an escallop Or, an ostrich-feather erect Argent quilled of the third.

𝕾ʳ 𝕰𝖉𝖜𝖆𝖗𝖉 𝕻𝖔𝖞𝖓𝖎𝖓𝖌𝖊𝖘.

Quarterly—1 and 4, Barry of six Or and Vert, a bend Gules; 2 and 3, Gules, three lions passant in pale Argent, a bendlet Azure (FITZ PAIN). *Crest*—A dragon's head, wings displayed, Sable. *Badge*—A key erect Argent, handle uppermost, ducally crowned Or.

𝕾ʳ 𝕵𝖆𝖒𝖊𝖘 𝕭𝖑𝖔𝖚𝖓𝖙.

Quarterly—1, Argent, two wolves passant Sable within a bordure Gules charged with ten pairs of lions' gambs in saltire Or (AYALA); 2, Or, a castle Azure (CASTILE); 3, Barry

c

nebulée of six Or and Sable (BLOUNT); 4, Vair (BEAUCHAMP); over all a mullet for difference. *Crest*—A wolf passant Sable between two cornets out of a ducal coronet Or.

Sr Davy Owen. Gules, a chevron Sable between three helmets close Argent garnished Or, a bend sinister of the last.

Sr John Fortescu. Azure, on a bend engrailed Argent between two cotises Or a mullet pierced Sable. *Crest*—An heraldic tiger passant Argent.

Sr John Haliwell. Quarterly—1 and 4, Or, on a bend Sable three antelopes Argent, attired of the field; 2 and 3, Argent, on a chevron Sable three bezants.

Sr John Reisley. Barry of ten Argent and Azure, a griffin segreant Or armed Gules, a crescent for difference. *Crest*—A man's head affrontée Sable, earrings Or, wreathed Argent.

Sr William Brandon. Barry of ten Argent and Gules, a lion rampant Or, ducally crowned per pale of the first and second.

Sr Thomas Milborn. Gules, a chevron between three escallops Argent.

Sr William Tyler. Vert, a bend between six passion nails Or. *Crest*—A bull statant "dunyshe," armed Or.

Sr John Treury.

Knightes made at the battell of Redmore ("a fair plaine neere Bosworth, about seaven miles west from Leicester"—*Yorke's Union of Honour*) anno primo of the Kinge after Kinge Richard was slayne :

Sr Gilbert Talbott. Quarterly—1, Azure, a lion rampant within a bordure Or; 2, Gules, a lion rampant within a bordure engrailed Or; 3, Argent, two lions passant Gules; 4, Argent, a bend between six martlets Gules. *Crest*—On a chapeau Gules turned up Ermine, a lion statant Or.

Sr John Mortemer. Azure, three bars Or, an inescucheon Ermine, on a chief of the first two pallets between as many gyrons of the second. *Crest*—In a ducal coronet Or a pyramid of leaves Azure.

Sr Walter Hungerforde. Quarterly—1 and 4, Sable, two bars Argent, in chief three plates ; 2 and 3, Paly wavy of six Or and Gules. *Crest*—Out of a ducal coronet Or a garb between two sickles erect proper.

Sr Robert Pointz. Quarterly—1 and 4, Quarterly per fess indented Argent and Azure (ACTON); 2 and 3, Quarterly Gules and Or, a bend Argent (FITZ NICHOLL). *Crest*—Five teazles Or, stalked and leaved Vert.

Sr Humfrey Stanley. Quarterly—1, Argent, on a bend Azure three bucks' heads cabossed Or, quartering, Or, on a chief indented Azure three plates; 2, Or, a chevron Gules between three martlets Sable ; 3, Azure, crusily and two organ-pipes chevronwise Or; 4, Gules, three lions passant Argent. *Crest*—An eagle, wings endorsed, Or standing over an infant, face proper, in its cradle Gules fretty Or. " Alibi, the creast a leopard's hed cabosed Argent, crowned Or, the crown full of ostryche-fethers Or, a crescent in the middest of the scucheon for a difference."

Sr Will'm Willoughby. Quarterly—1, Sable, a cross engrailed Or, quartering, Gules, a cross moline Argent, over all a crescent for difference ; 2 and 3, Gules, a cross patonce Or ; 4, Gules, four fusils in fess Argent, each charged with an escallop Sable. *Crest*—The bust of a man couped Sable ducally crowned Or.

Sr John Turberville. Argent, a lion rampant Gules ducally crowned Or.

Sr Res ap Thomas. Argent, a chevron between three Cornish choughs Sable.

Sr Hugh Persall. Quarterly—1 and 4, Or, three bars Gules ; 2 and 3, Ermine; all within a bordure Azure.

Sr Richard Edgecombe. Gules, on a bend Sable, cotised Or three boars' heads couped Argent.

Knightes made between the batell of Redmore and the Kinge's coronation :

The Baron of Carew. Sr John Bickenell.
Sr Will'm Courteney.

Sr Charles Somersett made Knighte by the Duke of Austria at or before this tyme.

Knightes of the Bathe made at the coronation of the Kinge the 30 day of Octobre Anno D'ni MCCCCLXXXV in the Halle within the Towre of London :

Edward, Duke of Buckingha'. France and England quarterly, within a bordure Argent. *Crest*—On a chapeau, turned up Ermine, a lion statant ducally crowned Or, collared Argent.

The Lord Fitzwalter. Or, a fess between two chevrons Gules. *Crest* —Out of a chapeau two wings Gules, united by a chain, therefrom depending a padlock Or above a sun in splendour of the second. " A wreath Or and Gules, and no chapeau."

Sᵣ Thomas Corbesey. Quarterly of six—1, Azure, a cross engrailed within a bordure Or; 2, Azure, crusily and a lion rampant Or; 3, Argent, on a bend Azure three cinquefoils Or; 4, Argent, a bend Sable, a label of three points Gules; 5, Argent, a bend Gules within a bordure counter-compony Or and Azure; 6, Argent, on a bend Gules three annulets of the field. *Crest*—A garb of cinquefoils Or, banded Gules.

Sᵣ Roger Lewkenor. Azure, three chevrons Argent. *Crest*—A unicorn's head couped Argent, spotted with annulets Sable, armed and maned Or. "Alibi, caput unicorni de Aseriâ absq. annulettis."

Sᵣ Henry Heydon. Quarterly Argent and Gules, a cross engrailed counterchanged. *Crest*—A talbot statant Argent, spotted Sable.

Sᵣ Reignold Bray. Argent, a chevron between three eagles' legs erased à-la-cuise Sable. *Crest*—A rabbit passant " dunyshe."

Sᵣ John Verney. Azure, on a cross Argent five mullets pierced Gules. *Crest*—A phœnix Azure, wings expanded Or, in flames Gules.

Sᵣ Nicholas Billesdon, late Maior of London (1483). Azure, a bend cotised Or, in sinister chief an eagle's head erased of the second.

Sᵣ Sampson Norton, dubbed in Bretaigne by Robert Wilughby, lorde Brooke. Azure, three swords in triangle pomel to pomel Argent, hilts Gules, on a chief Or a lion passant-gardant of the third between two maunches Ermine. *Crest*—A demi-winged lion rampant Gules guttée d'eau, holding in the dexter paw a sword proper.

Sᵣ Edward Wyngfeilde, made Knight in Granado by Sᵣ Edward Woodvill warringe on the infidels.

Sᵣ .... Cantelupe, made Knight in Grauado with Sᵣ Edward Wyngfeilde.

Sᵣ John Fenkell. Sable, a fess dancettée between three mullets Argent.

Knightes of London made the xiiᵗʰ day of Christmas in the first yere of the Kinge:

Sᵣ Hugh Brice, Maior of London (1485), dubbed in the tower. Argent fretty Gules, over all a cross of the first within a bordure Sable charged with eight cinquefoils Or. " Without cinquefoyles." *Crest*—A demi-woman, habited Gules, face proper, crined Or, holding in both hands also proper a chaplet of the second.

𝕾ʳ **Henry Collett,** Maior of London (1486), made on Twelfe day, the Kinge keepinge his Estate at the Whitehall beinge crowned.

Sable, on a chevron between three hinds statant Argent as many annulets of the field. *Crest—* A hind statant Argent.

𝕾ʳ **John Browne.**

Azure, a chevron between three escallops Or within a bordure engrailed Gules.

𝕾ʳ **Will'm Capell.**

Gules, crusily and a lion rampant Or. *Crest—* A demi-lion rampant Or, holding erect in both paws a cross-crosslet fitchée Gules.

𝕾ʳ **John Byron,** made Knight as the Kinge came from Yorke, Anno p'mo.

Quarterly—1 and 4, Argent, three bendlets enhanced Gules ; 2 and 3, Argent, on a bend Azure three bezants, in sinister chief a cross-crosslet fitchée of the second. *Crest—*A mermaid with her comb and mirror all proper.

𝕾ʳ **Roger Townesende,** Justice, dubbed at Worcester in the Kinge's chambre on Whitsonday, Anno p'mo.

Quarterly—1 and 4, Azure, a chevron Ermine between three escallops Argent ; 2 and 3, Gules, a chevron between three fleurs-de-lis Or.

𝕾ʳ **Will'm Hodie,** cheif baron of th'eschequer, dubbed at Westminster Anno s'c'do by the Kinge.

Gules, a fess between six cross-crosslets Argent (? ALBOROUGH).

𝕾ʳ **John Swpliard (Suliard),** Justice, dubbed at Westminster Anno 2.

Quarterly—1 and 4, Argent, a chevron Gules between three pheons Sable ; 2 and 3, Gules, a chevron between three lions rampant Or. " Leones argentei in aliis libris."

Banerettes made by the Kinge at the batell of Stoke besydes Newarke upon Trent the ixᵗʰ day of June in Anno Sec'do, wherof the first three wer made before the batell, and the other xi afterward :

𝕾ʳ **Gilbert Talbott.**
𝕾ʳ **John Cheyny.**
𝕾ʳ **Will'm Stonner.**

Arms and Crest as at p. 10.
Arms and Crest as at p. 9.
Quarterly—1 and 4, Azure, two bars indented and a chief Or ; 2, Azure, six lioncels rampant Argent, on a canton Or a mullet Gules ; 3, Argent, three roses Gules.

𝕾ʳ **John Arundell.**

Quarterly—1 and 4, Gules, a lion rampant Or ; 2 and 3, Sable fretty Or ; over all a crescent for difference. *Crest—*Out of a ducal coronet Gules a dragon's head, wings expanded Argent, beaked and eared of the first.

𝕾ʳ **Thomas Cokesey** alias **Grebell.**
𝕾ʳ **Edmonde Bedingfellde.**

Arms as at p. 12, but 2, not crusily, and 6, three round buckles Or instead of annulets.

Ermine, an eagle displayed Gules beaked and legged Or. *Crest—*An eagle displayed Or.

Sͬ John Fortescu. — Arms as at p. 10, without the mullet; the same Crest.

Sͬ Humfrey Stanley. · Arms quarterly and Crest as at p. 11.

Sͬ James Blount. — Arms quarterly and Crest as at p. 9, without the mullet for difference.

Sͬ Richard Delabere. — Azure, a bend Argent cotised Or between six martlets of the third. *Crest*—Out of a ducal coronet Or a plume of ostrich-feathers Argent.

Sͬ John Mortemer. — Arms and Crest as at p. 10.

Sͬ Will'm Troutbecke. — Quarterly—1 and 4, Azure, three trouts fretted Argent; 2 and 3, Argent, a fleur-de-lis between three Blackamoors' heads couped Sable. *Crest*—On three trouts fretted Argent a Blackamoor's head proper.

Sͬ Richard Croft. — Quarterly per fess indented Argent and Azure, in dexter chief a lion passant-gardant Gules. *Crest*—A wivern Sable, vulned in the side Gules.

Sͬ James Baskerville. — Argent, a chevron Gules between three hurts. *Crest*—A bunch of rosemary proper.

Knightes made at the foresayd batell of Stoke by Newarke :

Sͬ James Awdeley. — Quarterly—1 and 4, Gules, fretty Or ; 2 and 3, Ermine, a chevron Gules. *Crest*—A man's head in profile, "swart," crined Sable bound round the temples Argent.

Sͬ Thomas Poole. — Quarterly—1 and 4, Azure fleury Or, a lion rampant Argent; 2 and 3, Argent, a chevron Sable between three bucks' heads cabossed Gules. *Crest*—Out of a ducal coronet Gules a griffin's head Azure, beaked of the first.

Sͬ Robert Clyfford. — Chequy Or and Azure, a fess Gules. *Crest*—On a ducal coronet Or a wyvern Gules.

Sͬ Edward Borough. — Quarterly—1 and 4, Azure, three fleurs-de-lis Ermine ; 2 and 3, Or, a lion rampant Azure, a crescent Argent for difference ; quartering Or, three pales Azure ; over all a label of three points Gules. *Crest*—A falcon rising Ermine, beaked and ducally gorged Or.

Sͬ George Hopton of Swillington. — Argent, a chevron Azure, over all a label of three points Ermine. *Crest*—A friar's head proper, hooded Argent.

Sͬ Edward Norrys. — Quarterly—1 and 4, Argent, a chevron between three ravens' heads erased Sable ; 2 and 3, Bendy of six Azure and Or within a bordure Gules ; over all a label of three points Gules. *Crest*—A raven Sable.

Sr **William Tyrwhit** of Kettleby. — Gules, three lapwings Or. *Crest*—A demi-lapwing Or.

Sr **Thomas Green.** — Azure, three bucks statant Or. "Quarterly with MABLETHORP, Gules, a chevron betwene 3 cros-crosslets Gold, in chief a lion passant Argent." *Crest*—A buck's head Or.

Sr **Henry Willoughby.** — Or, on two bars Gules three water-bougets Argent. *Crest*—An owl statant gardant Argent, ducally crowned and clawed Or.

Sr **John Musgrave.** — Azure, six annulets Or.

Sr **Edward Pykeringe.** — Ermine, a lion rampant Azure, ducally crowned Or. *Crest*—A lion's gamb erect Azure, clawed Or.

Sr **Will'm Sandes.** — Argent, a cross ragulée Sable, a label of three points Gules. *Crest*—A goat's head Argent, attired Or, between two wings of the second.

Sr **Thomas Lovell.** — Argent, a chevron Azure between three squirrels sejant Gules each cracking a nut.

Sr **James Parker.** — Quarterly—1 and 4, Argent, three bucks' heads cabossed Sable; 2 and 3, Sable, a fess Or between three bezants. *Crest*—A buck's head Sable.

Sr **Anthony Browne.** — Quarterly—1 and 4, Sable, three lions passant in bend between two cotises Argent; 2 and 3, ARUNDELL as at p. 13, a mullet for difference; over all a crescent for difference. *Crest*—Out of a mound Vert seven sprigs of foxglove proper.

Sr **Maurice Barkley.** — Gules, a chevron between ten cinquefoils Argent. *Crest*—A bear's head Argent, muzzled Gules and Vert.

Sir **Will'm Carew.** — Or, three lions passant in pale Sable. *Crest*—Out of the round top of a mainmast Or a lion rampant issuing Sable.

Sr **Richard Fitzlewes.** — Sable, a chevron between three trefoils slipped Argent. "Quartred with Asure, a playne cross silver betwene 20 cross-crosslets Gold."

Sr **John Paston.** — Argent, six fleurs-de-lis Azure, a chief indented Or. *Crest*—A griffin sejant, wings endorsed, holding in the beak a chain ring Or.

Sr **Richard Poole (Pole).** — Per pale Or and Sable, a saltire counterchanged. *Crest*—A sea-gull Or, preying on a fish proper.

Sr **Roger Bellengham.** — Quarterly—1 and 4, Argent, a bugle-horn Sable garnished Or; 2 and 3, Argent, three bendlets Gules, on a canton of the second a lion passant of the field. *Crest*—A buck's head Or, collared Argent.

Sʳ **Edward Darell.** Azure, a lion rampant Or ducally crowned Argent, on the shoulder a crescent Gules for difference.

Sʳ **Thomas Hansard.** Gules, three mullets Argent.

Sʳ **Thomas of Walton.** Argent, three hawks' heads erased Sable. *Crest* —A wild man proper, holding a club Or.

Sʳ **Robert of Broughton.** Quarterly—1, Argent, a chevron between three mullets Gules ; 2, Argent, a chevron Sable ; 3, Azure, two lions passant-gardant Or ; 4, On a cross in middle chief an escallop.

Sʳ **Thomas Blount.** Quarterly—1 and 4, Barry nebulée of six Or and Sable ; 2 and 3, Ermine, a lion rampant Gules ducally crowned Or within a bordure engrailed Sable bezantée. *Crest*—On a chapeau Gules turned up Ermine, a lion statant of the first ducally crowned Or.

Sʳ **Will'm Vampage,** the first Knight that was dubbed in the feild that day. Azure, an eagle displayed Argent beaked and legged Or within a double tressure flory counter-flory of the second, a crescent for difference. *Crest*—A demi-lion rampant Or guttée de poix.

Sʳ **Pumfrey Savage.** Quarterly—1 and 4, Argent, a pale fusily Sable ; 2, Or, on a fess Azure three garbs of the field ; 3, Gules, a chevron between three martlets Argent. *Crest*—A unicorn's head erased Argent armed Or ; on both Arms and Crest a crescent Azure for difference.

Sʳ **John Sabcotts.** Quarterly—1 and 4, Sable, three dovecotes Argent ; 2 and 3, Argent, three square buckles Sable. *Crest*—A goat's head erased Argent, attired Or.

Sʳ **Gregory Lovell.** Arms as at p. 15.

Sʳ **Nicholas Vaulx.** Chequy Argent and Gules, on a chevron Azure three roses Or.

Sʳ **Will'm Trowtbeke.**

Sʳ **John Devenishe.**

Sʳ **Ampas Poulett.** (Sable,) three swords in pile (Argent, hilts Or).

Sʳ **Penry Bouldc.** Argent, a griffin segreant Sable beaked Gules. *Crest*—Out of a ducal coronet Gules a griffin's head Sable wings displayed Or.

Sʳ **Will'm Redmcyll.**

Sʳ **Robert Cheiney.** Arms and Crest as at p. 9, a mullet for difference.

Sʳ **John Wyndam.**

Sʳ **George Nevill** the Bastarde. Gules, a saltire Argent, a bendlet sinister Azure.

Sʳ **Rauf Shirley.** Paly of six Or and Azure, a canton Ermine.

Sr **Robert Brandon.** Arms as at p. 10; on the shoulder a crescent Sable.

Sr **John Digby.** Azure, a fleur-de-lis Argent charged with a mullet Gules. *Crest*—An ostrich Argent holding in the beak a horse-shoe Azure.

Sr **Will'm Litilton.** Quarterly—1, Argent, a bend cotised Sable, a bordure engrailed Gules bezantée; 2, Argent, a chevron between three escallops Sable; 3, Argent, a fess Azure between four sinister hands couped Gules; 4, Argent, two wolves passant Gules. "Quære quod genus animalis," *in a later hand;* "it should be two dogs, for PRESTON."

Sr **Chr'opher Wroughton.** Argent, a chevron Gules between three boars' heads couped close Sable.

Sr **Will'm Norrys.**
Sr **Thomas Lien.**
Sr **Maurice Abarow.** Sable, two swords in saltire Argent between four fleurs-de-lis Or.

Sr **Thomas Manyngton.**
Sr **James Parington.** Sable, a fret Argent.
Sr **John Longvile.** Gules, a fess dancettée between six cross-crosslets fitchée Argent. *Crest*—A talbot's head Gules, eared Argent, gorged with a fess dancettée of the second.

Sr **Thomas Tyrell.** Argent, two chevrons Azure within a bordure engrailed Gules.

Sr **George Herbert.** Per pale Azure and Gules, three lions rampant Argent. *Crest*—A maiden's head Sable, crined Or, the back hair plaited, wreathed round the temples Gules and of the second.

Sr **Rauf Langforth.**
Sr **Thomas Onley,** Merchant, dubbed at Coventry the same somer the Kinge's banner yet desplayed; he was of the same towne a burges.
Sr **Richard Todde,** Maior of York, and there dubbed.
Sr **Richard Yorke,** Maior of Azure, a saltire Argent. *Crest*—A monkey's the Staple, dubbed at Yorke head, "greenish," the face proper. the same tyme.
Sr **Richard Salkyld,** dubbed Argent, fretty Gules, a chief of the second. by the Kinge at Duresme.
Sr **Richard Clervaux,** dubbed Or, a saltire Sable, "campus niger, saltatorium at Croft by the Kinge on St Lau- aureum." *Crest* — "A crane in the nest rence Even the ixth of August. proper."

D

S͏ᵣ **John Warren**, dubbed by the Kinge at Ryppon on S͏ᵗ Bartholmew's Day. •

Quarterly—1 and 4, Chequy Or and Azure, on a canton Gules a lion rampant Argent; 2, Or, on a chevron Gules three martlets Argent; 3, Azure, three lozenges between eight crosscrosslets Or. *Crest*—Out of a ducal coronet Or, a pyramid of leaves Argent.

S͏ᵣ **Thomas Ashton**, dubbed at Rippon the same tyme.

Argent, a mullet Sable. *Crest*—A mower with his scythe, face and hands proper, habit and cap per pale Sable and Argent, handle of the scythe Argent, blade Sable.

S͏ᵣ **William Horn**, Maior of London (1487), dubbed by the Kinge in Hornsey Parke at his retourne to London, Anno 3.

Azure, a bugle-horn proper. *Crest*—A hunter blowing a horn held in his right hand, in the left a bow, at his back a sheaf of arrows, all proper.

S͏ᵣ **John Perceball**, dubbed in Hornsey Parke at the same tyme.

Quarterly—1 and 4, Per chevron Azure and Gules, three greyhounds' heads erased Argent, collared counterchanged; 2 and 3, Gules, a chief Or, over all a bend engrailed Sable, a crescent for difference. *Crest*—A lion sejant Gules.

S͏ᵣ **Thomas Fitzwill'm**, Recorder of London.

S͏ᵣ **Richard Nanfant**, dubbed by the Kinge before Christmas, who sent him in ambassade into Spayne; he was dubbed in the way towards Kingston, Anno quarto.

Quarterly—1 and 4, Sable, a chevron Ermine between three wings displayed Argent; 2 and 3, Argent, three wolves passant Azure, "quære quod genus animalis—puto Lupi." *Crest*—A spaniel dog passant Argent.

Knightes made at the coronation of Queene Elizabeth, wyf to Kinge Henry the Seventh, and eldest daughter to Kinge Edwarde the Fourthe, which was the xxvᵗʰ of Novembre Anno D'ni 1485, Anno p'mo of the Kinge:

Will'm, Lorde Courteney, sonne and heire of Edward, Erle of Devonshire.

Arms and Crest as at p. 9.

S͏ᵣ **Edward Sutton, Lord Dudley.**

Quarterly—1 and 4, Or, a lion rampant doublequeued Vert; 2, Or, two lions passant Azure, quartering Argent, a cross patonce Azure; 3, Argent, a saltire Gules, quartering Or, a lion rampant Gules. *Crest*—Out of a ducal coronet Or, a lion's head Azure langued Gules.

S͏ᵣ **Will'm Gascoigne.**

Quarterly—1, Argent, on a pale Sable a demilucy erect couped Or; 2, Gules, a saltire Argent, a crescent for difference; 3, Gules, a lion rampant Argent within a bordure engrailed gobony of the first and Or; 4, Vair

Sʳ **Thomas Boteler** of Warington.

Sʳ **Edward Barkley.**

Sʳ **Will'm Lucy.**

Sʳ **Thomas Hungerford.**

Sʳ **Guy of Wulston.**
Sʳ **Thomas Pomerey.**

Sʳ **Raulf Schelton.**

Sʳ **Thomas Pulteney.**

Sʳ **Hugh Conway.**

Sʳ **Hugh Loterell.**
Sʳ **Nicholas Lisle.**

Sʳ **Arnold Hake Van Sollge,** nat. Van Tyell, of Almaigne, dubbed by the Kinge the same yere, on Friday after the Conception of Our Lady.

Gules and Or. *Crest*—A demi-lucy's head erect Or.

Azure, a bend between six covered cups Or. *Crest*—A covered cup Or.

Quarterly—1 and 4, Gules, a chevron between ten crosses patée within a bordure Argent; 2 and 3, Argent, on a saltire Gules five estoiles Or (BETISHORNE). *Crest*—A mitre Argent charged with the Arms.

Quarterly—1 and 4, Barry of ten, impaling Gules, crusily and three lucies hauriant Argent; 2 and 3, Gules, a lion rampant tail forked Argent, ducally crowned Or.

Quarterly—1 and 4, HUNGERFORD, as at p. 10; 2 and 3, Argent, a lion rampant Sable ducally crowned Or within a bordure Azure; and the same Crest.

Or, a lion rampant Gules, a bordure engrailed Sable. *Crest*—A lion sejant Gules, holding in the dexter paw a bezant.

Azure, a cross Or. *Crest*—A friar's head proper, hood Argent, "alibi caputiu' depingitur ex auro et tegit caput Heremita."

Argent, a fess dancettée Gules, in chief three leopards' faces Sable. *Crest*—A leopard's head Sable.

Quarterly—1 and 4, Sable, on a bend cotised Argent a rose Gules between two annulets Or; 2 and 3, Azure, a cross double-voided Or. *Crest*—A Blackamoor's head Sable, wreathed Argent.

Azure, a bend between six martlets Argent.

Or, on a chief Azure three lioncels rampant of the field. *Crest*—A buck statant Argent, attired, collared, and lined Or.

Argent, two branches ragulée conjoined in pile Gules.

These three followinge came from High Almaigne to see this realme and to receave the ordre of Knighthoode of the Kinge, as they dyd :

Sʳ **Balthezar Canhauser.**
(*Sic, but* ? Tanhauser.)

Sable, an eagle's leg couped à-la-cuisse issuing from the sinister side Argent. *Crest*—Out of a ducal coronet Or, an eagle's leg erect Argent.

Sⁱ Christopher Van Silbermerg.

Gules, three spade-heads conjoined 2 and 1 Sable bordured Or. *Crest*—Out of a ducal coronet two spade-heads in bend, the one slightly behind the other, Sable bordured Or.

Sⁱ Adryan Van Crehnecke.

Quarterly—1 and 4, Gules, on a bend Sable a lion passant-gardant Or; 2 and 3, Argent, a chief invected. *Crest*—A cord embowed Or, out of each end ducally crowned of the second four feathers Argent, the bow resting on an oval cushion Gules, tasselled of the second.

These xxᵗ followinge were made Knightes of the Bathe at the creation of Prince Arthure and of his Bayne on Sᵗ Andrew's Eve in anno quinto of the Kinge :

1. **Prince Arthure.**

France and England quarterly, a label of three points Argent. *Crest*—On a chapeau Gules turned up Ermine a lion statant-gardant ducally crowned Or, charged on the breast with a label of three points Argent.

2. **Henry, Erle of Northumberlande,** then a warde et igitur nihil solvebat officiariis Armorum.

Quarterly—1, Or, a lion rampant Azure, quartering Gules, three lucies hauriant Argent ; 2, Azure, five fusils in fess Or ; 3, Barry of six Or and Vert, over all a bend Gules ; 4, Gules, three lions passant in pale Argent, a bend Azure ; on an escucheon of pretence—Or, three piles meeting at the base Azure. *Crest*—On a chapeau Gules turned up Ermine a lion statant Azure.

3. **The Lorde Maltravers.**

Quarterly—1, Gules, a lion rampant Or ; 2, Barry of eight Or and Gules ; 3, Argent, a fess and canton Gules ; 4, Sable, fretty Or, quartering Argent, a chief Azure ; over all a label of three points Azure. *Crest*—Out of a ducal coronet a dragon's head wings expanded Argent, beaked Gules, charged on the neck with a label of three points Azure.

4. **The Lorde Grey** of Ruthyn.

Quarterly—1 and 4, Barry of six Argent and Azure, in chief three torteaux ; 2 and 3, Or, a maunch Gules, quartering Barry of ten Argent and Azure, an orle of martlets Gules. *Crest*—On a chapeau Gules turned up Ermine a wyvern Or.

5. **The Lorde Stourton.**

Sable, a bend Or between six fountains. *Crest* —A demi-greyfriar proper, holding in the dexter hand a scourge handle Or of three lashes with knots Sable.

KNIGHTS MADE 1489. 21

6. **Sᵣ Thomas West,** the father.
Quarterly—1 and 4, Argent, a fess dancettée Sable; 2, Gules, crusily fitchée and a lion rampant Argent (DE LA WARR); 3, Azure, three leopards' heads jessant-de-lis Or (CANTELUPE). "Only La Warr and Cantelupe quarterly in the originall."

7. **Sᵣ John Saint John.**
Quarterly—1 and 4, Argent, a bend Gules, on a chief of the second two mullets pierced Or; 2 and 3, Gules, a fess between six martlets Or, a mullet for difference.

8. **Sᵣ Henry Vernon.**
Quarterly of six—1, Argent, fretty Sable; 2, Azure, three leopards passant in pale Argent; 3, Argent, a lion rampant double-queued Gules, collared Or; 4, Barry of six Or and Azure; 5, Argent, fretty Sable, a canton Gules; 6, Azure, crusily and two organ-pipes in chevron Or. *Crest*—A boar's head erased Sable, eared and tusked Or.

9. **Sᵣ John Hastings.**
Quarterly—1 and 4, Or, a maunch Gules; 2 and 3, Gules, a bend Argent. *Crest*—A mermaid with comb and mirror all proper.

10. **Sᵣ Will'm Griffiths.**
Quarterly—1, Gules, a chevron Argent between three men's heads couped of the second, wreathed Or, quartering Azure, crusily and a lion rampant Argent; 2, Argent, on a bend Azure three bucks' heads cabossed Or; 3, Argent, on a bend Azure three mullets Or; 4, Gules, a chevron Sable fretty Or between three bucks' heads cabossed Argent. *Crest*—A buck's head cabossed per pale Or and Argent.

11. **Sᵣ Will'm Tyndall.**
Quarterly—1 and 4, Argent, a fess dancettée and in chief three crescents Gules; 2, Or, a lion salient Gules; 3, Gules, six escallops Argent. *Crest*—Out of a ducal coronet Or, a plume of five feathers Ermines banded Argent.

12. **Sᵣ Nicholas Montgomery.**
Quarterly—1 and 4, Or, an eagle displayed Azure; 2 and 3, Ermine, on a bordure Gules eight horse-shoes Or.

13. **Sᵣ William Vupdall (Abedall).**
Quarterly—1 and 4, Argent, a cross moline Gules; 2 and 3, Azure, fretty Or. *Crest*—On each side of a chapeau Azure turned up Argent a feather Gules stuck within the turning up.

14. **Sᵣ Mathew Browne.**
Arms as at p. 15, without the difference. *Crest*—A griffin's head erased.

15. Sͬ **Thomas Darcy.** Quarterly—1 and 4, Azure, crusily and three cinquefoils Argent; 2 and 3, Azure, three bars-gemelles and a chief Or. *Crest*—A bull statant Sable, armed Argent.

16. Sͬ **Thomas Cheyny.** Quarterly of five—1 and 5, Quarterly Argent and Sable, over all a bend logenzy Gules; 2, Gules, three birds Or—quartering, 1, Barry of eight Argent and Azure, on a bend Gules three mullets of the first; 2, Gules, a fess dancetteé between six cross-crosslets Or ; and 3, Argent, a chevron Sable, in dexter chief a cinquefoil of the field ; 3, Chequy Or and Gules, a bend engrailed Sable ; 4, Argent, on a bend Sable three cross-crosslets fitchée of the field.

17. Sͬ **Edmond Gorges.** Quarterly—1, Lozengy Azure and Or, a chevron Gules ; 2, Argent, on a chief Gules three bezants ; 3, Gules, a lion rampant Ermine ; 4, Argent, a chevron between three dice Sable, each charged with four plates. *Crest* —A greyhound's head "swartishe," collared Gules bezantée.

18. Sͬ **Walter Denys.** Quarterly—1 and 4, Gules, a bend engrailed Azure between three leopards' heads Or, jessant-de-lis of the second; 2, Argent, a Cornish chough Sable within a bordure engrailed of the second bezantée ; 3, Argent, on a chief Gules three bezants.

19. Sͬ **Will'm Scott.** Argent, three Catherine wheels Sable, a bordure engrailed Gules.

20. Sͬ **John Gwyse.** Quarterly—1 and 4, Gules, seven lozenges conjoined 3, 3, and 1, Vair, on a canton Or a mullet Sable ; 2 and 3, Gules, a fess between six billets Or.

Sͬ **Albright** . . . ., brother to the Chauncellor of Denmarke, dubbed.

Sͬ **Thomas Stafford,** dubbed by the Kinge at the sea-syde when he sent his army into Brytaigne. Or, a chevron Gules, a canton Ermine, on the chevron a crescent Argent for difference.

Sͬ **John Podilston,** dubbed with Sͬ Thomas Stafforde. Gules, fretty Argent, a crescent Or for difference.

Sͬ **Lewys Carlton,** dubbed by the Kinge at Gwynes.

(? Sͬ **Gilbert Talbott.**) Quarterly of six—1, 2, 4, and 6, as 1, 2, 4, and 3 at p. 10; 3, Gules, a saltire Argent, a

	martlet Sable for difference ; 5, Or, fretty Gules; and the same Crest.
(Sr .... Nebill.)	Quarterly of five—1, Gules, on a saltire Argent a rose of the field ; 2, Chequy Or and Azure ; 3, Or, three chevrons Gules ; 4, Quarterly Argent and Gules, fretty Or, over all a bend Sable ; 5, Gules, a fess between six cross-crosslets Or, a crescent Sable for difference.
(? Sr .... Benstead.)	Quarterly—1 and 4, Gules, three bars-gemelles Argent ; 2 and 3, Azure, a fess dancettée Ermine between six cross-crosslets Argent.
....	Per pale Purpure and Azure, three lucies' heads erased and erect Or, in the mouth of each a spear-head Argent.
Sr .... Sabage.	Quarterly—1 and 2, as 1 and 2 at p. 16 ; 3, Gules, a chevron Argent between three falcons of the second, beaked, legged, and belled Or ; 4, Sable, a bend between two owls Argent.
....	Quarterly—1, Gules, a fess dancettée Argent ; 2, Azure, an eagle displayed Or, a bendlet Gules ; 3, Or, on a chief Gules two hands couped Argent, the one dexter, the other sinister ; 4, Gules, three lucies in pale Argent.
(Sr .... Pickering.)	Gules, on a chevron between three fleurs-de-lis Or as many pellets.
Sr George Darell.	Quarterly—1 and 4, DARELL, as at p. 16 ; 2 and 3, Argent, two bars-gemelles and in chief as many lions rampant Gules.
(...... Stanley.)	Quarterly—1 and 4, Quarterly, as at p. 11 ; 2 and 3, Gules, three legs flexed in triangle in armour Argent, spurred Or; over all on an escucheon of pretence—Azure, a lion rampant Argent.
(...... Courteney.)	Quarterly—1 and 4, Or, three torteaux ; 2 and 3, Or, a lion rampant Azure.
(...... Vere.)	Quarterly Gules and Or, in the first quarter a mullet Argent.
(......Fitzwarryn.)	Quarterly—1 and 4, Argent, a cross engrailed Gules between four water-bougets . Sable ; 2 and 3, Gules, billitée Or, a fess Argent.
Sr Robert Curson.	Argent, on a bend Sable between three wiverns' heads erased Gules a popinjay Argent beaked and legged Or.
Sr .... Gascoigne.	Quarterly—1 and 4 as 3, and 2 and 3 as 1, at p. 18.
Sr .... Beamont.	Azure, fleury and a lion rampant Or.

Sʳ **Will'm Browne.**   Argent, a chevron between three cranes Gules.

Sʳ . . . . **Evers.**   Quarterly—1 and 4, quarterly Or and Gules, on a bend Sable three escallops Argent ; 2 and 3, Or, a cross Gules.

Sʳ **Will'm Pawte.**   Quarterly—1 and 4, Or, a cross engrailed Gules ; 2 and 3, Per pale Azure and Gules, a lion rampant Ermine.

(? Sʳ . . . . **Mence.**)   Or, four pales Azure, on a chief Gules three crosses patée of the first.

Sʳ . . . . **Brereton.**   Quarterly—1 and 4, Argent, two bars Sable ; 2 and 3, Sable, on a bend Or three lozenges of the field.

Sʳ . . . . **Strange.**   Quarterly—1 and 4, Gules, two lions passant Argent, a bendlet Azure ; 2 and 3, Gules, on a bend Argent nine billets Sable.

Sʳ . . . . **Hungerforde.**   Arms of HUNGERFORD as at p. 10.

. . . .   Azure, a fess dancettée between three falcons Or belled proper.

In Anno nono on the Twelf day the Kinge dubbed these fowre followinge Knights in his chamber at Westminster :

Sʳ **Rauf Ostriche (Astry),** then Maior of London in Anno nono.
Sʳ **Will'm Martin,** late Maior of London.
The **Lorde Pothe** of Irelande.
The **Baron of Slane.**

These xxiii followinge were made Knights (of the Bath) at the creation of Henry Duke of Yorke on the Eve of All Sayntes, Anno decimo of the Kinge et Anno D'ni 1494 :

1. **Henry, Duke of Yorke.**   Arms as those of Prince Arthur at p. 20, the label Ermine.

2. **Thomas, Lord Darington.**   Quarterly of eight—1, Barry of six Argent and Azure, in chief three torteaux ; 2, Or, a maunch Gules ; 3, Barry of twelve Argent and Azure, an orle of martlets Gules ; 4, Gules, seven mascles conjoined, 3, 3, 1, Or ; 5, Azure, a cinquefoil Ermine ; 6, Argent, a fess and canton Gules ; 7, Sable, six mullets Argent, each charged with a torteaux ; 8, Sable, fretty Argent ; on the first three quarters a label of three points Ermine; on the first four another label of three points Azure. *Crest*—A unicorn passant Ermine armed Or, with Azure label as in the Arms.

3. **Henry, Lorde Clyfforde.**   Arms and Crest as at p. 14.

4. **Lorde Fitzwaryn.**   Quarterly—1 and 4, as at p. 23, a label of three points Azure each charged with as many fleurs-de-lis Or ; 2 and 3, Quarterly per fess indented · Argent and Gules. *Crest*—A wyvern Or.

5. **Lorde Dacre** of the South.   Quarterly—1 and 4, Azure, three lions rampant Or ; 2 and 3, Gules, three escallops Argent. *Crest*—An eagle's head Or, in the beak a round buckle.

6. **Sr Thomas Stanley.**   Quarterly—1, 2, 3, as 1, 2, 3 at p. 23 ; 4, Gules, two lions rampant Argent, quartering, 1, Argent, a fess and canton Gules ; 2, Or, a cross engrailed Sable ; over all a label of three points Argent, thereon another Azure ; the same escucheon of pretence. *Crest*—As at p. 11.

7. **Sr John Arundell.**   Quarterly—1 and 4, Sable, six swallows Argent; 2 and 3, Azure, a bend Or, a label of three points Gules ; over all, on an escucheon of pretence, Gules, an inescucheon within an orle of martlets Argent. *Crest*—A wolf passant Argent.

8. **Sr Walter Gryffithe.**   Quarterly—1 and 4, Gules, on a fess dancettée Argent between six lioncels rampant Or three martlets Sable ; 2 and 3, Azure, semée of cross-crosslets and three eagles displayed Or ; on an escucheon of pretence, Barry of six Argent and Gules, a bordure Azure charged with eight martlets Or. *Crest*—A maiden's head couped at the shoulders proper, vested Gules, crined Or.

9. **Sr Gervase Clyfton.**   Quarterly—1 and 4, Sable, semée of cinquefoils and a lion rampant Argent ; 2 and 3, Argent, a lion rampant double-queued Sable. *Crest* —Out of a ducal coronet Or a peacock's head Azure plumed of the first.

10. **Sr Robert Harecourt.**   Gules, two bars Or. *Crest*—On a ducal coronet Or a peacock proper.

11. **Sr Edmond Traforde.**   Quarterly—1 and 4, Argent, a griffin segreant Gules ; 2, Argent, on a bend Azure three garbs Or ; 3, Argent, on a bend Gules three escarbuncles Or. *Crest*—A thrasher with his flail all proper.

12. **Sr Henry Marney.**   Quarterly—1 and 4, Gules, a lion rampant-gardant Argent ; 2 and 3, Azure, two bars Argent. *Crest*—A chapeau Sable, lined Ermine, winged on the top Argent, corded Or.

13. **Sr Roger Newborough.**   Quarterly—1 and 4, Or, three bends Azure, a bordure engrailed Gules ; 2, Argent, three

E

14. r **Rauf Ryder.**

15. r **Thomas Bawde.**

16. r **John Speke.**

17. r **Humfrey Fulford.**

18. r **Robert Litton.**

19. r **Piers Edgecombe.**

20. r **Robert Clere.**

21. r **Thomas Fayrfax.**

22. r **Richard Knightley** de Falwesley.

23. r **John Choke.**

r **John Levesque,** a Breton, dubbed by the Kinge afterwarde, the ix day of November, the day of the tourney.

lions' heads erased Gules collared Or; 3, Argent, two bars Gules. *Crest*—A Blackamoor's head proper.

Quarterly—1 and 4, Azure, three crescents Or; 2 and 3, Gules, a lion rampant Argent on the shoulder a fleur-de-lis Azure. *Crest*—A man's leg and thigh couped Sable embowed at the knee, the foot upwards pointing to the sinister side, thereon a spur or.

Quarterly—1 and 4, Purpure, three chevrons Argent; 2 and 3, Gules, three wings Or. *Crest*—A Blackamoor's head in profile between two wings Sable.

Argent, two bars Azure, over all a spread-eagle Gules. *Crest*—A porcupine proper.

Quarterly—1 and 4, Sable, a chevron between three bears' heads erased Argent, muzzled Sable; 2 and 3, Azure, three bird-bolts erect Argent. *Crest*—A bear's head erect and erased Argent muzzled Sable.

Ermine, on a chief indented three ducal coronets Or. *Crest*—A bittern proper. "Avis quædam canens in arundine vel herbam aliquam ore tenens."

Quarterly—1 and 4, as at p. 11; 2 and 3, Azure, fleury and a lion rampant Argent. *Crest*—A boar's head, as in the Arms.

Quarterly—1 and 4, Argent, on a fess Azure three eagles displayed Or; 2 and 3, Argent, a cross moline Gules thereon an annulet of the field. *Crest*—Out of a ducal coronet Or, a plume of feathers Argent.

Quarterly—1 and 4, Argent, a lion rampant Sable debruised by three bars-gemelles Gules; 2 and 3, Argent, a chevron between three hinds' heads Sable. *Crest*—A lion's head erased Sable gorged with three bars-gemelles Gules.

Quarterly Or and Ermine, the first and fourth quarters charged with three pales Gules, a bordure Azure. *Crest*—A buck's head Argent, attired Or.

Argent, three cinquefoils per pale Azure and Gules. *Crest*—A crane's head proper. "Caput gruis."

Azure, a fess between three lions' faces Argent.

All these xxiii Knightes aforesayd of this Bayne payde all maner of fees to the Officers of Armes after their Estates and Degrees, viz., the high and mighty Prince the Duke of Yorke for his creation and all xx marks, the Lorde Harington l⁸, every baron xl⁸, and every bachelor xx⁸, with all their mantels, surcotts, girdels, laces, gloves, coyffes, and their blew gownes with their hoodes.

These xiiij followinge were made Baneretts at the batell of Blackheathe the xvii of June Anno D'ni 1497, Anno 12 of the Kinge, hadde agaynst the Co'mons of Cornwaill :

1. Sʳ **Thomas Lovell.** — Arms as at p. 15, a crescent Or for difference.
2. Sʳ **Charles Somersett.** — France and England quarterly within a bordure gobony Argent and Azure; over all a bendlet sinister Argent.
3. Sʳ **Reignald Bray.** — Arms as at p. 12, quartering Gules, three bends Vair.
4. Sʳ **Richard Guyleforde.** — Arms as at p. 9.
5. Sʳ **Robert Harecourt.** — Arms as at p. 25.
6. Sʳ **Res ap Thomas.** — Arms as at p. 11.
7. Sʳ **Henry Willoughby.** — Arms as at p. 15.
8. Sʳ **Richard FitzLewes.** — Arms as at p. 15.
9. Sʳ **John Saint John.** — Arms as at p. 21.
10. Sʳ **Thomas Greene.** — Arms as at p. 15.
11. Sʳ **Robert Broughton.** — Quarterly—1 and 4 as 1, and 2 and 3 as 2 and 3, at p. 16.
12. Sʳ **Nicholas Vaulx.** — Arms as at p. 16, quartering Gules, crusily and three lucies hauriant Or.
13. Sʳ **Will'm Tyrwhitte.** — Arms as at p. 15.
14. Sʳ **Thomas Tyrell.** — Arms as at p. 17. "In originali campus asorius reliqui argentei et fimbria de rubro."

The xiiij Banneretts beforesayd have payde their fees—v markes apeice.

Sʳ **John P** . . . . . dubbed at the bridgefoote at the Kinge's entringe of London after the battell of Blackheathe.
Sʳ **Morgan** . . . . . dubbed at the bridgefoote the same tyme.

Knightes made at Blackheathe feilde Anno 12 of the Kinge on Seint Botolphe's Day, the 17 of June Anno D'ni 1497, against the Comons of Cornwall.
(The 22 Knights following are each stated to have been "dubbed at the Battell of Blackheath:")

Sʳ **Edward Blount.** — Barry nebulée of six Or and Sable.
Sʳ **Will'm de la Poole,** brother to Edmond de la Poole, Erle of Suffolke; called Lord Will'm of Suffolke. — Quarterly—1 and 4, Azure, a fess between three leopards' faces Or ; 2 and 3, Argent, a chief Gules, over all a lion rampant double-queued Or. *Crest*—A Blackamoor's head in profile

proper wreathed and vested Argent charged with hurts and torteaux; on each a crescent for difference.

Sꞃ Thomas Brandon. Arms as at p. 10, a mullet Sable for difference.

Sꞃ John (Edward) Sabage. Arms quarterly as at p. 16, but falcons instead of martlets in the third coat.

Sꞃ Thomas Cornewall, Baron of Burforde. Ermine, a lion rampant Gules ducally crowned Or within a bordure engrailed Sable bezantée.

Sꞃ John Seymer of Wiltshire. Gules, a pair of "angels' wynges" conjoined in lure Or.

Sꞃ Gyles a Bruges. Quarterly—1 and 4, Argent, on a cross Sable a leopard's face Or; 2 and 3, Argent, a fess between three martlets Sable.

Sꞃ Edward Stanhope. Quarterly—1 and 4, Vert, three wolves passant in pale Or; 2 and 3, Sable, a bend between six cross-crosslets Argent (LONGVILLARS). "Quære de genere animalis, an sit Lupus vel vulpes."

Sꞃ Robert Lovell. Arms as at p. 15, a crescent Gules on a mullet Argent for difference.

Sꞃ Robert Tyrell. Arms as at p. 17.

Sꞃ John Ferrers. Gules, seven mascles conjoined, 3, 3, 1, Or.

Sꞃ Robert Drury. Argent, on a chief Vert two mullets pierced Or.

Sꞃ Henry Tay. Argent, a fess and in chief three martlets and in base a chevron Azure. *Crests*—Out of a ducal coronet Gules a tiger's head Or. A tiger sejant.

Sꞃ John Hussee. Quarterly—1 and 4, Or, a cross Vert; 2 and 3, Gules, three bars Ermine. *Crest*—A hind statant Argent.

Sꞃ John Rodney. Or, three eagles displayed Purpure.

Sꞃ Richard Pudsey. Vert, a chevron between three mullets Or, a crescent Azure for difference.

Sꞃ John Darell of Calehill in Kent. Arms as at p. 16, a fleur-de-lis Sable for difference.

Sꞃ Edmond Arundell of the West. Arms as at p. 25, without the quartering, a crescent Argent for difference.

Sꞃ Will'm Merynge. Argent, on a chevron Sable three escallops Or. *Crest*—A giraffe's head Sable spotted Argent, Or, and Gules, in the mouth a ring of the second. "The hedde of an oraffle" (see 'Sir John Mandevile's Travels,' by Halliwell. London, 1839; p. 289).

Sꞃ John Peche. Azure, a lion rampant Ermine ducally crowned Or.

Sꞃ Thomas Digby. Arms as at p. 17, without the mullet.

Sr Robert Payton.

Sable, a cross engrailed Or, in dexter chief a mullet Argent. *Crest*—A griffin sejant wings endorsed Or.

Sr John Hungerforde, dubbed at the bridge foote on the Kinge's entringe of London.

Arms as at p. 10, a mullet Argent for difference, quartering Argent, a lion rampant Sable ducally crowned Or, within a bordure Azure.

Sr John Fyneulx, Cheif Justice.

Vert, a chevron between three eagles displayed Or. *Crest*—A "phenix hedde" proper ducally crowned Gules.

Sr John Raynsforde.

Quarterly—1 and 4, Gules, a chevron engrailed between three fleurs-de-lis Argent ; 2 and 3, Gules, six eagles displayed Or (BROKSBURNE).

Sr George Taylboys, dubbed at the Battell of Blackheathe.

Argent, a saltire Gules, on a chief of the second three escallops of the field.

(The three Knights following are each stated to have been " dubbed at the bridge foote at the Kinge's entringe into London:")

Sr Bryan Sandforde.

Per chevron Sable and Ermine, in chief two boars' heads couped Or. *Crest*—On a ducal coronet Gules a boar's head couped Or, tusked Argent.

S^r . . . .

Argent, a chevron Gules.

Sr John Langforde.

Paly of six Or and Gules, over all a bend Argent. *Crest*—"Three chibolls (onion-heads) in a tufte of phesantes fethers." "Quære num iste Johannes Langforde portaret palatim de argento et rubeo in capite scuti asoreo leonem respicientem aureum. Constat namq. hæc esse insignia Langfordor. de com. Derby."

Sr Thomas Bryan.

Argent, three piles meeting at the base Vert.

(The seven Knights following are each stated to have been " dubbed at the Battell of Blackheath:")

Sr Philippe Calthorpe.

Quarterly—1 and 4, Chequy Or and Azure, a fess Ermine ; 2, Gules, on a chief Argent two mullets Sable ; 3, Azure, three wyverns passant Or, beaked and legged Gules.

Sr John Greene of Essex.

Gules, a lion rampant per fess Argent and Sable, ducally crowned Or.

Sr Roger Wentworthe.

Gules, on a bend Argent three escallops Azure.

Sr Robert Constable.

Quarterly Gules and Vair, over all a bend Or. *Crest*—A ship Or.

Sr John Skipwith de com. Lincoln.

Gules, three bars Argent, on a chief of the second a greyhound courant Sable.

Sᵣ John Williams. Azure, two organ-pipes in saltire between four crosses patée Argent.

Sᵣ Rouland de Veyllebylle. Argent, a lion rampant Gules charged on the breast with a bezant.

(The twelve Knights following are each stated to have been "dubbed at the Bridge foote in the King's enteringe of London :")

Sᵣ John Tate, then Maior of London. Per fess Or and Gules, a pale counter-changed, three Cornish choughs Sable beaked and legged Gules, a mullet Argent for difference.

Sᵣ John Shaa, then Shyrif of London. Argent, a chevron between three lozenges Ermines within a bordure Gules.

Sᵣ Robert Sheffeild, then Recorder of London. Argent, a chevron between three garbs Gules.

Sᵣ John Dunham. Azure, a chief indented Or, a label of three points Gules.

Sᵣ Thomas Rotherham. Vert, three bucks statant Or. "Quære an sit a robuck vel alterius generis." *Crest*—A buck's head Or between two branches Vert.

Sᵣ John Awdeley of Suffolke. Arms as at p. 14, a crescent for difference.

Sᵣ Philippe Cooke. Or, a chevron counter-compony Azure and Gules between three cinquefoils of the second.

Sᵣ John Bruerton. Argent, two bars sable.

Sᵣ Thomas de la Launde. Argent, a fess dancettée between three billets Gules.

Sᵣ Richard Lovelace.

Sᵣ Thomas Salisbury. Azure, on a saltire Argent five martlets Gules.

Sᵣ Richarde (John) Carewe. Arms as at p. 15.

Sᵣ Richard Waddon. Or, a man's leg couped at the middle of the thigh Azure. *Crest*—A man's leg couped at the middle thigh in armour proper embowed at the knee, the foot upwards, the toe pointing to the sinister side.

Sᵣ Andrew de Trevisano, a Venetian. Or, a chevron Azure. *Crest*—A man's head couped at the shoulders habited Azure, with three faces all proper, the middle one affrontée, the others in profile on either side, crined Argent.

Sᵣ Laurence Aylmer. Quarterly—1 and 4, Argent, on a cross engrailed between four martlets Sable five bezants within a bordure gobony Purpure and Azure ; 2 and 3, Argent, on a fess between three annulets Gules as many mullets of the field. *Crest*—An Indian goat statant Or, armed Sable.

These ten Banerettes followinge wer made in Scotland by Thomas, Erle of Surrey, the Kinge's Lieutenant, Anno 13 of the Kinge's reigne:

Sr William Gascoigne.
Sr John Nevill.
Sr John Hastinges.
Sr Thomas Darcy.
Sr Walter Gryffith.

Sr Rauf Ryder.
Sr Thomas Wortley.
Sr Roger Bellingham.
Sr Will'm Tyler.
Sr Edward Pykeringe.

Knightes in nombre 30 made in Scotland by Thomas, Erle of Surrey, the Kinge's Lieutenant, in Anno 13 of the Kinge's reigne:

Thomas Lord Howarde his sonne.
Sr Edward Howarde his sonne.
Sr Henry Scroope.
Sr Will'm Conyers.
Sr Will'm Bulmer.
Sr George Manners.
Sr Rauf Evers.
Sr Edward Savage.
Sr Roger Hopton.
Sr John Warbreton.
Sr Randolf Bruerton.
Sr Andrew Bruerton.
Sr Robert Aske.
Sr John Hotham.
Sr Henry Boynton.

Sr Edward Brampton's son, of Portugall, was dubbed by the Kinge at Wynchester Anno . .

Sr Robert Bellingham.
Sr Richard Woodrofe.
Sr Thomas Elderton.
Sr John Wlandisford.
Sr Roger Hastings.
Sr John Roclyff.
Sr Richard Cholmondeley.
Sr John Normanvile.
Sr Richard Aldeburgh.
Sr Richard Calverley.
Sr William Skargill.
Sr Richard Myrfeilde.
Sr Raulf Ellercar.
Sr Will'm Calverley.
Sr John Gower.

Other Knightes made in Scotlande by George, Lorde Strange, beinge there with Thomas, Erle of Surrey, Anno 13 of the Kinge's reigne:

Sr John Irelande.
Sr Will'm Bowthe.
Sr Richard Asheton.
Sr John Townley.
Sr Will'm Terbuke.

Sr Henry Halsall.
Sr Roger Pylston.
Sr Edward Hanmare.
Sr Humfrey Lysley.

Knightes of the Bathe made at the mariage of Prince Arthure the 17 day of Novembre, Anno 1501, Anno 17 of the Kinge's reigne:

Will'm, Lord Willoughby. Quarterly—1 and 4, Sable, a cross engrailed Or; 2, Gules, a cross moline Argent; 3, Or, a lion rampant double-queued Sable. *Crest* —As at p. 11.

Lorde Clynton.

Argent, six cross-crosslets fitchée Sable, on a chief Azure two mullets Or, on each a torteau. *Crest*—" A bushe of flagges or waterreedes Sable in a crowne Gules."

Sᵣ Thomas Englefcilde.

Quarterly—1 and 4, Barry of six Gules and Argent, on a chief Or a lion passant Azure ; 2 and 3, Sable, a fess between six martlets Or (RUSSALL). *Crest*—A spread eagle per pale Azure and Gules.

Sᵣ Nicholas Gryffyn.

Quarterly—1 and 4, Sable, a griffin segreant Argent beaked and armed Or ; 2 and 3, Gules, a cross patonce Or, a label of three points Sable. *Crest*—Six feathers per pale Or and Argent, over all a fess Azure.

Sᵣ Will'm Fylloll.

Vair, a canton Gules. *Crest*—A unicorn's head erased Sable.

Sᵣ Morgan Rydwelly.

Azure, a wolf salient Argent, collared countercompony Or and Gules. *Crest*—A goat's head Argent, armed Purpure and Azure.

Sᵣ Richard Fowler.

Quarterly—1 and 4, Or, three wolves' heads erased Gules within a bordure Azure charged with eight castles of the field; 2 and 3, Argent, a chief per pale Gules and Ermine, on the first an owl of the field.

Sᵣ Will'm Hartwell.

Quarterly—1 and 4, Sable, a buck's head cabossed Argent between the attires a cross patée pierced of the second ; 2 and 3, Gules, in chief five and in base three lozenges conjoined Argent. *Crest* — Surrounded with pales Or, a hart lodged Argent attired of the first.

Sᵣ Thomas Fenys.

Quarterly—1 and 4, Azure, three lions rampant Or ; 2 and 3, Gules, three escallops Argent; over all a crescent Argent for difference. *Crest*—An eagle's head holding in the beak a round buckle Or.

Sᵣ John Leghe of Stockwell.

Gules, a cross engrailed within a bordure Argent. *Crest*—A cock Gules with a ram's head Or, legged of the second.

Sᵣ Will'm Walgrave.

Quarterly—1 and 4, Per pale Argent and Gules ; 2 and 3, Barry of ten Argent and Azure. *Crest*—Out of a ducal coronet Or a plume of six feathers per pale Argent and Gules.

Sᵣ John Scroope of Castlecombe.

Quarterly—1 and 4, Azure, on the upper end of a bend Or a saltire engrailed Gules ; 2, Argent, a saltire engrailed Gules ; 3, Argent, a fess between two bars-gemelles Gules. *Crest*—

Out of a ducal coronet Or, two arms in armour counter-embowed Argent holding a ring jewelled Or.

Sᵣ Will'm Reade. Quarterly—1 and 4, Azure, three pheasants Or; 2 and 3, Per chevron Gules and Argent, three unicorns' heads couped counter-changed. *Crest*—A boar passant between two bucks' horns Sable.

Sᵣ John Ewardby. Argent, a saltire Sable, on a chief of the second two mullets pierced of the field. *Crest*—Out of a ducal coronet Or a maiden's head proper crined of the first, the back hair platted. " The heare loose and not thus woven in the originall, igitur quære."

Sᵣ Philip Bowthe. Quarterly—1 and 4, Argent, three boars' heads erased and erect Sable, an annulet of the second for difference; 2 and 3, Sable, on a fess Argent between six acorns Or, three oak-leaves Vert. *Crest*—A demi-St. Catherine proper, in the dexter hand a Catherine-wheel Or.

Sᵣ John Ley of Wiltshire. Argent, on a chief embattled Sable three plates. *Crest*—A wild ass's head proper. " Non constat cuius animalis caput hoc est." Note in pencil, " An onager's head."

Sᵣ Alnathe Malyverer. Gules, three greyhounds courant in pale Argent collared and ringed of the field studded Or. *Crest*—A greyhound statant as in the Arms, on the shoulder a crescent Sable for difference.

Sᵣ Thomas Laurance. Quarterly—1 and 4, Argent, a cross ragulée Gules; 2 and 3, Argent, two bars and in chief three mullets pierced Gules. *Crest*—A lucie's tail proper.

Sᵣ George Forster. Quarterly—1 and 4, Sable, on a chevron engrailed Argent a crescent of the field for difference; 2 and 3, Argent, on a chief Gules, three bucks' heads cabossed Or. *Crest*—Out of a ducal coronet Or a hind's head Gules. " Quære de capite isto, quale foret."

Sᵣ Thomas Grenefelde. Gules, three clarions Or. *Crest*—A garb of stalks Argent, leaved Vert, fructed Sable.

Sᵣ Robert Throgm'ton. Quarterly—1, Gules, on a chevron Argent three bars-gemelles Sable; 2, Argent, on a fess imbattled between six cross-crosslets fitchée Gules three crescents of the field (OLNEY); 3, Sable, a chevron Argent between three

F

crescents Or (SPYNEY); 4, Argent, three bird-bolts (BURGON). *Crest*—An elephant's head Sable, eared Gules, armed Argent.

Sʳ John Arondell of Trevyse. Quarterly—1, Sable, three chevronels Argent; 2, Argent, a bend Sable, on a chief Gules three mullets pierced Or; 3, Argent, a chevron Sable between three round buckles Gules; 4, Vert, a lion rampant-gardant Ermine debruised by a fess Gules. *Crest*—A buck's head couped affrontée Gules, attired Argent.

Sʳ John Philpott. Quarterly—1 and 4, Sable, a bend Ermine; 2 and 3, Or, two bars Gules, over all a bendlet Sable. *Crest*—A porcupine Argent.

Sʳ John Norton. Azure, a maunch Ermine, over all a bendlet Gules. *Crest*—A man's head " grayeshe," crined Sable.

Sʳ Hugh Lover. Or, six annulets Sable. *Crest*—A wyvern Argent, langued Gules.

Sʳ Walter Baskervile. Arms of BASKERVILE as at p. 14, quartering Gules, a fess Or between three escallops Argent. *Crest*—A garb of osiers Vert. "Oysyers."

Sʳ John Bassett. Quarterly—1 and 4, Barry wavy of six Argent and Gules; 2, Barry of six Vair and Gules; 3, Gules, a saltire Vair. *Crest*—A unicorn's head Argent armed and crined Or, charged on the neck with two bars indented Gules.

Sʳ Walter Stricklande. Quarterly—1 and 4, Sable, three escallops Argent; 2 and 3, Argent, a fess dancettée between ten billets Sable, four in chief and six in base. *Crest*—A garb proper.

Sʳ Lancelott Thyrkell. Argent, a maunch Gules. *Crest*—On the battlements of a church tower Argent, windows Sable, steeple Azure, a woman proper vested Gules, in her right hand a sword erect, in her left a baby swathed, all proper.

Sʳ Thomas Curwen. Argent, fretty Gules, a chief Azure. *Crest*—A unicorn's head Argent, armed and crined Or.

Sʳ George Hastynges, sonne and heir of George, Lord Hastinges. Quarterly—1, Argent, a maunch Sable, a label of three points Gules; 2, Sable, two bars Argent, in chief three plates; 3, Argent, a griffin segreant Gules, beaked and armed Or; 4, Paly wavy of six Or and Gules. *Crest* as that of HUNGERFORDE at p. 10.

Sʳ Henry Frowike. Quarterly—1 and 4, Azure, a chevron between three leopards' heads Or, a mullet Sable for difference; 2 and 3, Azure, three sturgeons naiant in pale Or, over all fretty Gules (STURGEON). *Crest*—Two arms counterembowed proper vested Azure, holding in the hands a leopard's head Or.

S⟨r⟩ **Roger Ormeston.** Sable, a chevron between three spear-heads Argent within a bordure Gules. *Crest*—A wyvern's head erased Vert.

S⟨r⟩ .... **Aston.** Per chevron Sable and Argent. *Crest*—An ass's head erased Sable. "Quære cuiusmodi caput sit."

S⟨r⟩ **Nicholas Byron.** Arms and Crest as at p. 13.

S⟨r⟩ **John Owgan.** Or, on a chief Sable three martlets of the field. *Crest*—A lion's paw erect Gules, unguled Azure.

S⟨r⟩ **Robert Waterton.** Barry of six Ermine and Gules, three crescents Sable. *Crest*—An otter "dunyshe," holding in the mouth a fish per fess Or and Argent.

S⟨r⟩ **John Gyffarde.** Argent, ten torteaux, 4, 3, 2, 1. *Crest*—A hand holding five gillyflowers all proper.

S⟨r⟩ **Will'm Ascu.** Sable, a fess between three asses passant Argent. *Crest*—An ass's head Argent.

S⟨r⟩ **George Putnam.** Quarterly—1 and 4, Sable, crusily fitchée and a stork Argent ; 2 and 3, Lozengy Azure and Or. *Crest*—A hind's head Gules. "Quære an sit caput vulpis vel damæ."

S⟨r⟩ **Gryffeth ap S⟨r⟩ Res Thomas.** Arms as at p. 11, with a label of three points Gules. *Crest*—Out of palisadoes Argent and Vert a demi-lion rampant Sable.

S⟨r⟩ **Robert Corbett.** Quarterly—1 and 4, Or, a crow Sable ; 2 and 3, Gules, crusily and three lucies hauriant Or. *Crest*—A squirrel sejant Or, cracking a nut.

S⟨r⟩ **Thomas Pawte.** Arms as at p. 24. *Crest*—Five branches Vert flowered with quatrefoils Argent.

S⟨r⟩ **Roger Strange.** Quarterly—1 and 4, Gules, two lions passant in pale Argent, over all a bendlet Or ; 2 and 3, Gules, on a bend Argent nine billets Sable. *Crest*—Two hands couped and clasped Argent.

S⟨r⟩ **Thomas Woodhouse.** Sable, a chevron Or billetée Gules between three cinquefoils Ermine. *Crest*—A demi-savage holding in his right hand and across his left shoulder a club, all proper.

S⟨r⟩ **Edward Fyldynge.** Argent, on a fess Azure three lozenges Or. *Crest*—Three filberts proper, leaved Vert.

S⟨r⟩ **Will'm Caylwey.** Quarterly—1 and 4, Argent, two glaziers' snippers in saltire Sable between four "peares in proper colour V. Ar. and G. lyke Catherine peares," within a borduro engrailed of the

S͇ʳ Richard de la Warre.

S͇ʳ John Cylpott.

S͇ʳ Henry Rogers.

S͇ʳ John Powlett.

S͇ʳ Thomas Longe.

S͇ʳ Thomas Sampson.

S͇ʳ John Trevilian.

S͇ʳ Will'm Scintmore.

S͇ʳ Will'm Martin.
S͇ʳ John Aston.
S͇ʳ Thomas Kempe.

second ; 2, Argent, a fess Gules, in chief a label of three points of the second ; 3, Azure, ten bezants, 4, 3, 2, 1. *Crest*—A cock Argent, combed and legged Azure.

Gules, crusily fitchée and a lion rampant Argent within a bordure engrailed Sable. *Crest*— An eagle's head Argent, beaked Gules.

Ermine, on a bend Sable three congers' heads erased Argent. *Crest*—A conger's head erased and erect Gules.

Quarterly—1 and 4, Argent, a chief Gules, a fleur-de-lis Or for difference; 2 and 3, Argent, fretty Sable, a chief Gules. *Crest*— Five branches leaved Vert fructed Gules.

Quarterly—1, POWLETT, as at p. 16; 2, Argent, fretty and a canton Sable ; 3, Argent, six martlets Sable; 4, Azure, a fess between three fleurs-de-lis Or. *Crest*—A falcon, wings expanded Or, ducally gorged. " The Lord S͇ᵗ John's creste."

Quarterly—1 and 4, Sable, crusily and a lion rampant Argent ; 2 and 3, Gules, two wings conjoined in lure Or. *Crest*—A demi-lion rampant Argent.

Quarterly—1 and 4, Gules, a cross counter-compony Argent and Sable ; 2 and 3, Or, a lion rampant Gules. *Crest*—Out of a ducal coronet Or six feathers Ermine.

Quarterly—1 and 4, Gules, a demi-horse Argent, hoofed and maned Or, issuing out of water in base proper ; 2, Argent, three bends Gules within a bordure Sable charged with ten bezants ; 3, Gules, a bend fusily Argent; 4, Ermine, three bows Gules. *Crest*—Two arms counter-embowed proper, habited Azure, cuffed Or, holding in the hands a pellet, thereon a parrot Vert beaked Gules.

Quarterly—1 and 4, Argent, two chevrons Gules, a label of three points ; 2, Or, crusily and a lion rampant Azure. *Crest*—A wolf passant " russett."

Argent, two bars Gules.
Argent, a fess and in chief three lozenges Sable.
Gules, three garbs Or. *Crest*—On a garb lying fessways Or a falcon with wings endorsed proper.

Knightes of the Sworde made at the sayd mariage of Prince Arthure :

Sͬ John Danvers of Dauncy. — Quarterly—1 and 4, Argent, on a bend Gules three martlets Or winged Vert ; 2 and 3, Gules, two bars Or, in chief two bucks' heads cabossed of the second ; over all a crescent for difference. *Crest*—Two hands conjoined in pile Argent.

Sͬ John Cottysmore. — Azure, a spread-eagle Argent, charged with an escucheon Gules, thereon a leopard's face Or. *Crest*—A unicorn sejant Argent, maned Or.

Sͬ Pumfrey Catisby. — Argent, two lions passant in pale Sable within a bordure engrailed Gules. *Crest*—A cat's head Ermine.

Sͬ John Vavasour, Justice. — Or, a fess dancettée Sable. *Crest*—A squirrel sejant Gules, cracking a nut Or.

Sͬ John Pounde. — Argent, on a fess Gules, between two boars' heads couped Sable in chief, and a cross patée fitchée of the third in base, three mullets pierced of the field. *Crest*—A gourd Or, leaved Vert.

Sͬ John Fogge.

Sͬ Lewes Bagott.

Sͬ Will'm Clopton.

Sͬ Will'm Perott.

Sͬ James ap Owen.

Sͬ Edmond Jenny.

Sͬ Thomas Barneston.

Sͬ Thomas Knight.

Sͬ Rauf Verney.

Sͬ Philippe Tilney.

Sͬ Thomas Danvers.

Sͬ Dedo de Aÿcbedo, a Spanyard.

Sͬ Ferdinando de Villa Lobos, a Spanyard.

Sͬ Thomas Woode, Cheif Justice. — Quarterly—1 and 4, Gules, three demi-woodmen Argent, holding clubs over their dexter shoulders Or ; 2 and 3, Argent, a pelican in piety Sable.

Sͬ Robert Reade, Justice. — Gules, on a bend wavy Argent three shovellers Sable beaked and legged Or. *Crest*—A shoveller close per bend Argent and Sable, beaked and legged Or.

Sͬ Thomas Tremayle, Justice. — Quarterly—1 and 4, Argent, a fess between three brogues Gules, a crescent for difference ; 2, Argent, a trivet within a bordure Sable ; 3, Sable, a chevron between three escallops Argent.

Sͬ Will'm Danvers, Justice. — Arms of DANVERS as above, quartering Ermine, on a bend Gules two chevrons Or.

Sͬ John Tymperley.

Sͬ John Champernoun.

Sͬ John Villers.

Sr Franciscus de Capello, a
Venetian, made at Greenwich
18 of May, anno 17.

A p Dave of Islande, a Scott.

Sr Thomas Frowyke, Cheif   Arms quarterly as at p. 34.
Justice of the Common Pleas,
made at Richmont in Christmas,
anno 18.

Sr Robert Taufelde, made   Argent, two chevrons between three martlets
Knight at the mariage of Prince   Sable.
Arthure.

Sr Bartholomew Rede, Mayre   Per pale Gules and Sable, a cross bottonée
. . . ., anno 18, dubbed at Bay-   fitchée Argent between four fleurs-de-lis Or.
nardes Castle with these fol-   *Crest*—A fleur-de-lis per pale Or and Argent.
lowinge (ut opinor):

These followinge were dubbed by the Kinge in his chamber at Baynardes Castle
betwene Ester and Whitsontyde after the death of the Queene, anno 18 :

Sr Rey Van Aubyll.   Azure, a wing Argent issuing from the sinister
side ; impaling, Barry of four Argent and
Gules. *Crest*—On a cushion Gules tasselled
Or a dog sejant gardant Argent, collared and
belled of the second.

Sr John Fisher.   Argent, on a chevron between three demi-
lions rampant Gules as many bezants.

Sr Edmond Lucy.

Sr . . . . Cotton of Cambrigeshire.

Sr Gilbert Debbenham.   Quarterly—1 and 4, Sable, a bend between two
crescents Or ; 2 and 3, Or, crusily and a
chevron Gules (BROCKHOLE).

Knightes of the Sworde dubbed at the creation of Prince Henry the 18 of
February, anno 19 of the Kinge's reigne :

Sr John Grey, Viscount Lysle.   Quarterly of six—1 and 2 as 1 and 2 at p. 20 ;
3, Gules, seven mascles conjoined, 3, 3, 1, Or,
quartering Azure, a cinquefoil pierced Ermine ; 4, Azure, a lion rampant within a
bordure Or, quartering Gules, a lion rampant
within a bordure engrailed Or ; 5, Gules, a
fess between six cross-crosslets Or, quartering chequy Or and Azure, a chevron Ermine ;
6, Gules, crusily and a chevron Argent,
quartering—1, Gules, a lion rampant gardant Argent ducally crowned Or ; and 2,
Sable, a chevron Ermine between three es-

callops Argent. *Crest*—A unicorn statant Argent armed Or, a crescent Gules for difference.

Lorde Dacres of the Northe. Gules, three escallops Argent. *Crest*—A bull statant Gules, armed, collared, and lined Or.

Sr Bryan Stapleton. Quarterly—1 and 4, Argent, a lion rampant Sable ; 2 and 3, Argent, a chevron Sable, in dexter chief a cinquefoil of the second. *Crest* —A Saracen's head in profile proper wreathed about the temples Argent.

Sr Rauf Grey. Gules, a lion rampant within a bordure engrailed Argent.

Sr Miles Bussy. Argent, three bars Sable.

Sr Edward Pomerey. Arms and Crest as at p. 19.

Sr John Mordant. Argent, a chevron between three estoiles Sable.

Sr James Hubert. Sable, an estoile of eight points Or between two flanches Ermine. *Crest*—A buffalo passant per pale Sable and Gules bezantée, armed Or, in the nostrils a gemel-ring of the third.

Sr Richard Emson. Quarterly—1 and 4, Argent, two bends Sable ; 2 and 3, Gules, three pears Or. *Crest*—A wild cat statant-gardant "browne."

Sr Davy Philippe. Per bend Or and Argent, a lion rampant Sable within a bordure gobony of the second and Vert.

Sr Hugh Vaughan. Quarterly—1 and 4, Azure, a fess Or between three horses' heads Argent erased of the second, bridled Gules, within a bordure gobony Argent and of the second ; 2 and 3, Per pale Azure and Purpure, three lucies' heads erased and erect Or, in the mouth of each a spear-head Argent. *Crests*—1, A lion's gamb erect Or unguled Azure ; 2, A lucie's head as in the Arms.

Sr Edmond Hampden. Argent, a saltire Gules between four eagles displayed Azure, beaked and legged of the second.

Sr Nicholas Waddam. Quarterly—1 and 4, Gules, a chevron between three roses Argent ; 2, Or, on a chevron Gules three martlets Argent ; 3, Argent, on a chief Gules three stags' heads cabossed of the field attired Or. *Crest*—The stump of a tree sprouting at the top per pale Argent and Vert, on the sinister side a bough of the second.

Sr William Perpount. Quarterly—1 and 4, Argent, a lion rampant Sable within an orle of eight cinquefoils

Gules ; 2, Argent, six annulets in pale, 3, 3, Sable ; 3, Azure, three porcupines Or.

S͛ John Southworthe. • Sable, a chevron between three cross-crosslets Argent. *Crest*—A goat's head erased Argent.

S͛ Adrian Fortescu. Arms as at p. 10, a crescent on the mullet for difference ; and the same Crest, with a crescent for difference.

S͛ John Lyngeyn. Barry of six Or and Azure, on a bend Gules three roses Argent. *Crest*—Out of a ducal coronet Or a garb Vert, fructed Argent, banded " quære quid foret."

S͛ John Everingham. Quarterly—1 and 4, Gules, a lion rampant Vair ; 2 and 3, Argent, a fess Azure, a label of three points Gules. *Crest*—A stag's head Argent, attired Or.

S͛ John Constable of Holder- Barry of six Or and Azure. *Crest*—A dragon's
ness. head Argent charged with three bars Gules, on each as many lozenges Or.

S͛ Henry Wyderington. Quarterly—Argent and Gules, a bendlet Sable. *Crest*—A bull's head Sable, armed and spotted Argent.

S͛ Thomas Trenchard.
S͛ Will'm Gyfforde. Arms and Crest as at p. 35.
S͛ Thomas Sutton. Argent, a canton Sable.
S͛ John Lysle of Throkston Arms and Crest as at p. 19.
in Wiltshire.
S͛ Thomas Fetyplace.
S͛ John Cutte.
S͛ Robert Southwell.
Lorde Henry Stafforde. Quarterly—1, France and England quarterly within a bordure Argent ; 2, Azure, a bend Argent cotised Or between six lioncels rampant of the last ; 3, Azure, on a bend Argent cotised Or between six lioncels rampant of the third three mullets Gules ; 4, Or, a chevron Gules ; over all a crescent Gules for difference. *Crest*—Out of a ducal coronet per pale Gules and Sable a swan, wings endorsed Argent.

S͛ John Wiltshire, dubbed by Per chevron Azure and Argent, in chief eight
the Duke of Julyers at the crosses patée Or. *Crest*—An eagle's leg erased
Kinge of Romane's comand- à-la-cuisse Sable.
ment.

𝕿𝖍𝖊 Names and Armes of those that were honoured with the Order of Knighthoode in the tyme of the triumphant reigne of

Kinge Henry the Eight.

(Cotton MSS., Claudius, c. iii., fol. 68–144.)

Sᵣ Robert Radcliff, Lord Fitz-walter.

Quarterly—1, Argent, a bend engrailed Sable ; 2 and 3, as under FITZWALTER, p. 11 ; 4, Argent, three bars Gules ; and the same Crest.

Sᵣ Henry Scroope, Lorde Scroope.

Quarterly—1 and 4, Azure, a bend Or ; 2 and 3, as 2 at p. 32 ; on an escucheon of pretence SCROOPE, with a label of three points Argent. *Crest*—Out of a ducal coronet a plume of feathers Azure.

Sᵣ Henry Daubeney, Lorde Daubeney.

Gules, five fusils in fess Argent. *Crest*—A holly-tree Vert, fructed Gules.

Sᵣ Robert Wyllughby, Lorde Brooke.

Quarterly—1, Quarterly as 1, 2 at p. 31, a crescent for difference ; 2, Gules, a cross patonce Or ; 3, Gules, on four fusils conjoined in fess Argent as many escallops Sable ; 4, Or, a chevron Gules within a bordure Sable. Crest as at p. 11.

The Lorde Fitzhugh.

Azure, three chevronels braced in base and a chief Or. *Crest*—On a mural coronet Or a wyvern Azure.

The Lorde Mountjoy.

Quarterly of six—1 and 6, 2, 3, and 4, same as 3, 1, 2, and 4 under Sir JAMES BLOUNT at p. 9 ; 5, Argent, three fleurs-de-lis Azure. The same Crest.

Sᵣ Henry Clyfforde.

Arms and Crest as at p. 14. On the coat a label of three points Gules.

Sᵣ Maurice Barkeley.

Quarterly of six—1, as at p. 19 ; 2, Gules, three lions passant gardant in pale Or, a label of three points Argent ; 3, Chequy Or and Azure ; 4, Gules, a lion rampant Argent ; 5, Sable, a lion rampant Argent, ducally crowned Or ; 6, Azure, crusily and a lion rampant Or ; and the same Crest.

Sᵣ Thomas Knyvett.

Quarterly of six—1, Argent, a bend within a bordure engrailed Sable ; 2, Argent, a chief Gules, a bend Azure ; 3, Chequy Or and Gules, a chief Ermine ; 4, Bendy of eight Gules and Argent, quartering chequy Or and Gules, a bend Ermine ; 5, Argent, three pales

G

Gules within a bordure Azure bezantée;
6, Or, four bendlets Azure, a canton Argent.
Crest—A demi-dragon, wings endorsed, Azure.

Sʳ Andrew Wyndesore.

Quarterly of six—1 and 6, Gules, a saltire Argent between twelve cross-crosslets Or; 2, Argent, on a bend cotised Sable three mullets of the field; 3, Azure, a cross moline quarter-pierced Argent; 4, Argent, on a cross Sable five bezants; 5, Gules, five lioncels rampant in cross Or. *Crest*—A buck's head Argent.

Sʳ Thomas Parre.

Quarterly—1 and 4, Argent, two bars Azure within a bordure engrailed Sable; 2 and 3, Or, three water-bougets Sable. *Crest*—Five roses Gules, stalked and leaved Vert.

Sʳ Thomas Bulleyn.

Quarterly of eight—1, Argent, a chevron Gules between three bulls' heads couped Sable; 2, Quarterly Sable and Argent; 3, Azure, a fess between six cross-crosslets fitchée Or; 4, Azure, three sinister hands couped Argent; 5, Ermine, on a chief Sable three crosses patée Argent; 6, Azure, fretty Argent, a chief Gules; 7, Argent, a bend wavy Sable; 8, Azure, three mullets Or, a chief indented Argent. *Crests*—1, A bull's head Sable, armed Or, langued Gules; 2, A wyvern sejant Or.

Sʳ Richard Wentworth.

Quarterly—1, Gules, on a bend Argent three escallops Azure; 2, Quarterly Argent and Gules fretty Or, over all on a bend Sable three mullets of the first; 3, Argent, a saltire engrailed Gules; 4, Barry of six Or and Gules, a canton Ermine. *Crest*—A griffin passant Or. "Huius Ricardi insignia paulo post inter baronettos melius et verius depinguntur."

Sʳ Henry Ittreight.

Quarterly—1 and 4, Gules, on a cross patonce Or five mullets Gules; 2 and 3, Ermine, a cross moline Sable. *Crest*—Out of a ducal coronet Or, a buck's head Azure, attired Or.

Sʳ Franceys Cheney.

Arms (without the difference) and Crest as at p. 9.

Sʳ Henry Wyatt.

Gules, on a fess Or between three boars' heads couped Argent, as many lions rampant Sable. *Crest*—A demi-lion rampant Sable, charged on the shoulder with a pheon Or, holding in the dexter paw an arrow of the second.

Sᵣ George Hastings.

Sᵣ Thomas Metham.

Sᵣ Gyles Alington.

Sᵣ John Trevepnon.

Sᵣ Thomas Bedingfeild.

Sᵣ John Schelton.

Sᵣ Will'm Crowmer.

Sᵣ John Heydon of Bacons-thorpe.

Sᵣ Godarde Oxenbridge.

Sᵣ Henry Sacheverell.

Sᵣ Stephan Jennyns, Maior of London (1508), dubbed the day of the coronation before dynner, payed his fee lyke a baron.

Arms and Crest as at p. 21.

Quarterly—1 and 4, Quarterly Azure and Argent, in the first quarter a fleur-de-lis Or; 2 and 3, Argent, a lion rampant Sable (ASHBY). Crest—A bull's head Sable, armed Or, between two bats' wings of the first. "Alæ vespertilionis."

Quarterly—1 and 4, Sable, a bend engrailed between six billets Argent; 2 and 3, Gules, three covered cups Argent. Crest—A talbot statant Ermine.

Quarterly—1 and 4, Argent, on a fess Azure between two chevrons Gules three escallops Or; 2 and 3, Argent, a lion rampant Gules. Crest—A stag statant quarterly Gules and Argent, attired Or.

Arms of BEDINGFEILD as at p. 13; quartering 2 and 3, Paly bendy of four Gules and Argent. The same Crest.

Arms and Crest as at p. 19.

Quarterly—1 and 4, Argent, a chevron engrailed between three crows Sable; 2 and 3, Argent, a squirrel sejant Gules, cracking a nut. Crest—A tiger statant regardant a mirror Argent.

Arms and Crest as at p. 12.

Quarterly—1 and 4, Gules, a lion rampant double-queued Argent within a bordure Vert escallopée Or; 2, Gules, crusily and a lion rampant Or; 3, Gules, a bend Argent, fretty Sable. Crest—A demi-lion rampant double-queued Argent holding in the dexter paw an escallop Or.

Quarterly—1, Argent, on a saltire Azure five water-bougets Or; 2, Gules, a pale fusily Argent (STATHAM); 3, Argent, a lion rampant Sable, ducally crowned Or, charged on the shoulder with a mullet of the field (MORLEY); 4, Argent, three squirrels playing on bagpipes Gules (HOPEWELL). Crest—A goat statant Argent.

Argent, a chevron Gules between three plummets Sable. Crest—A griffin's head Or, wings endorsed, holding in the beak a plummet Sable.

Sr **Hugh Odonell,** dubbed at the bankett at Westminster anno secundo.

Sr **Henry Guildeforde,** dubbed at Westminster the 20 day of Marche, the last day of the Parlement anno iij°.

Arms as at p. 9, a mullet Or for difference. *Crest*—A tree ragulée couped at the top Or, flamant Gules, a mullet Azure for difference.

Sr **Charles Brandon,** dubbed at Westm. the same day.

Quarterly—1 and 4, as at p. 10 ; 2 and 3, Azure, a cross moline Or, quartering lozengy Ermine and Gules. *Crest*—A lion's head erased Or, guttée de larmes, ducally crowned per pale Gules and Argent.

Sr **Henry Guildeforde,** dubbed by the Kinge of Arragon at Bruges in Castille the 15 day of Septembre anno d'ni 1511.

Arms as above, without the difference ; but on 1 and 4 a canton Argent charged with a pomegranate Gules, seeded Or ; the same Crest charged with a pomegranate as in the Arms.

Sr **Ulystan Browne,** dubbed at Bruges the same tyme.

Gules, a chevron between three lions' gambs erased and erect, within a bordure Argent ; over all a chief of the second, thereon an eagle displayed Sable armed and ducally crowned Or. *Crest*—A lion's gamb erased and erect Argent, holding a wing Sable.

Sr **Thomas Burghchier,** Lord Fitzwaryn.

Quarterly—1, Argent a cross engrailed Gules between four water-bougets Sable, quartering Gules, billitée Or, a fess Argent, over all a label of three points ; 2, Quarterly per fess indented Argent and Gules, quartering Argent, two bends wavy Sable ; 3, Gules, four fusils in fess Ermine, quartering Gules, three arches Or, two single, and one double in base (ARCHES). *Crest*—An old man's head in profile proper couped at the shoulders, habited Vert, collared Argent, on his head a ducal coronet Or, out of which a long cap hanging forward Gules, tasselled of the last.

Sr **Guyot de Heule,** Sr **de la Mote,** dubbed at Greenwiche the 18 day of Aprill anno tertio of the Kinge.

Quarterly Gules and Or, in the first and third quarters three bars Argent. *Crest*—A swan wings expanded Ermine, ducally crowned Or.

Sr **Henry Sherbourne.**

Quarterly—1 and 4, Or, on a chevron engrailed between three eagles displayed Gules as many plates ; 2 and 3, Gules, a lion rampant Or, langued Sable, a canton Ermine. *Crest*—A lion's gamb erect Or, grasping an eagle's head erased Gules.

Sʳ Thomas Lucy.

Quarterly—1 and 4, Gules, crusily and three lucies hauriant Argent; 2, Quarterly Or and Azure, in the first and third quarters an eagle displayed Sable, in the second and third a buck's head cabossed Or; 3, Barry of six Argent and Azure, on a bend three mullets, quartering, 1, Or, a cross between four martlets Gules; 2, Argent, billitée and a lion rampant Sable; 3, Azure, a fess between six cross-crosslets Argent. *Crest*—Out of a ducal coronet Gules a boar's head Ermine between two wings Sable billitée Or.

Sʳ John Burdett.

Quarterly—1 and 4, Azure, two bars Or, on each three martlets Gules; 2, Azure, a lion passant Argent; 3, Gules, a fess Or between six martlets Argent. *Crest*—A lion's head erased Sable, langued Gules.

Sʳ Anthony Utreight, made at Eltham.

Arms and Crest as at p. 42, on each a crescent Or for difference.

Sʳ Robert Morton.

Quarterly—1 and 4, Quarterly Gules and Or, in the first quarter a goat's head erased Argent, on a chief of the third three torteaux, each charged with an escallop of the second, a label of three points Azure; 2 and 3, Argent, on a chevron between three lapwings Sable two Ermine spots. *Crest*—A lapwing rising Argent, winged and legged Sable.

Sʳ Will'm Sidney, made in Bretaigne by the Duke of Norff., Lorde Admirall.

Or, a pheon Azure. *Crest*—A porcupine Azure, quilled, collared, and lined Or.

(The following 28 Knights are each stated to be a " Banneret.")

1. Sʳ John Peche.

Arms as at p. 28.

2. Sʳ Robert Brandon.

Arms of BRANDON as at p. 10, a crescent for difference.

3. Sʳ Henry Guildford.

Arms quarterly as No. 2 at p. 44.

4. Sʳ Edward Poyninges.

Arms as at p. 9.

5. Sʳ Andrew Wyndesore, Threasorer of the Kinge's Middle Warde.

Quarterly of five—1, 2, 3, 4, and 5, as at p. 42.

6. Sʳ John Reynsford.

Quarterly—1 and 4 and 2, as 1 and 2 at p. 29; 3, on a bend three roundles.

7. Sʳ Henry Wyatt.

Arms as at p. 42.

8. Sʳ John Seymour.

9. Sʳ Richard Carew.

Quarterly—1 and 4, CAREW, as at p. 15; 2 and 3, Quarterly Sable and Argent.

10. Sͬ **John Awdeley.**   Arms as at p. 30.

11. Sͬ **Anthony Ultreight.**   Arms as at p. 45.

12. Sͬ **Thomas West.**   . Quarterly—1 as 1, and 2 and 3 quarterly as 2 and 3, at p. 21 ; 4, MORTIMER. " Mortymer of Wigmore : beareth asure, 3 barres in the cheif 2 palettes in eche canton a gyron gold ; an inner scocheon Ermins."

13. Sͬ **Robert Dymoke,** Threasorer of the Kinge's Rerewarde.   Quarterly of six—1, Sable, two lions passant Argent ducally crowned Or ; 2, Or, a lion rampant double-queued Sable ; 3, Gules, a fess dancettée between six cross-crosslets Or ; 4, Barry of six Ermine and Gules, three crescents Sable ; 5, Vair, a fess Gules, fretty Or ; 6, Ermine, five fusils in fess Gules.

14. Sͬ **John Husee.**   Arms quarterly as at p. 28; but 2 and 3, Ermine, three bars Gules.

15. Sͬ **John Arundell** of the West.   Quarterly—1, Sable, six swallows Argent; 2, Gules, four fusils in fess Ermine, quartering Gules, three arches Argent bases Or ; 3, Gules, an escucheon within an orle of martlets Argent; 4, Azure, a bend Or, a label of three points Gules.

16. Sͬ **Richard Wentworthe.**   Quarterly of six—1, Sable, a chevron between three leopards' faces Or, a crescent Gules for difference ; 2, Quarterly Argent and Gules, fretty Or, over all on a bend Sable three mullets of the first ; 3, Argent, a saltire engrailed Gules ; 4, Argent, a fess between two bars-gemelles Gules ; 5, Barry of six Or and Gules, a canton Ermine ; 6, Azure, three lucies hauriant between as many crosscrosslets Or. *Crest*—A ewer wreathed Argent.

17. Sͬ **Randolf Brereton,** Mareschall of the Rerewarde.

18. Sͬ **Piers Edgecombe.**   Gules, on a bend Ermines cotised Or three boars' heads couped Argent.

19. Sͬ **Henry Clyfforde.**

20. Sͬ **Thomas Cornewall.**

21. Sͬ **Thomas Leighton.**

22. Sͬ **Thomas Blount.**

23. Sͬ **John Aston.**   Arms as at p. 36.

24. Sͬ **Will'm Perpount.**   Arms quarterly as at p. 39.

25. Sͬ **Henry Sacheverell.**   Arms quarterly as at p. 43.

26. Sͬ **George Wolforde.**

27. Sͬ **Henry Walsall.**

28. Sͬ **George Warbleton.**

(? S𝔯 **Thomas Barnardiston.**) Gules, a fess dancettée Ermine between three
cross-crosslets fitchée Argent, - a bendlet
sinister Or. *Crest*—A talbot's head Gules
eared Argent gorged with a fess dancettée
Ermine.

(Knightes made at Tourraine in the Church, after the Kinge came from Masse,
under his banner in the Church, 25 Decembre in the 5th yeare of his reigne—
Harl. MS. 6063.)

1. **John, Lorde Awdeley.** Arms quarterly and Crest as at p. 14.
2. **Lorde Cobham.**
3. **Lorde Richard Grey.** Quarterly of eight—1, 2, 3, same as 1 and 2 at
p. 20 ; 4, Gules, seven mascles conjoined,
3, 3, and 1, Or ; 5, Azure, a cinquefoil Ermine ; 6, Argent, a fess and canton Gules ;
7, Sable, six mullets Argent, on each a torteau ; 8, Sable, fretty Argent. *Crest*—A
sun in splendour Or behind a unicorn statant
Ermine, armed of the first.

4. **Lorde Edward Grey.**
5. **S𝔯 Anthonye Wynge=**
feilde. Quarterly—1 and 4, Argent, on a bend Gules
cotised Sable three pairs of wings conjoined
in lure of the field ; 2, quarterly Sable and
Or ; 3, Barry of six Or and Gules, a canton
Ermine, quartering chequy Or and Azure.
Crest—A bull passant quarterly Sable and
Or, horned of the second.

6. **S𝔯 Thomas Tyrell** of Gyp-
pynge. Arms as at p. 17, a martlet Or for difference.
Crest—A boar's head erect Argent, in the
mouth a peacock's tail proper, on the head
a martlet Sable for difference.

7. **S𝔯 Chr'opher Willughby.** Quarterly of six—1, Sable, a cross engrailed Or ;
2, Gules, a cross moline Argent ; 3, Gules, a
lion rampant Or, quartering Sable, fretty Or,
a crescent for difference ; 4, 5, and 6, as 2,
3, 4 under DYMOKE at p. 46 ; over all a
crescent Or for difference. *Crest*—Same as
at p. 11, a crescent Argent for difference.

8. **S𝔯 Edward Guildeforde.** Arms and Crest as No. 1 at p. 44, without the
difference.

9. **S𝔯 Will'm Compton.** Quarterly—1 and 4, Sable, a lion rampant
gardant Or between three helmets close
Argent ; 2 and 3, Argent, a chevron Vert
within a bordure Sable bezantée. *Crest*—A
demi-griffin erased Gules enfiled by a ducal
coronet Or.

10. Sr Richard Sacheverell.   Arms and Crest of SACHEVERELL as at p. 43, on each a crescent for difference.

11. Sr Thomas Tyrell.   .   TYRELL, as at p. 17, quartering Argent, a cross between four escallops Sable (COGGESHALL). Crest as at p. 47.

12. Sr Will'm Evers.   Arms of EVERS as at p. 24, a label Azure. *Crest* —A wild-cat statant gardant quarterly Or and Azure.

13. Sr Thomas Borough.   Quarterly—1, 2, and 4, as at p. 14 ; 3, Gules, on a chevron Or three estoiles Sable ; over all a label of three points Gules. Crest as at p. 14.

14. Sr Robert Tyrwhit.   Arms as at p. 15, a label of three points Argent. *Crest*—A lapwing Or.

15. Sr Thomas Fairfax.   Quarterly of six—1 and 6, and 2, same as 1 and 2 at p. 26 ; 3, Barry of eight Argent and Gules, on a canton Sable a cross patonce Or ; 4, Or, a bend Azure ; 5, Argent, a chevron between three martlets Sable. *Crest*—A goat's head erased Argent, armed and ducally gorged Or, debruised by three bars-gemelles Gules. " Alibi : couppe in originali."

16. Sr Edward Hungerforde.   Arms and Crest as at p. 10, the latter without the coronet.

17. Sr Giles Capell.   Gules, a lion rampant between three cross-crosslets Or, a label of three points Argent. *Crest*—An anchor erect Gules bezantée, ringed Azure.

18. Sr Edward Doon.   Azure, a wolf salient Argent. *Crest*—Five serpents entwined heads erect Vert, langued Azure.

19. Sr Edward Bellknape.   Quarterly—1, Azure, three eagles displayed in bend between two cotises Argent ; 2, Gules, a fess counter-compony Argent and Sable between six crosses patée fitchée of the second ; 3, Or, two bends Gules ; 4, Bendy of ten Or and Azure. *Crest*—A lizard Or, scaled Vert, ducally gorged and lined of the first.

20. Sr Edward Ferrers.   Arms as at p. 28. *Crest*—A unicorn statant Ermine, armed Or, a crescent Gules for difference.

21. Sr Will'm Musee.   Arms quarterly as at p. 9, a crescent Gules for difference. *Crest*—A hind couchant regardant Argent, ducally gorged and lined Or.

22. Sr Owen Perrott.

23. Sr Will'm Fitz William.   Quarterly—1 and 4, Lozengy Gules and Argent, a mullet for difference ; 2, quarterly, 1 and 4, Argent, three lozenges in fess Gules, quarter-

ing Or, an eagle displayed Vert, legged Gules—
2 and 3, Gules, a saltire Argent, a label of
three points compony of the second and Azure,
and a crescent for difference; over all on an
escucheon of pretence, quarterly—1, Gules,
a cross engrailed Argent; 2, Argent, on a
canton Gules a cinquefoil Or; 3, Azure, a
fess between three leopards' faces Or; 4,
Argent, on a fess dancettée Sable three bezants;
3, Gules, six martlets Argent, quartering,
1, Azure, a bend Or, a label of three points
Argent; 2, Argent, three garbs between six
cross-crosslets fitchée Gules; 3, Argent, a
bend fusily Sable.

24. Sr **Chr'opher Garneys.** Argent, a chevron Azure between three escallops
Sable. *Crest*—A cubit arm grasping a scimitar embrued all proper, hilt and pommel Or.

25. Sr **Henry Poole (Pole).** Quarterly of eight—1, France and England
quarterly, a label of three points Argent, on
each point a canton Gules; 2, Per pale Or
and Sable, a saltire engrailed counterchanged;
3, Gules, a saltire Argent, a label of three
points compony of the second and Azure; 4,
Gules, a fess between six cross-crosslets Or;
5, Chequy Or and Azure, a chevron Ermine;
6, Argent, three fusils in fess Gules; 7, Or,
an eagle displayed Vert; 8, Or, three chevronels Gules, quartering, Quarterly Argent
and Gules fretty Or, a bend Sable. *Crest*—
Out of a ducal coronet a demi-griffin Argent,
beaked and eared Gules.

26. Sr **John Veer.** Arms as at p. 23. *Crest*—A boar passant
Azure, bristled and tusked Or.

27. Sr **John Marney.** Quarterly—1, 2, and 4, as 1, 2, and 4 at p. 25;
3, Argent, a saltire Sable between twelve
apples Gules slipped Vert; the same Crest,
without the cord.

28. Sr **John Markham.** Azure, on a chief Or a demi-lion rampant
issuant Gules.

29. Sr **John Savage.** Arms quarterly and Crest as at p. 16, without
the difference.

30. Sr **Edward Stradlinge.** Paly of six Argent and Azure, on a bend Gules
three cinquefoils pierced Or.

31. Sr **John Raglande.** Per pale Or and Gules, three lions rampant
counterchanged.

32. Sr **Edward Chamberleyn.** Quarterly of six—1 and 6, Gules, an inescucheon
Argent within an orle of cinquefoils Or; 2,

Gules, a chevron between three escallops Or ;
3, Ermine, a chief indented Gules ; 4, Azure,
two lions passant-gardant in pale Or, a label
of three points Argent ; 5, Azure, on a bend
cotised Argent three saltires Gules. *Crest*—
An ass's head Argent.

33. **Sʳ Will'm Gryffith.**   Arms quarterly as at p. 21, but the chevron in
the last quarter Argent instead of Sable,
fretty Or ; and the same Crest. "Gules, a
chevron, in the upper part two Sarraceyns'
heds with towels coupe, in the nether part a
man's head rased Argent."

34. **Sʳ Will'm Parre.**   Arms quarterly (with a crescent for difference)
and Crest as at p. 42.

35. **Sʳ Edward Nevyll.**   Arms quarterly of five as at p. 23. *Crest*—A bull
statant Ermine, armed, collared, and lined Or.

36. **Sʳ Will'm Essex.**   Quarterly—1 and 4, Azure, a chevron Ermine,
surmounting another engrailed Or between
three eagles displayed Argent ; 2 and 3,
Sable, a chevron Or between three crescents
Ermine. On an escucheon of pretence : Quarterly—1 and 4, Argent, on a chief Or a fleur-
de-lis Gules ; 2 and 3, Ermine, a chief per
pale indented Or and Gules. *Crest*—A demi-
griffin Or, in the beak a talon Gules.

37. **Sʳ Rauf Egerton.**

38. **Sʳ James Framelingham.**   Quarterly—1 and 4, Argent, a fess Gules between three choughs Sable ; 2 and 3, Argent,
a chevron Ermines between three crescents
Sable. *Crest*—A panther's head erased Or,
spotted Azure and Gules.

39. **Sʳ John Nevyll** of Lever-
sege.   Argent, a saltire Gules, a label of three points
Vert, a mullet Or for difference. *Crest*—A
hound's head Or, charged with a label of
three points Vert between as many pellets
1 and 2.

40. **Sʳ John Maynwaringe.**   Quarterly—1 and 4, Argent, two bars Gules ;
2 and 3, Gules, a scythe Argent. *Crest*—
An ass's head erased Sable, haltered "lyke
hempe."

41. **Sʳ Will'm Tyler.**   Sable, on a fess Or between two wild-cats passant-gardant Argent a cross patée between
as many crescents Gules. *Crest*—A demi-
wild-cat erased Or, spotted Sable, charged
with a cross patée out of a crescent Gules.

42. **Sʳ John Sharpe.**   Argent, three falcons' heads erased Sable each
charged with a chess rook Or within a bor-

dure engrailed Azure bezantée. *Crest*—A leopard's head erased per pale Sable and Or ducally gorged counterchanged.

43. Sr **Thomas Lovell**, Junior.   Arms as at p. 15.

44. Sr **Richard Jerningham.**   Quarterly—1 and 4, Argent, three square buckles Gules; 2 and 3, Gules, three bars-gemelles Or, a canton Argent (FITZOSBORNE). *Crest*—A demi-eagle (? falcon) Azure, wings expanded Gules, penoned Or, charged with three bars-gemelles of the last.

45. Sr **Lewes Orell.**   Argent, three torteaux between two bendlets Gules, a chief Sable.

46. Sr **Geffrey Gates.**   Quarterly—1 and 4, Per pale Gules and Azure, three lions rampant-gardant Or; 2 and 3, Gules, a cinquefoil Argent. *Crest*—A demi-lion rampant-gardant Or.

47. Sr **Richard Tempest.**   Argent, a bend between six martlets Sable.

48. Sr **Will'm Brereton.**   Argent, two bars Sable. *Crest*—A bear's head erased Sable, muzzled Gules.

49. Sr **Henry Owen.**   Quarterly—1 and 4, OWEN as at p. 10, quartering Gules, a chevron between three lions rampant Or; over all a bendlet sinister Argent; 2, Or, a cross Azure, quartering 1, Argent, a bend Gules, on a chief of the second two mullets Or—2, Sable, a chevron Ermine between three men's heads Argent crined Or—3, Vair, a canton Gules; 3, Paly of six Or and Gules, on a chief Argent three lozenges of the second, quartering 1, Argent, a bend between two cotises and six lions rampant Sable—2, Azure, on a bend Argent three mullets Gules—3, Ermine, a fess counter-company Or and Azure.

Sr **John Gyfforde.**   Azure, three stirrups Or. *Crest*—A panther's head Or, spotted Azure and Gules, breathing fire proper.

Sr **Henry Longe.**   Quarterly—1 and 4 and 3, as 1 and 4 and 2 at p. 36; 2, Argent, on a chief Gules a bezant between two stags' heads cabossed Or. *Crest*—A lion's head erased Argent, in the mouth a human arm erased and bleeding proper. " Alibi a demy lyon Argent."

Sr **Will'm Hansarde.**   Quarterly—1 and 4, Gules, three mullets Argent; 2 and 3, Gules, a cross flory Argent, in dexter chief an escallop Or. *Crest*—A falcon rising Azure, penoned Gules, beaked and belled Or.

Sr **Will'm Ascu.**   Arms as at p. 35.

Sr John Gleymham.

Sr Arthur Plantagenet, dubbed the xiiijth day of Octobre.

Sr Symon Harccourt.   *   Arms and Crest as at p. 25.

Sr John Zowkett de Germania.

Sr Lewes de Waldencourte de Hannonia.

Sr Rauf Verney.

Sr Richard Walden.

Sr James Darell.

Sr Anthony Hungerforde.

Sr Will'm Kingeston.   Azure, a cross Or between four leopards' heads Argent. *Crest*—A goat erect Argent, armed Or, browsing on an ivy-tree Vert. "Alibi the gote Sable igitur quære."

Sr Peter Vavasour.   Quarterly—1 and 4, Or, on a fess dancettée Sable a mullet Argent ; 2, Gules, three covered cups within a bordure engrailed Or (BUTLER of Bensherhall in Com. Lanc.) ; 3, Argent, three escallops Gules between two bendlets Sable (DELAHAY). *Crest*—A squirrel sejant Gules devouring a nut Or, a mullet for difference.

Sr Edward Wadham.

Sr John Hampden.

Sr John Talbot.   Quarterly of six—1, 2, 4, and 6, the same as 1, 2, 3, and 4 at p. 10 ; 3, Gules, a saltire Argent, a martlet Sable for difference; 5, Or, fretty Gules ; over all a crescent Argent on another Azure for difference. The same Crest, with the difference as in the Arms.

Sr Edward Grey.   Quarterly—1 and 4, Quarterly, 1, Barry of six Argent and Azure, in chief three torteaux—2, Or, a maunch Gules, quartering Barry of ten Argent and Azure, an orle of martlets Gules— 3, Or, a cinquefoil pierced Ermine; 2, Argent, on a bend Azure three wolves' heads erased of the field ; 3, Argent, on a chevron Gules, between three lions' heads erased Sable ducally crowned Or, as many bezants. *Crest* —A wivern sejant Or, a martlet Sable for difference.

Sr Will'm Barantine.   Quarterly—1, Sable, three eagles displayed Argent ; 2, Azure, a bend between six cross-crosslets fitchée Or, ; 3, Argent, on a chief Gules two stags' heads cabossed Or ; 4, Ermine, on a fess Gules three billets Or. *Crest*—An eagle displayed Or.

Sr Nicholas Barington.
Sr John Bruges.
Sr Will'm Fynche.　　Quarterly—1 and 4, Argent, a chevron engrailed between three griffins passant Sable ; 2, Azure, three eagles displayed between two bendlets Argent ; 3, Sable, three shovellers in pale Argent, billed Gules. *Crest*—A finch Vert, wings expanded Or, standing on a bur-stalk proper.

Sr George Darby.　　Quarterly—1 and 4, Gules, on a bend Argent three trefoils slipped Vert ; 2, Sable, a lion rampant Argent within a bordure gobony of the second and first. *Crest* — A leopard statant gardant Sable platée, collared and chained Or, holding in the dexter paw a trefoil slipped Vert.

Sr Nicholas Peydon.
Sr Lyonell Dymoke.　　Arms quarterly of six the same as at p. 46. *Crest* —The ears of a hare " grey."

Sr Edward Bensted.　　Gules, three bars-gemelles Or.
Sr Will'm Smythe.
Sr John Daunce.　　Per pale Argent and Or, a fess nebulée between three lions' heads erased Gules, out of each mouth the head of a spear Azure. *Crest*— A horse's head Azure bezantée, bridled Argent.

Sr Thomas Clynton.　　Arms and Crest the same as at p. 32.
Sr Richard Whethill.　　Per fess Azure and Or, a pale counterchanged, three lions rampant of the second.

Sr Will'm Thomas.　　Argent, on a cross Sable five crescents Or within a bordure gobony of the first and Vert, the latter bezantée. *Crest*—A roebuck's head Sable between two branches of nettles Vert.

Sr John Wiseman.

Of the Lorde Chamberleyn's Warde at the same tyme, the 13 day of Octobre, anno　　, were made Knightes :

S^r . . . . De la Zouche, sonne and heire of the Lorde Zouche.
S^r . . . . Sutton, sonne and heire of the Lorde Dudley.
Sr Arthure Hopton.　　Quarterly—1, Ermine, two bars Sable, on each three mullets pierced Or ; 2, Argent, a chevron Azure, a label of three points Ermine ; 3, Argent, on a bend Gules three

mascles Or ; 4, Gules, a griffin segreant Or. *Crest*—A griffin passant Argent, armed Or, holding in the dexter claw a pellet.

Sᵣ Edmond Bray.
Sᵣ George Saintleger.
Sᵣ Will'm Morgan.
Sᵣ Edward Greville.

Sable, on a cross engrailed Or five pellets within a bordure engrailed of the second.

Sᵣ Thomas Philipps.
Sᵣ Thomas Gamage.
Sᵣ Richard Herbert.
Sᵣ Will'm Mathew.
Sᵣ Chr'opher Baynham.

Quarterly—1, Gules, a chevron between three bulls' heads cabossed Argent, horned Or, a crescent Sable for difference ; 2, Gules, on a bend Ermine a mastiff courant Sable, a crescent Argent for difference (WALWYN); 3, Vert, six gouttes d'eau, 3, 3, in pale (GREYNDOR) ; 4, Or, a fess between six cross-crosslets Gules (GREYNDOR). *Crest*—A wild ass statant Sable, eared and legged Gules, spotted with estoiles Or.

Sᵣ Richard Vaughan.
Sᵣ Chr'opher Ascu.
Sᵣ Andrew Bylisby.
Sᵣ Thomas Hanmer.

Sᵣ John Thimbilby.
Sᵣ Symon FitzRichard.
Sᵣ Will'm Bawdryppe.

Knights dubbed at Lysle the 14 day of Octobre, anno   :

Sᵣ .... Nevill, sonne and heire to the Lorde Latymer.

Quarterly of six—1, Gules, a saltire Argent, a torteau for difference ; 2, Gules, a fess between six cross-crosslets Or ; 3, Chequy Or and Azure, a chevron Ermine ; 4, Gules, crusily patée and a chevron Argent; 5, Gules, a lion passant-gardant Argent ducally crowned Or ; 6, Argent, a bend Gules. *Crest*—A griffin passant Or.

Sᵣ Gilbert Talbott.

Arms quarterly of six the same as at p. 52, over the whole a label of three points Argent, and a crescent Azure for difference. The same Crest, without a difference.

Sᵣ Symon de Ferrato.
Sᵣ Thomas Fuchs.
Sᵣ Paul Armesdroffer.

" Gules, a man havinge a hedde pece, a cuirasse, gantlets, and sabbottes of harneys and gorget, all the rest mayle with a hoode of the same about his shoulders, holding in the dexter

Sᵣ **Will'm de Houton.**
Sᵣ **John de la Souche.**

Sᵣ **John Lepke.**
Sᵣ **Edward Croft.**
Sᵣ **Will'm Grysley** (**Gresley**).
Sᵣ **Thomas Cokayn.**

Sᵣ **Richard Bassett.**
Sᵣ **John Maynweringe** of
Ightfeilde.

Sᵣ **Richard Bossum.**
Sᵣ . . . . **Cressenor.**
Sᵣ **Alexander Radclyff.**

Sᵣ **Will'm Stanley.**
Sᵣ **Will'm Poole.**

Sᵣ **Will'm Leylonde.**

Sᵣ **Alexander Orbaston.**
Sᵣ **John Holforde.**

Sᵣ **Edward Belyngham.**
Sᵣ **Robert Nevyll** of Leversege.
Sᵣ **Will'm Lysle.**
Sᵣ **Walter Calverley.**

hand a battle-axe erect Argent." *Crest*—Out of a ducal coronet Or a demi-man Or, and the arms holding a mace of the first.

Quarterly—1 and 4, Gules, twelve bezants, 3, 3, 3, 2, 1, on a canton Ermine a crescent Azure; 2 and 3, Barry of six Argent and Azure, quartering Or, three piles Gules, a canton Vair. *Crest*—On a staff couped and ragulée Or sprouting at the dexter end, a falcon with wings expanded Argent, a crescent for difference.

Arms as at p. 14.
Vair, Ermine and Gules.
Azure, three cocks Gules, combed, beaked, and legged Azure. *Crest*—A cock's head as in the Arms.

Quarterly—1 and 4, Argent, two bars Gules, a crescent Or for difference; 2 and 3, Chequy Argent and Sable. *Crest*—An ass's head erased "dunne" in a hempen halter proper, a crescent Or for difference.

Arms as at p. 41. *Crest*—A bull's head erased Sable, ducally gorged, lined and horned Or.

Arms quarterly as p. 14. *Crest*—A stag's head cabossed Gules, the attires barry of six Or and Azure.
Argent, on a fess Sable a lion passant between two escallops of the field, in chief nine ears of wheat Gules, 3, 3, 3, each placed one in pale and two in Saltire and banded Or. *Crest*—A dove's head Argent, wings endorsed Azure, in the beak Gules three ears of wheat Or.

Argent, a greyhound passant Sable. *Crest*—A greyhound as in the Arms.

Sᵣ **Thomas Wentworth.**

Sᵣ **John Rodney.**   Arms as at p. 28, a label of three points Azure.
                  •   *Crest*—A boar's head couped Sable, tusked
                     Or.

Sᵣ **John Burton.**

Sᵣ **Thomas Rokeley.**

Sᵣ **Thomas Rynardeston.**

Sᵣ **John Tremayle.**   Arms quarterly as at p. 37, without the difference.

Knightes (35 in number) made at the battaill of Branston Moore otherwise called Flodden field: which field was faughten the ixᵗʰ day of September in the yere of our Lord God 1513 beinge the fifte yere of the reigne of Kinge Henry the Eight betwene the Kinge of Scottes and his people to the nombre of 60000 on the one partie, and the Erle of Surrey Threasoror and Marshall of England and Lieutenant Generall in the north partes and certein nobles and subiectes of the Kinge of England to the nombre of 30000 on the other partie. At what tyme as the Scottishe Kinge and dyvers of his Noblemen wer slayne.

The Lorde Scroope of Upsalle.   Azure, a bend Or, a label of three points Argent.

Sᵣ **Will'm Percy.**   Quarterly of five—1, 2, 3, 4, as under HENRY,
                    Earl of NORTHUMBERLAND, p. 20 ; 5, as on the
                    escucheon of pretence ; and the same Crest, a
                    crescent for difference.

Sᵣ **Edmond Howarde.**   Quarterly—1, Gules, on a bend between six
                    cross-crosslets fitchée Argent an escucheon
                    Or charged with a demi-lion rampant within
                    a double tressure flory counter-flory of the
                    first ; 2, Gules, three lions passant-gardant in
                    pale Or, a label of three points Argent
                    (BROTHERTON); 3, Chequy Or and Azure
                    (WARREN) ; 4, Gules, a lion rampant Or
                    (MOWBRAY) ; a crescent Argent for difference.
                    Crest—On a chapeau Gules, turned up Ermine,
                    a lion statant gardant, the tail extended Or,
                    ducally crowned Argent and gorged with a
                    label of three points of the last, a crescent
                    Sable for difference.

Sᵣ **George Darcy.**   Arms quarterly and Crest as at p. 22.

Sᵣ **Will'm Gascoigne,** Junior.

Sᵣ **Will'm Mydilton.**

Sᵣ **Will'm Mauleberer.**

Sᵣ **Thomas Barkeley.**   Arms and Crest as at p. 41, a crescent for dif-
                    ference.

Sᵣ **Marmaduke Constable,**   Arms and Crest as at p. 29, a crescent for dif-
Junior.   ference.

Sᵣ **Xpofer Dacre.**

Sᵣ **John Rowthom.**

Sᵣ Nicholas Appleyarde.   Quarterly—1 and 4, Azure, a chevron between three owls Or ; 2 and 3, Argent, a chief Or, over all a lion rampant Azure debruised by two bendlets Gules. *Crest*—A demi-tiger rampant quarterly Azure and Gules, maned Or, holding in the mouth an apple proper slipped Vert.

Sᵣ Edward Gorge.   Arms quarterly as at p. 22. *Crest*—A greyhound's head "dunne," collared Gules.

Sᵣ Rauf Ellercar, Junior.   Azure, fretty and a chief Argent.

Sᵣ John Willughby.   Arms and Crest as at p. 47, a crescent for difference.

Sᵣ Edward Echingham.   Azure, a fret Argent. *Crest*—A demi-griffin Vert.

Sᵣ John Stanley, bastarde.   Or, three eagles' legs erased à-la-cuisse Gules, on a chief indented Azure as many bucks' heads cabossed of the field. *Crest*—An eagle's head Or, charged with three pellets, in the beak a lion's paw Gules, clawed Argent.

Sᵣ Walter Stonner.   Arms of STONNER as at p. 13.

Sᵣ Nynyan Markynfild.   Sᵣ Thomas Burgh.
Sᵣ Rauf Bowes.   Sᵣ Will'm Roos.
Sᵣ Bryan Stapleton.   Sᵣ Will'm Newton.
Sᵣ Guy Dawney.   Sᵣ Roger Grey.
Sᵣ Rauf Salvayn.   Sᵣ Robert Colyngwod.
Sᵣ Richard Mauleverer.   Sᵣ Roger Farewell.
Sᵣ Will'm Constable of Hatfeld.   Sᵣ Thomas Stranguishe.
Sᵣ Will'm Constable of Carethorp.   Sᵣ John Bulmer.
Sᵣ Christopher Danby.

Sᵣ . . . . W(alsingham).   Sable, a chevron Argent between three cinquefoils pierced Or.

Lorde Ogle.   Quarterly—1 and 4, Argent, a fess between three crescents Gules ; 2 and 3, Or, an orle Azure (BERTRAM).

Sᵣ Edmond Walsingham.   Gules, bezantée, a cross humetée counter-compony Argent and Azure.

Sᵣ Thomas West.   Quarterly—1, 2, 3, as 1, 2, 3 at p. 21 ; 4, Gules, three bendlets enhanced Or. *Crest*—Out of a ducal coronet per pale Gules and Azure a griffin's head Argent, beaked and eared Gules, collar indented Sable.

Sᵣ John Dawtrey.   Azure, five fusils in fess Argent. *Crest*—A fox per pale Sable and Gules between two wings Or.

I

Sʳ Ꮃill'm Butler, then Maior of London (1515).

Argent, on a fess counter-compony Azure and Purpure between six cross-crosslets Sable three annulets Or. *Crest*—A boar's head per pale Purpure "or Gules" and Azure, tusked Or.

Sʳ Ꮃill'm FitᴢᎳilliam of Geynsparke Hall in Essex.

Arms of FITZWILLIAM and Crest as at p. 48, on each a fleur-de-lis out of a roundle Or for difference.

Sʳ John Peyron, dubbed at Wyndesore the 3 day of January anno nono.

Sable, a chevron Ermine between three herons close Argent. *Crest*—A heron's head erased Ermine "vel Argent," ducally gorged Or.

Sʳ Richard Ꮃeston, dubbed at Wyndesor the same tyme.

Quarterly—1 and 4, Ermine, on a chief Azure five bezants ; 2 and 3, Argent, three camels Sable. *Crest*—A Saracen's head proper.

Sʳ Thomas Dynham.

Gules, four fusils in fess Ermine between three arches Argent, capitals and bases Or, two single in chief and one double in base, a pile of the last. *Crest*—" An Ermyn in his kynde with a lace aboute his necke and goinge und'r him golde, standinge betwene two (lighted) tapers gobony " (Or and Sable, flames Gules).

Sʳ Thomas Exmew, then Maire of London (1517).

Argent, a chevron counter-compony of the first and Purpure between three escallops Sable, within a bordure Gules charged with five leopards' heads Or and as many plates alternately. *Crest*—A dove Argent holding in the beak a text E.

Sʳ James Ꮲerforde, then Maior of London (1519).

Argent, on a chevron Sable between three goats' heads erased Azure as many lozenges Or, on a chief Gules as many escallops of the fourth. *Crest*—A goat's head erased Azure, attired Or, charged with three escallops of the second.

Sʳ Thomas Seymour, dubbed by the Kinge at Callais in anno 12 of his reigne.

Sable, on a fess embattled counter-embattled Argent between three wings Or as many pellets. *Crest*—A swan's head bendy of six Argent and Gules.

Sʳ Lawrence Stayber of Noremberge in high Almaigne.

Per bend sinister Sable and Or, a mastiff courant counterchanged, on a chief Azure a lion passant-gardant of the second within a bordure gobony Argent and Gules. *Crest*—Out of a ducal coronet Or a demi-lion rampant-gardant Or gorged with a label of three points Argent on each a fess Gules, between two horns Sable.

Sʳ Ꮃill'm Gascoigne of Cardington in com. Bedf.

Sᵣ **Edmonde Came.**   Argent, a dragon segreant Vert and a lion ram-
                            pant Azure ducally crowned Or combatant.
Sᵣ **Will'm Denys.**   Arms quarterly as at p. 22.

Knightes made by the Duke of Norfolke, Lorde Threasorer of Englande, in
Scotlande in the 14 yere of the Kinge :

Sᵣ **Arthur Darcy.**   Sᵣ **Will'm Cary.**
Sᵣ **Thomas Clyfforde.**   Sᵣ **John Harbey.**
Sᵣ **Phillip Dacres.**   Sᵣ **Edward Grey** of Fyllyngham.
Sᵣ **Richard Brereton.**   Sᵣ **Nich'as Ryddeley.**
Sᵣ **Will'm Ogle.**   Sᵣ **Will'm Eldrecare.**
Sᵣ **Rauf Fenwyke.**

Knightes made by my Lord of Suffolke in Fraunce at a towne called Roye,
in the tyme of Warre, he beinge the Kinge's Lieutenant, anno d'ni 1523, on All-
hallowen day in the 15 yere of the Kinge's reigne :

Lord Herbert, sonne and heire to the   Sᵣ **Arthur Poole,** brother to the
Erle of Worcester.   Lorde Montagu.
Lord Powes.   Sᵣ **Thomas Wentworthe.**
Sᵣ **Olyver Maners,** brother to the   Sᵣ **Richard Corbett.**
Lorde Roos.   Sᵣ **Will'm Stourton.**
Sᵣ **Robert Jerningham.**   Sᵣ **Richard Sandes.**
Sᵣ **Edmonde Beningfeilde.**   Arms and Crest as at p. 43.
Sᵣ **Edward Seymour.**   Quarterly—1, Gules, two wings conjoined in
                                  lure Or; 2, Vair; 3, Argent, three demi-
                                  lions rampant Gules; 4, Argent, on a bend
                                  Gules three leopards' heads Or.
Sᵣ **George Warham.**   Gules, a fess Or between a goat's head couped
                                  in chief and three escallops in base Argent
                                  within a bordure engrailed of the second, a
                                  crescent Azure for difference. *Crest*—An
                                  arm embowed vested quarterly Argent and
                                  Azure, holding downwards in the hand proper
                                  a sword Sable, hilted Or, on the blade three
                                  plates on each a cross Gules.
Sᵣ **Walter Mantell.**   Argent, a cross engrailed between four martlets
                                  Sable.

Item, the said Lorde of Suffolke at the same tyme made these two Knightes on
the Ryver of Some :

Sᵣ **John Dudley.**
Sᵣ **Robert Utreight.**   Arms and Crest as at p. 42.

Item, at Valenciennes the sayde Lorde of Suffolke made these two Knightes the
3 day of Decembre at the same tyme :

Sᵣ **Will'm Penyngton.** | Sᵣ **Bartholomew Tate.**

Sr Thomas Wrryothesley alias
Garter Kinge of Armes, dubbed
by Don Ferdinando, Archduke
of Austria, at Nuremberge in
Germany in anno 16 of the
Kinge's reigne.

Quarterly—1 and 4, Azure, a cross Or between
four doves Argent; 2, Argent, fretty Gules
within a bordure engrailed Sable, on a canton
of the second a lion passant Or; 3, Argent,
a pale fusily Gules within a bordure Azure
bezantée. *Crest*—A buffalo's head erased
Sable, ducally crowned, ringed and guttee
d'or. " A bugle's hed."

Sr Will'm Bayly, then Maior
of London, dubbed in anno
d'ni 1525 by the Kinge at
Brydewell.

Gules, a fess Vair, in base three martlets Argent,
in chief on a bezant between two estoiles Or
an anchor Sable. *Crest*—A dexter arm
embowed habited Argent, on the arm a fess
Vair cotised Azure, the hand proper, supporting a staff Or. " A woodhous arme
Argent."

Sr Thomas Baldry, then Maior
of London.

Sable, on a chevron engrailed Or between three
demi-griffins segreant Ermine as many martlets Gules. *Crest*—Out of a daisy proper
leaved Vert, a demi-maiden proper habited per
pale Or and Sable, girdle and sleeves counterchanged, crined of the second, the head encircled with " a garland Gules budded Gold."

Sr .... FitzJames.

Quarterly—1 and 4, Azure, a dolphin embowed
Argent between three mullets pierced Or ;
2 and 3, Argent, a cross engrailed Sable, in
the first quarter an eagle displayed Gules.

. . . .

Gules, three lions rampant Or.

. . . .

Sable, a cross engrailed Or.

Sr Roger Maynors, dubbed
at Wyndesore on Corpus Chr'i
day anno 19 of the Kinge.

Sable, an eagle displayed Or armed Gules, on a
chief Azure a chevron Argent between two
crescents in chief and a rose in base Or,
within a bordure of the fourth.

Sr Thomas Elyott.

Quarterly—1 and 4, Argent, a fess Gules between
two bars-gemelles wavy Azure ; 2 and 3,
Argent, a chevron Gules between three towers
Sable.

Sr Thomas Wharton.

Sable, a maunch Argent.

Sr Edward Gower.

Quarterly—1 and 4, Argent, four bars Gules,
over all a cross patonce Sable ; 2 and 3,
Ermine, a cross patonce Gules.

Sr Will'm Fayrfax.

Arms of FAIRFAX as at p. 26.

Sr Robert Shargyll.

Ermine, a saltire Gules.

. . . .

Or, a cross flory Sable.

Sr George Lawson.

Paly of four Gules and Vert, on a chevron Argent
a greyhound's head erased Sable between two
cinquefoils pierced Azure, on a chief of the
third a pellet charged with a demi-lion

rampant of the third between two crescents of the fourth each charged with three plates. *Crest*—An ass's head erased Argent gorged Vert between three pellets.

Sʳ Edward Boughton of Wolwiche in Kent. Gules, on a fess between three goats' heads Argent erased and attired Or as many fleurs-de-lis Azure. *Crest*—A goat's head per pale Sable and Gules platée erased and attired Or.

Sʳ Thomas Speke. Arms and Crest as at p. 26.

Sʳ James Metcalfe. Argent, three calves passant Sable.

Sʳ George Carew. Arms and Crest as at p. 15, in the latter, the top of the mainmast set off with pallisadoes Or.

Knightes made by the Kinge at Yorke place now called Whitehall in the Parlement tyme Anno D'ni 1529, the 21 yere of his reigne:

Sʳ Will'm Russee.
Sʳ Geoffrey Poole.
Sʳ John Milton.
Sʳ Robert Payton.
Sʳ Richard Greenfeilde.
Sʳ Richard Page.
Sʳ Phillippe Butler of Hertfordshire.
Sʳ Thomas Straunge.
Sʳ John Russell.
Sʳ Robert Cheyffelde.
Sʳ Raufe Dodmere, Maior of London.
Sʳ .... Pargeter, Maior of London.
Sʳ James Stranguische.
Sʳ James Spencer.
Sʳ Will'm Stretton.
Sʳ Rauf Langforde.
Sʳ Anthony Babington.
Sʳ .... Basset of Blowre.

Sʳ Thomas de Curton.
Sʳ .... Norwyche, Justice.
Sʳ .... Shelley, Justice.
Sʳ John Rudstone.
Sʳ John Mundy.
Sʳ Bryan Tuke.
Sʳ Robert Leghe.
Sʳ John Clerke.
Sʳ John Dannet.
Sʳ Edward Pykeringe.
Sʳ Osburne Echingham.
Sʳ Will'm Pondre.
Sʳ Lyonell Norres.
Sʳ John Chamoun.
Sʳ .... Smythe of Chester.
Sʳ James Leybourne.
Sʳ Richard Lampley at Wolton.
Sʳ Richard Clement.

Sʳ John Allen. Or, three pellets each charged with a talbot passant of the field, on a chief Gules a lion passant between two anchors Argent.

Sʳ Thomas Spert. Azure, two tilting-spears Or barbed Argent saltirewise between four hearts of the second, on a chief of the same "a shipp Sable sette on fyre Gules."

Sʳ Henry Farmour. Argent, on a saltire Sable between four lions' heads erased Gules a martlet Or between as many bezants, on a chief Azure between two pales an anchor of the fourth.

Knightes made at Callais on All-hallowen day anno d'ni 1532 in the xxiiij yere of the reigne of the Kinge :

S͏ʳ **Thomas Darcy** of Essex.

S͏ʳ **Humfrey Forster** of Bark-　Quarterly—1, Sable, a chevron engrailed between
shire.　　　　　　　　　　three arrows Argent ; 2, Gules, two lions
　　　　　　　　　　　passant in pale Argent ; 3, Quarterly—1 and 4,
　　　　　　　　　　　Argent, on a chief Gules two stags' heads
　　　　　　　　　　　cabossed Or—2 and 3, Gules, bezantée,
　　　　　　　　　　　a chevron Argent ; 4, Or, a bend fusily Sable.

S͏ʳ **John Ackett** of Waterton in Ireland.
S͏ʳ **George Somersett** of Northampton.
S͏ʳ **George Gryffith** of Staffordshire.
S͏ʳ **Will'm Neweman** of Northampton.
S͏ʳ **Edmond Aston** of Staffordshire.
S͏ʳ **Thomas Palmer**, capitayne of Newenham bridge,
　　dubbed by the Kinge the 10 of Novembre.

These Knightes followinge were made at Greenewiche before the coronation of Queene Anne Bulleyn on the Sonday before Whit Sonday :

S͏ʳ **Chr'opher Danby.**
S͏ʳ **Chr'opher Wylyarde.**　　Azure, a chevron Argent between three mullets
　　　　　　　　　　　　Or.
S͏ʳ **Bryan Hastings.**　　　Arms and Crest as at p. 21.
S͏ʳ **Thomas Metham.**　　　Arms quarterly as at p. 43.
S͏ʳ **Will'm Walgrave.**　　　Per pale Argent and Gules.
S͏ʳ **Will'm Feldynge.**　　　Argent, on a bend Azure three lozenges Or.
S͏ʳ **Thomas Butteler.**　　　Arms as at p. 19.

Knightes of the Bathe made at the coronation of the most excellent Princesse Queene Anne the 25 yere of the reign of Kinge Henry the Eight on Whitsonday, the last day of May, 1533 ; shee was crown'd at Westminster :

Marquyse Dorsett.　　　Arms as those of THOMAS, Lord HARINGTON,
　　　　　　　　　　at p. 24, without the second label. *Crest*—
　　　　　　　　　　In front of a sun in splendour Or, a unicorn
　　　　　　　　　　passant Ermine, armed of the first.
Erle of Derby.　　　　Arms and Crest as those of Sir THOMAS STANLEY
　　　　　　　　　　at p. 25, without the label.
Lorde Clifford.　　　　Quarterly—1, CLIFFORD as at p. 14 ; 2, Sable,
　　　　　　　　　　a bend flory counter-flory Or ; 3, Or, a cross
　　　　　　　　　　Sable ; 4, Gules, six annulets, 2, 2, 2, Or,
　　　　　　　　　　quartering Vert, three flint-stones Argent ;
　　　　　　　　　　and the same Crest.
Lorde Fitzwalter.　　　Quarterly—1, Quarterly, 1 and 4, and 2 and 3,
　　　　　　　　　　same as 1 and 2 at p. 41 ; 2, Argent, a lion
　　　　　　　　　　rampant Sable ducally crowned Or within a

bordure Azure ; 3, Gules, three luces hauriant Argent; 4, Argent, three bars Gules.
Crest as at p. 41.

Lorde Hastinges. Arms quarterly as at p. 34.   *Crest*—A bull's
head erased Sable, armed and ducally gorged
Or, a label of three points.

Lorde Mounteagle. Quarterly—1 and 4 as 1 and 2, and 3 as 2, under
DERBY as above without the escucheon, a
crescent for difference ; and the same Crest.

Lorde Vaulx. Quarterly of five—1, Chequy Argent and Gules,
on a chevron Azure three roses Or, quarter-
ing Argent, on a chevron Gules between
three eagles' heads erased Sable, beaked Or,
as many crescents of the last ; 2, Azure, three
bucks statant Or; 3, Gules, crusily fitchée
and three luces hauriant Or ; 4, Argent, three
chevronels Sable ; 5, Gules, crusily a chevron
and in chief a lion passant Or.   *Crest*—An
eagle's head Sable, beaked Or.

Sr Henry Parker, sonne of the Quarterly—1, Argent, a lion passant Gules
Lorde Morley.
between two bars Sable, on the first two
bezants, on the second one, in chief three
stags' heads cabossed of the third ; 2, Argent,
a lion rampant Sable, ducally crowned Or ;
3, Barry undy of six Or and Gules, quartering Azure, a lion rampant within an orle of
fleurs-de-lis Argent ; 4, Gules, a bend lozengy
Or ; over all a label of three points Azure.
Crest—A bear's head Sable, ducally gorged
and muzzled Or, a label of three points
Argent.

Sr Will'm Wyndesore. Quarterly of six—1, 3, 4, 5, 6, as 1, 2, 3, 4, 5
at p. 42 ; 2, Barry undy of six Or and Sable ;
quartering—1, Argent, two wolves passant
Sable within a bordure Or charged with ten
saltires Gules ; 2, Or, a tower triple-towered
Azure ; 3, Vair.   *Crest*—A buck's head affrontée Argent.

Sr John Mordant. Quarterly of ten—1, Argent, a chevron between
three estoiles Sable ; 2, Gules, a cross patonce
Or ; 3, Quarterly per pale indented, in the
first and fourth quarters five lozenges in
cross Gules ; 4, Argent, a lion rampant Gules
charged with a shield Or, thereon three martlets Azure ; 5, Argent, on a bend Sable a
lure Or ; 6, Gules, a cross lozengy Argent ;
7, Quarterly per fess indented Or and Azure,

a crescent Gules for difference; 8, Gules, a griffin segreant Or, charged with a label of three points Azure; 9, Argent, three lozenges in pale Gules; 10, Gules, an eagle displayed Argent within a bordure engrailed Or. "Upon the pendant of the lable about the gryfon's neke 3 flour de lyce golde." *Crest* —A Saracen's head proper, crined Sable, wreathed Argent and Purpure, collared Or.

Sr Francys Weston. Arms quarterly (with a label of three points Gules) and Crest as at p. 58.

Sr Thomas Arundell. Arms quarterly as at p. 46, a crescent for difference. *Crest*—A wolf passant Argent, a crescent Gules for difference.

Sr Henry Savell. Quarterly of six—1, Argent, on a bend Sable three owls of the field; 2, Or, six fleurs-de-lis Azure, a chief Argent; 3, Gules, three bars-gemelles Argent; 4, Gules, two bars between nine martlets Argent; 5, Argent, a bend Sable between a dove volant Vert beaked and legged Gules in chief and a cross-crosslet of the second in base; 6, Gules, a cross patée Or. *Crest*—A maiden's head proper vested Gules, crined and ducally crowned Or, out of the crown a plume of feathers proper.

Sr John Huddelston. Gules, fretty Argent. *Crest*—Two arms dexter and sinister embowed proper, holding in their hands "the scalpe of a manne's hedde, the ynner syde rawe and bluddy, the outesyde heary."

Sr Thomas Poyninges. Quarterly as at p. 9, a bendlet sinister Argent; and the same Crest.

Sr George Fitzwilliam. Quarterly—1 and 4, Argent, a chevron between three cross-crosslets Sable within a bordure Sable bezantée; 2 and 3, Argent, two bars engrailed Sable. *Crest*—A phœnix in flames of fire proper.

Sr John Tyndall. Quarterly—1, 2, and 3, as 1, 2, and 3 at p. 21; 4, Argent, three fleurs-de-lis Gules; and the same Crest.

Sr John Jermy. Quarterly—1 and 4, Argent, a lion rampant-gardant Gules; 2 and 3, Gules, a bend between six martlets Or. *Crest*—A griffin statant Gules, armed Azure.

Knightes made with the sworde at the same coronation, anno 25 of the Kinge's reigne :

Sʳ John Willughby.   Arms and Crest as at p. 15.

Sʳ George Calveley.   Argent, a fess Gules between three calves passant Sable.

Sʳ Andrew Brereton.   Arms as at p. 51, quartering Argent, a chevron between three crescents Gules; and the same Crest.

Sʳ John Chaworthe.

Sʳ George Gresley.   Vair Argent and Gules.

Sʳ John Constable.

Sʳ Thomas Umpton.   Quarterly—1 and 4, Azure, on a fess engrailed Or between three spear-heads Argent a greyhound courant Sable; 2 and 3, Gules, two chevrons Argent. *Crest*—A demi-greyhound Sable, gorged Or, holding in the mouth a broken spear of the second. " Quære si foret caput leporarii."

Sʳ Thomas Russhe.   Purpure, on a fess Or between three horses passant Argent as many hurts. *Crest*—A leopard's head erased Vert, guttée d'eau.

Sʳ John Seintelere.

Sʳ Anthony Wyndesore.   Arms quarterly of six and Crest as at p. 42.

Sʳ Marmaduke Tunstall.   Sable, three combs Argent. *Crest*—A cock Argent, combed and beaked Or, wattled Gules.

Sʳ Henry Farington.   Quarterly—1 and 4, Gules, three cinquefoils pierced Argent; 2 and 3, Argent, a chevron Gules between three leopards' heads Sable. *Crest*—A wivern Vert, breast Or, langued Gules.

Sʳ Thomas Halsall.   Quarterly—1 and 4, Argent, three dragons' heads erased Azure; 2 and 3, Gules, three unicorns' heads erased Or.

Sʳ Edward Fytton.   Argent, two chevrons and a canton Gules. *Crest*—On a chapeau Purpure turned up Ermine a cinquefoil erect proper.

Sʳ Edward Madeson.

Sʳ Richard Lygon.

Sʳ Robert Nedham.   Azure, a bend between two bucks' heads cabossed Argent.

Sʳ George Coquiers.   Azure, a maunch Or.

Sʳ Humfrey Ferrers.   Quarterly of five—1, FERRERS as at p. 28; 2, Or, a cross patonce Gules; 3, Or, a saltire engrailed Sable; 4, Vair, a fess Gules; 5, Bendy of ten Or and Azure. *Crest*—A plume of peacocks' feathers proper.

𝔖ʳ .... 𝕷oṅgforð.   Quarterly—1 and 4, Paly of six Or and Gules, over all a bend Argent ; 2 and 3, Quarterly Gules and Argent. *Crest*—"Three chibolls (onion-heads) in a bushe of phesants' fethers."

𝔖ʳ 𝕎ill'm 𝔙enables, Baron of Kynderton.   Azure, two bars Argent.

𝕿homas, 𝕷orðe 𝕮romwell, dubbed at the breakenge up of the Parlement anno 28.

𝔖ʳ .... 𝕻owlett, dubbed the same tyme anno 28.

𝔖ʳ 𝕿homas 𝕎yatt, dubbed on Ester-day anno 28, the 18 day of March 1536.

𝔖ʳ .... 𝕯e la 𝕸oyte, dubbed the same tyme.

𝔖ʳ 𝕲eorge 𝕾peeke, dubbed at Wyndesore the 16 of October anno 28.

𝔖ʳ 𝕿homas 𝕮arewe, dubbed at Wyndesore the same day.

𝔖ʳ 𝕎ill'm 𝕎est, dubbed anno 28.

𝔖ʳ 𝕵ohn 𝕯awney of Yorkshire, dubbed on Candlemas-day anno 33 (*sic*).

Knightes made at the creation of the Erle of Hertforde and Southampton, on Thursday the 18 day of Octobre anno d'ni 1537, anno 29 of the Kinge :

𝔖ʳ 𝕿homas 𝕻ennage.   Quarterly—1 and 4, Argent, a greyhound courant Sable between three wolves' heads erased Gules "hyndes heddes alibi" within a bordure Azure charged with ten cinquefoils of the field ; 2, Or, three garbs Gules, quartering Gules, a cross patonce between four trefoils slipped Or ; 3, Barry of six Argent and Gules, a canton of the second (CORBET). *Crest*—On a cinquefoil Purpure a greyhound's head couped Sable, collared Or.

𝔖ʳ 𝕿homas 𝕾eymour.   Quarterly of five—1, 2, 3, 5, as 1, 2, 3, 4 at p. 59 ; 4, Per bend Argent and Gules, three roses in bend counterchanged. *Crest*—A phœnix Or, wings expanded Azure, in flames proper.

𝔖ʳ 𝕽ichard 𝕷onge.   Quarterly—1 and 4, Sable, crusily and a lion rampant Argent ; 2, Argent, on a chief Gules a bezant between two stags' heads cabossed Or ; 3, Gules, two wings conjoined Or. *Crest*—A demi-lion rampant Argent, holding in the mouth a human arm couped proper.

𝔖ʳ 𝕎ill'm 𝕮offyn.   Quarterly—1 and 4, Azure, three bezants within seven cross-crosslets Or ; 2 and 3, Argent, a chevron between three mullets pierced Sable.

𝔖ʳ 𝕸ichael 𝕷yster (𝕷ytster).   Quarterly—1 and 4, Azure, on a cross Argent between four magpies Or five torteaux on each an estoile of the third ; 2 and 3, Gules, semée of crescents and a lion rampant Argent. *Crest*—On a mound a buck statant Sable bezantée, attired and ducally gorged Or.

Sᵣ **Robert Dormer.** Azure, ten billets, 4, 3, 2, 1, Or, on a chief of the second three Cornish choughs Sable. *Crest*—A wolf passant Sable between two wings Argent.

Sᵣ **John Williams.** Arms as at p. 30. *Crest*—A fish-weir.

Sᵣ **Henry Knyvett.** Arms quarterly of six and Crest as at p. 41.

Sᵣ **Hugh Powlett.** Quarterly of eight—1 and 8, POULETT as at p. 16 ; 2, Azure, six mascles in fess, 3 and 3, Argent ; 3, Azure, on a chief Or a demi-lion rampant issuant Gules ; 4, Gules, three lions passant in pale Argent ; 5, Barry of six Argent and Gules ; 6, Argent, a chevron between three garbs Gules, banded Vert ; 7, Argent, a fess between three cinquefoils Gules. *Crest*—An arm embowed habited Sable, in the hand proper a sword Argent, hilt and pomel Or.

Sᵣ **Stephen Pecocke.** Gules, on a fess engrailed Argent between three bezants, on each a peacock's head erased Azure, as many mascles Sable. *Crest*—A peacock's head Or, wings expanded Azure, holding in the beak a serpent Vert.

Sᵣ **Edward Montagu.** Argent, three lozenges conjoined in fess Gules within a bordure engrailed Sable. *Crest*—A griffin's head Or, wings endorsed and beak Sable.

Sᵣ **Humfrey Browne.** Arms and Crest as at p. 44.

Sᵣ **Gervase Clyfton.** Arms quarterly as at p. 25. *Crest*—Out of a ducal coronet Or a peacock's head per pale Argent and Sable, wings expanded counter-changed.

Sᵣ **Robert Bowes.** Ermine, three bows in pale Gules, a crescent for difference. *Crest*—A sheaf of arrows Or, feathered Argent, banded Sable, buckled of the first.

Sᵣ **Rauf Evers.** Arms as at p. 24. Crest as at p. 48.

Sᵣ **Edward Wyndham.** Azure, a chevron between three lions' heads erased Or. *Crest*—A fetterlock Or chained of the first and Argent, within the chain a lion's head erased of the first.

Sᵣ **Chr'opher Morrys.** Azure, a battle-axe in bend sinister surmounted by a tilting-spear in bend dexter Or headed Argent, between four cannons of the second, on a chief of the same a fleur-de-lis of the field between a demi-rose Gules, emitting rays of the third and the stump of a tree eradicated and couped at the top Gules. *Crest*—A tower Or inflamed Gules.

Sr Rauf Warren.

Azure, on a chevron between three lozenges Argent as many griffins' heads erased of the first, on a chief chequy Or and Gules a hound courant Ermine. *Crest*—Two hounds' heads erased addorsed Gules and Argent, eared Sable, gorged with a wreath counterchanged.

Sr Roger Cholmeley.

Gules, a sword in fess Argent hilted Or, point dexterwards, between a helmet close in chief and two garbs in base Or, a martlet for difference. *Crest*—On a royal helmet Gules a garb Or.

Sr Richard Gresham.

Argent, a chevron between three mullets pierced Sable, on a chief Gules a pelican of the first winged Or between two lions' gambs erased of the last. *Crest*—A grasshopper proper.

Sr Percyvall Harte.

Per chevron Azure and Gules, two bucks, their sterns in chief, drinking at a mural well in base Or. *Crest*—Out of a heart Purpure, between two wings Or, three sprigs of cinquefoil of the first, stalked Vert.

Sr Rauf Ferney.

Arms and Crest as at p. 12.

Sr Thomas Wriothesley.

Quarterly—1, WRIOTHESLEY quartering 2 and 3 as at p. 60 ; 2, Per pale indented Gules and Azure, over all a lion rampant Or; 3, Argent, a chevron Gules between three Cornish choughs Sable, a crescent for difference ; 4, Sable, a chevron Or between three cross-crosslets fitchée Argent. The same Crest.

Sr Robert Southwell.

Quarterly—1 and 4, Argent, three cinquefoils pierced Gules, each charged with five bezants ; 2 and 3, Ermine, a gemel-ring Sable, on a chief of the second three crosses patée Argent. *Crest*—A demi-Indian goat Argent, eared and hoofed Gules, charged on the body with three annulets in pale of the second.

Sr Nicholas Hare.

Gules, two bars and a chief indented Or. *Crest*—A demi-lion rampant Argent, holding erect a cross botonny fitchée Gules.

Sr Anthony Kyngeston.

Arms of KINGSTON as at p. 52, quartering Argent, a lion's head Or between a chevron and a chief Sable. The same Crest.

Sʳ Richard Cromwell. Gules, three chevronels Argent, over all as many lions rampant Or. *Crest*—A demi-lion rampant Or, charged with three chevronels Gules, holding between the paws a plummet Azure.

Sʳ Thomas Pope. Per pale Or and Azure, on a chevron between three griffins' heads erased four fleurs-de-lis all counterchanged. *Crest*—Two griffins' heads erased addorsed Or and Azure, ducally gorged counterchanged.

Sʳ John Arundell. Arms quarterly as at p. 46. Crest as at p. 64, without the difference.

Sʳ John Baker. Azure, on a fess between three swans' heads erased Or, ducally gorged Gules, as many cinquefoils of the last. *Crest*—An arm embowed habited Vert, holding in the hand proper a swan's head erased Or.

Sʳ Nicholas Forman. Barry nebulée of six Argent and Azure, on a chevron Sable three martlets Or, on a chief Gules a lion passant-gardant between two anchors of the fourth. *Crest*—A demi-dragon rampant proper.

Sʳ Will'm Hollyes. Sable, on a bend between a talbot courant in chief and a dolphin embowed in base Argent three torteaux. *Crest*—An arm embowed vested bendy of six Argent and Sable, the hand proper cuffed of the second holding up a bunch of holly also proper.

Sʳ John Gresham. Argent, a chevron Ermines between three mullets pierced Sable, on a chief Or a trefoil slipped Azure between two hinds' heads erased of the second, double gorged of the first, a martlet Or for difference. *Crest*—A grasshopper, in the mouth a heartsease proper.

Sʳ Antony Leghe. Argent, on a fess Azure between three unicorns' heads erased Sable as many columbines of the first slipped and leaved Or. *Crest*—A falcon Or winged Gules preying on "an egle's foot" Azure.

Sʳ Martin Bowes, Maior of London. Ermine, three bows in pale Gules, on a chief Azure a swan Argent in the beak a ring, between two leopards' heads Or. *Crest*—A demi-lion rampant-gardant Gules holding up a sheaf of arrows Or, feathered Argent, bound Azure.

Sʳ Henry Howard, Erle of Surrey, attaynted. Arms quarterly and Crest as at p. 56, on the Arms a label of three points Azure, and on the Crest label Argent, another Azure.

Sr William, Lord Parre.

Quarterly of six—1, 2, 3, as 1, 2, and 3 at p. 42 ; 4, Vair, a fess Gules; 5, Or, three chevronels Gules, a chief Vair ; 6, Barry of eight Argent and Gules, a fleur-de-lis Sable; and the same Crest.

Sr John Vernon.

Arms of VERNON and Crest as at p. 21.

Sr Anthony Ruybet, Porter of Callais.

Arms quarterly of six and Crest as at p. 41.

Sr Richard Manners.

Quarterly—1 and 4, Or, two bars Azure, a chief Gules; 2, Gules, three water-bougets Argent, quartering, 1, Azure, a Catherine-wheel Or, 2, Gules, three wheels Argent, and 3, Argent, a fess between two bars-gemelles Gules ; 3, Quarterly—1, Gules, three lions passant-gardant Or within a bordure Argent ; 2 and 3, Argent, a saltire engrailed Gules ; 4, Or, a lion rampant Gules. *Crest*—A peacock in pride proper.

Sr John Nevill.

Argent, a saltire Gules. *Crest*—A parrot Vert, beaked Gules.

Sr Thomas Borough.

Quarterly—1, 2, 3, 4, as 1, 3, 2, 4 at p. 48, without the label. Crest as at p. 14.

Sr Rauf Sadler, of Stondon in com. Hertford.

Per pale Or and Azure, guttée and a lion rampant all counterchanged, on a canton of the second a buck's head cabossed Or. *Crest*— A demi-lion rampant Azure guttée d'or. *Added,* Or, a lion rampant per fess Azure and Gules. *Crest*—A demi-lion rampant Azure ducally crowned Or.

Sr Edmond Knightley.

Arms as at p. 26, on an escucheon of pretence, Quarterly of five—1, Quarterly Gules and Or, on the first a mullet Argent; 2, Gules, on a bend between six cross-crosslets fitchée Argent an Ermine spot; 3, Gules, six escallops Argent ; 4, Or, a chevron Gules, a bordure engrailed Sable ; 5, Per chevron Sable and Argent, in chief three leopards' faces Or. Crest as at p. 26.

Sr Chr'opher More of Hampshire.

Azure, on a cross Argent five martlets Sable, in the first quarter an annulet Or.

Sr James Foulerhampe.

Quarterly—1 and 4, Sable, a bend between six escallops Or ; 2, Argent, a bend Azure crusily Or ; 3, Argent, a chevron between three escallops Gules. *Crest*—A leg couped at the thigh per pale Sable and Or, wreathed at the knee Azure and Argent, spurred of the third. Another added, " ung chatloup," quarterly Sable and Or.

Sͬ John Gostwyke.

Argent, a bend Gules between six Cornish choughs Sable, beaked and legged of the second, on a chief Or three horses' heads couped Sable, bridled Argent. *Crest—* "A gryffon's hed betweene two wynges plated."

Sͬ John Gascoigne.

Arms of GASCOIGNE as at p. 18.

Sͬ Pumfrey Wyngefeilde.

Arms quarterly and Crest as at p. 47.

Sͬ Rauf Lane.

Argent, a lion rampant Gules within a bordure Sable.

Sͬ Edward Carne.

Sable, a Julian cross Argent, in chief a crescent Or.

Sͬ .... Partriche.

Sͬ Richard Pollard.

Quarterly—1 and 4, Argent, a chevron Azure between three escallops Gules, a crescent for difference ; 2 and 3, Argent, a chevron Sable between three mullets pierced Gules. *Crest—* A demi-polecat Or.

Sͬ Michael Dormer.

Azure, ten billets, 4, 3, 2, 1, Or, on a chief of the second a lion rampant issuant Sable, a mullet for difference. *Crest—*A wolf statant Sable, in the mouth a wing Argent.

Sͬ Richard Edgecombe.

Arms as at p. 46.

Sͬ John Guildeforde.

Quarterly of six—1 and 2 as at p. 9 ; 3, MOR-TIMER, on the escucheon three nails points in base Sable ; 4, Ermine, on a chevron Sable three crescents Or ; 5, Argent, a fess between three leopards' heads erased Sable ; 6, Vair, a canton Gules. Crest as No. 1 at p. 44, without the difference.

Sͬ John Harington.

Quarterly—1, Sable, a fret Argent ; 2, Argent, a cross flory Sable ; 3, Argent, a lion rampant double-queued Azure ; 4, Gules, three escallops Argent.

Sͬ Will'm Willoughby.

Quarterly of seven—1, Or, on two bars Gules three water-bougets Argent ; 2, 3, 4, 5, 6, and 7, as 1 to 6 at p. 47, a crescent for difference.

Sͬ Thomas Moyle of Kent.

Quarterly—1, Gules, an ass statant within a bordure Argent ; 2, Gules, a greyhound Or between two bars Argent and three martlets Sable thereon, in chief as many plates ; 3, Argent, a saltire Sable between four estoiles Gules ; 4, Quarterly per fess and per pale embattled Argent and Sable. *Crest—*Two demi-dragons addorsed and interlaced, the one Gules, the other Or.

Sr Walter Herbert. Quarterly—1 and 4, Per pale Gules and Azure, three lions rampant Argent; 2, Argent, a chevron between three Cornish choughs Sable; 3, Sable, a chevron between three spear-heads Argent imbrued Gules. *Crest*—A maiden's head couped Sable at the shoulders, crined and eared Or.

Sr Thomas Johanes. Argent, a chevron between three Cornish choughs Sable within a bordure engrailed Gules bezantée, a mullet for difference. *Crest*—Two battle-axes in saltire, handles Azure, heads Or, between the upper ends a Cornish chough Sable, "alibi no byrde here."

Sr Will'm Vaughan. Sable, a chevron between three boys' heads couped at the shoulders Argent, crined Or, their necks encircled with serpents Azure.

Sr Robert Acton. Gules, a fess and a bordure engrailed Ermine. *Crest*—An arm in armour embowed proper, holding erect in the hand a sword Argent, hilted and pomelled Or, on the point a boar's head couped Sable, the neck distilling blood.

Sr Edmond Peckham (note, Richard), Cofferer in the Kinge's howse. Quarterly—1 and 4, Sable, a chevron Or between three cross-crosslets fitchée Argent; 2 and 3, Or, on a fess Gules between three mullets Sable as many cross-crosslets fitchée Argent. *Crest*—A lion's head affrontée Sable pierced with three cross-crosslets fitchée Argent.

Sr Rowland Hyll. Azure, two bars Argent, on a canton Sable a chevron between three pheons Argent, on the chevron a hind's head erased between two mullets of the third. *Crest*—A hind's head erased Azure, collared Argent, in the mouth a trefoil slipped Vert.

Sr George Cotton. Azure, a chevron between three cotton twists Argent, a mullet for difference. *Crest*—An eagle with wings expanded Argent, beaked and legged Or, holding in the dexter claw a cornet Or, "alibi, holdinge a buckle Or, thonge B."

Sr Reignold Scotte of Kent. *Crest*—A demi-griffin wings endorsed Sable, beaked Or.

Sr John Candyshe. Quarterly—1, Argent, three piles wavy Gules; 2 and 3, Sable, a chevron Or between three cups uncovered Argent; 4, Barry of six Ermine and Sable. *Crest*—A greyhound's head Azure, collared Or.

S͏ʳ Donugans Macampce of Irelande, dubbed at Grenwiche the first day of October, anno 34, and **S͏ʳ Arthure Makenpce,** also then dubbed, who bare these armes with a crescent difference.

Argent, a hart statant Gules, attired or. " No roe bucke, but a harte."

S͏ʳ John Arundell of Treryse.

Quarterly of six—1, Sable, a hound courant between six swallows Argent; 2, Sable, three chevronels Argent; 3, Argent, a bend engrailed Sable, on a chief Gules three mullets Or on each a hurt; 4, Argent, a chevron Sable between three bucks statant Gules; 5, Vert, a lion rampant-gardant Argent, over all a fess Gules; 6, GREENFIELD.

S͏ʳ John Cotes of London, Maire.

Per pale Or and Azure, two dolphins hauriant addorsed and counterchanged, on a chief Sable a covered cup of the first between as many dove-cotes Argent. *Crest*—An arm erect habited paly of six Or and Azure, holding in the hand proper a covered cup Or.

S͏ʳ Will'm Herbert, dubbed anno 35.

Quarterly—1, HERBERT as at p. 17, a bordure gobony Or and Gules, the latter bezantée; 2, Crusily and three boars' heads couped; 3, Argent, three bendlets engrailed Gules, a canton Or; 4, Gules, three leopards' heads jessant-de-lis Or; over all a crescent for difference. Crest as at p. 72, a crescent for difference.

S͏ʳ Robert Tyrwhite.

Arms same as at p. 15. *Crest*—A demi-savage Argent, cinctured Vert, holding in both hands a club of the first.

S͏ʳ Will'm Peter.

Gules, on a bend Or between two escallops Argent a Cornish chough Sable beaked and legged of the first between as many cinquefoils Azure, on a chief of the second a rose of the first seeded of the second between two demi-fleurs-de-lis of the fourth. *Crest*—Two hounds' (probably should be lions') heads erased and addorsed, the first Azure, the second Or, collared and in the mouth of each an annulet all counterchanged.

S͏ʳ John Fogge.

Quarterly—1 and 4, Argent, on a fess between three annulets Sable as many mullets pierced of the field; 2, Paly wavy of six Or and Gules; 3, Azure, three baskets Or. *Crest*—A unicorn's head Argent, maned Sable, armed Or.

Sᵣ Will'm Pagett, Lord Pagett of Beaudesert, wrytten then of Bromley in com. Stafford. •

Azure, on a cross engrailed between four eagles displayed Argent five lions passant Sable. *Crest*—A demi-heraldic tiger salient Sable, tufted and ducally gorged Argent.

Sᵣ Foulke Grevell.

Arms as at p. 54.

Sᵣ Richard Manners.

Arms quarterly as at p. 70, but 1 and 4 the chief quarterly Azure and Gules, in the first and fourth two fleurs-de-lis, and in the second and third a lion passant-gardant Or ; and the same Crest.

Sᵣ Edward Stradlinge.

Quarterly—1 and 4, STRADLINGE as at p. 49 ; 2 and 3, Azure, a chevron between three crescents Or, quartering chequy Or and Gules, a fess Ermine. *Crest*—A buck statant Argent, about his neck a scarf Or.

Sᵣ Rauf Ellercar.

Quarterly—1, as at p. 57 ; 2, Ermine, a cross patonce Gules ; 3, Argent, a saltire engrailed Sable between four cinquefoils Gules; 4, Argent, three Cornish choughs Sable, beaked and legged Gules. *Crest*—Two dolphins hauriant and addorsed Azure and Or enfiled with a ducal coronet per pale counterchanged.

Sᵣ Richard Southwell, dubbed at the Parlement Anno 33, who with these 3 following ar placed in the originall before Sᵣ Richard Edgecombe :

Sᵣ Edward Marvyn.   **Sᵣ Edward North.**   **Sᵣ Will'm Denham.**

Knightes (58 in number) made in Scotland by the Erle of Hertforde, the Kinge's Lieutenant Generall, of whom 41 were made at Leith the 11 day of May Sonday after the destruction of Edenborough and other townes in anno 36 of the Kinge's reigne (6 at Leith marked * on the 13th, and 11 at Butterden marked † on the 18th of the same month—Harl. MS. 6063) :

Edward, Lorde Clynton.

Quarterly—1 and 4, as at p. 32 ; 2 and 3, Quarterly Or and Gules. *Crest*—" Owte of a crowne Gules six feathers Argent with a blew lace."

John, Lorde Cognyers.

Quarterly—1 and 4, Azure, a maunch Or, an annulet Sable for difference ; 2 and 3, Azure, crusily and 3 cinquefoils Argent, quartering Azure, three bars-gemelles and a chief Or. *Crest*—A sinister wing Gules.

Sᵣ Will'm Wroughton.

Arms as at p. 17.

Sᵣ Thomas Holcrofte.

Quarterly—1 and 4, Argent, a cross and bordure engrailed Sable; 2, Argent, a squirrel Gules devouring a nut Or ; 3, Argent, an eagle Sable standing on a child proper swathed Gules, a crescent for difference.

Crest—A raven Sable, wings endorsed, holding erect in the dexter claw a sword in pale Argent, hilt and pomel Or, a crescent of the last for difference.

Sʳ Edward Darrell. Quarterly—1 and 4, Arms of DARRELL as at p. 16, the crescent surmounting a lozenge fitchée ; 2 and 3, Argent, two bars and in chief as many lions rampant Gules. *Crest*—Out of a ducal coronet Or a Saracen's head in profile couped at the shoulders proper, bearded Sable, wreathed about the temple Argent and Sable, on the head a chapeau Azure fretty of the third.

Sʳ John Lutterell. Or, a bend between six martlets Sable.

Sʳ John Jenyns of London, Skynner. Quarterly—1 and 4, Argent, on a fess Gules three bezants ; 2 and 3, Gules, a bull's head cabossed Argent, armed Or. *Crest*—A demi-lion erased holding erect in both paws a mace Azure.

Sʳ Thomas Waterton of Yorkshire. Arms as at p. 35.

* Sʳ Charles Howarde. Arms quarterly as at p. 56, but 3 and 4 transposed, with difference and Crest as at p. 69.

* Sʳ George Blount. Arms quarterly as at p. 16. *Crest*—"An armed foote in the sonne."

† Sʳ Peter Mewtas. Azure, a unicorn salient Ermine, armed Or.

† Sʳ Edward Warner. Quarterly—1 and 4, Per bend indented Sable and Argent, quartering Azure, a fleur-de-lis Or ; 2 and 3, Vert, a cross engrailed Argent; over all a crescent for difference. *Crest*—A double plume of feathers Or, a crescent for difference.

Sʳ Rauf Bulmer. Gules, billitée and a lion rampant Or.

Sʳ Hugh Cholmeley. Gules, two helmets close Argent in chief, a garb Or in base, a fleur-de-lis on a crescent of the last for difference. Crest as at p. 68.

Sʳ Thomas Lee, Doctor. Quarterly—1 and 4, Azure, two bars Argent, a bend gobony Or and Gules, a crescent for difference ; 2 and 3, Argent, two bars Gules, on a canton of the second a maunch of the first. *Crest*—An arm embowed habited chequy Or and Gules, cuffed Argent, holding erect in the hand proper a sword of the third, hilt and pomel of the first, the point transfixing a dragon of the third.

Sʳ Richard Lee of St. Alban's. Per chevron Or and Gules, in chief two lions rampant Sable combatant. *Crest*—A dexter arm embowed in armour holding a sword, from the blade flames of fire issuing, all proper.

Sᵣ **Peter Lee.**

Sᵣ **John Legh** of Bowthe.

Sᵣ **Lawrence Smythe.**   •   Azure, two bars wavy Ermine, on a chief Or a demi-lion rampant issuing Sable, on the breast three wounds Gules. "One wound on the lion's breast." *Crest*—An ostrich's head quarterly Azure and Or between two wings expanded Gules, in the beak a horse-shoe of the second.

Sᵣ **Will'm Vavasour.**   Arms quarterly and Crest as at p. 52. *Motto*— "Je le veul bien."

Sᵣ **Richard Sherbourne.**   Quarterly—1 and 4, Argent, a lion rampant-gardant Vert ; 2 and 3, Vert, an eagle displayed Argent. *Crest*—A unicorn's head Argent, armed Or.

Sᵣ **Robert Stapleton.**   Quarterly—1 and 4, as at p. 39 ; 2, Argent, on a fess Azure three fleurs-de-lis Or, quartering Argent, a bend between six martlets Gules ; 3, Bendy of six Argent and Azure. Crest as at p. 39.

Sᵣ **Thomas Holte.**

† Sᵣ **Will'm Davenporte.**   Argent, a chevron between three cross-crosslets Sable. *Crest*—A man's head in profile couped at the shoulders and a rope round the neck, all proper.

† Sᵣ **Rauf Leycester.**   Azure, a fess between three fleurs-de-lis Or.

† Sᵣ **Thomas Bradbourne.**

Sᵣ **Thomas Malyverer** of Alderton in Yorkshire.   Quarterly—1 and 4, Gules, three greyhounds courant in pale Argent, quartering Gules, a bend gobony Argent and Azure, over all a chief Or ; 2 and 3, Azure, on a bend between six martlets Argent a crescent Gules for difference. *Crest*—A greyhound statant Argent, collared Azure.

† Sᵣ **Franceys Pothome** of Yorkshire.   Barry of ten Argent and Azure, on a canton Or a martlet Sable.

† Sᵣ **John Massy.**   Gules, a lion passant Argent.

Sᵣ **Leonarde Beckwythe.**   Argent, a chevron Gules fretty Or between three hinds' heads erased of the second, on a chief of the same a saltire engrailed of the third between two roses of the field, at each end of the chief a demi-fleur-de-lis of the same. *Crest*—A stag's head erased quarterly Or and Azure, the attires counterchanged.

Sᵣ **Thomas Cokeyn** of Ashburne in com. Derby.   Arms (quartering Argent, two bars Vert) and Crest as at p. 55.

S⟨r⟩ Peter Frecheville of Staveley in com. Derby.	Azure, a bend between six escallops Argent.
S⟨r⟩ Richard Egerton.	Argent, a lion rampant Gules between three pheons Sable. *Crest*—A lion's gamb Gules, holding a sword per pale Argent and Azure, hilt and pomel Or.
S⟨r⟩ Anthony Nevyll.	Gules, a saltire Ermine.
† S⟨r⟩ John Nevyll.	
S⟨r⟩ Will'm Radcliffe of Ordesale.	Gules, a bend engrailed Argent. Crest as at p. 55.
S⟨r⟩ George Bowes of the Byshopryke.	Arms and Crest as at p. 67.
* S⟨r⟩ Uryan Breerton. ⎱	
S⟨r⟩ Will'm Brereton. ⎬	Arms quarterly and Crest as at p. 65.
* S⟨r⟩ Roger Breereton. ⎰	
S⟨r⟩ Edward Warren.	Arms quarterly and Crest as at p. 18.
S⟨r⟩ Bryan Layton of Lancashire.	Sable, on a bend Argent three escallops Gules. *Crest*—A lion's head erased Sable charged with three escallops between two bars Argent.
S⟨r⟩ Robert Wortesley (Worseley).	Quarterly—1 and 4, Argent, on a chief Gules a crescent of the field for difference; 2 and 3, Azure, three lozenges Or. *Crest*—Out of a ducal coronet Or ten feathers Argent.
S⟨r⟩ Thomas Talbot of Bashall.	Argent, three lions rampant Purpure. *Crest*—A talbot statant Sable.
S⟨r⟩ Hugh Calveley.	Arms as at p. 65. *Crest*—Out of a ducal coronet Or a calf's head Sable.
S⟨r⟩ Thomas Clere of Norff.	Quarterly—1 and 4, Argent, on a fess Azure three eagles displayed Or; 2 and 3, Ermine, on a chief Gules three lozenges of the field. *Crest*—A sun in splendour Or between two wings Azure on each a crescent Argent.
S⟨r⟩ Richard Hollande.	Per fess Azure and Gules, three fleurs-de-lis Argent.
S⟨r⟩ Thomas Venables, made Knight at Edenborough.	Azure, two bars Argent. *Crest*—A wivern passant Gules issuing from a weir Argent.
S⟨r⟩ John Constable of Yorkshire.	
S⟨r⟩ Edmond Trafford of Lancashire.	Arms quarterly and Crest as at p. 25.
S⟨r⟩ John Atherton.	Gules, three sparhawks Argent, beaked, legged, and belled Or. *Crest*—Out of a ducal coronet Or a swan Argent, wings endorsed, beaked Gules.
S⟨r⟩ Richard Cholmeley of Yorkshire.	Arms and Crest as at p. 75, but the crescent Ermine.

78 KNIGHTS MADE 1544.

* Sr Philippe Egerton.

Sable, a chevron between three pheons Argent. *Crest*—A buck's head erased.

† Sr Hugh Wyllughby.

Arms as at p. 15. *Crest*—A griffin passant.

† Sr Thomas Constable of Yorkshire.

Arms and Crest as at p. 29.

* Sr Will'm Woodhous of Norf. quære si fuit miles.

Sable, a chevron Or goutté Gules between three cinquefoils Ermine, a crescent Argent for difference. *Crest*—A demi-woodman per pale Gules and Or, the head proper, holding in both hands a club ragulée of the second. "Alibi, the woodman whole standing on his feete."

† Sr Edmond Sabage.

Arms quarterly and Crest as at p. 16, without the difference ; but 1 and 4 the tinctures reversed, and the Crest not erased.

Sr Thomas Gerarde.

Azure, a lion rampant Ermine ducally crowned Or. *Crest*—A lion's gamb erased Ermine resting on a lure Or.

Sr Humfrey Style, dubbed Knight at Dover by the Kinge when he came from the wynninge of Boleyn, he being then Shirif of Kent.

Quarterly—1 and 4, Sable, a fess engrailed fretty of the field between three fleurs-de-lis Or within a bordure of the last; 2 and 3, Argent, a wolf statant Sable, quartering Argent, three turnpikes Sable. *Crest*—A wolf's head Sable gorged with three bezants between two bars Or, the neck fretty of the second, eared and langued Gules. "His wief bare g. 3 crescents or. Creast a gote's hedde razed b. 3 gouttes horned and bearded wreath or v."

Sr Will'm Woodhouse, belonging to the Shippes, after Vice-Admirall.

Quarterly Ermine and Azure, in the second and third quarters a leopard's face Or, a crescent for difference.

Knightes made by the Kinge at Bolleyne after the conquest of the Towne on the morowe after Michelmasse day the laste of September, in the 36 yere of his reigne :

Erle of Rutlande.

Arms quarterly and Crest as those of Sir RICHARD MANNERS at p. 74, but the Crest on a chapeau Gules turned up Ermine.

Lorde Nebill.

Quarterly—1 and 4, Gules, a saltire Argent ; 2, Gules, three lions passant-gardant in pale Or within a bordure Argent ; 3, Or, fretty Gules, on a canton per pale Ermine and Or a lymphad Sable. *Crest*—Out of a ducal coronet Or a bull's head Argent, armed Or, tipped Vert. On both shield and crest a label of three points.

Lord Fitzwalter.

Quarterly of eight—1, Argent, a bend engrailed Sable; 2, Or, a fess between two chevrons Gules; 3, Argent, a lion rampant Sable ducally crowned Or within a bordure Azure; 4, Argent, a saltire engrailed Sable; 5, Gules, three lucies haurant Argent; 6, Argent, three bars Gules; 7, Or, flory Sable; 8, Argent, an eagle Sable preying on a child swathed Gules. *Crest*—An arm erect in armour Argent grasping in the hand proper a wivern Or, the tail encircling the arm.

Lorde Bray.

Arms quarterly as at p. 27. On an escucheon of pretence, Quarterly—1, Or, on a bend Gules three goats passant Argent; 2, Sable, a chevron engrailed between three bulls' heads cabossed Argent; 3, Gules, a fess counter-compony Argent and Sable between six crosses patée fitchée of the second, quartering—1, Or, two bends Gules; 2, Bendy of eight Or and Azure; and 3, Sable, a cross between four bees Or. *Crest*—A lion passant-gardant Or between two wings vair.

Lorde John Grey.
Lorde Edward Grey.

Arms quarterly of eight and Crest as at p. 47.

The same Arms and Crest, on each a crescent for difference.

Lorde Powre of Irelande.

Or, a chief indented Sable.

Sr Henry Dudley, dubbed by the Kinge at Boleyn the xxth of January, anno 36.

Quarterly of six—1, Or, two lions passant Azure, quartering Argent, a cross patonce Azure; 2, Gules, a fess between six cross-crosslets Or; 3, Chequy Or and Azure, a fess Ermine; 4, Gules, crusily patée and a chevron Argent; 5, Or, a fess between two chevrons Sable; 6, Barry of six Argent and Azure, in chief three torteaux and a label of three points; quartering—1, Gules, a lion rampant within a bordure Or, a crescent for difference; 2, Or, a maunch Gules; and 3, Barry of ten Argent and Azure, an orle of martlets Gules. Crest as under Sir EDWARD SUTTON, p. 18. On both shield and crest a label of three points.

Sr Ingram Clyfforde.

Quarterly of eight—1, 3, and 4, as 1, 2, 3 at p. 62, 5 and 6 as 4, the quarterings reversed; 2, Azure, three spears Or; 7, Barry of six Or and Azure, on a canton Gules a cross patonce Argent; 8, Argent, on a chief indented Gules an annulet between two mullets Or. The same Crest.

S͛ Anthony Denny.

Quarterly—1 and 4, Gules, crusily patée Or, a saltire Argent; 2, Or, a fess dancettée Gules, in chief three martlets Sable; 3, TROUT-BECKE, a mullet pierced Or for difference. *Crest*—An arm erect habited Azure, charged with a quatrefoil Argent, holding in the hand proper a garb Or.

S͛ Thomas Carden.

Quarterly—1 and 4, Sable, a sling in bend between two pheons Argent; 2 and 3, Argent, three bends engrailed Gules. *Crest* — A hind statant Sable, holding in the mouth an arrow Argent. "Quære quod genus animalis, forsan equus."

S͛ Philippe Hobby.

Argent, on a chevron embattled counter-embattled Gules between three griffins' heads erased Azure each holding in the beak a cinquefoil slipped of the third and Or as many roses of the last. *Crest*—A falcon belled, holding in the dexter claw a thistle proper leaved Vert.

S͛ Thomas Paston.

Quarterly—1, Argent, six fleurs-de-lis Azure, a chief indented Or, quartering Or, on a chevron between three lions' heads erased Gules as many bezants; 2, Azure, a cross Or; 3, Argent, a chevron between three bears' heads erased Sable, muzzled Gules, quartering—1, Ermine, on a chief indented Gules three crowns Or; 2, Sable, a fess between two chevrons Or; and 3, Argent, a fess between three crescents Gules; over all a crescent for difference. Crest as at p. 15.

S͛ John Barkeley.

Arms quarterly of six and Crest as at p. 41.

S͛ Charles Brandon.

Arms quarterly as at p. 44, a bendlet sinister Or, and the same Crest.

S͛ Francis Askue of Lincolnshire.

Sable, a fess Or between three asses passant Argent. *Crest*—An ass's head erased Argent, haltered proper.

S͛ Rauf Vane.

Azure, three dexter gauntlets Or, a bendlet sinister Gules. *Crest*—An arm erect in armour Or, gauntlet Gules, grasping three branches of heartsease proper. "Alibi the gauntlett only: no part of the arme."

S͛ Richard Wynybanke.

Vert, on a chevron between three falcons volant Or as many trefoils slipped Sable. *Crest*—Out of a mound Vert four vine-branches of the second bearing grapes proper.

S͛ Nicholas Wentworthe of Essex.

Arms of WENTWORTH as at p. 46, without the difference, quartering Gules, three escucheons Argent; over all an annulet for difference. Crest as at p. 46, with the same difference, per pale Or and Gules.

Sᵣ Rauf Popton. Gules, crusily fitchée and a lion rampant Or, a crescent Sable for difference. *Crest*—A lion's head erased Or charged with a bend Gules, thereon three cross-crosslets of the first.

Sᵣ John Powlett, now Marquyse of Wynchester. Quarterly of nine—1, POWLETT as at p. 16; 2, Gules, three fleurs-de-lis Ermine; 3, Barry of six Or and Vert; 4, Argent, on a chief Gules two mullets pierced Or; 5, Gules, two lions passant-gardant Argent; 6, Barry of six Ermine and Gules; 7, Azure, a fess between three fleurs-de-lis Or; 8, Argent, fretty and a canton Sable; 9, Argent, six martlets Sable; over all a label of three points. Crest as at p. 36.

Sᵣ Thomas Morgan of Wales. Quarterly—1 and 4, Or, a griffin segreant Sable; 2, Argent, guttée and a cross patonce Sable; 3, Argent, a unicorn salient within a bordure engrailed Sable. *Crest*—A buck's head cabossed double attired Or.

Sᵣ Robert Stafforde. Quarterly of six—1 and 6, Or, a chevron Gules and a canton Ermine, a mullet for difference; 2, Ermine, a fess Sable between three beehives Or; 3, Azure, a cross Argent; 4, Azure, two bars Argent, each charged with three martlets Gules; 5, Per fess Gules and Azure, a lion rampant Or. *Crest*—Out of a ducal coronet per pale Or and Gules a boar's head Sable.

Sᵣ Will'm Blount. Quarterly—1 and 4, BLOUNT as at p. 16; 2 and 3, Quarterly paly of four Or and Gules and Ermine within a bordure Azure, impaling Argent, a cross flory Sable, on a canton Gules a lion's head erased of the first crowned Or; and the same Crest.

Sᵣ Andrew Flamocke. Argent, on a cross between four mullets pierced Gules five acorns Or. *Crest*—A tree ragulée Vert flamant Gules.

Sᵣ Richard Wyngefeilde. Arms quarterly as at p. 47. *Crest*—A bull statant quarterly Sable and Or. On each an annulet for difference.

Sᵣ Maurice Barkleye. Arms quarterly of six as at p. 41, and Crest as at p. 19.

Sᵣ John Wellisbourn. Quarterly—1 and 4, Gules, a chief counter-compony Or and of the first, over all a griffin segreant of the second, debruised by a bend

Ermine; 2, Sable, a fess counter-compony Or and Azure between three goats' heads erased Argent; 3, Argent, a tower triple-towered between three covered cups Azure, quartering Ermine, on a canton Gules an owl Argent. *Crest*—A harpy Or without wings, but with a peacock's tail displayed proper. "Alibi no byrde but haulfe the body of a mayden the armes and brestes seene downe to the nether ribbes and behind it the pecock's fethers."

Sʳ Will'm Buttes.

Azure, on a chevron between three estoiles Or as many lozenges Gules. "Party per pale Or and B., the whole counterchanged." *Crest*—Two hands Gules, the dexter above the sinister, both grasping a (?) caduceus Or.

Sʳ George Baynham.

Arms quarterly and Crest as at p. 54. On an escucheon of pretence, Azure, a cross Or between four leopards' faces Argent, quartering Ermine, a leopard's face Or between a chief and a chevron Sable.

Sʳ Richard Candysbe, Capetayne of Blacknesse, dubbed in Scotland by the Erle of Hertforde the 23 of September, anno 37 of the Kinge's reigne.

Arms quarterly and Crest as at p. 72.

Sʳ Will'm Larton, dubbed at the Pallas of Westm' anno 37 of the Kinge's reigne, on Sonday the 7 of February, he then beinge Maior of London.

Argent, a chevron engrailed counter-compony Ermine and Sable between three griffins' heads erased Gules guttée d'Or. *Crest*—A griffin's head per pale Or and Vert, collared counterchanged.

Sʳ George Cornwall, dubbed at Bulleyn by the Erle of Hertforde anno 37 of the Kinge's reigne.

Quarterly—1 and 4, as at p. 28; 2, On a bend cotised three mullets, quartering, 1, Barry of six Argent and Azure, and 2, Sable, a bend lozengy Argent; 3, Gules, three bars gobony Argent and Sable, quartering Barry of six Or and Azure, a bend Gules. *Crest*—A lion statant Gules, ducally crowned Or.

Knightes made in Scotlande by the Erle of Hertforde, the Kinge's Lieutenant, the 23 day of September, anno d'ni 1545, anno regis 37, being then encamped by our Lady Churche by Norham Castle, at his cominge home after he had ben in Scotland 25 dayes :

John, Lorde Latymer.

Quarterly of eleven—1, Gules, a saltire Argent, an annulet for difference ; 2, Or, fretty Gules, on a canton per pale Ermine and of the first a lymphad Sable ; 3, Gules, a fess between six cross-crosslets Or ; 4, Chequy Or and Azure, a chevron Ermine ; 5, Argent, a fess between two bars-gemelles Gules ; 6, Gules, a lion passant-gardant Argent ducally crowned Or ; 7, Argent, a chevron Gules ; 8, Gules, crusily patée and a chevron Argent ; 9, Quarterly Or and Vert, quartering, 1, Quarterly Gules and Or, in the first quarter a mullet Argent— 2, Gules, on a bend between six cross-crosslets fitchée Argent an Ermine spot— and 3, Gules, six escallops Argent ; 10, Or, a chevron Gules within a bordure engrailed Sable ; 11, Per chevron Sable and Argent, in chief three leopards' faces Or. *Crest*— A griffin passant Or.

Sr Thomas Wharton, sonne and heire to the Lorde Wharton.

Sable, a maunch Argent, a label of three points. *Crest*—A bull's head erased Argent, armed Sable, ducally gorged per pale Gules and Or ; a similar label.

Sr John Tempest.

Arms as at p. 51.

Sr George Radclyffe.

Arms as at p. 55, at the upper end an escallop Argent, "or els a molet"; the same Crest.

Sr Francys Hastyngs.

Arms quarterly and Crest as at p. 21.

Sr Will'm Seint Quintin.

Or, three chevronels Gules, a chief Vair.

S^r Xp'opher Metcalf.

Argent, three calves passant Sable.

Sr Thomas Dacres.

Arms as at p. 39, a bendlet sinister Azure ; and the same Crest.

Sr Will'm Stafforde.

Arms quarterly of six and Crest as at p. 81.

Sr Thomas Grey of Horton.

Gules, a lion rampant Argent charged on the shoulder with a boar's head couped within a bordure engrailed of the second.

Sr Will'm Calverley.

Sable, an inescucheon within an orle of owls Argent.

Sr Will'm Ingleby.

Quarterly—1 and 4, Sable, an estoile of six points Argent ; 2, Argent, a chevron between three leopards' heads Gules ; 3, Gules, a lion rampant Argent within a bordure per pale indented Sable and Or. *Crest*—A boar's head erect Argent, tusked Or.

Sr Roger Fenwyke.

Per fess Gules and Argent, three martlets in chief and as many in base counterchanged.

Knightes dubbed by the Kinge sythence his retourne from Bulleyn :

Sr Francys Leyke.

Argent, on a saltire engrailed Sable nine annulets Or.

S͛ **Robert Townshende** of Norf., dubbed on Trinity Sonday anno 37.

Quarterly—1 and 4, and 2, as at p. 13 ; 3, Argent, crusily and a lion rampant Gules ducally crowned Or, a crescent for difference.

S͛ **Michael Stanhope**, dubbed anno 37 at Hampton Courte.

Quarterly—1, Quarterly Ermine and Gules ; 2 and 3, as 1 and 2 at p. 28; 4, Argent, three saltires engrailed Sable ; over all a crescent for difference. *Crest*—Out of a tower Azure, a lion rampant Or ducally crowned Gules, holding between the paws a flint-stone Argent. " Alibi, a rynge, no stone."

S͛ **John Pylston**, dubbed . . . .
S͛ . . . . **Pogan.**

S͛ **Richard Rede**, Doctor, anno 37 de Redbourne juxta Sᵗᵉ Alban's.

Argent, on a cross between two hurts each charged with a dove Argent in chief and as many Cornish choughs Sable beaked and legged Gules in base, a lion rampant Or at the top and bottom ends and another passant at the side ends. " These two lyons gardant. Alibi two hurts with a white dove as above and not the Cornish choughs." *Crest*—A buffalo's head Sable, fretty armed and ringed Or.

S͛ **Will'm Cavendishe**, Threasurer of the chamber, dubbed in anno 37 on Ester-day.

Quarterly—1 and 4, Sable, three stags' heads cabossed Argent attired Or, a crescent for difference ; 2 and 3, Argent, a chevron Gules between three crosses botony Sable. *Crest*— A snake nowed Vert.

S͛ **John Perpent** of Hertfordshire, anno 37.

Gules, three crescents Argent. *Crest*—On a mound a parrot Vert, beaked and legged Gules, holding in the dexter claw a pear Or, slipped and leaved of the first. On each a mullet for difference.

S͛ **Francis Barnarde**, a Venetian, anno 37.

Per bend Argent and Gules, demi-fleurs-de-lis issuing from all sides, a rose counterchanged, a sinister quarter quarterly, 1, Sable, a lion passant-gardant Or; 2 and 3, voided of the field ; 4, also Sable, a fleur-de-lis also Or. *Crest*—An elephant's head Sable, tusked Or, collared Argent, charged with three roses Gules.

S͛ **John Pakington**, anno 37.

Per chevron Sable and Argent, in chief three mullets pierced Or, in base as many garbs Gules on each a rose of the third. *Crest*— A demi-hare Azure, thereon four bezants.

S͛ **Thomas Bromley**, Justice, dubbed at the Parlement anno 37.

Quarterly per fess indented Or and Gules. *Crest*—Two arms embowed, the dexter vested Or, the sinister Azure, each cuffed Ermine, holding in the hands proper a bunch of broom.

Sᵣ **Peter Gambow**, Spanyard, dubbed by the Kinge at Yorke Place, anno 38.

Vert, " a wolf silver in a nette Sable," impaling Argent three fig-leaves stalks upwards Vert.

Sᵣ **Will'm Farmour** of Norf.

(*added*) Argent, a chevron between four lions' heads erased Gules, on a chief Azure an anchor between two pales Or, a martlet for difference.

Sᵣ **Humfrey Acton.**

Sᵣ .... **Wynde**, Justice, made at the Parlement, anno 37.

Sᵣ **Thomas Palmer.**

The Names and Armes of those that were advanced to the honorable Ordre of Knighthode in the happy reigne of

Kinge Edward the Sixt.

(Cotton MSS., Claudius ciii., fol. 151–178.)

On Sonday the 6 of February, Kinge Edward the Sixt, in the first yere of his reigne, was made Knighte by Edward, Erle of Hertford his uncle, Lorde Protector, and the same tyme the sayd Kinge dubbed these two followinge :

Sᵣ **Henry Houblethorne**, Maior of London, dubbed by the Kinge at the Toure the 6 of February before the coronation.

Sable, a mascle within a tressure flory counter-flory Argent. *Crest*—An elephant's head Azure, gorged Gules bezantée, tusked Or, on the top of the head leaves Vert.

Sᵣ **John Portman**, Justice, dubbed at that tyme, the 6 of February, before the coronation.

Quarterly—1 and 4, Or, a fleur-de-lis Azure ; 2 and 3, Azure, a chevron Argent between three pears Or.

Knightes dubbed by the Kinge on Sonday, the day of his coronation, the 20 of February, being crowned, to the nombre of 40, in lieu of the Bathe, w'ch then could not be perfourmed accordinge to all ceremonyes thereto belonginge, the tyme for that pourpose beinge to shorte :

Duke of Suffolke.

Quarterly of nine—1, BRANDON as at p. 10 ; 2, Azure, a cross moline Or ; 3, Lozengy Ermine and Gules ; 4, Sable, a cross engrailed Or ; 5, Gules, a cross moline Argent ; 6, Gules, a lion rampant Or, quartering Sable, fretty Or, over all a crescent for difference ; 7, Or, a lion rampant Sable ; 8, Gules, a fess dancettée between six cross-crosslets Or ; 9, Barry of six Ermine and Gules, three crescents Sable. *Crest*—BRANDON as at p. 44.

Erle of Oxford.

Quarterly of eight—1, VERE as at p. 23 ; 2, Argent, fretty Gules, on each joint a bezant ; 3, Argent, a lion rampant Gules, over all on a fess Or three crosses patée fitchée Sable ; 4, Argent, three chevronels Sable ; 5, Argent, a chevron Sable between twelve pears Gules slipped Vert ; 6, Argent, a fess between two bars-gemelles Gules ; 7, Barry wavy of six Argent and Azure ; 8, Vert, a lion rampant Argent, a wound on the shoulder distilling blood. *Crest*—VERE as at p. 49.

Erle of Hertforde.

Quarterly of six—1, Or, flory Azure, on a pile Gules three lions passant-gardant of the field ; 2, 3, 4, 5, and 6, as Sir THOMAS SEYMOUR, p. 66. *Crest*—Out of a ducal coronet Or a phœnix in flames proper with wings expanded of the first. *Motto*—"A l'amy fidel pour jamais."

Erle of Ormonde.

Quarterly—1 and 4, Or, a chief indented Azure ; 2, Ermine, a saltire Gules ; 3, Gules, three covered cups Or. *Crest*—In a ducal coronet Or a plume of feathers Argent, thereon a falcon rising of the last.

Lorde Maltravers.

Arms quarterly and Crest as at p. 20.

Lorde Talbot.

Quarterly of nine—1, 2, 5, 6, 7, and 8, the same as 1, 2, 3, 4, 5, and 6 at p. 52 ; 3, Argent, five bends Gules ; 4, Gules, three garbs Or, quartering Barry of ten Argent and Azure, an orle of martlets Gules ; 9, Argent, a lion rampant per fess Gules and Sable ; over all a label of three points. *Crest*—A lion statant Or, on the neck a label of three points.

Lorde Strange.

Quarterly of eight—1, Argent, on a bend Azure three bucks' heads cabossed Or ; 2, Or, on a chief indented Azure three plates ; 3, as 2 under STANLEY at p. 23 ; 4, Chequy Or and Azure ; 5, Gules, two lions passant Argent ; 6, Argent, a fess and canton Gules ; 7, Or, a cross engrailed Sable ; 8, Azure, a lion rampant Argent ; over all a label of three points. Crest as under STANLEY at p. 11.

Lorde Herbert.

Quarterly—1 and 4, Or, on a fess France and England quarterly within a bordure gobony Azure and Argent ; 2, Per pale Gules and Azure, three lions rampant Argent ; 3, Argent, a fess and canton Gules. *Crest*—"A

John, Lord Lysle, sonne and heire of John, Erle of Warwyke.

panther Argent, spotted Or, Gules, and Azure," charged with a label of three points.

Quarterly of six—1-5, as 1-5 under Sir HENRY DUDLEY at p. 79 ; 6, Gules, a lion passant-gardant Argent ducally crowned Or ; and the same Crest.

Lorde Charles Brandon.

Arms quarterly of nine as under the Duke of SUFFOLK at p. 85, and Crest as under BRANDON p. 45 ; on each a crescent for difference.

Lorde Cromewell.

Quarterly per fess indented Azure and Or, four lions passant counterchanged. *Crest*—On a chapeau Gules turned up Ermine a pelican in piety Or guttée d'Azure.

Lorde Hastinges.

Quarterly of seven—1, Argent, a maunch Sable, quartering, 1, Per pale indented Gules and Vert, a chevron Or—2, Sable, two bars Argent and in chief three plates—and 3, Barry of six Ermine and Gules ; 2, Azure, three garbs Argent banded Gules, a chief Or ; 3, Argent, three toads erect Sable ; 4, Argent, a griffin segreant Gules, clawed Azure ; 5, Paly wavy of six Or and Gules ; 6, Argent, two bars Gules and in chief three torteaux ; 7, Or, three torteaux, a label of three points Azure bezantée ; over all a label of three points. *Crest*—A bull's head erased Sable, horned and ducally gorged Or.

Lorde Scroope's sonne and heire.

Quarterly—1, 2, and 3, as 1, 2, and 3 at p. 32 ; 4, Azure, a bend Or, an annulet Sable and a label of three points Argent for difference. *Crest*—Same as at p. 41. On each a label of three points.

Sr Thomas Wyndesore, sonne and heire to the Lord Wyndesore.

Arms quarterly of eight—1, as 1 ; 2, 3, 4, 5, as 2 ; 6, as 3 ; 7, as 4 ; 8, as 6 ; and an escucheon of pretence as 5, at p. 63 ; and the same Crest.

Sr Francys Russell.

Quarterly—1, Argent, a lion rampant Gules, on a chief Sable three escallops of the field, quartering Azure, a tower embattled with a cupola Argent, port Gules ; 2, Gules, three lucies hauriant in fess Argent ; 3, Sable, a griffin segreant between three cross-crosslets fitchée Argent ; 4, Sable, three chevronels Ermine, a crescent Or for difference. *Crest*—A goat passant Argent attired Or. On each a label of three points.

S͠ʳ Richard Devereulx. — Quarterly—1 and 4, Argent, a fess Gules, in chief three torteaux; 2 and 3, Vair Or and Gules. *Crest*—Out of a ducal coronet Or a talbot's head Argent, eared Gules. On each a label of three points. *Motto*—"Loyal suis."

S͠ʳ Anthony Browne. — Quarterly—1, Quarterly same as at p. 15; 2, Gules, a saltire Argent, a label of three points and a crescent Sable for difference, quartering, 1, Argent, three lozenges in fess Gules—and 2, Or, an eagle displayed Vert; 3, Gules, three lions passant-gardant Or within a bordure Argent, quartering, 1, Argent, a saltire engrailed Gules—and 2, Or, a lion rampant Gules; 4, Gules, a cross engrailed Argent, quartering, 1, Argent, on a canton Gules a rose Or—2, Azure, a fess between three leopards' faces Or, an annulet Sable for difference—3, Argent, on a fess dancettée Sable three bezants. *Crest*—A stag statant proper, attired, ducally gorged, and lined Or.

S͠ʳ Henry Seymour. — Arms quarterly of six and Crest as those of the Earl of HERTFORD at p. 86; on each a crescent for difference.

S͠ʳ John Gates. — Arms quarterly and Crest as at p. 51.

S͠ʳ Anthony Cooke of Essex. — Quarterly of eight—1 and 8, COOKE as at p. 30; 2, Sable, a fess between three pheons Argent; 3, Or, a spread-eagle Sable, charged with a fleur-de-lis Argent; 4, Three eagles displayed between two bendlets; 5, Gules, a fess counter-compony Argent and Sable between six crosses patée fitchée of the first; 6, Or, two bends Gules; 7, Bendy of ten Azure and Or. *Crest*—A unicorn's head Or between two wings Azure. "Bothe the wynges behynde the hedd."

S͠ʳ Alexander Umpton of Oxfordshire. — Arms of UMPTON as at p. 65, and the same Crest without the collar.

S͠ʳ George Norton of Somersetshire. — Quarterly—1 and 4, Argent, three escallops in bend cotised between two lions rampant Sable, a crescent for difference; 2 and 3, Per pale Azure and Gules, three lions rampant-gardant Argent. *Crest*—A greyhound's head "dunyshe," collared Gules bezantée, a crescent Sable for difference.

S͠ʳ Valentine Knightley. — Arms and Crest as at p. 26.

S͠ʳ Robert Lytton. — Arms as at p. 26.

Sr George Vernon of the Peke.

Arms quarterly of six and Crest as at p. 21. *Motto*—" Mais si je puis."

Sr John Porte of Derbyshire.

Azure, a fess between two cotises engrailed and three pigeons Or beaked Sable.

Sr Thomas Josselyn.

Quarterly—1, Azure, a josselyn Argent and Sable belled Or ; 2, Gules, on a saltire engrailed Or five torteaux, a chief Ermine (HYDE) ; 3, Gules, a griffin segreant within a bordure engrailed Or (BATTELL) ; 4, Azure, a fess Or. *Crest*—A falcon's leg Or erased Gules, belled of the first.

Sr Chr'opher Barker alias Garter Kinge of Armes.

Quarterly—1 and 4, Azure, three bears' heads Argent muzzled Gules, in chief as many bezants ; 2 and 3, Argent, on a chevron between three Cornish choughs Sable as many estoiles Or. *Crest*—A bear's head per pale Or and Azure, muzzled Gules, between two wings counterchanged.

Sr Edmonde Molyneux, Serjeant at the Lawe.

Azure, a cross moline pierced Argent, a crescent Gules on another Or for difference. *Crests* —1, A garb of peacock's feathers proper banded Or and Azure, a similar difference ; 2, " A hare in p'per colour sittinge on a rushe hill."

Sr James Hales.

Argent, on a chevron Sable between three chaplets Gules, each enclosing a fleur-de-lis of the second, as many estoiles Or, on a chief Azure as many quill-pens points downwards Or.

Sr Will'm Babthorpe.

Quarterly—1 and 4, Sable, a chevron Or between three crescents Ermine ; 2 and 3, Barry of six Argent and Gules, three crescents Sable.

Sr Thomas Brudenall.

Quarterly—1, Argent, on a chevron Gules between three chapeaux (? should be *steel caps*) Azure an escallop Or ; 2, Sable, a buck's head cabossed Argent, attired Or, between the attires a cross patée fitchée, in the mouth an arrow of the second ; 3, Ermine, on a chevron Gules three escallops Or ; 4, Azure, a bend cotised between six cross-crosslets fitchée Or. *Crest*—An arm embowed covered with leaves Vert, elbow proper, in the hand also proper a spiked club Or slung to the arm with a line of the last.

Sr Thomas Nevill of the Holte.

Quarterly—1 and 4, Gules, a saltire Ermine ; 2 and 3, Lozengy Or and Azure, a canton Ermine. *Crest*—A bull's head Ermine, armed Or.

Sᵣ **Angell Marian** de Cremona, Italian. | Or, a bend Gules. *Crest*—A sea-dog's head Sable.

Sᵣ **John Holcroft.** | . Arms quarterly and Crest as at p. 74.

Sᵣ **John Cutte** of Essex. | Quarterly—1 and 4, Argent, on a bend engrailed Sable three plates each charged with a martlet of the second within a bordure gobony Gules and Or ; 2, Argent, a bend cotised Sable ; 3, Argent, on a chevron between three bugle-horns Sable as many mascles Or. *Crest*— A greyhound's head erased Argent, collared gobony Or and Gules.

Sᵣ **Henry Tyrell** of Heron. | Arms quarterly as at p. 48, and Crest as at p. 47.

Sᵣ **Will'm Scharington.** | Quarterly—1 and 4, Gules, two crosses patée of the first fimbriated Or between as many flaunches chequy Argent and Azure ; 2, Azure, a bend Argent (LA VALL); 3, Per pale indented Or and Azure, six martlets in pale, 3 and 3, counterchanged (FRANKHAM). *Crest*—A scorpion in pale Or, tail in chief between two elephant's teeth, the upper part chequy Argent and Azure, the lower Gules, each charged with a cross voided as in the Arms.

Sᵣ **Wymond Carew.** | Arms as at p. 15, and Crest as at p. 61.

Sᵣ **Will'm Snathe.** | Argent, a chevron between three ravens' heads erased Sable.

Knightes of the Carpett dubbed by the Kinge on Tuesday the 22 day of February in the aforesayd first yere of his reigne :

Sᵣ **John Radclyffe.** | Arms quarterly as under FITZWALTER at p. 62, without the label. Crest as at p. 11.

Sᵣ **Will'm Stanley.** | Quarterly—1 and 4 as 1 and 2, and 3 as 2 and 3, at p. 25 ; and the same Crest. On each a crescent for difference.

Lorde Thomas Grey. | Arms quarterly of eight and Crest as at p. 52; on each a martlet for difference.

Sᵣ **Anthony Aucher.** | Ermine, on a chief Azure three lions rampant Or. *Crest*—A bull's head erased Gules, armed Or.

Sᵣ **John Shelton** of Suff. | Arms and Crest as at p. 19.

Sᵣ **Edward Sabcottes.** | Quarterly—1, 2, and 4, as at p. 16 ; 3, Argent, on a cross Gules five escallops Or ; and the same Crest.

Sᵣ **Richard Cotton.** | Arms as at p. 72, a crescent for difference ; the same Crest but a buckle Or, strapped Azure,

Sʳ **John Mason.**

Sʳ **Thomas Newnam.**

Sʳ **John Wyndham.**

Sʳ **Philippe Calthorpe.**
Sʳ **Mauryce Denys** of Gloucestershire.
Sʳ **Anthony Kenyngham.**

Sʳ **Rowland Moreton.**
Sʳ **John Wentworthe** of Essex, father to the Lady Maltravers.
Sʳ **Thomas Dyer.**
Sʳ **John Godsalve.**

Sʳ **Thomas Barneston.**
Sʳ **Thomas Gyfforde.**
Sʳ **Roger Gyfforde** of Devonshire.
Sʳ **John Savage.**
Sʳ **Edward Rogers.**

instead of a cornet. "This fowle close, his wyngs asure."
Quarterly—1 and 4, Or, a two-headed lion rampant Azure, a wound on the shoulder Gules; 2, Quarterly Gules and Argent, a lion rampant counterchanged (LANGSTON); 3, Argent, a chevron Gules between three snakes nowed Sable, a crescent for difference (RADLEY). *Crest*—A mermaid proper.
Azure, three demi-lions rampant Argent guttée de sang. *Crest*—A demi-lion rampant Argent guttée de sang between two wings expanded Gules.
Arms and Crest as at p. 67, the lion's head in the Crest on an escucheon Azure.
Chequy Or and Azure, a fess Ermine.
Arms quarterly and Crest as at p. 22. "Quære si forte sederet vel hoc modo surgeret lupus."
Quarterly—1 and 4, Quarterly Or and Gules within a bordure Sable escallopée Argent; 2, Ermine, three chevronels Sable; 3, Argent fleury Gules; on an escucheon of pretence, Quarterly Or and Azure. *Crest*—An old man's head sidefaced proper, habited Gules and collared with two bars Or, on his head a cap Azure turned up Ermine charged with three guttés and tasselled of the second.

Gules, on a bend Argent three escallops Azure, "untrue." *Crest*—Out of a ducal coronet Gules a unicorn's head Argent.
Sable, three goats passant Argent, attired Or.
Per pale Gules and Azure, on a fess nebulée between four crosses patée Or three crescents Sable. *Crest*—A griffin's head erased per pale indented Argent and Sable, in the mouth a heartsease slipped proper, stalked and leaved Vert.
Azure, a fess dancettée Ermine.
Arms and Crest as at p. 51.
Sable, three fusils conjoined in fess Ermine.

Crest—A unicorn's head Argent.
Argent, a chevron between three stags passant Sable, a mullet Or for difference. *Crest*—A stag passant Sable platée, attired and ducally gorged Or.

Sr **Walter Bucler** (Will'm added).

Sable, on a fess between three dragons' heads erased Or as many estoiles of the field. *Crest*— A dragon's head Sable charged with two bars between eight guttés d'Or.

Sr **Roger Blewett.**

Or, a chevron between six eagles displayed Vert.

Sr **Humfrey Stafford.**

Quarterly of six—1, 2, 3, 4, 5, as at p. 81 ; 6, Vair, three bars Gules ; and the same Crest.

Sr **John Percy.**

Gules, a chief Argent. *Crests*—1, Out of a ducal coronet Or a Blackamoor's head Sable ; 2, On a mound Or a porcupine proper, "russett," quilled Argent.

Sr **John Perpount** of Nottinghamshire.

Arms quarterly as at p. 39. *Crest*—A lion rampant Sable holding in the dexter paw a cinquefoil Or.

Sr **Francys Englefeilde.**

Arms quarterly as at p. 32. *Crest*—An arm erect vested per pale Azure and Gules, cuffed Argent, holding in the hand proper a branch of three cinquefoils Or, leaved and slipped Vert.

Sr **Thomas Fitzherbert.**

Quarterly—1 and 4, Gules, three lions rampant Or ; 2 and 3, Argent, a bend Sable and a chief vair Or and Gules.

Sr **John Sprynge.**

Argent, on a chevron between three mascles Gules as many cinquefoils pierced Or, in each five hurts. *Crest*—A demi-stag salient quarterly Argent and Or, holding in the mouth a branch of columbine proper.

Sr **Thomas Hawnarc.**

Vert, two dolphins addorsed in pale Argent. "These be the Hawmers' Armes, and this man's Armes ar Argent, two lyons passant-regardant Asure." *Crest*—A sea-dog statant Azure, finned and webbed Or, in the mouth a fish proper.

Sr **John Grevill.**

Quarterly of six—1, Sable, on a cross Or five pellets within a bordure engrailed of the second ; 2, Azure, crusily and a lion rampant Or ; 3, Argent, on a bend Azure three cinquefoils pierced Or ; 4, Argent, a bend Sable, a label of three points Gules ; 5, Argent, a bend Gules, a bordure chequy Or and Azure ; 6, Argent, on a bend Gules three round buckles Or. *Crest*—A greyhound's head Sable, collared Gules bezantée.

Sr **John Brokett.**

Sr **Thomas Bell** of Gloucestershire.

Argent, on a chevron between three hawks' bells Gules two bars-gemelles of the first, on a chief of the second a hawk's lure between two martlets of the field. *Crest*—An arm erect vested Gules, holding also erect in the hand proper a battle-axe, staff of the first, head Azure.

Sʳ **John Horsey.**   Quarterly—1 and 4, Azure, three horses' heads couped Argent, bridled Or ; 2, Azure, a chevron between three cross-crosslets fitchée, within a bordure engrailed Or ; 3, Argent, four bars wavy Gules, a saltire Or. *Crest*—A horse's head couped Argent, armed Or, bridled Azure, and plumed of the second and third.

Sʳ **Res Gryffythe** of Wales.   No Arms given. " Arma in originali sunt de rubro super barram dancé de Argento 3 merlettos de nigro inter 6 leones aureos rapaces, de quibus dubitari potest." *Crests*— 1, A buck's head cabossed per pale Or and Argent ; 2, A man's head erased proper, crined Sable, wreathed round the temples Or and Azure.

Sʳ **John Salisbury** of Wales.   Gules, a lion rampant Argent between three crescents Or.

Sʳ **Thomas Hollyes.**   Arms as at p. 69, a crescent Or for difference, and the same Crest.

Sʳ **Will'm Raynsforde.**   Quarterly—1 and 4, Azure, an eagle displayed Argent ducally gorged Or ; 2 and 3, Argent, a cross Sable. *Crest*—A buck's head erased Ermine.

Sʳ **Thomas Wrothe.**   Argent, on a bend Sable three lions' heads erased of the field, ducally crowned Or. *Crest*—A lion's head erased Argent ducally crowned Or.

Sʳ **Will'm Pykeringe.**   Gules, on a chevron Argent between three fleurs-de-lis Or as many hurts. *Crest*—An arm embowed habited Or two bars Gules, holding in the hand proper a fleur-de-lis of the first.

Sʳ **John Cary.**
Sʳ **Henry Doyle.**   Azure, three bucks' heads cabossed Argent.
Sʳ **Uryan Brereton.**   Arms of BRERETON and Crest as at p. 65.
Sʳ **Will'm Drury.**   Argent, on a chief Vert a tau Or between two mullets of the third, on each a torteaux. *Crest*—A greyhound passant Sable, eared Argent. "A hounde Sable, the snowte Argent."
Sʳ **John Butteler** of Hertfordshire.
Sʳ **George Harper.**   Argent, a lion rampant within a bordure engrailed Sable. *Crest*—A boar passant Or, collared and lined Gules.
Sʳ **Thomas Kempe.**   Arms and Crest as at p. 36.

Sʳ 𝕵𝖔𝖍𝖓 𝕹𝖔𝖗𝖙𝖔𝖓 of Kent.

Quarterly—1 and 4, Gules, a cross potent Ermine ; 2 and 3, Ermine, a cross engrailed Gules. *Crest*—A talbot's head erased between two wings Or.

Sʳ 𝕽𝖔𝖇𝖊𝖗𝖙 𝕷𝖆𝖓𝖌𝖊𝖑𝖊𝖞.

Quarterly—1 and 4, Argent, a cockatrice Sable ; 2 and 3, Gules, a mermaid Argent crined mirror and comb Or (Prestwich).

Sʳ 𝕿𝖍𝖔𝖒𝖆𝖘 𝕹𝖊𝖛𝖎𝖑𝖑.

Quarterly—1 and 4 (with an annulet for difference), as at p. 78 ; 2 and 3, as 3 at the same page, without the label. *Crest*—A griffin passant Or.

Sʳ 𝕵𝖔𝖍𝖓 𝖆𝖕 𝕽𝖊𝖘 (𝕬𝖕𝖗𝖞𝖈𝖊).

Sable, on a chevron between three leopards' heads Argent as many spear-heads of the field, on a chief of the second as many cocks Gules. *Crest*—A cock Gules, combed and legged Or, charged on the neck with two bars of the second, holding in the beak a heartsease. " Sine flore in originali."

Sʳ 𝕵𝖔𝖍𝖓 𝖁𝖆𝖚𝖌𝖍𝖆𝖓 of Wales.
Sʳ 𝕿𝖍𝖔𝖒𝖆𝖘 𝕲𝖗𝖆𝖛𝖊𝖓𝖔𝖗.

Sʳ 𝖂𝖆𝖑𝖙𝖊𝖗 𝕸𝖞𝖑𝖉𝖒𝖆𝖞.

Per fess Argent and Sable, a fess nebulée per fess of the second and Or between three greyhounds' heads couped counterchanged, collared Gules bezantée, a martlet for difference. *Crest*—A leopard's head erased Or, ducally gorged and lined Azure, on the neck beneath the coronet three pellets.

Sʳ 𝕮𝖑𝖊𝖒𝖊𝖓𝖙 𝕾𝖒𝖞𝖙𝖍𝖊.

Argent, a cross Gules between four peacocks Azure. *Crest*—An arm erect vested chequy Vert and Argent ("alibi or et b."), holding in the hand proper three arrows Or.

Sʳ 𝕵𝖔𝖍𝖓 𝕵𝖊𝖗𝖒𝖞𝖓 of Suffolk.

Quarterly—1, Sable, a crescent between two mullets in pale Argent ; 2, Sable, a fess between three roses Or ; 3, Azure, a lion rampant Or, ducally gorged Argent ; 4, Henyngham. *Crest*—A greyhound's head Sable, eared Gules, gorged with a bar-gemelle Or.

Sʳ 𝕵𝖆𝖒𝖊𝖘 𝕭𝖆𝖘𝖈𝖆𝖗𝖛𝖎𝖑𝖑𝖊.

Arms and Crest as at p. 34.

Sʳ 𝕵𝖆𝖒𝖊𝖘 𝕮𝖗𝖔𝖋𝖙𝖊𝖘, dubbed at Westm. 24 of Novembre, anno primo.

Arms and Crest as at p. 14, the wivern statant.

Sʳ 𝕬𝖓𝖙𝖍𝖔𝖓𝖞 𝕮𝖔𝖕𝖊, dubbed at Westm. the 24 of Novembre, anno primo.

Sʳ 𝖧𝖊𝖓𝖗𝖞 𝖂𝖍𝖆𝖗𝖙𝖔𝖓, dubbed at Westm. anno secundo vel p'mo.

Quarterly—1 and 4, Sable, a maunch Ermine within a bordure Or, charged with eight pairs of lions' paws saltirewise erased Gules ; 2 and 3, Ermine, on a chief Azure three lions rampant Argent, quartering Quarterly Gules and Argent, a bend Or. *Crest*—A bull's head erased Argent, horned and crined Sable, ducally gorged per pale Or and Gules, a crescent Sable for difference.

Sᵣ Robert Curson of Norf., anno p'mo.

Quarterly—1 and 4, Ermine, a bend gobony Sable and Argent, a crescent for difference ; 2 and 3, Gules, two lions passant in pale Ermine, ducally crowned Or. *Crest*—Out of a crescent Azure thereon an estoile Or two demi-griffins, the one Argent, the other of the second, respecting each other.

Knightes Bannerettes and Bachelor Knightes made in the campe besydes Rockesburgh in Scotland in anno primo of the Kinge's reigne, by the handes of the high and mighty Prynce Edward, Duke of Somersett, Generall of all the Kinge's Armyes by lande and by sea, and Governour of his royall person and protectour of all his realmes, dominions, and subjectes :

Sᵣ Francys Bryan, Bannerett.

Argent, three piles wavy meeting at the base Vert, a bordure Azure bezantée. *Crests*—1, A tiger passant Argent bezantée, tusked and maned Or ; 2, A beacon proper.

Sᵣ Rauf Sadler, Bannerett.

Arms and Crest as at p. 70.

Sᵣ Raufe Vane, Bannerett.

Arms and Crest as at p. 80. "The gantlet onely, no parte of the arme."

Lord Grey of Wylton.

Quarterly—1 and 4, Barry of six Argent and Azure ; 2 and 3, Gules, three lions rampant Argent, ducally crowned Or. *Crest*—A falcon belled proper, wings expanded, standing on a gauntlet Argent, and encircled by a branch of columbine Azure, leaved Vert, issuing from the gauntlet.

Lorde Edward Seymour.

Arms quarterly of five, same as 2, 3, 4, 5, 6 at p. 66, and Crest as under Hertford at p. 86, without the coronet and difference.

Lorde Waldyke.

Or, an estoile Sable.

Sᵣ Thomas Dacres.

Quarterly of six—1, Gules, three escallops Argent ; 2, Barry of twelve Argent and Azure, three chaplets Gules ; 3, Gules, three cushions Ermine, tasselled Or ; 4, Vair Or and Gules, in dexter chief a lion rampant Or, quartering Gules, a fess counter-compony Argent and Sable between six crosses patée fitchée of the second ; 5, Azure, fleury and fretty Or ;

6, Chequy Or and Gules. Crest as at p. 39. On each a label of three points.

Sᵣ John Botevill alias Thynne.
Quarterly—1 and 4, Barry of ten Or and Sable; 2 and 3, Argent, a lion rampant tail forked and double nowed Gules. *Crest*—A reindeer Or, attired and erased Sable.

Sᵣ John Gresham.
Arms (with a label of three points Or) and Crest as at p. 68.

Sᵣ Miles Partrige.
Gules, on a fess between two bars-gemelles and three partridges volant Or as many torteaux, on a pile of the second a demi-rose Gules emitting rays. *Crest*—A partridge in the beak an ear of wheat Or. "Alibi, de rubro 3 bezantes inter 2 gemellos aureos in fece inter 3 perdices ut hic et non torteaux in fece de auro. Verius, le fece inter duos coticcs et non gemelles."

Sᵣ Franceys Hemynge.
Gules, a chevron between three owls Argent. *Crest*—A demi-sea-dog Sable, eared and finned Or.

Lorde Charles Stourton, executed for murther.
Quarterly—1, Sable, a bend Or between six fountains; 2, Or, a cross engrailed Sable; 3, Gules, an escocheon within an orle of martlets Argent; 4, Argent, on a bend Sable three calves passant Or. *Crest*—A sea-dog Sable, finned Or.

Sᵣ Edmonde (Edward) Bruges.
Quarterly—1 and 4, and 3, as at p. 28; 2, Or, a pile Gules; over all a label of three points. *Crest*—A Saracen's head in profile couped at the shoulders proper, habited paly of four Argent and Sable, studded with pellets and plates and wreathed about the temples of the first and second.

Sᵣ Nicholas Strange.
No Arms given. "In originali de rubro 2 leones peditantes de Argento." *Crest*—A wolf passant Argent, in the mouth a child proper.

Sᵣ John Talbot of Grafton.
Arms quarterly of six as at p. 52. *Crest*—A talbot statant Argent. On both shield and crest a crescent for difference. "In originali hæc arma fuerunt de Argento cum tribus leonibus de purpuro. Crista hujusmodi canem de nigro."

Sᵣ Franceys Salveyn.
Quarterly—1 and 4, Argent, on a chief Sable three mullets pierced Or; 2 and 3, Or, a bend Sable.

Sᵣ John Southworthe.
Arms as at p. 40. *Crest*—A bull's head erased Sable, armed Argent.

Sr **Thomas Danby** of Yorkshire.

Quarterly of six—1, Vert, three chevronels braced Or, on a chief Argent three mullets pierced Sable ; 2, Vert, a bend Or; 3, Gules, three cushions Argent tasselled Or, quartering Argent, on a saltire Sable five guttes d'eau ; 4, Argent, a saltire Gules; 5, Gules, a chevron Ermine between three lions rampant Or ; 6, Gules, six billets Ermine.

Sr **John Foster.**

Argent, a chevron Gules between three bugle-horns Azure, garnished and stringed Or. *Crest*—An arm in armour embowed proper, the hand grasping a baton Gules.

Sr **John Horseley.**

Azure, a fess Or between three horses' heads erased Argent, bridled Gules, within a bordure gobony of the second and Vert.

Sr **Rauf Bagnall.**

Sable, on an escucheon Ermine within an orle of martlets Argent a leopard's face Gules.

Lorde Thomas Howarde.
Sr **Richard Conway.**

Azure, a lion passant-gardant paly of six Or and Argent, between three dexter gauntlets of the third, plated of the second, within a bordure engrailed of the same. *Crest*—A crane's head paly of six Argent and Sable, charged on the neck with two bars Or.

Sr **Gyles Poole.**

Arms quarterly as at p. 14. Crest as at p. 55.

Sr **Olyver Laurence.**

Argent, a cross ragulée Gules. *Crest*—A luce's tail proper.

Sr **Henry Gates.**

Arms quarterly and Crest as at p. 51.

Sr **Edward Hastinges.**

Arms quarterly of eight and Crest as at p. 87, without the label, but each bearing a mullet for difference.

Sr **Will'm Skipwithe.**

Quarterly—1, SKIPWITH as at p. 29 ; 2, Quarterly Sable and Or, a bend Argent; 3, Or, fretty Azure, on a canton Gules a cross moline of the field ; 4, Or, on a chevron Azure between three fleurs-de-lis Vert as many martlets of the field. *Crest*—A reel or turnstile proper.

Sr **Will'm Buttes.**

Per pale Or and Azure, on a chevron between three estoiles as many lozenges all counterchanged. Crest as at p. 82.

Sr **George Blage.**

Argent, two bends Gules each surmounting another engrailed Sable.

Sr **Will'm Fraunces.**

Gules, a saltire between four crosses flory Or.

Sr **Francys Knolles.**

Quarterly—1 and 4, Azure, crusily and a cross moline voided throughout Or; 2 and 3, Gules, on a chevron Argent three roses of

o

	the field. *Crest*—A ram's head Argent, armed Or.
Sr Will'm Thorneborough.	Ermine, fretty and a chief Gules.
Sr George Howarde.	Arms quarterly as at p. 75 and Crest as at p. 69.
Sr James Wylforde.	Gules, a chevron engrailed between three leopards' faces Or.
Sr Rauf Copynger.	Gules, three bends Or, on a fess Vert three plates within a bordure Purpure. *Crest*—An arm embowed Gules fesswise, holding in the hand proper a hawk's lure also proper.
Sr Thomas Wentworth.	Arms quarterly of six and Crest as at p. 46, on each a label of three points.
Sr John Mervyn.	Argent, a demi-lion rampant Sable.
Sr Hugh Ascue.	Arms and Crest as at p. 35, but the latter erased; on each a crescent Or on another Gules for difference.
Sr Richard Towneley.	Argent, a fess and in chief three mullets pierced Sable, "quartered with Sable, three gotes rampant Argent for GAYTFORD." *Crest*—On a perch Or a falcon close proper, belled and lined of the first.
Sr Marmaduke Constable.	Arms (with a label of three points) and Crest as at p. 29.
Sr George Awdeley.	Arms quarterly and Crest as at p. 14.
Sr .... Barteville, a Frenchman.	Quarterly per fess indented Or and Gules. *Crest*—A swan Argent.
Sr Andrew Dudley.	Quarterly of eight—1, Or, two lions passant Azure; 2, Barry of six Argent and Azure, in chief three torteaux, a label of three points thereon a crescent for difference; 3, Gules, a lion rampant within a bordure engrailed Or; 4, 5, 6, 7, and 8, as 4, 3, 5, 6, 7 under Lord LYSLE at p. 87; and the same Crest. On each a crescent for difference.
Sr Xp'ofer Dyes.	
Sr Thomas Chaloner.	
Sr Rowland Clerke.	

Knightes made at Newcastle the first day of October in anno primo aforesayde by the handes of Edward, Duke of Somersett, Lord Protectour:

Sr Walter Bonham.	Gules, a chevron wavy between three crosses patée fitchée Argent. *Crest*—A snake erect on its tail Argent nowed Azure, with the head of a maiden proper crined Or.
Sr Henry Hussee.	Quarterly—1 and 4, Ermine, three bars Gules; 2, Azure, a pheon Or; 3, Azure, on a chief

indented Argent three mullets pierced Sable. *Crest*—A talbot statant Argent, collared and lined Or.

Sʳ Robert Branlyn. Quarterly—1 and 4, Gules, a cross patonce and in dexter chief an escallop Argent ; 2 and 3, Per pale indented Argent and Or, three escallops Gules. *Crest*—The stump of a tree ragulée couped and erect, from the top issuing flames of fire, from the sinister two sprigs with acorns and leaves, all proper.

Sʳ Jaques Granado. Quarterly—1 and 4, Sable, three eagles' talons couped Argent ; 2 and 3, Argent, a Blackamoor's head couped Sable wreathed Argent, on an escucheon of pretence Argent, a pomegranate slipped Vert. *Crest*—A pomegranate slipped proper.

Knightes made at Berwyke by the hands of John, Erle of Warwyke, Lieutenant of the Kinge's Army in anno primo in Scotland :

Sʳ Richard Buckley. Argent, three bulls' heads couped Sable. *Crest*—A bull's head per pale Argent and Sable, armed Or and of the first.

Sʳ Anthony Strelley. Paly of six Argent and Azure. *Crest*—A man's head " greyish " wreathed Gules, belled Or.

Sʳ Arthur Manwerynge. Arms quarterly and Crest as at p. 55, without the difference, and the ass's head Sable.

Sʳ John Rybande, dubbed at Newcastle.

Sʳ Andrew Corbet, dubbed at Newcastle.

Sʳ Thomas Nevill, second son to Raufe, Erle of Westmerlande. Arms quarterly and Crest (without the label and crest coronet) as at p. 78. On each a crescent for difference.

Sʳ Peter Negro.
Sʳ Alounce de Ville Seige.
Sʳ Will'm Cobham, dubbed at Westminster the first day of December anno 2. Quarterly—1, Gules, on a chevron Argent a lion rampant Sable ducally crowned Or ; 2, Gules, on a chevron Or three lions rampant Sable ; 3, Azure, a fess between three leopards' faces Or, an annulet Sable for difference ; 4, Argent, seven mascles conjoined, 3, 3, 1, Gules. *Crest*—A Blackamoor's head Sable, wreathed Argent and Azure. On each a label of three points Argent.

Sʳ Thomas Cornwalles, dubbed as above. Arms quarterly of six as in the ' Visitations of Suffolk, 1561, 1577, 1612,' p. 21. *Crest*—A

Sr **Richard Corbett**, dubbed as above.

buck lodged and regardant Vert, attired Or, on the dexter side an oak-branch proper. Argent, two bars and a canton Gules.

Sr **Dompnike Bollonus**, Embassador of Venyce.

Or, two bends Gules, on the upper ends a rose proper. *Crest*—An angel proper, wings expanded Argent, crowned and the crown surmounted by a cross patée Or, the hands outstretched. *Motto*—" Otiosus nunquam."

Sr **Henry Amcottes**, Maior of London.

Crest—A squirrel sejant Gules, devouring a nut Or, leaved and slipped Vert.

Sr **Will'm Locke**, Sherife of London.

Per fess Azure and Or, a pale counterchanged, three falcons of the second. *Crest*—A falcon's wings endorsed Or, in the mouth a padlock proper.

Sr **John Awlyf**, Sherif of London.

Argent, on a chevron Sable between three estoiles Gules, on each a bezant, as many stags' heads cabossed of the field. *Crest*— Out of a coronet Or charged with torteaux nine stems leaved Vert.

Sr **Thomas Gargrave** of Yorkshire.

Lozengy Argent and Sable, on a bend Gules three crescents of the first.

Sr **Richard Sakeville**, Chancelor of the Augmentacion Courte.

Quarterly Or and Gules, a bend Vair. *Crest*— A ram's head erased Sable, armed Or.

Sr **John Yorke**, Sherif of London.

Arms as at p. 17, a mullet for difference.

Sr **John de la Zouche**, dubbed at Westminster the 10 day of November in anno 3 of the Kinge's reigne, and with him these that followe.

Quarterly—1 and 4, as at p. 55; 2 and 3, Argent, two chevrons Gules, a label of three points Azure, quartering Or, crusily and a lion rampant Azure; the same Crest, without the difference.

Sr **John Pollarde**.

Arms quarterly and Crest as at p. 71, a crescent Sable for difference.

Sr **Arthur Champernoun**.

Quarterly of six—1 and 6, Gules, billetée Or, a saltire vair; 2, Bendy of six Gules and Argent, a bordure Sable bezantée; 3, Argent, a lion rampant Gules, a bordure Sable bezantée; 4, Argent, on a chevron between three eagles' heads erased Sable as many acorns Or; 5, Sable, a chevron Ermine between three shovellers Argent. *Crest*—Out of a ducal coronet Or an ostrich Argent, in the mouth a horseshoe Or, a crescent for difference.

Sr **Gyles Stranguishe** (**Strangwayes**).

Quarterly of six—1, Sable, two lions passant in pale paly of six Argent and Gules; 2, Or, a chevron Gules, a bordure engrailed Sable;

3, Sable, fretty Or; 4, Per fess Azure and Gules, three crescents Argent; 5, Argent, six lioncels rampant Gules; 6, Azure, three bars-gemelles Argent. *Crest*—A boar's head erased Sable between two wings Azure billittée Or out of a ducal coronet of the last. "Or els the creast is one of the lyons in the first cote."

Sᵣ John More. Ermine, on a chevron Gules three quatrefoils Argent, on each a bezant. *Crest*—An arm proper, holding a sword Argent, hilted and pomelled Or.

Sᵣ Thomas Woodhouse. Arms as those of Sir WILLIAM "belonginge to the Shippes" at p. 78.

Sᵣ Will'm Herbert.
Sᵣ Walter Herbert. Arms as at p. 17. *Crest*—A maiden's head couped at the shoulders Sable, habited Gules, face and hair Sable, wreathed Argent and Azure, earrings Or.

The Duke of Luninborough, dubbed at Westminster the 17 of November, anno 3 of the Kinge's reigne, and with him these fyve followenge :
.... **Lorde Fitzwarin,** sonne and heir to the Erle of Bathe.

Sᵣ .... Pelham. Quarterly—1 and 4, Azure, three pelicans in piety Argent ; 2, Gules, two demi-belts pale-ways, the buckles in chief Argent; 3, Or, fretty Azure. "The first cote only in the original." *Crest*—A peacock in pride Argent, tail proper.

Sᵣ Ambrose Dudley, sonne to the Erle of Warwyke. Quarterly of eight—1, Or, a lion rampant Vert ; 2, 3, 4, 5, 6, 7, and 8, as 1, 2, 3, 5, 4, 6, and 8 at p. 98 ; and the same Crest and difference.

Sᵣ John Parrett. Gules, three pears Or, on a chief Argent a lion passant Sable. *Crest*—On a mount Vert a parrot proper, winged of the first and beaked Gules.

Sᵣ Thomas Russell. Quarterly—1, Argent, a chevron between three cross-crosslets fitchée Sable ; 2, Gules, a saltire Argent within a bordure Sable mullettée Or ; 3, Argent, on a bend Gules three round buckles Or ; 4, Argent, on a bend Azure three cinquefoils pierced Or ; 5, Barry undy of six Argent and Gules, on a bend

Sable three bezants ; 6, Argent, on a bend engrailed between two cotises Sable three mullets of the field. *Crest*—A demi-lion collared and charged with a chevron, holding in both paws a cross-crosslet fitchée.

Sᵣ Thomas Essex.
Sᵣ Chr'opher Heydon of Norf. Quarterly—1 and 4, HEYDON as at p. 12 ; 2, Chequy Or and Azure, on a canton Gules a lion rampant Argent; 3, Per pale Azure and Or, a lion rampant Gules ; and the same Crest. " Potius sic. Quarterly of seven— 1, HEYDON ; 2, Argent, a windmill Sable ; 3, Azure, a garb Or ; 4, Quarterly Vert and Gules, a lion rampant counterchanged ; 5, as 2 above ; 6, Or, on a chevron Gules three swans Or ; 7, Azure, crusily and three lozenges."

Sᵣ Thomas Pomerey. Arms as at p. 19. *Crest*—A lion's gamb erased and erect Or, charged with a gutte de sang, in the paw a heart of the second.

Sᵣ John Sydnam. Argent, three rams' heads cabossed Sable, armed Or.

Sᵣ Henry Bedingfeilde. Arms quarterly and Crest as at p. 43.
Sᵣ Roger Vaughan.
Sᵣ Thomas Goldynge. Quarterly—1 and 4, Gules, a chevron Argent between three bezants ; 2 and 3, Gules, a chevron Argent, fretty Azure, between twelve cinquefoils pierced Or. *Crest*—A dragon's head erased Vert, langued Gules, collared and ringed Or.

Sᵣ John Saintloe.
Sᵣ Paule Baptist Spynola of Geane. Or, a fess chequy Argent and Gules, in chief a mortcour of the second between a rose of the same and a portcullis Azure studded with torteaux. *Crest*—An arm erect habited Vert, guttée d'Or, the hand proper holding a sword Argent, hilted and pomelled of the second.

Sᵣ Nicholas Arnolde. Gules, a chevron engrailed Ermine between three pheons Or. " Quarterly with Sable a chevron gold 3 lewres of hauks silver." *Crest (added)*—A demi-lion rampant Or, billitée Sable, holding in both paws a fire-ball Sable emitting flames proper.

Sᵣ Will'm Allerton.
Sᵣ Francys Jobson. Paly of six Argent and Azure, a chevron Ermine between three eagles displayed Or.

Sʳ **Anthony Gwydott.**
Per saltire Argent and Barry nebulée of six Or and Azure, two crescents voided in pale Gules, on a chief of the third a lion passant-gardant between three fleurs-de-lis Or, one in chief and on either side. *Crest*—A falcon rising Argent, wings Or, pennoned Gules, holding in the dexter claw a branch slipped Vert, fructed Or.

Sʳ **Thomas Saunders.**
Quarterly—1 and 4, Sable, a chevron Ermine between three bulls' heads cabossed Argent; 2 and 3, Or, three lions passant-gardant in pale Sable. "Alibi, Argent, 3 lions Sable, non gardantes ut hic, igitur quære." *Crest* —A demi-bull salient per pale Gules and Sable, armed and eared Argent and Or counterchanged, holding between the fore-legs three ears of a cereal fructed Or, leaved and slipped Vert. *Motto*—"Dum spero serviam."

Sʳ **Richard Blount.**
Arms of BLOUNT and Crest as at p. 75, the shoe Argent.

Sʳ **Andrew Judde.**
Quarterly—1 and 4, Gules, a fess ragulée between three boars' heads couped Argent; 2 and 3, Azure, three lions rampant and a bordure Argent. *Crest*—A boar's head per pale Gules and Or.

Sʳ **Gilbert Dethike** alias Garter Kinge of Armes.
Quarterly—1 and 4, Argent, a fess vair Or and Gules between three water-bougets Sable; 2, Argent, a chief Gules, on a bend Azure three escucheons of the first, on each a chief Gules; 3, Or, a bend Gules, on a canton Argent five guttes de poix. *Crest*—A horse's head Argent. On each a mullet on a crescent for difference.

Sʳ **Will'm Cicill**, Secretary.
Quarterly of six—1 and 6, Barry of ten Argent and Azure, over all six escucheons Sable, on each a lion rampant of the first; 2, Per pale Gules and Azure, a lion rampant Argent holding in both paws a tree eradicated Vert; 3, Sable, a plate between three towers triple-towered Argent; 4, Argent, on a bend cotised Gules three cinquefoils Or; 5, Argent, a chevron between three chess-rooks Ermines. *Crests*—1, A sheaf of arrows Or, feathered Argent, banded Gules, covered with a salade of the second; 2, A garb Or, banded Azure, between two lions rampant respecting each other, the one Azure, the other Argent.

Sʳ Henry Nevill.   Quarterly—1, Gules, on a saltire Argent a cinquefoil ; 2, as at p. 28 ; 3, as 3, quartering 4 ; and 4, as 5, on the same page. Crest as at p. 50.

Sʳ Henry Sidney.   Arms and Crest as at p. 45.

Sʳ John Cheeke.   Gules, a chevron Or between three crescents Argent.

Sʳ Will'm Walderton.   Azure, fleury Or, a chief per pale Argent and Gules, on the dexter side a flower of the third slipped and leaved Vert, on the sinister a lion passant of the third. *Crest*—Two elephants' proboscies, one Argent, the other Azure.

Sʳ Will'm FitzWilliam of Ireland, in the privy chambre to the Kinge, who lyeth buryed at Wyndesore.   Gules, on a bend cotised Argent three popinjays Vert beaked and legged of the field, a crescent Or for difference. *Crest*—In front of a peacock's tail proper a demi-tiger quarterly Argent and Azure, holding in both paws a branch flowered Gules leaved and slipped Vert, a crescent for difference.

Sʳ Robert Chestre, dubbed at Waltham.   Gules, two lions' hind feet issuing from the dexter and sinister sides meeting in fess Or between three hawks' lures Argent. *Crest*—A lion's gamb erased and erect Gules, holding a broken sword Argent, hilt Or.

Sʳ Rauf Ellercar.

Sʳ James Stumpes, buryed in St. Gregorye's Churche at Westminster.   Per chevron Argent and Sable, three griffins' heads erased counterchanged. *Crest*—Out of clouds proper emitting rays Or a demi-horse Gules, maned of the second.

Sʳ Thomas Smythe, Secretary.   Sable, a fess dancettée Argent billitée between three lioncels rampant-gardant of the second, each supporting an altar Or flaming proper. " This cote is quartered with Argent, on a bend Sable three cross-crosslets Argent, in the sinister corner a martlet Sable." *Crests* —1, An eagle Sable holding in the dexter claw a torch Argent flaming Gules ; 2, " A salimander in the fyre."

Sʳ Thomas Stradlinge.   Arms quarterly and Crest as at p. 74.

Sʳ Thomas Wyatt the yonger.   *Crests*—1, A horse-barnacle Argent, tied together at the bottom Or ; 2, As at p. 42.

Sʳ James Dyer, Sergeant at the lawe.   Sable, three goats statant Argent, a mullet Or for difference.

Sʳ John Sentleger.

The Names and Armes of those that receaved the honorable Ordre
of Knighthode in the tyme of the reigne of

Queene Mary.

(Cotton MSS., Claudius, C. iii., fol. 182–195.)

(Knightes of the Bath, 15 in number, made in the Tower of London at the
Coronacon of Queen Mary—Harl. MS. 6063.)

Edward, Erle of Devonshire. Quarterly—1, Quarterly France and England
within a bordure quarterly Gules and Azure,
the first and fourth quarters charged with
three lions passant-gardant, and the second
and third with as many fleurs-de-lis Or;
2 and 3, Or, three torteaux; 4, Or, a lion
rampant Azure. *Crest*—Out of a ducal
coronet Or a plume of feathers Argent.

Thomas, Erle of Surrey. Arms quarterly and Crest as those of Sir
HENRY HOWARD at p. 69.

Lorde Herberte of Cardyff. Quarterly of seven—1, Per pale Azure and
Gules, three lions rampant Argent; 2, Sable,
a chevron between three spear-heads Argent
imbrued Gules; 3, Argent, three cocks Gules,
beaked, wattled, and legged Or; 4, Argent, a
lion rampant Sable ducally crowned Or; 5,
Azure, crusily and three boars' heads couped
Argent; 6, Argent, three bends engrailed
Gules, a canton Or; 7, Gules, three leopards'
heads jessant-de-lis Or. Over all a label of
three points. *Crest*—A wivern vert, gorged
and lined Or. On each a crescent for difference.

Lorde of Burgaveny. Quarterly of five—1, Gules, on a saltire Argent
a rose of the field; 2, Chequy Or and Azure;
3, Or, three chevronels Gules; 4, Quarterly
Argent and Gules fretty Or, over all a bend
Sable; 5, Gules, a fess between six cross-
crosslets Or, a crescent Sable for difference.
Crest—A bull statant Ermine, horned, gorged,
lined, and ringed Or, the ring holding two
drawn staples of the second, points Argent.

Lorde Barkley. Arms quarterly of six and Crest as at p. 41.

Lorde Lumley. *Crest*—A pelican in piety proper.

Lorde Mountjoy (Blount). Quarterly of six—1, 2, 3, 4, as 3, 1, 2, 4
under Sir JAMES BLOUNT at p. 9; 5, Ar-
gent, three fleurs-de-lis Azure; 6, Argent,
a fess and in chief three covered cups Gules;
and the same Crest.

P

Sr **Robert Rochester**, Comp-   *Crest*—A demi-antelope salient Azure, armed
troller of the Queen's howse.   and gorged Or, langued Gules.

Sr **Henry Jerningham.**   Arms quarterly as at p. 51, a crescent for difference. *Crest*—On a ducal coronet Or a
falcon, wings expanded, Argent, a crescent
Gules for difference.

Sr **William Powlett.**   Arms quarterly of nine and Crest as at p. 81.

Sr **Henry Clynton.**   Arms quarterly and Crest as at p. 74. On each
a label of three points.

Sr **Hugh Ryche.**   Quarterly Or and Azure, a chevron between
three roundles, on each a lion rampant, all
counterchanged. *Crest*—A talbot's head
per pale Or and Gules. On each a label of
three points.

Sr **Henry Pagett.**   Quarterly—1 and 4, as at p. 74 ; 2 and 3, Argent, two bars Gules, on a canton of the
second a cinquefoil of the field ; and the same
Crest. On each a label of three points.

Sr **Henry Parker.**   Arms quarterly as at p. 63. *Crest*—Out of a ducal
coronet Or a boar's head Sable muzzled of
the first, a label of three points.

Sr **Will'm Dormer.**   Arms as at p. 67. *Crest*—A wolf passant proper
between two wings Argent, holding in the
mouth another Or.

Huc usque Equites Balnei.

Lorde (*struck out*) **Garrett.**   Argent, a saltire Gules. *Crest*—An ape proper,
banded, lined, and clogged Or.

Lorde **Burghe.**   Arms quarterly and Crest as those of Sir THOMAS
BOROUGH at p. 48, without the difference.

Sr **Thomas Stanley.**   Arms quarterly of eight as under STRANGE at
p. 86, and Crest as at p. 11, a crescent for
difference.

Sr **Edmonde Wyndesore.**   Quarterly of thirteen—1, 2, 3, 4, 6, 7, 9,
and 10, as the shield at p. 87 ; 5, Azure,
fretty Argent ; 8, Argent, on a cross Sable
five bezants ; 11, Argent, a chevron Sable
between three mullets pierced Gules ; 12,
Ermine, a lion passant Gules ; 13, Argent,
a pale lozengy Gules, a bordure Azure bezantée. The same Crest.

Sr **Henry Radclyffe.**   Quarterly of eight—1 and 2 same as 1 quarterly,
and 3, 5, 6 same as 2, 3, 4, at p. 90 ; 4, Or,
a saltire engrailed Sable ; 7, Or, flory Sable ;
8, Argent, an eagle Sable standing on an
infant swathed Gules fretty Or. *Crest*—As
under FITZWALTER at p. 11, an estoile Or
instead of a sun in splendour.

Sʳ **Thomas Hastinges.** — Arms quarterly of eight and Crest as at p. 97, a crescent for difference.

Lord Dudley. — Quarterly—1 and 4, Or, a lion rampant double-queued Vert; 2, Or, two lions passant in pale Azure, quartering Argent, a cross patonce Azure ; 3, Argent, a saltire engrailed Gules, quartering Or, a lion rampant Gules. *Crest*— Out of a ducal coronet Or a lion's head Azure.

Sʳ **Edward Walgrave.** — Quarterly—1, Quarterly as at p. 32 ; 2, Gules, an eagle displayed Ermine, armed Or ; 3, Or, a fess (?) vair Gules and Azure; 4, Argent, two bars and in chief three mullets Sable ; over all a crescent for difference. *Crest*—As at p. 32.

Sʳ **George Powlett.** — Arms quarterly of nine and Crest as at p. 81, a crescent for difference.

Sʳ **Thomas Rypvett.** — Arms quarterly of six and Crest as at p. 41, but the bend in the second quartering engrailed.

Sʳ **Robert Wyngefeilde.** — Arms quarterly and Crest as at p. 47.

Sʳ **Robert Peckham.** — Arms quarterly and Crest as at p. 72.

Sʳ **John Bourne,** Secretary. — Argent, a chevron Gules between three lions rampant Sable, a chief Ermines. *Crest*—A demi-wivern per pale Or and Gules, gorged with two bars per pale Azure and Argent, holding in both claws three flowers of marigold Or, leaved and slipped Vert.

Sʳ **Leonard Chamberleyne.** — Quarterly of six—1, 2, 3, 4, and 5, as at p. 49, but in the first quarter mullets ; 6, Argent, a saltire engrailed Azure. *Crest*—Out of a ducal coronet Or an ass's head Argent.

Sʳ **John Tyrell.** — Arms quarterly and Crest as at p. 90.

Sʳ **Henry Lee.** — Arms and Crest as those of Sir ANTHONY LEGHE at p. 69.

Sʳ **Thomas Cave.** — Azure, fretty Argent, over all on a bend Or a greyhound courant Sable within a bordure of the last pelletée. *Crest*—Out of a honeysuckle flower Or, stalked and leaved Vert, a greyhound's head per pale Argent and Sable guttée counterchanged.

Sʳ **Will'm Calloway** (**Caylwey**). — Quarterly—1, 2, and 4, as 1, 3, and 2 at p. 35 ; 3, Ermine, on a chief three lions rampant. *Crest*—A cock Gules, combed, beaked, and legged Azure

Sʳ **George Gyfforde.** — Gules, three lions passant in pale Argent, a crescent Or for difference. *Crest*—An arm erect vested bendy Or and Azure, holding in the hand Gules two bucks' antlers of the last.

Sr Thomas Metham. — Arms quarterly and Crest as at p. 43.

Sr Edward Litleton. — Quarterly—1, 2, 4, as at p. 17 ; 3, Gules, a fess Or.

Sr Chr'opher Allen. — Sable, a fess Ermine between three talbots passant Or, collared and ringed Gules.

Sr Robert Lane. — Quarterly—1 and 4, Per pale Azure and Gules, three saltires Or ; 2, Argent, two bars Azure, a bordure engrailed Sable, quartering Or, three water-bougets Sable ; 3, Gyronny of eight Sable and Or, on a canton Gules a covered cup of the second. *Crest*—Two griffins' heads issuant out of a crescent Or, the dexter Azure, the sinister Gules, beaks of the first

Sr John Chichester. — Quarterly—1, Chequy Or and Gules, a chief Vair ; 2, Gules, a bend Vair; 3, Vair, quartering Gules, a saltire Vair ; 4, Sable, three chevronels Ermine. *Crest*—A bittern proper, beaked and legged Vert, in the beak an adder Azure.

Sr John Tregonell. — Argent, three pellets in fess cotised Sable between as many Cornish choughs of the second, beaked and legged Gules. *Crest*—A griffin's head erased Sable, the beak Or, a chaplet of the second and Gules.

Sr Thomas Palmer. — Or, two bars Gules, on each three trefoils slipped Argent, in chief a greyhound courant Sable, collared Gules. *Crest*—A demi-panther rampant-gardant holding in both paws a holly branch with leaves and berries all proper.

Sr Richard Tate. — Per fess Or and Gules, a pale counterchanged, three Cornish choughs Sable. *Crest*—An arm embowed vested per pale Gules and Or, in the hand proper a branch of pears of the second, leaved Vert.

Sr Thomas Fynche. — Arms quarterly and Crest as at p. 53.

Sr John a Lye (Leigh or Alley). — Quarterly—1 and 4, Gules, a cross and a bordure engrailed Argent; 2, Barry of six Argent and Vert ; 3, Argent, a bend nebulée Gules. *Crest*—A cockatrice Azure, beaked, combed, collared, legged, and guttée d'or.

Sr John Farmour. — Quarterly—1 and 4, Argent, on a fess Sable between three lions' heads erased Gules as many anchors Or ; 2 and 3, Per pale indented Argent and Or, a chevron between three escallops Gules. *Crest*—A cock's head Gules, combed and beaked Or, in the beak a branch of flowers Argent, leaved Vert.

Sᵣ Edmond Maliverer. — Arms and Crest as at p. 33, without the difference.

Sᵣ Thomas Tyndall. — Arms quarterly and Crest as at p. 21.

Sᵣ Richard Molineux. — Quarterly—1 and 4, Azure, a fer-de-moline Or ; 2 and 3, Azure, escallopée Argent, a lion rampant-gardant Or. *Crest*—As No. 1 at p. 89, without the difference.

Sᵣ Henry Joanes. — Argent, on a cross ragulée Azure between four pheons Gules five bezants. *Crest*—A raven's head erased Sable, holding in the beak a branch reversed Vert.

Sᵣ Edward Fytton. — Arms as at p. 65. *Crest*—On a chapeau Azure turned up Ermine a fleur-de-lis Or.

Sᵣ Thomas Baskervill. — Arms quarterly and Crest as at p. 34.

Sᵣ Thomas Gerarde. — Arms as at p. 78, quartering Argent, three torteaux in bend between two cotises Gules; the same Crest.

Sᵣ Henry Stafforde. — Or, a chevron Gules, a label of three points Azure. *Crest*—Out of a ducal coronet per pale Or and Gules a demi-swan Argent, beaked of the second.

Sᵣ Richard Brugys. — Arms quarterly and Crest as at p. 96, the coat without the label, but with a crescent for difference.

Sᵣ Thomas Wayman. — Sable, on a fess Argent between three anchors Or as many leopards' heads erased Gules. *Crest*—A cock's head Gules, combed and beaked Or.

Sᵣ Will'm Wygston. — Per chevron Ermine and Ermines, a chevron per chevron Sable and Argent, on the first three estoiles Or. *Crest*—A wolf's head erased per pale Gules and Azure guttée d'or.

Sᵣ Will'm Fitzwilliam. — Quarterly of ten—1, Lozengy Argent and Gules ; 2, Chequy Or and Azure ; 3, Argent, a chief Gules, over all a bend Azure ; 4, Ermine, a fess Gules ; 5, Argent, three cinquefoils and a canton Gules ; 6, Chequy Or and Gules, a chief Ermine ; 7, Azure, a lion rampant Or ; 8, Azure, three garbs Or ; 9, Azure, a wolf's head erased Argent ; 10, Argent, a cross engrailed Gules, quartering Chequy Or and Azure, a bordure Gules. *Crest*—As at p. 49. On each a crescent for difference.

Sᵣ Thomas Throgmorton. — Arms quarterly and Crest as at p. 33, in the second quartering the three escallops omitted.

Sᵣ Richard Stapleton. — Quarterly—1, STAPLETON as at p. 76 ; 2, Or, two bars nebulée Gules, quartering—1, Azure, billitée and a fess dancettée Or—2, Argent, a lion rampant Sable, ducally crowned Or, within a bordure Azure—and 3, Azure, fleury and a lion rampant-gardant Argent ; 3, Azure, fleury and a lion rampant Or, quartering— 1, Azure, three garbs Or—2, Azure, three cinquefoils Or—and 3, Quarterly Gules and Argent, in the first quarter an eagle displayed Or ; 4, Argent, a chevron and in dexter chief a cinquefoil Sable ; the same Crest.

Sr William Warham.

Arms as at p. 59, and the same Crest, but on the sword-blade three roses Argent.

Sr James Fitz James.

Quarterly—1, 3, and 4, as at p. 60 ; 2, Sable, billitée and a cross flory Or. *Crest*—A chapeau Azure turned up Ermine, the peak in the mouth of a dolphin embowed Argent.

Sr John Huddleston.

Arms and Crest as at p. 64.

Sr Thomas Beringer.

Or, a cross Vert and a bend Gules. *Crest*—A cockatrice Vert, wings per pale Or and Vert, expanded of the first.

Sr Thomas Whyte, Maior of London.

Gules, a bordure Sable, estoilée Or, on a canton Ermine a lion rampant of the second. *Crest* —A pewit proper.

Sr William Merynge.

Arms and Crest as at p. 28.

Sr William Courteney.

Arms quarterly as at p. 23. Crest as at p. 9.

Sr James Williams.

Or, on a fess between three ravens Sable as many crescents Or, in chief a spear-head Azure. *Crest*—A raven rising Sable guttée d'or.

Sr Richard Stranguishe.

Quarterly of six—1, STRANGUISHE as at p. 100 ; 2, Azure, a bend Or, a label of three points Argent ; 3, Gules, a saltire Argent, a fleur-de-lis Sable for difference ; 4, Argent, a lion rampant Azure ; 5, Azure, crusily and three cinquefoils Argent ; 6, Azure, three bars-gemelles and a chief Or. *Crest*—A lion statant per pale as in the Arms.

Sr Davy Brooke, Lord Chief Baron of the Exchequer.

Gules, on a chevron Argent a lion rampant Sable ducally crowned Or, a crescent Azure on another of the third for difference. *Crest* —A Blackamoor's head proper wreathed Argent and Sable.

Sr John Warbelton (Warburton).

Quarterly of six—1, Argent, a chevron between three cormorants Sable ; 2, Quarterly Argent and Gules, on the second and third quarters a fret Or (DUTTON) : 3, Argent, three chevronels Gules, on a canton of the second a mullet Or (WARBURTON, Ancient); 4, Azure, a garb between two bezants (GROSVENOR); 5, Argent, an orle within eight martlets Sable (WINNINGTON); 6, Sable, a cross patonce Argent (PULFORD).

Sr John Constable. Quarterly of six—1, CONSTABLE as at p. 40; 2, Argent, three chaplets Gules; 3, Quarterly Argent and Gules, on a bend Sable three escallops of the first, a crescent for difference; 4, Gules, a saltire Argent, a mullet Sable for difference; 5, Argent, a cross patonce Or; 6, Sable, a fess between three garbs Argent; the same Crest.

Sr Rauf Chamberleyne. Quarterly—1 and 4, Argent, fretty Sable, on a chief of the second three plates; 2, Or, three chevronels Gules, on each five fleurs-de-lis Argent; 3, Three chevronels. *Crest*—An ass's head erased proper, ducally gorged Or.

Sr George Stanley. Or, three lions' gambs erased Gules, on a chief indented Azure as many bucks' heads cabossed of the field. *Crest*—An eagle's head Or, charged on the neck with three pellets, in the beak a lion's gamb erased.

Sr Thomas Peshett. Quarterly of five—1, Argent, on a bend Sable three garbs Or; 2, Barry of six Argent and Azure, in chief three lozenges Gules; 3, Argent, a cross patonce Sable; 4, Argent, a fess Gules; 5, Sable, three crescents each enclosing a mullet Argent. *Crest*—A garb banded Azure.

Sr Edward Grevell. Quarterly of six—1, Sable, a cross engrailed and a bordure Or; 2, 3, 4, 5, and 6, as at p. 92. *Crest*—A garb Or banded Gules.

Sr Richard Freston. Quarterly—1 and 4, Azure platée, on a fess Or three leopards' faces Gules; 2 and 3, Argent, on a bend cotised Sable three roses of the field. *Crest*—A demi-talbot Sable holding in both paws a plate.

Sr Ambrose Jermyn. Quarterly—1 and 4 as 1 and 2, and 3 as 2, at p. 94; and the same Crest.

Sr Philippe Parrys. Gules, three unicorns' heads couped within a bordure engrailed Or.

Sr Thomas Lovell. Quarterly—1 and 4, LOVELL as at p. 15; 2 and 3, Vert, two chevrons Argent, on each three cinquefoils Gules. *Crest*—A garb of peacock's feathers proper banded Gules.

Sʳ Rauf Egerton.

Arms as at p. 77. *Crest*—A lion's gamb erect Gules grasping a sword Argent, hilted Or.

Sʳ Thomas Dawney.

Argent, on a bend cotised Sable three cinque-foils Or.

Sʳ Edward Greene.

Arms as at p. 29.

Sʳ Will'm Stanforde (Stain-forth), dubbed knighte the 22 day of January anno primo et secundo Philipi et Marie.

Argent, three bars Azure, on a canton Or a fess and in chief three mascles Sable. *Crest*—A dexter hand and wrist gauntletted, grasping a broken sword Argent, hilt and pomel Sable.

Sʳ John Lyons, Maior of London.

Azure, on a fess Or between three plates Azure, on each a griffin's head erased Sable, a lion passant between two cinquefoils Gules. *Crest*—On a pink proper a lion's head couped quarterly Ermine and Ermines.

Sʳ Henry Asheley (Maseley).

Argent, a fess Gules between three hazel-nuts Or, husks and stalks Vert.

Sʳ George Mathew.

Gyronny of eight Gules and Sable, a lion rampant Or within a bordure Azure, crusily of the third.

Sʳ John Cotton.

Quarterly—1 and 4, Azure, an eagle displayed Argent ; 2, Vair Argent and Sable, a canton Gules ; 3, Gules, a chevron Ermine between three eagles displayed Argent.

Sʳ Robert Broke, Lord Cheif Justice of the Com'on Pleas.

Quarterly—1 and 4, Chequy Argent and Gules, on a chief Or a brock statant proper ; 2, Argent, a cross patonce Sable. *Crest*—On a mount Vert a brock statant proper.

Sʳ John Spencer.

Azure, a fess engrailed Ermine between three eagles' heads erased Argent. *Crest*—An eagle's head Argent.

Sʳ Edward Saunders.

Per chevron Sable and Argent, three elephants' heads erased counterchanged, a martlet for difference.

Sʳ Will'm Gryseley (Gresley). Arms as at p. 55.

Sʳ Olyver Leader.

Or, on a fess Sable between three pellets on each an escallop Argent, a leopard's head erased between two boars' heads couped of the field, within a bordure engrailed Azure. *Crest*—An embowed arm habited barry of six Gules and Vert, holding in the hand proper a bunch of cinquefoils Azure, leaved Vert.

Sʳ Thomas Verney.

Arms and Crest as at p. 12.

Sʳ Clement Higham.

Sable, a fess chequy Or and Azure between three horses' heads erased Argent.

Sʳ John Wyndout.

Per fess Gules and Or, a lion rampant per fess Argent and Azure guttée counterchanged between three escallops also counterchanged.

𝔖ᵣ **Robert Whitney.** Vert, a cross counter-compony Or and Gules.

𝔖ᵣ **Will'm Garrat,** Maior of London. Argent, on a fess Sable a lion passant of the field. *Crest*—A leopard sejant proper.

𝔖ᵣ **Richard Walwyn.** Sable, a fess between three leopards' faces Argent.

𝔖ᵣ **Thomas Pakington.** Arms and Crest as at p. 84, the latter without the bezants.

𝔖ᵣ **Henry Gascoigne.** Arms quarterly and Crest as at p. 18.

𝔖ᵣ **Roger Woodhouse.** Arms and Crest as No. 1 at p. 78, the chevron billitée without the difference.

𝔖ᵣ **Francys Stonner.** Quarterly—1, 2, and 3, as 1, 2, 3 at p. 13 ; 4, Argent, a bend Sable surmounted of another dancettée of the field, quartering Argent, a fret Sable, on a chief Gules three bezants.

𝔖ᵣ **Edward Gage.** Quarterly—1 and 4, Per saltire Azure and Argent, a saltire Gules ; 2 and 3, Azure, a sun in splendour Or. *Crest*—A ram passant Argent, armed Or.

𝔖ᵣ **Robert Denys.** Quarterly—1, Ermine, three battle-axes Gules ; 2, Per pale Argent and Sable, a spread eagle counterchanged, beaked, legged, and ducally gorged Or ; 3, Gules, two demi-leopards passant-gardant in pale Or ; 4, Argent on a fess Sable three escallops of the field. *Crest*— A dragon's head erased quarterly Argent and Gules. On each a label of three points.

𝔖ᵣ **Thomas Offcley.** Argent, on a cross flory Azure between four Cornish choughs Sable beaked and legged Gules, a lion passant-gardant Or. *Crest*—A demi-lion rampant quarterly Or and Azure, gorged counter-compony of the first and Sable, holding in both paws a branch, fructed Or, leaved Vert.

𝔖ᵣ **Will'm Chester.** Per pale Sable and Argent, a chevron engrailed between three rams' heads erased, all counter-changed within a bordure Azure bezantée. *Crest*—A ram's head erased Argent, armed Or.

𝔖ᵣ **Thomas Percy,** created Erle of Northumb'land and after rebelled in anno . . . . of Queene Elizabeth, and therfore was behedded at Yorke. Quarterly of twelve—1, 2, 3, 4, 5, as at p. 56 ; 6, Sable, two bars nebulée Ermine ; 7, France and England quarterly, a bordure gobony Argent and Azure ; 8, Gules, a fess between six cross-crosslets Or ; 9, Chequy Or and Azure, a chevron Ermine ; 10, Gules, crusily patée and a chevron Argent ; 11, Gules, a lion passant-gardant Argent ducally crowned Or ; 12, Azure, three icicles in bend Or. Crest as under NORTHUMBERLAND at p. 20.

Q

Sr Henry Percy.	The same Arms and Crest, a crescent for dif-. ference.
Sr Thomas Curteys.	Barry wavy of six Sable and Argent, a chevron Or between three plates, on a chief of the third two dolphins addorsed Azure between as many anchors Gules. *Crest*—Out of a crescent Or an arm erect habited Azure, holding in the hand proper a branch of columbines Azure leaved and slipped Vert.
Sr Will'm Cordell, the Quene's Sollicitor.	Quarterly—1 and 4, Gules, a chevron engrailed Ermine between three griffins' heads erased Argent ; 2 and 3, Paly of six Ermine and Azure, a chevron between three lions passant-gardant Or. *Crest*—A cockatrice proper, beaked and legged Gules, ducally gorged Or.
Sr William Damsell.	Ermine, on a cross engrailed Sable, a tower Argent between four crescents, each enclosing a mullet of the third. *Crest*—A harpy proper.
Sr John Sulyard.	Arms quarterly as at p. 13, in 2 and 3 the lions Argent. *Crest*—A buck's head proper.

The Names and Armes of those that were addaunced to the honorable Ordre of Knighthode in the godly quyet and fortunate reigne of

Queene Elizabeth.

(Cotton MSS., Claudius, C. iii., fol. 198—232, with additions in parentheses from Harl. MS. 6063, up to 1586, and then continued from the latter MS. and other MSS. indicated *post*.)

(Knights of the Bath at the Coronation, A° 1°.)

1. **Lord Darcy** of the North.	Quarterly of eleven—1 and 2, as 1 and 2 at p. 22; 3, Argent, a bend between six martlets Sable, an annulet for difference ; 4, Azure, a fess between three fleurs-de-lis Or; 5, Gules, three goats' heads couped Or ; 6, Azure, a cross patonce voided Argent ; 7, Gules, three lucies hauriant Argent ; 8, Argent, two bars Azure, a fleur-de-lis Or ; 9, Argent, three chaplets Gules ; 10, Argent, a boar statant Sable ; 11, Or, a helmet close Gules. The same Crest.

2. **Lord Sheffeilde.**   *Crest*—A boar's head erased Or, langued Gules.

3. **Lorde Darcy** of Chyche.   Quarterly of five—1, Argent, three cinquefoils Gules; 2, Argent, a fess Ermine double cotised Sable; 3, Gules, a goat salient, attired Or; 4, Argent, a saltire Sable, an annulet of the second for difference. *Crest*—A demi-maiden, face proper, habited and crined Or, holding in her right hand a branch of cinquefoils also proper.

4. **Sr Robert Riche.**   Arms and Crest as at p. 106.

5. **Sr Roger Northe.**   Azure, a lion passant Or between three fleurs-de-lis Argent, a label of three points. *Crest*—A dragon's head erased Sable, ducally gorged Or, a similar label.

6. **Sr John de la Zouche.**   Quarterly of twelve—1, as 1 at p. 55; 2, Barry of six Argent and Azure; 3, Or, a lion rampant Azure; 4, Or, three pales Sable; 5, Gules, three garbs within a double tressure flory-counterflory Or; 6, Barry of ten Argent and Azure, an orle of martlets Gules; 7, Or, three escucheons barry of six Vair and Gules; 8, Gules, a bend lozengy Or; 9, Argent, on a chief Azure three crosses patée fitchée of the field; 10, Sable, three garbs Argent; 11, Or, three piles meeting at the base Gules, a canton Vair; 12, Or, a fess Gules. Crest as at p. 55, a crescent for difference.

7. **Sr Henry Weston.**   Quarterly of six—1 and 2, as 1 and 2 at p. 58; 3, Ermine, a lion rampant Sable, ducally crowned Or; 4, Argent, three chaplets Gules; 5, Sable, a cross Argent, in dexter chief a cinquefoil of the second; 6, Argent, a maunch Gules. *Crest*—A dromedary Sable, the hump Argent, gorged and hoofed Or.

8. **Sr Edward Umpton.**   Quarterly—1, 2, and 4, as 1, 2, and 4 at p. 65; 3, Azure, three griffins segreant Argent; and the same Crest.

9. **Sr Nicholas Pointz.**   Quarterly of six—1, Barry of eight Or and Gules; 2 and 3, as 1 and 2 at p. 10; 4, Paly of six Or and Azure, on a fess Gules three mullets of the first; 5, Argent, a fess between three boars passant Sable, a crescent for difference; 6, Or, a chevron between three cinquefoils Azure, a mullet for difference. *Crest*—An arm erect fist clenched proper.

10. **Sr John Barkley.**   Arms quarterly and Crest as at p. 19.

11. **Sr George Speake.**   Arms and Crest as at p. 26.

, (Knights Bachelor the same year and the next.)

Sʳ Thomas Parry (of Wales, Thresurer of the Queene's hous-. hold).
Quarterly of six—1, Sable, a chevron between three boys' heads couped at the shoulders Argent, round each neck a serpent Azure; 2, Sable, a chevron between three spear-heads Argent, the points dropping blood Gules; 3, Argent, three cocks Gules, combed and legged Or; 4, Argent, a lion rampant Sable, ducally crowned Or; 5, Argent, a bull's head couped Gules, armed Or, between three mullets of the second; over all a crescent for difference. *Crest*—An arm erect proper grasping the neck and entwined by the body of a serpent Vert.

Sʳ Henry Cary, after created Baron of Hunsdon.

Sʳ Thomas Leighe (Maior of London).
Gules, on a cross engrailed Argent between four unicorns' heads erased Or five roundles Ermines. *Crest*—A unicorn's head erased Or, collared Argent, studded Gules.

Sʳ Nicholas Bacon, Lorde Keeper of the Greate Seale, dyed at London on Friday the 21 February 1578, and was buried in Powles on Monday the 9 of Marche following.
Quarterly—1 and 4, Gules, on a chief Argent two mullets Sable; 2 and 3, Barry of six Or and Azure, a bend Gules. *Crest*—A boar passant Ermine. On each a crescent for difference.

Sʳ Robert Catelyne, Cheif Justice.
Per chevron Azure and Or, three lions passant-gardant in pale counterchanged, a chief Argent. *Crest*—A lion's head affrontée Argent, ducally gorged between two wings Azure.

Sʳ Thomas Gresham.
Argent, a chevron Ermines between three mullets pierced Sable. Crest as at p. 68.

Sʳ Will'm Hewet, Maior of London.
Azure, on a fess flory-counterflory Or between three lions passant Argent as many lapwings proper. *Crest*—A lapwing proper.

(These twelve were knighted at Barwick by the Duke of Norfolk, 1560.)

1. **Sʳ George Bowes.**
Arms and Crest as at p. 67, without the difference.

2. **Sʳ Arthure Grey**, now Lorde Grey of Wylton.
Crest as at p. 95, a glove Argent instead of a gauntlet.

3. **Sʳ Bernaby Fitz Patrike** (of Ireland).
Sable, a saltire Argent, on a chief of the second three torteaux, a mullet of three points Azure. *Crest*—A lion Sable springing on the back of a dragon statant-regardant Vert.

4. **Sr Edward Bray.** Arms quarterly as at p. 27. Crest as at p. 12, "russet."

5. **Sr William Mallory.** Quarterly—1, Or, a lion rampant double-queued Gules, gorged Argent ; 2, Azure, a maunch Ermine ; 3, Argent, a bend between six martlets Sable ; 4, Argent, two bars Gules, on a chief Sable three mullets of the field. *Crest*—A horse's head Gules.

6. **Sr Edward Litleton.** Blazon given in a later hand thus : "Arg't, a chevron with 3 escallops Sab., with a crescent for difference." *Crest*—A buck's head cabossed Sable, between the attires Or and depending from them by its string Sable a bugle-horn Argent.

7. **Sr William Babthorpe.** Arms quarterly as at p. 89.

8. **Sr John Conway** (of Warwickshire). Arms quarterly and Crest as at p. 19.

9. **Sr Walter Aston** (of Staffordshire). Quarterly of six—1, Argent, a fess and in chief three lozenges Sable ; 2, Argent, a chevron between three escallops Sable; 3, Barry of ten Argent and Gules, a bend ; 4, Sable, on a chevron between three leopards' heads erased Or as many cinquefoils of the field ; 5, Argent, three bends Gules ; 6, Argent, a lion passant Sable, debruised by a fess countercompony Or and Azure.

10. **Sr Richard Newporte.** Quarterly—1, Argent, a chevron Gules between three leopards' faces Sable ; 2, Argent, three bars-gemelles Sable; 3, Barry of six Argent and Azure ; 4, Argent, on a fess dancettée Sable three bezants. *Crest*—A lion's head erased Azure between two dragons' wings Gules, in the mouth a broken spear Or.

11. **Sr William Fairfax** (of Gilling). Quarterly of six—1, 2, and 6, same as 1, 2, and 4 at p. 26 ; 3, Barry of eight Argent and Gules, on a canton Sable a cross patonce Or ; 4, Or, a bend Azure ; 5, Argent, a fess between two lions passant-gardant in pale Sable ; and the same Crest.

12. **Sr Richard Fulmerston.** Or, on a fess between three doves Azure a rose between two garbs of the field. *Crest*—A goat's head erased proper platée, attired Or, in the mouth a branch of roses Argent leaved Vert.

(**Sr William Chester,** Lord Maior of London, 1560.)

(**Sᵣ William Butler**, 1560.)

Sᵣ Owen Hopton, dubbed at Mr. Will'm Walgrave's house in Essex (Suffolk) anno d'hi 1561.

Arms quarterly and Crest as at p. 53.

Sᵣ Will'm Harper, Maior of London, dubbed at Westminster the 15 of February, anno d'ni 1562.

Azure, on a fess between three eagles displayed Or, a fret between two martlets of the field. *Crest*—Out of a crescent Argent, charged with a fret between two martlets Azure, an eagle displayed of the last.

Sᵣ Thomas Lodge, Maior of London, dubbed at Westm. (1562).

Azure, a lion rampant Argent, crusily fitchée Gules, within a bordure flory of the second. *Crest*—A demi-lion purpure supporting upright in both paws a cross fitchée Gules.

Sᵣ Adryan Poyninges.

Arms and Crest as at p. 9, on each a bendlet sinister.

Sᵣ John White, Maior of London, anno d'ni 1563.

Per fess Azure and Or, a pale counterchanged, three leopards' heads erased Gules between as many roundles barry wavy of six Argent and Vert. *Crest*—A lion's head erased quarterly Or and Azure, guttée counterchanged.

Sᵣ Henry Cheyny, now Lorde Cheyny, called by wrytte to the Parlement holden at Westm. anno .... (knighted by the Queen's own hand, 1563).

Quarterly of seventeen—1, Azure, six lioncels rampant, 3 and 3, Argent, a canton Ermine; 2, Ermine, on the dexter side of a chief per pale indented Or and Gules a rose of the last ; 3, Argent, a chevron between three mullets Gules ; 4, Argent, three Blackamoors' faces Sable ; 5, Sable, a chevron Ermine between three bird-bolts Argent ; 6, Argent, on a chevron Gules three fleurs-de-lis Or; 7, Quarterly Argent and Gules, a bend of the second ; 8, Quarterly per fess indented Or and Azure ; 9, Gules, a bend Vair between six escallops Or ; 10, Sable, a saltire engrailed Argent ; 11, Argent, on a cross Azure five escallops Or ; 12, Barry of six Argent and Sable ; 13, Argent, a horse-barnacle Sable ; 14, Gules, a fess dancettée between six crosscrosslets Or ; 15, Or, a cross engrailed Vert ; 16, Azure, two lions passant-gardant in pale Or ; 17, Argent, on a chevron Sable a fleur-de-lis of the field. *Crest*—An heraldic tiger statant Vert bezantée, ducally gorged and lined Or.

Sᵣ Henry Williams alias **Cromwell** (by the hand of the Queen, 1563).

Quarterly of six—1, Sable, a lion rampant Argent ; 2, Sable, three spear-heads Argent, their points imbrued Gules ; 3, Argent, a chevron between three fleurs-de-lis Sable ; 4, Gules, three chevronels Argent ; 5, Argent, a lion rampant Sable ; 6, Argent, on a chevron Gules a mullet of the field. *Crest*—A demi-lion Argent holding in the dexter paw a ring Or.

Sᵣ Edward Capell. Quarterly of six—1 and 6, Gules, a lion rampant between three cross-crosslets fitchée Or ; 2, Argent, a chevron Gules between three torteaux, on a chief Azure a fret between two cinquefoils Or ; 3, Argent, on a chevron Azure three garbs Or ; 4, Sable, a chevron Ermine between three escallops Argent ; 5, Gules, a chevron between three fleurs-de-lis Or. *Crest*—A demi-lion Argent holding in both paws a cross-crosslet fitchée Or.

Sᵣ Richard Mallory, Maior of London, dubbed at Westm. the 18 of February, anno d'ni 1564. (**Sᵣ Owin Oswilifant** of Ireland, 1564.) **Sᵣ James Harington,** dubbed by the Erle of Leycester at the Queene's com'andment anno d'ni 1565.

Or, a lion rampant within a bordure Gules. *Crest*—A horse's head Gules, the face and ears Argent, maned and ducally gorged Or.

Sᵣ Richard Champyon, Maior of London, dubbed at Grenwiche by Thomas, Erle of Sussex, on Sonday the 17 of February, anno d'ni 1565.

Argent, on a fess Gules between three trefoils slipped Ermines, an eagle displayed Or, a bordure engrailed Azure bezantée. *Crest*—An arm erect vested Gules, three bars Argent, holding in the hand proper three roses Gules, leaved and slipped Vert.

Sᵣ Thomas Robby, dubbed at Grenwiche on Sonday the 9 of Marche, anno d'ni 1565.

Quarterly of six—1, Argent, a fess between three hawks Sable, beaked and belled Or, quartering—1, Gules, three battle-axes in fess Or—2, Argent, three bottoms in fess Gules ; 2, Sable, an eagle displayed Argent ; 3, Argent, a lion rampant Sable, langued and ducally crowned Or ; 4, Sable, a pomegranate Or, seeded proper, leaved and slipped Vert ; 5, Gules, a lion rampant-regardant Argent ; 6, Argent, a chevron between three boars' heads couped Sable. *Crest*—A falcon rising proper, ducally gorged and belled Or.

Sᵣ Henry Darcy, dubbed at Fodringhay anno d'ni 1566 (by the Erle of Leycester).

Quarterly of six—1 and 6 as 1, and 2, 3, 4, and 5 as 2, 3, 4, 5, at p. 114, but in the last the goats' heads erased. *Crest*—A buck's head Ermine, attired Or.

Sr Richard Knightley (the like).

Quarterly of twelve—1, Quarterly Ermine and barry of six Or and Gules, a bordure Azure ; 2, Azure, a buck's head cabossed Argent, attired Or ; 3, Argent, on a saltire Sable five swans of the field, beaked and legged Gules (BURGH); 4, Argent, a lion rampant within a bordure engrailed Sable (COWLEY) ; 5, Sable, a chevron between three pairs of wings conjoined Argent (SKINERTON); 6, Argent, a bend Gules surmounted of another lozengy Or (HARWEDON) ; 7, Barry of six Argent and Gules, a canton Ermine (ST. JOHN) ; 8, Argent, a chevron Gules between three Cornish choughs (? should be martlets) Sable (BAGOTT); 9, Argent, a lion rampant Gules (LIONS) ; 10, Gules, a lion rampant Vair ; 11, Argent, a fess Azure between three crescents Gules ; 12, Gules, on a chief Argent five lozenges conjoined in fess of the field. Crest as at p. 26.

Sr George Hastinges, dubbed at Kenilworth anno d'ni 1566.

Crest—A bull's head erased Sable, armed and ducally gorged Or.

Sr Will'm Devereulx (the like).

Quarterly of nine—1 and 2, as at p. 88 ; 3, Gules, seven mascles conjoined, 3, 3, 1, Or ; 4, Gules, a cinquefoil pierced Ermine ; 5, Gules, three garbs within a tressure flory-counterflory Or ; 6, Argent, an escucheon within a tressure flory-counterflory Gules ; 7, Sable, three garbs Argent ; 8, Azure, a wolf's head erased Argent ; 9, Or, a fret Gules ; over all a crescent for difference. Crest as at p. 88.

Sr John Throgmorton (the like).

Arms quarterly and Crest as at p. 33.

Sr Foulke Grevill (the like).

Quarterly of twenty-three—1, Or, a cross and bordure engrailed Sable, the first bezantée ; 2, Ermine, a fess counter-compony Or and Azure ; 3, Quarterly per fess indented Argent and Azure, in the first quarter a crescent Gules ; 4, Sable, a cross engrailed Or ; 5, Gules, a cross potent Argent ; 6, Gules, a cross patonce Or ; 7, Sable, a fess between three fleurs-de-lis Argent ; 8, Gules, five fusils in fess Argent, on each an escallop Sable ; 9, Gules, three mullets pierced Argent ; 10, Azure, a cross flory Or ; 11, Gules, a lion rampant Argent ; 12, Argent, a cross flory Gules ; 13, Gules, three bars Or ; 14, Or, a chevron Gules, a bordure engrailed Sable ; 15, Argent, six lions rampant Gules ; 16, Or, a fret Sable ; 17, Azure, a fess cotised Or ; 18, Per fess Azure and Gules, three crescents Argent ; 19, Gules, billitée Or, a saltire Vair ; 20, Or, on a bend Sable three horse-shoes Argent ; 21, Azure, an eagle displayed Or ; 22, Gules, a fess between six martlets Or, a mullet Sable for difference ; 23, Argent, on a fess Azure three fleurs-de-lis Or. *Crest*—A greyhound's head erased Sable, gorged Argent.

Sᵣ John Litleton (the like). Quarterly of twelve—1, 2, 3, as at p. 17 ; 4, Argent, a lion rampant Sable, debruised by a fess counter-compony Or and Azure ; 5, Azure, a lion rampant and a bordure Or ; 6, Gules, a lion rampant and a bordure engrailed Or ; 7, Gules, a saltire Argent, thereon a martlet Sable for difference ; 8, Argent, a bend between six martlets Gules ; 9, Or, a fret Gules ; 10, Argent, two lions passant in pale Gules ; 11, Azure, six fleurs-de-lis Argent, a chief Or ; 12, Argent, a chevron between three leopards' heads erased Gules. Crest as at p. 117.

Sᵣ George Turpyn (the like). Quarterly of six—1 and 6, Gules, on a bend Argent three leopards' heads erased Sable ; 2, Gules, a fess counter-compony Or and Sable between six cross-crosslets Argent ; 3, Argent, a cross patonce between four crescents Gules ; 4, Gules, a cross patonce Argent ; 5, Sable, an escucheon quarterly Or and barry of eight Argent and Gules within an orle of dolphins embowed of the third. *Crest*—A lion's head erased Sable, ducally gorged Argent.

Sᵣ Thomas Lucy, dubbed at his owne house in Warwykshire anno d'ni 1566. Quarterly of eight—1 and 2, as 1 and 2 at p. 19 ; 3, Or, an eagle displayed Sable, gorged Argent ; 4, Azure, a buck's head cabossed Or ; 5, Barry of six Argent and Azure, on a bend Gules three mullets Or ; 6, Argent, billitée and a lion rampant Sable ; 7, Azure, a fess between six cross-crosslets Argent ; 8, Or, a cross between four martlets Gules. *Crest*—Out of a ducal coronet Gules, a boar's head Argent guttée de poix between two wings Sable billitée Or.

R

Sᵣ Edmoyd Brudenell, dubbed at Sᵣ Thomas Lucye's house anno d'ni 1566.

Quarterly of twelve—1, Argent, a chevron Gules between three chapeaux Azure; 2, Ermine, on a chevron Gules three escallops Argent; 3, Gyronny of eight Or and Sable; 4, Azure, a bend cotised between six cross-crosslets Or; 5, Sable, a buck's head cabossed Argent attired Or, in the mouth an arrow of the last; 6, Argent, a chevron Gules between three squirrels Sable; 7, Paly of six Argent and Azure, on a chief Sable two swords in saltire of the first, hilted Or; 8, Sable, three fusils in fess Argent; 9, Gules, a horse-barnacle Argent, a chief Sable; 10, Argent, a horse-barnacle Gules; 11, Argent, six cinquefoils, 2, 2, 2, Gules, on a canton Sable a mullet of the field; 12, Argent, a fess dancettée Gules, in chief three leopards' faces Sable. *Crest*—A sea-horse Argent, mane and tail Or.

Sᵣ Henry Norreys, dubbed at Rycott his owne house anno d'ni 1566. After called by writte to the Parlement holden at Westminster anno d'ni . . . . to be Lorde Norreys.

Quarterly of ten—1 and 2, as 1 and 2 at p. 14; 3, Or, two bars nebulée Gules; 4, Azure, billitée and a fess dancettée Or; 5, Argent, a lion rampant Sable, ducally crowned Or, a bordure Azure; 6, Azure, fleury and a lion rampant-gardant Argent; 7, Azure, fleury and a lion rampant-gardant Or; 8, Azure, three garbs Or; 9, Azure, three cinquefoils pierced Or; 10, Quarterly Gules and Azure, in the first quarter an eagle displayed Or. The same Crest.

Sᵣ Richard Wayneman, dubbed at Rycott the same tyme, anno d'ni 1566.

Quarterly of seven—1, as Wayman at p. 109; 2, Gules, three lions passant in pale Argent; 3, Argent, a chevron between three martlets Sable; 4, Chequy Argent and Gules, on a chevron Azure three roses of the first; 5, Ermine, on a chevron engrailed Gules three quatrefoils Argent; 6, Gules, a chevron Ermine between three lions rampant Or; 7, Argent, on a chevron Azure between three lozenges Sable as many bucks' heads cabossed Or. The same Crest.

Sᵣ Xpopher Browne, dubbed at Bradname anno d'ni 1566.

Quarterly—1 and 4, Sable, on a chevron Argent three mounds growing tulips Vert, a bordure Or; 2 and 3, Argent, on a chevron Sable between three pellets as many cinquefoils Or. *Crest*—A mound Vert growing tulips Or, leaved and stalked of the first.

Sr **John Arondell**, dubbed at the Courte the 27 of Novembre anno d'ni 1566.

Quarterly of six—1 and 2, as 1 and 2 at p. 25 ; 3, Ermine, on a cross Gules five martlets Or ; 4, 5, 6, as 3 and 2 quarterly at p. 46 ; and Crest as at p. 25.

Sr **Anthony Browne**, Justice of the Comon Pleas, dubbed by Thomas Erle of Sussex at the Parlement-house the 2 day of February anno d'ni 1566.

Quarterly—1 and 4, as 1 at p. 88 ; 2 and 3, Azure, a chevron between three ducks Argent, beaked and legged Gules, quartering Per bend sinister Sable and Or, a lion rampant counterchanged. Crest as at p. 88, a crescent Gules for difference.

Sr **Henry Cumpton**, dubbed by Robert Erle of Leycester at Arondell-house in London the 16 of February anno d'ni 1566.   After made Lord Compton by writte to the Parlement holden at Westm. anno . . . .

Crest—Out of a ducal coronet Or a demi-dragon erased Gules.

Sr **Xpopher Draper**, Maior of London, dubbed at Westm. on Sonday the 16 of February anno d'ni 1566.

Argent, two chevronels Sable, each charged with five martlets of the field between three escallops of the second.   *Crest*—A dexter arm embowed in armour proper, holding an anchor Or.

(Sr **Dermond Arlye**, 1567.)

Sr **Thomas Sakevile**, dubbed at Westm. the 8 of June anno d'ni 1567 (by the D. of Norff.) and the same day created Baron of Buckhurst.

Arms and Crest as at p. 100.

Sr **Thomas Mylomay**, dubbed at Richmond by Robert Erle of Leycester the 23 day of June anno d'ni 1567.

Arms and Crest as at p. 91.

Sr **Roger Martin**, Maior of London, dubbed at Westm. by Robert Erle of Leycester the 14 day of March anno d'ni 1567.

Gules, on a fess engrailed between three swans' heads erased Argent ducally gorged Azure as many mascles Sable.   *Crest*—A cockatrice's head proper.

Sr **George Penrodocke**, dubbed at Hatfeild by Robert Erle of Leycester the 7 day of August anno d'ni 1568.

Quarterly—1, Gules, a bend ragulée Argent ; 2, Per chevron Sable and Ermine, in chief two boars' heads couped Or ; 3, Sable, six annulets, 3 and 3, in pale Or ; 4, Azure, a fess between three martlets Or.   *Crest*—A demi-dragon Sable, wings Or, a crescent for difference.

Sr **Lewes Mordant** (1568).

Sr **Edward Montague** (1568).

Arms and Crest as at p. 67.

Sᵣ 𝕽𝖎𝖈𝖍𝖆𝖗𝖕 𝕵𝖊𝖓𝖕𝖘 (1568). Quarterly—1 and 4, Azure, three lions rampant Or ; 2, Argent, five mullets in cross Sable on each a bezant ; 3, Argent, two chevronels Sable between three roses Gules. Crest as at p. 32, a crescent for difference.

Sᵣ 𝕳𝖊𝖓𝖗𝖕 𝖀𝖀𝖆𝖑𝖑𝖔𝖕𝖕𝖊, dubbed at Basinge anno d'ni 1569. Quarterly—1 and 4, Argent, a bend wavy Sable ; 2 and 3, Paly wavy of six Argent and Sable, on a chief Or a saltire Gules (VALANS). *Crest*—A mermaid proper.

Sᵣ 𝖀𝖀𝖎𝖑𝖑'𝖒 𝕶𝖎𝖓𝖌𝖊𝖘𝖒𝖕𝖑𝖑, dubbed at Basinge anno d'ni 1569. Argent, crusily fitchée Sable, a chevron Ermines between three fers-de-moline of the second, a chief of the third.

Sᵣ 𝕿𝖍𝖔𝖒𝖆𝖘 𝕽𝖔𝖊, Maior of London, dubbed at Westm. anno d'ni 1569. Argent, on a chevron Azure between three trefoils slipped per pale Gules and Vert as many bezants, a crescent Sable for difference. *Crest*—A stag's head Gules, attired Or.

Sᵣ 𝖀𝖀𝖎𝖑𝖑'𝖒 𝖀𝖀𝖊𝖘𝖙, dubbed at Hampton Courte anno d'ni 1569, and was then created Lorde De la Ware. Quarterly of five—1, 2, and 4, as 1, 2, 4 at p. 57 ; 3, Azure, two bars-gemelles Or, in chief a lion passant of the second ; 5, Lozengy Gules and Vair. *Crest*—Out of a ducal coronet Or a griffin's head Azure, beaked of the first.

Sᵣ 𝕵𝖔𝖍𝖓 𝕲𝖔𝖔𝖉𝖊𝖜𝖕𝖓𝖊, dubbed at Eythorpe in Waddesdone at Sᵣ Will'm Dormer's house anno d'ni 1570 by the Erle of Leycester at the Queene's com'andment. Quarterly—1, Per pale Or and Gules, a lion rampant between three fleurs-de-lis all counterchanged ; 2, Argent, a saltire Gules fretty of the first between four escallops of the second ; 3, Per chevron Sable and Ermine, in chief two foxes combatant Argent, a bordure Azure fleury Or (BLEDLOW); 4, Argent, a stork Sable, beaked and legged Gules (STARKY). *Crest*—A demi-lion Argent, ducally gorged Gules.

Sᵣ 𝕰𝖉𝖒𝖚𝖓𝖉 𝕬𝖘𝖍𝖋𝖊𝖎𝖑𝖉, dubbed at Eythorpe 1570.

Sᵣ 𝕲𝖊𝖔𝖗𝖌𝖊 𝕻𝖊𝖈𝖐𝖍𝖆𝖒 (the like). Quarterly of six—1 and 3, as 1 and 2 at p. 72 ; 2, Chequy Argent and Sable, on a chief Or three leaves Vert ; 4, Barry nebulée of six Or and Sable ; 5, Argent, a lion rampant Gules, ducally crowned Or, a bordure Sable bezantée ; 6, Gules, two lions passant in pale Or. Crest as at p. 72.

Sᵣ 𝕽𝖔𝖇𝖊𝖗𝖙 𝖀𝖀𝖍𝖎𝖙𝖓𝖊𝖕, dubbed at Wyndesore anno (1570). Azure, a cross chequy Argent and Gules. *Crest*—A bull's head Sable, armed paly of four Gules and Argent.

(Sᵣ 𝕰𝖉𝖜𝖆𝖗𝖉 𝕬𝖘𝖙𝖔𝖓, 1570.)
Sᵣ 𝕬𝖑𝖊𝖝𝖆𝖓𝖉𝖊𝖗 𝕬𝖛𝖊𝖓𝖔𝖓, Maior of London 1569, dubbed (at Somerset-house) anno d'ni 1570. Ermine, on a pale Gules a cross flory, on a chief Sable a billet Or within a mascle between two escallops Argent. *Crest*—An eagle's head

erased Vert, gorged with two bars Or between two wings expanded per pale Azure and Gules, in the beak a branch of three leaves slipped Vert.

𝔖ᵣ 𝕽𝖔𝖜𝖑𝖆𝖓𝖉𝖊 𝕳𝖆𝖞𝖜𝖆𝖗𝖉𝖊, Maior of London 1570 (the like).

Quarterly—1 and 4, Gules, a lion rampant Argent, ducally crowned Or ; 2, Argent, two pales engrailed Sable ; 3, Argent, on a saltire engrailed Gules five fleurs-de-lis of the field. *Crest*—An ibex statant Or.

𝔖ᵣ 𝕿𝖍𝖔𝖒𝖆𝖘 𝕾𝖈𝖔𝖙𝖙𝖊 of Kente, dubbed at Somersett-place in London anno d'ni 1570.

Quarterly of six—1, Argent, three Catherine-wheels Azure, a bordure engrailed Gules ; 2, Barry of six Gules and Argent, a chief Vair ; 3, Purpure, a lion rampant double-queued Or ducally crowned Argent ; 4, Argent, a saltire Sable between twelve pears Gules slipped Vert ; 5, Gules, a fess Ermine between six cross-crosslets fitchée Argent ; 6, Gules, a chevron between three leaves slipped Argent. *Crest*—A demi-griffin segreant Sable.

𝔖ᵣ 𝕵𝖆𝖒𝖊𝖘 𝕻𝖆𝖑𝖊𝖘, 1570.

Gules, three arrows Argent, barbed Or. *Crest*—An arm embowed in armour proper, wreathed Argent, holding an arrow as in the arms.

𝔖ᵣ . . . 𝕷𝖚𝖈𝖆𝖘. (This entry probably refers to Sᵣ Thomas Lucas at p. 126, *post*.)

Quarterly—1 and 4, Argent, a fess between six annulets Gules ; 2, Gules, on a bend Argent seven billets Sable (MORIEUX) ; 3, Gules, a saltire between four cross-crosslets fitchée Or (BRAMPTON). *Crest*—Out of a ducal coronet Or a demi-griffin wings expanded Gules.

Knights dubbed by Thomas Erle of Sussex at Barwick the 11 May 1570 :

𝔖ᵣ 𝖂𝖎𝖑𝖑𝖎𝖆𝖒 𝕯𝖗𝖚𝖗𝖞 of Suffolk.
𝔖ᵣ 𝕿𝖍𝖔𝖒𝖆𝖘 𝕸𝖆𝖓𝖓𝖊𝖗𝖘.
𝔖ᵣ 𝕽𝖔𝖇𝖊𝖗𝖙 𝕮𝖔𝖓𝖘𝖙𝖆𝖇𝖑𝖊.

Quarterly of nine—1, as at p. 29, a crescent for difference ; 2, Chequy Or and Gules, on a chief Argent a lion passant-gardant Sable (COMBERWORTH) ; 3, Argent, two bars engrailed Sable (STANES) ; 4, Argent, a chevron between three martlets Sable (ARGUM) ; 5, Gules, an eagle displayed Argent, a crescent for difference (SUTHILL) ; 6, Argent, a bend Sable (PANNELL) ; 7, Gules, a cinquefoil Argent (POWCHER) ; 8, Gules, a lion rampant Vair (EVERINGHAM) ; 9, Or, on a cross Sable five crescents Argent (ELYS).

𝔖ᵣ 𝕲𝖊𝖔𝖗𝖌𝖊 𝕮𝖆𝖗𝖞.

Knights dubbed by Thomas Erle of Sussex at Carlyle the 28 of August 1570 :

𝔖ʳ 𝔙alentyne 𝔅rowne. — Argent, three martlets in pale Sable between two flaunches of the second, on each a lion passant of the first. *Crest*—A griffin Argent guttée de poix, wings expanded Sable guttée d'eau.

𝔖ʳ 𝔈dward 𝔥astings.

𝔖ʳ 𝔣rancis 𝔯ussell.

𝔖ʳ 𝔚illiam 𝔥ilton.

𝔖ʳ 𝔥enry 𝔠urwen. — Quarterly—1 and 4, Argent, fretty Gules, a chief Azure ; 2 and 3, Azure, a lion rampant Argent charged with three billets Or. Crest as at p. 34.

𝔖ʳ 𝔖imon 𝔐usgrave.

𝔖ʳ 𝔥enry 𝔊ray.

𝔖ʳ 𝔯obert 𝔖tapleton.

(𝔖ʳ 𝔍erome 𝔅owes.)

𝔖ʳ 𝔍ohn 𝔠utte (at Mr. Altham's in Essex, p. Erle of Lest. 1571). — Arms quarterly as at p. 90.

𝔖ʳ 𝔗homas 𝔏ucas (p. Erle of Lest. 1571). — Quarterly of six—1, 2, and 6, as 1, 2, and 4 at p. 125 ; 3, Gules, a chevron Argent between three eagles' heads erased Or (GEDDINGE) ; 4, Azure, three chevronels Or (ASPALL) ; 5, Argent, a fess between two chevrons Gules (PECHE). The same Crest, without the wings.

(𝔖ʳ 𝔗homas 𝔅arrington at Greenwich, 1571.)

𝔖ʳ 𝔊eorge 𝔠alveley (1571). — Quarterly of ten—1, Argent, a fess Gules between three calves passant Sable ; 2, Sable, on a chevron Argent between three cross-crosslets Or as many cinquefoils Gules ; 3, Argent, on a bend Sable three gemel-rings Or ; 4, Ermine, a fess Gules, a crescent for difference ; 5, Argent, on a saltire Sable five swans of the field ; 6, Sable, two hinds counter-trippant in fess Argent ; 7, Azure, a scimetar erect Argent, hilt Or, within a bordure engrailed of the third ; 8, Argent, on a mound Vert a stag lodged Gules ; 9, Sable, a chevron between three bulls' heads cabossed Argent ; 10, Gules, a fess dancettée Ermine between three bugle-horns Or. *Crest*—Out of a ducal coronet Or a calf's head Sable.

(𝔖ʳ 𝔥umfrey 𝔊ilbert in Ireland, 𝔖ʳ 𝔍ohn 𝔊ilbert at Westminster, 1571.)

𝔖ʳ 𝔚illiam 𝔄llen (Lord Maior, at Whitehall, 1571). — Per fess Sable and Or, a pale engrailed and counterchanged, three talbots passant of the second, collared Gules bezantée. *Crest*—A talbot passant Sable, eared Or, collared of the second studded Gules.

Sr **Walter Waller** (1572).   *Crest*—A tree eradicated Vert.

(Sr **Charles Somerset**, 1572, of Wales.)

(Sr **William FitzWilliams** of Northamptonshire, 1572.)

(Sr **Edward Mauncell** of Monmouthshire, 1572.)

Sr **Lionell Duckett**, Maior of London, dubbed anno 1574 (at Greenwich on Candlemas Day 1572).

Quarterly—1, Sable, a saltire Argent, thereon a mullet Gules for difference ; 2, Gules, three cushions Ermine, tasselled Or; 3, Gules, a lion rampant Argent, langued Or, on the shoulder a fleur-de-lis Azure; 4, Gules, crusily Or, a saltire Argent, thereon a mullet Sable for difference. *Crest*—A garb of lavender Vert, flowered Azure, banded Or.

Knightes dubbed in Kent in the progresse anno d'ni 1573 (at Rye, 12 August):

Sr **Thomas Guildeforde.**

Sr **Alexander Colepeper.**

Sr **Thomas Shirley.**

Sr **Thomas Walsingham.**

(Sr **Thomas Palmer.**)

Sr **John Pelham.**

Sr **Richard Baker** (at Dover, ult. August).

Quarterly of eight—1, as at p. 69 ; 2, Argent, a fess Sable, in chief a mullet of the second between two pellets (DINGLEY); 3, Gules, three garbs Or (COMYN) ; 4, Argent, on a bend engrailed Azure three croncls Argent (FOXCOTT); 5, Azure, a bend Or, a label of three points Gules (CHENDUT); 6, Gules, three lions rampant Or (FITZHERBERT) ; 7, Gules, a lion rampant-gardant, double-queued Ermine (STOKES) ; 8, Gules, six escallops Or (BRYMTON). Crest as at p. 69, the swan ducally gorged Gules.

Sr **Thomas Vane** (the like).

Sr **Will'm Winter.**

Sable, a fess and in chief a crescent Ermine, on a canton of the second a lion rampant of the field.

Sr **John Herbert** (? Thomas Herbert, at Greenwich, or Thomas Fitzherbert, 1573).

Sr **Will'm Drury** (1574).

Sr **Edmond Stradlinge** (at Greenwich, 1573 or 1575).

(Sr **John Rivers**, Lord Maior, at Greenwich, 1574.)

Sr **Richard Barkley** de com. Glouc., with these 22 followinge was .dubbed in the progresse to Bristowe anno d'ni 1574 :

Quarterly—1 and 4, Gules, crusily patée Or, a chevron Ermine ; 2 and 3, Or, a saltire engrailed Sable.

1. Sr **John Tracy.**

2. Sr **Thomas Porter.**

3. Sr **John Yonge.**

4. Sr **Will'm Morgan.**

5. Sr **John Sidnam.**

6. Sr **John Stowell.**

7. **Sr John Horner**, hath no armes.
8. **Sr George Rogers.**
9. **Sr Henry Portman.**
10. **Sr John Clifton.**
11. **Sr Edward Herbert.**
12. **Sr John Horsey.**
13. **Sr John Hungerford.**
14. **Sr Henry Knyvet.**
15. **Sr James Mervin.**
(**Sr John Huband**, Warwickshire, 1574.)

16. **Sr Thomas Wroughton.**
17. **Sr John Danvers.**
18. **Sr Henry Sherington.** Arms quarterly and Crest as at p. 90.
19. **Sr Mathew Arondell.**
20. **Sr Edward Baynton.**
21. **Sr John Norton.**
22. **Sr Will'm Babington.**

Sr Christopher Wray, Lord Cheif Justice, dubbed at Hampton Courte in November 1574. — Azure, a chevron engrailed Ermine between three scimitars (*sic*) Argent, on a chief Or as many martlets Gules.

Sr James Hawes, Maior of London, dubbed anno d'ni 1575. — Azure, on a chevron Or three cinquefoils Gules, a canton Ermine. *Crest*—Out of a ducal coronet Or a buck's head Argent, attired of the first.

Sr Charles, Lord Howarde of Effingham, dubbed in Aprill 1575, and immediately after elected Knighte of the Garter.

Knightes dubbed at Kenelworth in the progresse anno 1575 :

Sr Henry Cobham.
Sr Thomas Sicill (Cecill).
Sr Thomas Tresham.

Sr Thomas Stanhop.
Sr Arthur Bassett de com. Cornub.
Quarterly of fifteen—1, Per chevron Argent and Sable, three trefoils slipped Vert in chief and as many in base; 2, Sable, fretty Argent; 3, Argent, a cross patonce voided Gules; 4, Argent, two bars Azure, a bordure engrailed Sable; 5, Or, three water-bougets Sable; 6, Azure, three chevronels braced and a chief Or; 7, Barry of ten Argent and Gules, a fleur-de-lis Sable; 8, Gules, crusily and a bend Or; 9, Barry of six Argent and Azure, on a bend Gules three martlets Or; 10, Vair, a fess Gules; 11, Barry of ten Or and Azure, an eagle displayed Gules; 12, Or, three chevronels Gules, a chief Vair; 13, Gules, a chevron between three cross-crosslets and in chief a lion passant Or; 14, Gules, a lion rampant between three crescents Argent; 15, Argent, a chevron between three eagles' heads erased Sable. *Crest*—A boar's head Sable, bristled and ducally crowned Or, in the mouth a trefoil Vert.

Sᵣ Francys Wylughby de com. Nottingh'm, dubbed at Mydelton, his owne house, in the progresse anno 1575.

Sᵣ Will'm Catesby de com. Northamp., dubbed at Mydelton, Mr. Willughbie's house, in the progresse anno 1575.

Sᵣ John Fetyplace de com. Berks, dubbed at Woodstock in the progresse anno 1575.

Quarterly—1 and 4, Gules, two chevrons Argent; 2, Ermine, three torteaux; 3, Sable, a lion passant-gardant Argent, ducally crowned Or. *Crest*—A griffin's head erased Vert, beaked and eared Gules.

(**Sᵣ Edmond Fetyplace,** his cosen ; the like.)

Sᵣ Gerard Croker de com. Oxon (the like).

(**Sᵣ George Hastings,** 1575.)

Sᵣ Ampas Powlet de com. Wilt., dubbed at Wyndesor in October anno 1575.

Sᵣ Ambrose Nicholas, Maior of London, dubbed at White-hall on Sonday the 19 day of February 1575 in the parlement tyme.

Or, three fleurs-de-lis Azure, on a chief Gules a lion passant of the field. *Crest*—A unicorn's head Gules bezantée, armed and maned Sable.

Sᵣ Richard Rogers de com. Dorsett, dubbed at Westminster on Sonday the 25 of Marche, being the day of the Anuntiation of our Lady 1576.

Quarterly—1 and 4, Argent, a mullet Sable, on a chief Or a fleur-de-lis Gules ; 2 and 3, Argent, fretty Sable, a chief Gules. *Crest*—A fleur-de-lis per pale Or and Argent.

Sᵣ John Kelligrewe de com. Cornub., dubbed at Westm' the 25 of Marche in anno 1576, being the day of the Anuntiation of our Lady and the first day of the yere of our Lord 1576.

Quarterly of eight—1, Argent, a spread-eagle Sable within a bordure of the second bezantée ; 2, Sable, a chevron between three eagles displayed Or ; 3, Argent, three mascles Gules ; 4, Argent, on a chevron Sable between three torteaux as many bezants ; 5, Azure, on a bend Or three leaves of the field ; 6, Argent, a lion rampant Gules ; 7, Gules, a bend between six lozenges Or ; 8, Azure, a bend Or, a label of three points Gules. *Crest*—A demi-lion rampant Sable charged with three bezants.

Sᵣ Will'm Courteney, anno 1576.

Sᵣ Will'm Moore de com. Surrey, anno 1576.

Azure, on a cross Argent five martlets Sable. *Crest*—On a ducal coronet an heraldic tiger passant Argent.

Sᵣ Francis Carew de com. Surrey, dubbed anno 1576.

Quarterly of eleven—1, Or, three lions passant in pale Sable ; 2, Argent, three serpents nowed Vert ; 3, Gules, an arm habited in a maunch Ermine issuing from the sinister side, the hand proper holding a fleur-de-lis Or ; 4, Quarterly Argent and Sable ; 5, Azure, a fess between six cross-crosslets Or ; 6, Azure, three dexter hands appaumée couped Argent; 7, Ermine, a gemel-ring, on a chief Sable three crosses patée Argent; 8, Azure, fretty Argent; 9, Or, a lion rampant Sable, quartering Gules, a fess dancettée between six cross-crosslets Or; 10, Barry of six Ermine and Gules, three crescents Sable; 11, Argent, three piles Vert, a bordure Azure bezantée.

S͏ʳ Thomas Browne of Becheworthe Castell in Sussex, anno 1576.

Knights dubbed at . . . . anno 1576 :

S͏ʳ Will'm Drury de com. (Bucks, Lo. Deputy).
S͏ʳ Will'm Waldegrave de com. Essex.
S͏ʳ John Peter de com. Essex.
S͏ʳ Robert D'Oyley.   Crest—A demi-dragon Gules, winged and clawed Vert.
S͏ʳ Will'm Herbert de com. . . . . (Wales).
S͏ʳ John Smithe de com. Essex.
S͏ʳ Robert Bell, made Lord Chief Baron of the Exchequer, and dubbed in January 1576.   Sable, a fess Ermine between three bells Argent. Crest—On a mount Vert an eagle rising Argent, beaked and legged Sable, on the breast three Ermine spots.
S͏ʳ Richard Bulkeley de com. Cestre, dubbed on Shrove Sonday the 17 of February 1576, at Whitehall, the day before his maryage.
S͏ʳ John Langley, Maior of London, dubbed at Westminster anno 1576, in Marche.
(S͏ʳ Owen Arlye, 1576.)

Knightes dubbed at Gorambery, the house of Sir Nicholas Bacon, Lord Keeper of the Great Scale, in May, anno 1577 :

S͏ʳ John Brocket de com. Hertf.
S͏ʳ Henry Cocke de com. Hertf.   Quarterly Gules and Argent.
S͏ʳ Thomas Boteler de com. Lanc.
S͏ʳ Rauf (Randall) Breerton de com. Cestr.
S͏ʳ Will'm Bouthe de com. Linc.

———

S͏ʳ John Geoffrey, Seriaunt at the Lawe, made Lord Chief Baron of the Exchequer, and dubbed at Wyndesore in October, anno 1577.   Quarterly—1 and 4, Azure, fretty Or, on a chief Argent a lion passant-gardant Gules; 2 and 3, Argent, a cross potent Sable between four crescents Gules.
S͏ʳ Richard Grenevile, dubbed at Windesore anno 1577.
S͏ʳ Francis Walsingham, Principall Secretary, dubbed at Wyndesore anno 1577 in Novembre.   Quarterly of nine—1, Barry of six Argent and Sable, a fess Gules; 2, Gules, bezantée, a cross humetée counter-compony Argent and Azure; 3, Sable, a lion rampant Or (Nor-

TOFT) ; 4, Ermine, on a chief indented Sable a fleur-de-lis between two annulets Argent (BAMME); 5, Gules, guttée and a fess nebulée within a bordure Argent (DRYLAND); 6, Gules, a chevron between three garbs Argent and as many cross-crosslets fitchée, two in base and one in chief, Or (ROYTON); 7, Sable, a bend Argent, surmounted by another wavy of the first, in chief a cross-crosslet fitchée of the second (WRITTLE); 8, Argent, two bars and a canton Gules, over all a bendlet Sable (BOYS); 9, Sable, a chevron between three rams' heads couped Argent (RAMSEY). *Crest*—Out of a mural coronet Gules a griffin's head Or, langued of the first, ducally gorged Azure. On each a crescent for difference.

Sr Christopher Hatton, Vice-Chamberleyn and Captayne of the Guarde (the like). Quarterly of fourteen—1, Azure, a chevron between three garbs Or; 2, Barry lozengy Argent and Gules; 3, Or, a fess Gules, six fleurs-de-lis, 3 and 3, in pale counterchanged; 4, Argent, a cross patonce between four martlets Gules; 5, Argent, an eagle displayed Sable; 6, Argent, three piles meeting near the base Sable; 7, Argent, on a bend Sable three covered cups of the field; 8, Sable, a cross engrailed Ermine; 9, Or, a saltire Sable; 10, Sable, a fess couped Argent, a crescent for difference; 11, Azure, five cinquefoils in cross Argent; 12, Argent, three bends Sable, on a canton of the second a tower triple-towered of the first; 13, Argent, on a chief Gules three fleurs-de-lis Or; 14, Ermine, on a fess Azure three cross-crosslets Or. *Crest* —A hind passant Or.

Sr Thomas Heneage, Threasorer of the Chambre (the like).

(**Sr Henry Bagnol,** 1577.)

Sr Edward Horsey, Captaine of the Isle of Wight, dubbed at Hampton Court in December, anno 1577.

Sr Thomas Boynton of Aclam in com. Ebor., dubbed at Hampton Courte anno 1577, in January. Or, a fess between three crescents Gules.

Sr John Radcliff of Ordesall in com. Lancastre, dubbed at Hampton Court on Shrove Sonday, anno 1577, in February.

Sr Edward Longe of Wiltshire, dubbed anno 1578.

S^r 𝔉rancys 𝔚ynde de Com. Cambridg (the like).

S^r 𝔗homas 𝔯amsey, Maior of London, dubbed at Greenwiche on May-day anno 1578.

S^r 𝔠hr'opher 𝔚olyard of Yorkshire, dubbed at Greenwiche the 4 of May anno 1578.

S^r 𝔈dmond 𝔗rafforde of . . . ., dubbed on Sonday the 25 of May 1578.

S^r 𝔊eorge 𝔠olt, dubbed at his house called (Colts) Hall in Suff. the first of August 1578 in the progresse.

Quarterly—1 and 4, Argent, a fess between three colts courant Sable ; 2 and 3, Gyronny of eight Ermine and Azure. *Crest*—A horse's head Argent, three Ermine spots.

Knightes dubbed in the progresse at Bury St. Edmond on Saturday the first of August 1578 :

S^r 𝔓hilip 𝔓arker.

S^r 𝔄rthur 𝔥eveningham.

S^r 𝔯obert 𝔍ermyn.

S^r 𝔚ill'm 𝔖pringe.

S^r 𝔗homas 𝔯itson.

S^r 𝔗homas 𝔅ernardeston.

Knightes dubbed in the progresse at Norwich the 22 of August 1578 :

S^r 𝔯aufe 𝔖helton. S^r 𝔈dward 𝔠leere. S^r 𝔚ill'm 𝔓aston.

S^r 𝔑icholas 𝔅acon (at Norwich, son to the Lo. Keeper).

S^r 𝔗homas 𝔯upvet.

Quarterly of sixteen—1, Argent, a bend and a bordure engrailed Sable ; 2, Argent, three bars Gules, a bordure Azure bezantée ; 3, Or, a saltire engrailed Sable ; 4, Bendy of six Or and Azure, a canton Ermine ; 5, Chequy Or and Gules, a bend Ermine ; 6, Bendy of ten Argent and Gules ; 7, Argent, a chief Gules, a bend Azure ; 8, Ermine, a fess Gules ; 9, Argent, three cinquefoils and a canton Gules ; 10, Chequy Or and Gules, a chief Ermine ; 11, Argent, a cross engrailed between four water-bougets Gules, a label of three points, on each a lion rampant ; 12, Gules, billitée Or, a fess Argent ; 13, Quarterly Or and Vert ; 14, Argent, a chevron between three griffins' heads erased Gules (TILNEY); 15, Barry of ten Argent and Gules, a bend engrailed Sable; 16, Quarterly Or and Gules, a bordure Sable bezantée. Crest as at p. 70, a crescent for difference. "TILNEY bringeth these cotes : ROOS DE TYD, ROCHEFORD, LIMESEY, HILLARY, THORPE, GORBRIGE, NORWOOD, ASPALL."

S^r 𝔯obert 𝔚loode, Maior of Norwich.

(S͏ʳ **Henry Knyvett,** 1578.)

S͏ʳ **Thomas Gawdy,** dubbed at Woodrysinge in the progresse the 26 of August being Tuesday 1578.

S͏ʳ **Henry Woodhouse** (the like).

S͏ʳ **Roger Woodhouse,** dubbed on Wensday the 27 of August 1578 at S͏ʳ Edward Cleere's house in Thetford.

S͏ʳ **Roger Manwoode,** one of the Justices of the Kinge's Benche, dubbed on Saturday the 15 of Novembre 1578 at Richmond.

Sable, two pales Or, on a chief of the second a demi-lion rampant issuant of the first. Crest— Out of a ducal coronet a lion's head affrontée Or.

(S͏ʳ **Richard Pipe,** Lo. Maior, 1578.)

S͏ʳ **Will'm Herbert,** dubbed at Richmond on S͏ᵗ Thomas Day being Sonday the 21 of Decembre 1578.

S͏ʳ **Thomas Fayrfax,** dubbed at Westminster in May 1579.

S͏ʳ **Thomas Bromley,** dubbed at Westminster in May 1579, and immediately made Lorde Chancelor of England.

S͏ʳ **Thomas Layton** (**Leighton,** Shropshire), dubbed at Westminster in May 1579.

S͏ʳ **Gilbert Gerard,** Attorney Generall, dubbed at Grenwiche on Sonday the fifte of July 1579.

S͏ʳ **Drewe Drewry** (of Norff.), dubbed at Wanstead in Essex in Septembre 1579.

S͏ʳ **Henry Hudleston** (Edmond, 6063), dubbed with S͏ʳ John Heigham ; this S͏ʳ . . . . Hudleston was then Shiriff of Essex. "Quære an sit Sir Edmond Hodleston." (*Note.*—A Sir Edward Hudleston was Sheriff of Essex 20 Eliz.)

S͏ʳ **John Higham,** dubbed at Mulsham, S͏ʳ Thomas Mildmaye's house, in Essex, 1579 in Septembre.

S͏ʳ **Godfrey Foulgeam** de com. Derby, dubbed on Sonday the 24 of January 1579 at Westminster.

Quarterly of twenty-four—1, 2, 3, as 1, 2, 3 at p. 70 ; 4, Lozengy Argent and Gules, a mullet for difference ; 5, Chequy Or and Azure ; 6, Or, a chief Azure ; 7, Quarterly Or and Gules, a bend Sable, a label of five points Argent ; 8, Or, an orle Azure ; 9, Gules, six martlets Argent ; 10, Azure, on a bend Or an annulet Sable, a label of three points Argent ; 11, Or, crusily fitchée and three garbs Gules ; 12, Argent, a bend fusily Azure ; 13, Gules, a saltire Argent, a label of three points Argent, on each point a bar Azure, a crescent for difference ; 14, Argent, three fusils in fess Gules ; 15, Or, an eagle displayed Gules ; 16, Azure, flory and a lion rampant-gardant Argent ; 17, Three lions passant-gardant, a bordure ; 18, Or, two bars Gules, in chief three torteaux ; 19, Argent, a saltire engrailed Gules ; 20, Or, a lion rampant Gules ; 21, Gules, a cross engrailed Argent ; 22, Argent, on a canton

Gules a rose Or ; 23, Azure, a fess between three leopards' faces Or, an annulet Sable for difference ; 24, Argent, a fess dancettée Sable three bezants. Crest as at p. 70.

Sʳ John Byron (the like).

Knightes dubbed at Westm. on Sonday the 7 of February 1579 :

Sʳ Nicholas Woodrofe, Lord Maior of London.
Sʳ John Chichester.
Sʳ Thomas Rivett.

Sʳ Francis Godolphin, dubbed at Richmond on Sonday the 20 day of Novembre 1580, de com. Cornub.

Sʳ Thomas Sainctpoll of Lincolnshire, dubbed at Richmond on Sonday the 20 of Novembre 1580.

Sʳ George Bromley de com. Salope, Attorney to the Duchy of Lancaster, dubbed at Nonsuch in Surrey on Friday the 3 of June 1580.

Sʳ Henry Woderington (Widdrington) of Northumberland, dubbed 1580, after Sir George Bromley and yet before Sir Francys Godolphin and Sʳ Thomas Sᵗ Poll.

(**Sʳ William Cavendish**, 1580.)

Sʳ John Dawnay of Yorkshire, dubbed at Richemond on Wensday the 30 of Novembre 1580, beinge Sᵗ Andrewe's Day the 30 and last of that moneth.

Sʳ John Branche, Maior of London, dubbed at Westm. on Shrove Sonday the fifte day of February 1580.

Sʳ Francis Drake, dubbed at Depford neere Greenewiche by the Queene's Maᵗie, beinge in the shippe wherwith he had traveyled about the world, on Tuesday the 4 of Aprill 1581.

Sʳ George Hart, dubbed at Sᵗ James' neere Westminster in Aprill 1581, sonne and heire of Sʳ Percivall Hart of Kent.

(**Sʳ James Hales**, Kent, 1581.)

Sʳ Charles Framlingham of Suffolk, dubbed at Westminster on Sonday the last day of December 1581.

Sʳ James Harby, Maior of London, dubbed at the Court at Greenwich on Sonday the 6 of May 1582, after Sʳ Edmond Anderson.

Sʳ Edmond Anderson, Lord Chief Justice of the Com'on Pleas, dubbed at the Court at Grenwich on Thursday the 3 of May 1582.

Sʳ Edward Hobby, dubbed at Somerset Place in London on Tuesday the 22 of May anno 1582 the day after his mariage with the Baron of Hunston's daught'r.

Sʳ (John) Selby, Knight Porter of Berwike, dubbed at Nonesuche in July 1582.

Sʳ Charles Cavendish, dubbed anno 1582.

Sʳ Peregrine Bertie, Lord Wilughby of Eresby, dubbed at Windesore on Sonday the 13 of January 1582, and was that day installed of the Order for the Kinge of Denmark.

Sʳ Philippe Sidney, dubbed at Windesore on Sonday the 13 of January 1582, and was on that day lykewise installed for Duke John Cazimer Conte Palatine and Duke of Bavier.

Sʳ Thomas Sandes of Throwley in Kent, dubbed at Barne Elmes neere Fulham at Shrovetyde anno 1582 the 11 of February.

(S𝖗 **Francis Willoughby** of Wolterton, 1582.)

S𝖗 **Thomas Blanke**, L. Maior of London, dubbed at Grenwiche on Sonday the fifte of May 1583.

S𝖗 **Will'm Mohun**, dubbed on Sonday the 16 of June 1583.

S𝖗 **Tyrlow O'Brian** of the House of Towmont in Ireland, dubbed by the Lord of Hunsdon 1583 at Otlandes (by the Quene).

S𝖗 **John Orelly** of the Brenne in Ireland (the like).

S𝖗 **Edmond Stafford**, dubbed in October 1583 at his goenge Embassad'r resiaunt into France, at Otlandes.

S𝖗 **Will'm Haydon** of Norf., dubbed on Sonday the 3 of Novembre 1583 by the Erle of Leycester at S𝗍 James'.

S𝖗 **Philip Boteller** de com. Hertford (the like).

S𝖗 **George Penneage** of Lincolnshire, dubbed on Sonday the 8 of Decembre 1583 at S𝗍 James' by the . . . .

S𝖗 **Robert Savell** de com. Lincoln, nothus Henrici Savell equitis (the like).

S𝖗 **John Harington**, dubbed at the L. Lumleye's house on the Tower Hill the 9 of January 1583.

S𝖗 **Edward Osbourn**, L. Maior of London, dubbed at Westm. on Candlemasse-day 1583, the second of February.

S𝖗 **Richard Maliverer**, dubbed at the L. Lumleye's house on the Tower Hill the 9 of January 1583.

Quarterly—1 and 4, Gules, three greyhounds courant in pale Argent collared Or, a crescent for difference ; 2, Gules, a chief Or, over all a bend gobony Azure and Argent; 3, Azure, a bend between six martlets Argent, a crescent for difference. On an escucheon of pretence, Quarterly—1 and 4, as above, without the difference ; 2 and 3, as 3 above. *Crest*—A greyhound statant Argent, collared Or.

S𝖗 **George Sydenham**, dubbed the first of Marche anno d'ni 1583 at Whitehall.

S𝖗 **Rauf Burghchier** of Yorkshire, dubbed at Westm. Whitehall the 6 of Marche anno 1583.

Quarterly—1 and 4, Argent, a cross engrailed Gules between four water-bougets Sable, quartering, 1, Gules, billitée Or, a fess Argent; 2, Quarterly Or and Vert ; 3, Argent, a chevron between three eagles' heads erased Gules ; all within a bordure engrailed Sable. Over all a label of three points Azure, on each a lion rampant Or. 2 and 3, Argent, a cross patonce Sable, quartering Argent, three bars Sable, a bend Ermine. Crest as at p. 44.

(S𝖗 **John Berham**, 1584.)

S𝖗 **George Chaworth** of Wyverton in com. Nottingham, dubbed at Greenwiche on Sonday the 17 of May 1584.

Edward, Erle of Roteland, dubbed at Greenwich 1584.

S𝖗 **Edward Dymoke** of Lincolnshire, dubbed 1584, in August.

S𝖗 **Walter Rawley**, dubbed at Greenwiche on the Twelveth day 1584.

S𝖗 **Thomas Pullyson**, L. Maior of London, dubbed at Somersett House the 14 of February 1584.

Sr **Moyle Fynche** of Kent, dubbed at Greenwich the 7 of May 1584.

Sr **Henry Berkley** de Stoke in com. Som'sett, dubbed 1584.

Sr **Richard Dyer,** sonne and heire to the late L. Chief Justice of the Comon Pleas, dubbed 1585, the 4 of Aprill.

Sr **Cotton Gargrave** of Yorkshire, dubbed 1585.

Sr **Thomas Scroope,** sonne and heire to the L. Scroope, dubbed at Greenwiche the 13 of Aprill 1585.

Sr **Anthony Thorold** of Lincolnshire, dubbed the 6 of May 1585.

Sr **Robert Southwell,** dubbed at Thibaldes on Friday the 18 of June 1585.

Sr **Henry Coningesby,** dubbed at Thibaldes the same tyme on the removing day 1585.

Sr **John Aroudell,** dubbed at Richmond the 14 of October 1585, of Tolverne.

Sr **Bernard Drake,** dubbed at Greenwich on Sonday the 9 of January 1585.

Sr **Wolstan Dixi,** L. Maior of London, dubbed at Greenwich on Sonday the 6 of February 1585, anno reg. R. Eliz. 28.

(Sr **Monogh Allarchy,** 1585.)

Sr **Will'm Bowes** of Stretlam in the Bishopprik of Durham, dubbed at Grenwich anno 1586, reg. R. Eliz. 28.

Sr **Andrew Noel** of Dalby in com. Leyce'shire, dubbed at Greenwiche on Wensday the 2 of March 1585, anno 28 reg. Elizabethæ.

Sr **Chr'opher Wandesford** of Kirtlington in Yorkshire, dubbed at Greenwich anno 1586, reg. R. Eliz. 28.

Sr **Richard Molyneulx** of Sefton in Lancashire, dubbed at Greenwich on Midsomer day, beinge Thursday the 24 of June 1586, anno 28 R. Eliz.

Sr **John Monson** of Lincolnshire (the like).

(Sr **John Wingfield,** 1586.)

(Sr **Anthony Spillman,** 1586.)

(Sr **Edward Wingfield** of Kimbolton, 1586.)

Knights made by Robert Erle of Lecester in Holland in a° 1586 :

Sr **John Norrys.**
Robert E. of Essex.
George Lord Audly.
Sr **William Russell.**
Sr **Henry Palmer.**
Sr **Edward Denny.**
Sr **William Hatton.**
Sr **Henry Umpton.**
Sr **Henry Norris.**
Sr **Henry Noell.**
Sr **Robert Sydney.**
Sr **John Borrugh.**
Sr **Charles Blount.**
Sr **Francis Knowles.**
Sr **Henry Goodyear.**

Sr **George Farrer.**
Sr **Edward Wingfeild.**
Sr **George Digby.**
Sr **Phillip Butler.**
Sr **Thomas Dennys.**
Sr **Roger Williams.**
Sr **William Read.**
Sr **Edward Stanley.**
Sr **Edward Norris.**
Sr **Thomas Horsey.**
Sr **Richard Dyer.**
Sr **Edward Cary.**
Sr **John Paston.**
Sr **John Lloyd.**
Sr **Hugh Cholmely.**

Sʳ George Savile, 1587.
Sʳ Henry (? Andrew) Nowell, 1587.
Sʳ Edward Aston, 1588.

Knights made by the Lo. Admirall at Sea 1588 :

The Lo. Thomas Howard.
The Lo. Edm. Sheffeild.
Sʳ Roger Townsend.

Sʳ John Hawkins.
Sʳ Martin Frobisher.
Sʳ George Beeston.

Knights made by the Lord Willoughby in the Low Countries 1588 :

Sʳ Thomas Wilford.
Sʳ Francis Vere.
Sʳ John Pooley.
Sʳ John Pointz.
Sʳ Nicholas Parker.

Sʳ Thomas Knowles.
Sʳ John Scott.
Sʳ Ed. Uvedall.
Sʳ Charles Danvers.
Sʳ Christopher Blount.

Sʳ Edward Denny, 1589.   Sʳ Thomas Shirley, Jun., 1589.

Knights made by the French Kinge 1591 :

Sʳ Thomas Challoner.
Sʳ Devereux Poole.

Sʳ Christopher Lydcote.
Sʳ Thomas Wilkes.

Knights made by Robert, Erle of Essex, before Roane 1591 :

Sʳ Charles Perry.
Sʳ William Brooke.
Sʳ Thomas Conisbye.
Sʳ Thomas Gerrard.
Sʳ John Tracy.
Sʳ John Wootton.
Sʳ Richard Acton.
Sʳ Henry Jones.
Sʳ Francis Allyn.
Sʳ Edward Yorke.
Sʳ Mathew Morgan.

Sʳ Thomas Fairfax.
Sʳ Nicholas Clifford.
Sʳ Edmond Yorke.
Sʳ Robert Drury.
Sʳ Thomas Jermyn.
Sʳ William Woodhowse.
Sʳ William Dawtrey.
Sʳ Griffin Markham.
Sʳ Henry Danvers.
Sʳ Edward Hastinges.
Sʳ Ferdinando Gorge.

Knightes made by the Lo. Admirall and the Erle of Essex at Cales 1596 :

The E. of Sussex.
Don Christophero.
Count Lodovick.
The Lo. Herbert.
The Lo. Burke.
Sʳ Sam. Bagnall.
Sʳ Arthur Savage.
Sʳ William Howard.
Sʳ George Devereux.

Sʳ Henry Nevill.
Sʳ Edwin Rich.
Sʳ Anth. Ashley.
Mounseir Lavins.
Mounseir Edmarker.
Sʳ Henry Lennard.
Sʳ Richard Lewson.
Sʳ Horatio Vere.
Sʳ Arthur Throgmorton.

T

Sʳ Miles Corbet.
Sʳ Edward Conway.
Sʳ Oliver Lambert.
Sʳ Anthony Cooke.
Sʳ John Townsend.
Sʳ Christopher Paidon.
Sʳ Francis Popham.
Sʳ Phillip Woodhowse.
Sʳ Alexander Clifford.
Sʳ Moris Barkley.
Sʳ Charles Blount.
Sʳ George Gifford.
Sʳ Robert Crosse.
Sʳ John Scudamour.
Sʳ William Leigh.
Sʳ John Lea.
Sʳ Richard Waynman.
Sʳ Richard Weston.
Sʳ James Wootton.
Sʳ Richard Ruddall.
Sʳ Robert Mansell.
Sʳ William Mounson.
Sʳ John Bowlles.

Sʳ Edward Bowes.
Sʳ Humfrey Drewell.
Sʳ Amyas Preston.
Sʳ Robert Remington.
Sʳ John Butts.
Sʳ John Morgan.
Sʳ John Aldrigg.
Sʳ John Shelton.
Sʳ William Ashendon.
Sʳ Mathew Browne.
Sʳ Thomas Acton.
Sʳ Thomas Gates.
Sʳ Gulliam Merrick.
Sʳ Thomas Smyth.
Sʳ William Poley.
Sʳ Thomas Palmer.
Sʳ Robert Lovell.
Sʳ John Stafford.
Sʳ John Gilbert.
Sʳ William Harby.
Sʳ John Gray.
Sʳ Baldwin Medker.
Sʳ Gerrat Harby, Bedfordsh.

Knights made at the Island 1597 :

The E. of Southampton.
Sʳ Thomas Egerton.

Sʳ Thomas Vabasor.
Sʳ Lodovick Grevill.

Sʳ Jonathan Trelany at Whitehall on Shrove Tuesday, 1597.
Sʳ . . . . Strowde ⎰ ditto.
Sʳ Geo. More ⎱
Sʳ Geo. Cary of Cockington at Whitehall, ult. Feb.
Sʳ Thomas Fane of Kent, 25 Maii 1598.
Sʳ Mihill Sands ⎰ at Greenw'ch,
Sʳ Thos. Reresby ⎱ 18 Junii 1598.
Sʳ Henry Lo. Cobham at Nonsuch, July.
Sʳ Renald Mohun, 25 Martii 1599.
Sʳ Stephen Soham at Greenw'ch, Lo. Maior, 25 April.
Sʳ Rich. Ch'mp'non.

Sʳ Rich. Haughton, January.
Sʳ Rich. Lassells.
Sʳ Edm. Withepole.
Sʳ Nich. Moseley, Lo. Maior, August 1600.
Sʳ Francis Leake.
Sʳ Edward More.
Sʳ Robert Oxenbridg.
Sʳ Percivall Hart, June 1, 1601.
Sʳ William Ryder, Lo. Maior.
Sʳ John Norris, Novemb. 1601.
Sʳ Edward Hungerford.
Sʳ Carew Rawly.
Sʳ Hamden Powlet.
Sʳ Edmond Ludlow.
Sʳ . . . . Leigh.

The Names of all such as have beene advanced to the honorable Order of Knighthood in the tyme of the godlie Prudent and prosperous Reign of

King James.

(Cotton MS., Claudius, C. iii., fol. 239—264.)

This part of the MS. has been compared with "A Perfect Collection or Catalogue of all Knights Batchelaurs made by King James since his comming to the Crown of England; Faithfully extracted out of the Records by J. P. (John Philipot), Esq., Somerset Herald, a devout Servant of the Royal Line; London 1660;" additions from which are distinguished by a †, and variations between the book and the MS. are given in italics; the counties added are from the book. The Knights of the Bath are added from Lansd. MS. 866.

1603.

At Edenborough, 28 March:

Sr John Payton. Norf.

At Barwick, 6 of Aprill:

Sr William Selby. Northumb.
Sr Ralph Grey. „

At Widerington, 9 of Aprill:

Sr Henry Widerington. Northum.
Sr Nicholas Forster. „
Sr William Fenwicke. „
Sr Edward Gorges.

At Newcastle, 13 Aprill:

Sr Robert Delavall. Northumb.
Sr Christopher Lowther. Cumb.
Sr Nicholas Curwen. „
Sr James Bellingham. Westm'l'd.
Sr Nicholas Tufton. Kent.
Sr John Conyers. York.
Sr Bertram Bulmer.

At Yorke, 17 Aprill:

Sr William Cecil.
Sr Edmond Trafford. Lanc.
Sr Thomas Holcroft. Lanc.
Sr John Mallorie. York.
Sr William Ingelby. „
Sr Robert Watter, Mayor of Yorke.
Sr Philip Constable. Durham.
Sr Christopher Hil(d)yard. York.
Sr Robert Swift. „
Sr Richard Wortley. „
Sr Henry Bellasis. „
Sr Thomas Fairfax. „
Sr Henry Griffith. „
Sr Francis Boynton. „
Sr Henry Cholmeley. „
Sr Richard Gargrave. „
Sr Marmaduke Grimston. „
Sr Lancelot Alford. „
Sr Ralph Ellerker. „
Sr George Frevill. Durham.
Sr Mauger Vavasor. York.
Sr Ralph Babthorpe. „

At Grimston, 18 Aprill:

Sr Roger Aston. Chesh.
Sr Thomas Aston. „

Sᵣ Thomas Holte.   Chesh.
Sᵣ James Harrington.   Rutl.
Sᵣ Charles Montague. North'ton.
Sᵣ Thomas Dawney.   York.
Sᵣ William Bamborough.   „
Sᵣ Francis Lovell.   Norf.
Sᵣ Thomas Beaufeld.
Sᵣ Thomas Gerard.   Lanc.
Sᵣ Ralph Coningsbie.   Hertf.
Sᵣ Richard Musgrave.   York.

At Worksop, 21 Aprill :

Sᵣ John (? James) Manners.
       Derby.
Sᵣ Henry Gray.   Bedford.
Sᵣ Edward Loraine.   Derby.
Sᵣ Henry Perpoint.   Notts.
Sᵣ Francis Newport.   Salop.
Sᵣ Henry Beaumont.   Leic.
Sᵣ William Skipwith.   „
Sᵣ Hugh Smith.   Somerset.
Sᵣ Walter Cope.   Oxon.
Sᵣ Edmond Lucie.   Warw.
Sᵣ Edmond Cockaine.   Derby.
Sᵣ John Harper.   „
Sᵣ Thomas Gresley.   Notts.
Sᵣ John Byron.   „
Sᵣ Percival Willoughby.   Linc.
Sᵣ Peter Frechvile.   Derby.
Sᵣ Richard Checkston.   York.
Sᵣ Thomas Stanley.   Derby.

At Newarke, 22 Aprill :

Sᵣ John Parker.   Sussex.
Sᵣ Robert Brett.   Devon.
Sᵣ Lewis Lewkener.   Sussex.
Sᵣ Richard Mompesson.   Bucks.
Sᵣ Francis Duckett.   Salop.
Sᵣ Richard Warburton.   Chesh.
Sᵣ Richard Wigmore.   Heref.
Sᵣ Edward Fox.   Salop.
Sᵣ William Davenport.   Chesh.

Uppon the way to Beavercastle (Belvoir Castle, co. Leic.) :

Sᵣ Roger Askewe.   Chesh.
Sᵣ William Sutton.   Notts.
Sᵣ John Stanhop.   Derby.
Sᵣ Brian Lassells.   York.

At Beavercastle, 23 Aprill :

Sᵣ Oliver Manners.   Linc.
Sᵣ William Willoughby.   „
Sᵣ Thomas Willoughby.   „
Sᵣ Gregory Cromwell.   Hunts.
Sᵣ George Manners.   Leic.
Sᵣ Henry (? George) Hastings.
       Leic.
Sᵣ William Pelham.   Linc.
Sᵣ Philip Tirwhitt.   „
Sᵣ Valentine Browne.   „
Sᵣ Roger Dallison.   „
Sᵣ Thomas Grantham.   „
Sᵣ Anthony Markham.   Oxon.
Sᵣ William Carre.   Linc.
Sᵣ John Thorold.   „
Sᵣ Edward Ascue.   „
Sᵣ Henry Pagenham.   „
Sᵣ Edmund Bussie.   „
Sᵣ Edward Tirwitt.   „
Sᵣ Edward Carre.   „
Sᵣ Everard Digbie.   Rutl.
Sᵣ William Ermine.   Linc.
Sᵣ Nicholas Sanderson.   „
Sᵣ Richard Ogle.   „
Sᵣ Hugh (Hamon) Wichcote.
       Linc.
Sᵣ Edward Rosseter.   „
Sᵣ William Wichman.   „
Sᵣ Thomas Beaumont.   Leic.
Sᵣ William Jepson.   Hants.
Sᵣ Thomas Cave.   Leic.
Sᵣ Philip Sherard.   „
Sᵣ William Skeffington.   „
Sᵣ William Faunt.   „
Sᵣ Basil Brooke.   Salop.

Sr William Turpine.   Leic.
Sr William Lambert.
Sr John Zouche.   Derby.
Sr John Thornegh.   Notts.
Sr Edward Swift.   York.
Sr Philip Stirley (? Strelley). Leic.
Sr John Ferrers.   Warw.
Sr Edward Littleton.   Salop.
Sr William Feilding.   Warw.
Sr John Wentworth.   Essex.
Sr Walter Chute.   Kent.
Sr Edward Commes.
Sr William Fairfax.
Sr John Tyrell.
Sr Edward Cleare.
Sr Hamond Southcote.

At Theobald's, 7 May :

Sr William Killegrewe.   Cornw.
Sr Michaell Stanhope.   Suff.
Sr Francis Barrington.   Essex.
Sr Rowland Litton.   Hertf.
Sr William Peter.   Essex.
Sr John Brograve.   Hertf.
Sr William Cooke.   Essex.
Sr Henry (? Arthur) Capell. Hertf.
Sr Herbert Croft.   Heref.
Sr Edward Grevill.   Warw.
Sr Henry Butler.   Hertf.
Sr Henry Maynard.   Essex.
Sr Richard Spencer.   Hertf.
Sr John Leventhorpe.   „
Sr Thomas Pope Blunt.   „
Sr Richard Giffard.
Sr Thomas Metcalfe.   York.
Sr Henry Fanshawe.   Hertf.
Sr Gamaliel Capell.   Essex.
Sr William Smithe.   „
Sr John Ferrers.   Hertf.
Sr Richard Baker.   „
Sr Vincent Skinner.   Midd.
Sr Hugh Beeston.   Chesh.
Sr John Lee.

Sr Thomas Bishop.   Sussex.
Sr Gervaise Elwes.
Sr Edward Lewis.   Glam.

At the Charterhouse, 11 of May :

Sr Charles Howard.   Sussex.
Sr Ambrose Willoughbie. Linc.
Sr Edward Howard.   Surrey.
Sr Henrie Hastings.   Leic.
Sr Giles Allington.   Cambr.
Sr William Pinde.   „
Sr Richard Verney.   Warw.
Sr John Thinne.   Wilts.
Sr William Fitz Williams. Linc.
Sr Edward Carrell.   Sussex.
Sr Edward Bacon.   Suff.
Sr Francis Anderson.   Bedf.
Sr John Poultney.   Notts.
Sr Edward Darcie.   York.
Sr John Sidenham.   Somerset.
Sr John Tufton.   Kent.
Sr Thomas Griffin.   North'ton.
Sr Valentine Knightley.   „
Sr Ralphe Wiseman.   Essex.
Sr William Ayloffe.   „
Sr Edward Watson.   North'ton.
Sr James Cromer.   Kent.
Sr Thomas Cheeke.   Essex.
Sr Thomas Rouse.   Suff.
Sr John Rodney.
Sr Henry Vaughan.
Sr John Smith.   Kent.
Sr Charles Cornewallis.   Suff.
Sr John Hannam.   Chesh.
Sr Thomas Meede.   Kent.
Sr Eusebius Isham.   North'ton.
Sr Arthur Cooper.   Surrey.
Sr Robert Wingfeild.   North'ton.
Sr Thomas Josseline.   Hertf.
Sr Henry Goodricke.   York.
Sr Maximilian Dallison.   Kent.
Sr William Cope.   North'ton.
Sr George Fleetewood.   Bucks.

Sʳ Peter Evers.   Linc.
Sʳ Henry Clerc.   Norf.
Sʳ Edward Francis.
Sʳ Francis Wolley.   Linc.
Sʳ Arthur Manwaring.   Chesh.
Sʳ Edward Waterhouse.   York.
Sʳ Will. Twisden (created
  Baronet 29 June 1611). Kent.
Sʳ Patton Cheeke.
Sʳ Henry Goring.   Sussex.
Sʳ Richard Sandes.   Kent.
Sʳ Robert Cotton.   Hunts.
Sʳ Oliver Luke.   Beds.
Sʳ Thomas Knivett.   Norf.
Sʳ Henry Seckford.   Suff.
Sʳ Edwin Sands.   Kent.
Sʳ John Ashley.   „
Sʳ William Fleetwood.   Beds.
Sʳ Walter Mildmay.   Essex.
Sʳ Arthur Atye.   Midd.
Sʳ Edward Lewkenor.   Suff.
Sʳ Miles Sandes.   Cambr.
Sʳ William Kingsmill.   Hants.
Sʳ Thomas Kempe.   Kent.
Sʳ Edward Tirrell.   Bucks.
Sʳ Thomas (? William) Russell.
                          Worc.
Sʳ Richard Tichborne.   Hants.
Sʳ Thomas Cornwall.   Salop.
Sʳ John Cutts.   Cambr.
Sʳ Richard Farmer.   Norf.
Sʳ John Tasborough.   Suff.
Sʳ John Shirley.   Sussex.
Sʳ Thomas Preston.   Dorset.
Sʳ William Stafford.   Hunts.
Sʳ Thomas Carrell.   Sussex.
Sʳ Thomas Palmer.   Kent.
Sʳ Robert Newdigate.   Beds.
Sʳ George Rawley.   Essex.
Sʳ Thomas Beaufoe.   Warw.
Sʳ William Lower.   Cornw.
Sʳ Charles Fairfax.   York.
Sʳ Henry Sidney.   Norf.

Sʳ Pexall Brocas.   Hants.
Sʳ Walter Tichborne.
Sʳ Henry Crispe or Cripps. Kent.
Sʳ George Herbey.   Essex.
Sʳ John Heveningham.   Norf.
Sʳ William Bowyer.   Bucks.
†Sʳ Jerom Weston.   Essex.
†Sʳ Edmond Bowyer.   Surrey.
Sʳ Nicholas Halswell (? Hasel-
  well) or Haselwood.   North'ton.
Sʳ John Jenninges.   Worc.
Sʳ Ambrose Turbile.   Linc.
Sʳ John Luke.   Beds.
Sʳ John Dormer.   Bucks.
Sʳ Richard Sanders.   Linc.
Sʳ John Shirley.
Sʳ Thomas Wainman.   Oxon.
Sʳ Goddard Pemberton.
Sʳ Thomas Metham.   York.
Sʳ Edward Bellingham.   Cumb.
Sʳ John Warrington.   York.
Sʳ Edward Warrington.   „
Sʳ William Dier.   Somerset.
Sʳ John Wentworth.   „
Sʳ Walter Montague.   „
Sʳ Guy Palmes.   Rutl.
Sʳ Edward Apsley.   Sussex.
Sʳ Henry Ashley.   Surrey.
†Sʳ Thomas Baker.
Sʳ Thomas Fachell.
Sʳ Thomas Baskerville.
Sʳ Thomas Stukeley.   Sussex.
Sʳ William Leake.
Sʳ Hugh Losse.   Midd.
Sʳ William Lygon.   Worc.
Sʳ Thomas le Grosse.   Norf.
Sʳ Thomas Fowler.   Midd.
Sʳ Eusebius Andrewes.   North'tⁿ.
Sʳ Robert Lucy.   Warw.
Sʳ William Walter.
Sʳ Richard Blount.   Oxon.
Sʳ Anthony Deering.   Kent.
Sʳ John Carewe.   Somerset.

Sᵣ **William Alford.**   York.
Sᵣ **Robert Lee.**   Linc.
Sᵣ **Thomas Beaumont.**   Leic.
Sᵣ **Robert** (? George) **Markham.**   Oxon.
Sᵣ **Francis Castilion.**   Berks.
Sᵣ **Robert** (? John) **Marshall.**
Sᵣ **George Savill.**   York.
Sᵣ **Robert Cleveland.**
Sᵣ **Robert Townesend.**   Salop.

At the Tower, 13 May :

Sᵣ **William Dethicke,** Garter.
Sᵣ **Robert Mackland** (? Maickland) or **Macklarand.**   Oxon.
Sᵣ **George Morton.**   Dorset.
Sᵣ **Edmund Bell.**   Norf.
Sᵣ **Thomas Peyton.**   Kent.
Sᵣ **David Fowles.**
Sᵣ **William Gardener.**   Surrey.
Sᵣ **John Deane.**   Essex.
Sᵣ **John Trevor.**   Flint.
Sᵣ **Thomas Smithe.**   Kent.
Sᵣ **Thomas Hubart.**   Norf.

At Greenewich, 20 May :

Sᵣ **Julius Cæsar,**
Sᵣ **Roger Wilbraham,**   } Masters of yᵉ Request.

Sᵣ **William Wade,**
Sᵣ **Thomas Smithe,**
Sᵣ **Thomas Edmonds,**   } Clerks of the Counsell.
Sᵣ **Thomas Leeke,**
Sᵣ **John Wood,**

At Greenewich, 22 May :

Sᵣ **Robert Lee,** Lord Maior of London.
Sᵣ **John Crooke,** Recorder.
Sᵣ **Edward Coke,** Attorney-General.

At Greenewich, 22 May :

Sᵣ **John Morrys.**   Essex.
Sᵣ **Edward Seymour.**   Devon.
Sᵣ **Warwick Pele.**   „
Sᵣ **Thomas Arundell.**   Cornw.

At Greenewich, 10 June :

Sᵣ **William Selby.**   Kent.

At Bedington, at Sᵣ Francis Carew's :

Sᵣ **Nicholas Throckmorton.**   Surrey.
Sᵣ **Edward Gorges.**   Somerset.
Sᵣ **Alexander Brett.**   „

At Hendon, at Sir John Fortescue's :

Sᵣ **William Fleetwood.**   Bucks.
Sᵣ **Thomas Hesketh,** Attorney of the Wards.   Lanc.

At Sion, — June :

Sᵣ **Robert Wrothe.**   Essex.
†Sᵣ **William Norton.**   Hants.
Sᵣ **Thomas Tirringham.**
Sᵣ **Marmaduke Wyvell.**   York.
Sᵣ **Robert** (? Francis) **More.**   Berks.

At Hanworth, — July :

Sᵣ **Thomas Gardener.**   Surrey.
Sᵣ **Thomas Grimes.**   „
Sᵣ **George Trenchard.**   Dorset.
Sᵣ **John Foliott.**   Worc.
Sᵣ **Henry Poole.**   Wilts.
Sᵣ **John Pawlett.**   „
Sᵣ **Thomas Crompton.**   Heref.
Sᵣ **John Langton.**   Lanc.

At Windsor, 9 July :

Sᵣ **Thomas Tempest.**   Bucks.
Sᵣ **John Roper.**   Kent.
Sᵣ **William Pogan.**   Pembr.
Sᵣ **John Hogan.**   „
Sᵣ **Richard Cholmeley.**   York.

Sʳ John York. York.
Sʳ John Chamberlaine. Oxon.
Sʳ Francis Trappes. York.
Sʳ William Milliard. „
Sʳ Thomas Bellasis. „
Sʳ Richard (Chʳ) Lowther. Cumb.
Sʳ Edward Plumpton. York.
Sʳ Bryan (? George) Palmes.
                       Hants.
Sʳ Mathewe Redman. York.
Sʳ Mathew Tenant.
Sʳ Thomas Samford. Westmin.
Sʳ Stephen Tempest. York.
Sʳ William Paddy. Oxford.
Sʳ John (? Henry) Babthorpe.
                       Devon.
Sʳ Amias Bamfeild. „
Sʳ William Greene.
Sʳ Michael Greene. Oxon.
Sʳ Francis Stidolfe.
Sʳ Thomas Brown. Devon.
Sʳ Martin Gamon. „
Sʳ Thomas Preston. Dorset.
Sʳ Edward Stodder. Surrey.

At Sʳ Alexander Hampden's, — July :

Sʳ Alexander Hampden. Bucks.
Sʳ Henry Barker. Berks.
Sʳ William Willoughby. Bucks.
Sʳ Edward Pinchon. Essex.

At Sʳ John Fortescue's :

Sʳ William Dunche. Berks.
Sʳ John Dive. Beds.
Sʳ Gerard Throckmorton. Glouc.
Sʳ John Crooke. Oxon.
Sʳ Richard Chetwood. North'ton.
Sʳ Robert Hartwell. „
Sʳ Richard Price. Hunts.
Sʳ James Hayden. Norf.
Sʳ Thomas Snagge. Beds.
Sʳ Francis Cheney. Bucks.
Sʳ Henry Longvile. „

Sʳ Henry Drurie. Bucks.
Sʳ William Burlacie. „
Sʳ Thomas Denton. „
Sʳ Anthony Tirringham. „
Sʳ John Sands. „
Sʳ Richard Huntley.
Sʳ Thomas Hill. Kent.
Sʳ Thomas Cave. North'ton.
Sʳ Edmund Conquest. Beds.
Sʳ John Carrell. Sussex.
Sʳ John Townsend. Salop.
Sʳ Adrian Scroope. Linc.
Sʳ Robert Strickland.
Sʳ Edmund Morrell.
Sʳ John Langton.
Sʳ Thomas Temple.
Sʳ Henry Billingsley. London.

At Sʳ George Farmor's, — July :

Sʳ Hatton Farmor. Bucks.
Sʳ Edward Lee.
Sʳ Thomas Woodhouse. Norf.
Sʳ Francis Curson. Salop.
Sʳ Richard Conquest. Beds.
Sʳ Raphe Tempest. York.
Sʳ Edward Randall. Surrey.
Sʳ Anthony Chester. Heref.
Sʳ Gerrard Fleetwood. Bucks.
Sʳ Walter Vaughan. Heref.

At Sʳ William Fleetwood's :

Sʳ William Pawlett. Wilts.
Sʳ Thomas Monke.
Sʳ Thomas Somervile.
Sʳ Arthur Porter. Glouc.
Sʳ Francis Harris.
Sʳ Edward Walles.
Sʳ Richard Saunders.
Sʳ James Perrott.
Sʳ William Southland.
Sʳ Henry Billingsley.
Sʳ William Foster.
Sʳ William Walsh.
Sʳ Thomas Eversfield.

At Sʳ John Paginton's house, July :

Sʳ **William Smith.**

At Hampton Court, 20 July :

Sʳ **John Games.**   Radnor.

Sʳ **William Cave.**

At Whitehall, 23 of July, before the coronation of the King :

Sʳ **Baptist Hicks.**

Sʳ **John Bennett.**   London.

Sʳ **Francis Gawdie.**   Norf.

Sʳ **Thomas Walmesley.**   Lanc.

Sʳ **Robert Clerke.**   Essex.

Sʳ **Edward Fennor.**   Midd.

Sʳ **John Savill.**   York.

Sʳ **George Ringsmill.**   Hants.

Sʳ **Peter Warburton.**   Chesh.

Sʳ **Christopher Helberton.**   Norf.

Sʳ **John Hele.**   Devon.

Sʳ **Edward Phillips.**   Somerset.

Sʳ **John Harris.**   Essex.

Sʳ **David Williams.**

Sʳ **William Danyell.**   London.

Sʳ **Edward Heron.**   Linc.

Sʳ **Henry Hubert.**   Norf.

Sʳ **Thomas Fleminge.**   Hants.

Sʳ **Francis Bacon.**   Hertf.

Sʳ **Henry Montague.**   North'ton.

Sʳ **Edward Stanhop.**   York.

Sʳ **John Tindall.**   Norf.

Sʳ **Mathewe Carew.**   London.

†Sʳ **George Carew.**   ,,

Sʳ **Daniel Dun.**

Sʳ **Christopher Perkins.**   Kent.

Sʳ **Richard Swale.**   York.

Sʳ **Thomas Crompton.**   London.

Sʳ **John Gibson.**   York.

Sʳ **George Coppin.**   Norf.

Sʳ **Richard Coningsbie.**   Lond.

Sʳ **John Drommond.**   Scotus.

Sʳ **Thomas Conway.**   London.

Sʳ **John Willoughbie.**   Linc.

Sʳ **Edward Colepeper.**   Sussex.

Sʳ **John Morley.**   London.

Sʳ **John Tirrell.**   Essex.

Sʳ **Philip Scudamore.**   Heref.

Sʳ **Thomas Dabridgcourt.**   Hants.

Sʳ **William Roper.**   Kent.

Sʳ **John Gilbert.**   Suff.

†Sʳ **Thomas Smith.**   Chesh.

Sʳ **Francis Vincent.**   Surrey.

Sʳ **John Cotton.**   Cambr.

Sʳ **Robert Lane.**   Warw.

†Sʳ **Robert Edwards.**   Kent.

Sʳ **Nicholas Gilborne.**   ,,

Sʳ **Samuel Sandes.**   Worc.

Sʳ **Thomas Mildmay.**   Herts.

Sʳ **Thomas Hanmer.**   Chesh.

Sʳ **John Whitton.**

Sʳ **Alexander Cave.**

†Sʳ **John Tracy.**   Glouc.

Sʳ **Samuel Saltonstall.**   Lond.

†Sʳ **Thomas Beake.**

Sʳ **Robert Varnam.**   Chesh.

Sʳ **Thomas Penruddocke.**   Wilts.

Sʳ **Edward Cooke.**   Essex.

Sʳ **Thomas Humphry.**

Sʳ ....   Leicester.

Sʳ **Thomas Windebanke.**   Berks.

Sʳ **Thomas Clarke.**   Essex.

Sʳ **John Wood.**   ,,

Sʳ **Raphe Lawson.**   Kent.

Sʳ **William Meredith.**

Sʳ **George Selby.**   Northumb.

Sʳ **Walter Rice.**

Sʳ **Lewis Maunsell.**   Glam.

Sʳ **Richard Hawkins.**   Kent.

Sʳ **John Rogers.**

Sʳ **Robert Alexander.**   Hertf.

Sʳ **John Browne.**   Dorset.

Sʳ **Richard Skipwith.**   Leic.

Sʳ **Thomas Barnardiston.**   Essex.

Sʳ **William Gerrard.**   Berks.

Sʳ **Thomas Palmer.**   Kent.

Sʳ **Richard Aston.**   Chesh.

Sʳ William Thornegh.	Notts.
Sʳ Francis Bayldon.	York.
Sʳ Edward Duncombe.	
Sʳ William Hanmer.	Chesh.
Sʳ Henrie Longvile.	Bucks.
Sʳ John Meeres.	Kent.
Sʳ Charles Dymocke.	Linc.
Sʳ Valentine Browne.	,,
Sʳ George Reynell.	Devon.
Sʳ John Reade.	Linc.
Sʳ John Leigh.	,,
Sʳ Edward Pitts.	Wilts.
†Sʳ Thomas Roe.	London.
Sʳ George Knighton.	Notts.
†Sʳ Henry Savile.	York.
Sʳ Goddard Pemberton.	
†Sʳ Walter Treadway.	North'ton.
Sʳ Henry Jones.	
†Sʳ Edward Poynter.	
Sʳ Edward Wingfeild.	
Sʳ Anthony Everard.	Essex.
Sʳ Raphe Bosvill.	Kent.
Sʳ Thomas Bridges.	Glouc.
Sʳ Robert Stroude.	
Sʳ Stephen Borde.	Sussex.
Sʳ Thomas May.	,,
Sʳ John Bedell.	Hunts.
Sʳ Thomas Bedell.	,,
†Sʳ Henry Day.	
Sʳ John Windham.	
Sʳ Henry Hawley (*Rowley*).	Essex.
Sʳ John Fitz.	
Sʳ Francis Smithe.	
†Sʳ Henry Drury.	Norf.
Sʳ Lewis Stukeley.	
Sʳ Thomas Parris.	
Sʳ George Chowne.	Kent.
Sʳ Arthur Ackland.	Devon.
Sʳ Thomas Reynell.	,,
Sʳ Richard Verney.	
Sʳ William Barnes.	Kent.
Sʳ Robert Monson.	Linc.
Sʳ Henry Askewe.	
Sʳ Charles Hussey.	Linc.
Sʳ James Pitts.	Worc.
Sʳ William Bond.	
Sʳ Thomas Heneage.	Linc.
Sʳ Edmund Thorold.	
Sʳ Henry Boule.	
Sʳ Walter Lawson.	Westm'l'd.
Sʳ Edmund Montford.	Norf.
†Sʳ John Montford.	
Sʳ Thomas Lambert.	Norf.
Sʳ William Rigdon.	Linc.
Sʳ John Thornborough.	,,
Sʳ Francis Zouche (*Sowth*).	
Sʳ William Somervile.	Somerset.
Sʳ Nicholas Coote.	
Sʳ Henry Copinger.	Midd.
Sʳ Henry Blomer.	Glouc.
Sʳ Edward Thimblethorp.	Norf.
Sʳ Nicholas Lusher.	Surrey.
Sʳ Robert Philipps.	Somerset.
Sʳ Robert Hide.	Cambr.
Sʳ John Philipott.	Hants.
Sʳ Thomas Nevill.	Berks.
Sʳ Christopher Roper.	Kent.
Sʳ Robert Chichester.	Devon.
Sʳ Christopher Harte.	Kent.
Sʳ John Newdigate.	Beds.
Sʳ Edward Gorges.	Somerset.
Sʳ Martine Barnham.	Kent.
Sʳ William Dorrington.	Dorset.
Sʳ Edward Giles.	Devon.
Sʳ Richard Etherington.	
Sʳ Anthony Colepeper.	Sussex.
Sʳ Richard Cooper.	Surrey.
Sʳ John Granger.	Midd.
Sʳ William Reade.	,,
Sʳ Henry Rainsford.	Surrey.
Sʳ John Chamberlaine.	Oxon.
Sʳ Richard Leechford.	Kent.
Sʳ Tho. Septuans *al's* Harfleete.	Kent.
†Sʳ Thomas Dutton.	Chesh.
Sʳ Francis Dowse.	Somerset.

Sʳ Thomas Roberts.	Kent.
Sʳ Henry Williams.	
Sʳ Henry Bowyer.	London.
Sʳ Thomas Duckett.	Berks.
Sʳ Thomas Darnell.	Linc.
Sʳ Robert Ashbie.	Essex.
Sʳ Thomas Hartwell.	
Sʳ Edward Avery.	Glouc.
Sʳ George Sommers.	Dorset.
Sʳ Richard Portman.	Kent.
Sʳ Thomas Hunte.	Norf.
Sʳ John Wildegos.	Kent.
Sʳ George Peter.	Essex.
Sʳ Simon Steward.	Cambr.
Sʳ Nicholas Gascoigne.	Surrey.
Sʳ Bernard Whetston.	Linc.
Sʳ George Waldegrave.	Suff.
Sʳ Samuel Lennard.	
Sʳ William Barrowe.	Suff.
Sʳ John Wentworth.	„
Sʳ Guilford Slingesbie.	York.
Sʳ Richard Smith.	Kent.
Sʳ Arnold Lygon.	Worc.
Sʳ Edward Albanie.	
Sʳ George Yonge.	Somerset.
Sʳ John Skinner.	Essex.
Sʳ Conyers Darcie.	York.
Sʳ William Harman.	
Sʳ Anthony Browne.	Essex.
Sʳ Nicholas Poynty.	Glouc.
Sʳ Thomas Marvin.	
Sʳ Owen Oglethorpe.	Oxon.
Sʳ George Wilmore.	Notts.
Sʳ Gregory Wolmore.	Linc.
Sʳ George Buck.	„
Sʳ Thomas Conny.	„
Sʳ Thomas Barney.	Norf.
Sʳ Marke Steward.	Cambr.
Sʳ John Buck.	Worc.
Sʳ Richard Weston.	Surrey.
Sʳ Matthew Gamble.	Linc.
†Sʳ John Gamble.	„
Sʳ Henry (*Thomas*) May.	Sussex.

Sʳ Thomas Blennerhasset.	
Sʳ William Gresham.	
†Sʳ Leonard Hassell.	
Sʳ Francis Barneham.	Kent.
Sʳ George Fane.	„
Sʳ Anthony Roper.	„
Sʳ Henry Stoner.	Oxon.
Sʳ John Carowse.	
Sʳ Leonard Hide.	Hertf.
Sʳ Charles Morgan.	Heref.
Sʳ Rowland Morgan.	„
Sʳ .... Hartgill.	
Sʳ Thomas Hardres.	Kent.
Sʳ Richard Beaumont.	Leic.
Sʳ Thomas Harewood.	
Sʳ Henry Cholmeley.	Chesh.
Sʳ Edward Peacocke.	Midd.
Sʳ .... Wyatt.	
Sʳ Henry Williams.	
Sʳ Drew Drurie.	Norf.
Sʳ Richard Gresham.	„
Sʳ Henry Rolle, Sen.	Devon.
Sʳ Henry Rolle, Jun.	„
Sʳ John Hatcher.	
Sʳ William Blackston.	Durham.
Sʳ Thomas Mildmay.	Essex.
Sʳ Rowland Lacie.	Oxon.
Sʳ William Goodyeere.	Berks.
Sʳ Timothie Lowe.	Kent.
Sʳ Gideon Awnsham.	Midd.
Sʳ Thomas Skinner.	Essex.
Sʳ James Croft.	Heref.
Sʳ Will'm Worthington.	Essex.
Sʳ John Dorrington.	Notts.
Sʳ Anthony Denton.	Bucks.
Sʳ John Needham.	North'ton.
†Sʳ Thomas Wauton.	
Sʳ Edward Onley.	North'ton.
Sʳ Thomas Seymore.	Somerset.
Sʳ Henry Helmes.	Norf.
Sʳ William Leighton.	Salop.
Sʳ William Mynne.	Rutl.
Sʳ James Stonehouse.	London.

Sʳ **Mark Ibes.**	Essex.
Sʳ **Charles Pelverton.**	Norf.
Sʳ **James Thomas.**	Carnarvon.
Sʳ **Edward Capell.**	Norf.
†Sʳ **William Morris.**	Carnarvon.
Sʳ **Morris Griffith.**	
Sʳ **Andrew Ashley.**	
Sʳ **Edward Sulliard.**	Suff.
Sʳ **Benjamin Pellett.**	Sussex.
†Sʳ **Andrew Pascall.**	Essex.
Sʳ **Anthony Rowse.**	Cornw.
Sʳ **Edward Raleigh.**	Warw.
Sʳ **Penry Anderson.**	
Sʳ **Richard Edgcombe.**	Devon.
Sʳ **Richard Vaughan.**	Heref.
Sʳ **William Cobbe.**	Norf.
Sʳ **Francis Cleare.**	,,
Sʳ **George Forster.**	
Sʳ **James Calthorp.**	Norf.
Sʳ **Thomas Darrell.**	
Sʳ **Penry Disney.**	Linc.
Sʳ **William Slingesby.**	York.
Sʳ **John Sulliard.**	Suff.
Sʳ **William Gainsford.**	
Sʳ **Philip Coningsbie.**	Hertf.
Sʳ **George Cotton.**	Cambr.
Sʳ **Nicholas Smithe.**	
Sʳ **Edward Penruddocke.**	
Sʳ **William Morgan.**	
Sʳ **Rowland Morgan.**	
Sʳ **Edward Butler.**	Heref.
Sʳ **Penry Thinne.**	Wilts.
Sʳ **Richard Egerton.**	Staff.
Sʳ **Edward Ashford.**	
Sʳ **Raphe Gibbes.**	Linc.
Sʳ **John Gunter.**	
Sʳ **Penry Jenkins.**	
Sʳ **James Bourchier.**	
Sʳ **William Cray.**	Norf.
Sʳ **Robert Dinley.**	
Sʳ **George Selbie.**	
Sʳ **Daniell Norton.**	Hants.
Sʳ **George Gill.**	Hertf.

Sʳ **Clipesby Gawdie.**	Suff.
Sʳ **William Worthington.**	
Sʳ **William Withen.**	Kent.
Sʳ **Hugh Wyrrall.**	
Sʳ **Engleby Daniell.**	
Sʳ **Richard Saltonstall.**	London.
Sʳ **....Fitzwilliams.**	
Sʳ **Roger Porton.**	
Sʳ **Vincent Fulnetby.**	
Sʳ **Francis Egeoke.**	Worc.
Sʳ **.... Aneslie.**	
Sʳ **Philip Reighley.**	
Sʳ **William Harris.**	Essex.
Sʳ **Thomas Dallison.**	Linc.
Sʳ **John Dormer.**	Bucks.
Sʳ **Francis Tanfeild.**	Norf.
Sʳ **Weston Browne.**	
Sʳ **Thomas Standish.**	
Sʳ **George Belgrave.**	Linc.
Sʳ **Clement Spilman.**	Norf.
Sʳ **Edward Sheffeild.**	York.
Sʳ **Calthrope Parker.**	Suff.
†Sʳ **Edward Marbury.**	Linc.
†Sʳ **Richard Tracy.**	Glouc.
Sʳ **John Dauncie.**	Chesh.
Sʳ **John Powell.**	
Sʳ **Robert Edolfe.**	Kent.
Sʳ **David Woodroffe.**	
†Sʳ **Manwood Penruddock.**	Wilts.
†Sʳ **Thomas Harwell.**	Worc.
Sʳ **Richard Manwaring.**	Chesh.
Sʳ **Thomas Bigges.**	Worc.
Sʳ **Edward Blenerhasset.**	Norf.
Sʳ **Robert Welsh.**	Sussex.
Sʳ **George Snelling.**	,,
Sʳ **John Claxton.**	Durham.
Sʳ **John Oteley.**	
Sʳ **Thomas Bromley.**	
Sʳ **.... Rudyard.**	
Sʳ **.... Sherborne.**	
Sʳ **George Parkins.**	Kent.
†Sʳ **Ralph Maddison.**	,,
Sʳ **Edward Filmore.**	

†Sr Richard Wyber.	
S^r .... Buckmore.	
Sr Robert Stanford.	Staff.
Sr Robert Chester.	Hertf.
Sr Thomas Gresham.	Surrey.
Sr Henry Warner.	Suff.
Sr Thomas Hayes.	
Sr Henry Ashley.	Kent.
Sr Robert Winde.	Norf.
Sr Edward Clayborne.	
Sr Francis Curson.	Salop.
Sr William Reynard.	
Sr William Steede.	Kent.
Sr William Aprice.	Hunts.
Sr Walter Devereux.	
Sr William Hudson.	North'l'd.
Sr Edward Pinchon.	Dorset.
Sr Thomas Freake.	,,
Sr Thomas Prideaux.	Devon.
Sr Robert Miller.	Dorset.
Sr Fleetwood Dormer.	Bucks.
Sr Henry Maxey.	Essex.
Sr Henry Bokenham.	Norf.
Sr William Samuel.	
Sr John Acton.	Devon.
Sr Barthol. Samborne.	Som.
Sr Thomas Rockley.	York.
Sr Alexander Barlow.	Lanc.
Sr Roger Portington.	York.
Sr Henry Whiteheade.	Hants.
Sr William Thomas.	
Sr Reynold Scriven.	Salop.
Sr John Thorney.	
Sr Francis Hildesley.	York.
Sr Richard Pell.	Hants.
Sr Thomas Bartlett.	Glouc.
Sr Anthonie Irebie.	Linc.
Sr Anthony Pelham.	
Sr Thomas Southwell.	Norf.
Sr Edward Parham.	Linc.
Sr John Bentley.	Derby.
Sr Edward South (? Zouch).	Som.
Sr John Hubert.	Norf.

Sr James Bugges.	
Sr Thomas Fowler, Jun.	Midd.
Sr Charles Relke.	Linc.
Sr Walter Ayscough.	,,
Sr Thomas Ingham.	
Sr Richard Conquest.	Bedf.
Sr John Bynde.	
Sr Giles Howland.	London.
Sr Francis Ventris.	North'ton.
Sr Henry Bunbury.	Chester.
Sr Thomas Eden.	Suff.
Sr Henry James.	Kent.
†Sr Edward Awbrey.	Pemb.
†Sr William Awbrey.	,,
†Sr William Howson.	Linc.
Sr William Wraye.	Cornw.
Sr Richard Michelborne.	Sussex.
Sr Isaake Apleton.	Essex.
Sr Toby Chauncey.	North'ton.
Sr William Chauncey.	,,
Sr Thomas Varnam.	York.
Sr Christopher Hodson.	Bucks.
Sr John Locton.	
Sr Thomas Smithe.	
Sr John Pawlett.	Wilts.
Sr Charles Barneby.	York.
Sr Thomas Drewe.	Devon.
Sr George Southcote.	,,
Sr Robert Browne.	Dorset.
Sr Anthony Drury.	Norf.
Sr Richard Cocks.	
Sr Hugh Brawne.	London.
†Sr Henry Windham.	Norf.
Sr Robert Drurie.	Suff.
Sr John Prettiman.	,,
Sr William Barrowe.	
Sr William Pawlett.	Wilts.
Sr William Gray.	
Sr John Elmer (*Aylmer*).	Linc.
S^r .... Darcy.	
Sr Thomas Hanmer.	Flint.
Sr Jasper Moore.	
Sr William Crayford.	Kent.

Sʳ **Robert Cotton.** Hunts.
Sʳ **George Grenvile.** Cornw.
Sʳ **George Selbie** (*Gilby*). Linc.
Sʳ **Richard Fettiplace.** Berks.
Sʳ **Jeremy Horsey.** Bucks.
Sʳ **Francis Goldsmith.** Kent.
Sʳ **Thomas Elliott.** Surrey.
Sʳ **Robert Prideaux.** Devon.
Sʳ **Nicholas Stoddard.** Kent.
Sʳ **Robert Penruddocke.** Wilts.

At Whitehall, 24 of July :

Sʳ **Richard Browne.** Essex.
Sʳ **Marmaduke Darrell.** Bucks.
Sʳ **Raphe Weldon.** Kent.
Sʳ **Richard Cock** *alias* **Cookes.**
　　　　　　　　　　　　　Hertf.
Sʳ **Bartholomew Fowkes.** ,,

———

Knights of the Bathe made at the Coronac'on of K. James, 25 July, 1603 :

Sʳ **Philip Herbert**, after Earl of Pembroke.
Sʳ **Thomas Barkley**, son to Lord Barkley.
Sʳ **William Evers**, after Lord Evers of Malton.
Sʳ **George Wharton**, son to Lord Wharton.
Sʳ **Robert Riche**, after Earl of Warwick.
Sʳ **Robert Carr**, after Earl of Somersett.
Sʳ **John Egerton**, after Earl of Bridgewater.
Sʳ **Henry Compton**, brother to the Earl of Northampton.
Sʳ **John Erskinne**, son of the Earl of Marr.
Sʳ **William Anstruther.**
Sʳ **Patrick Murray**, Earl of Tullibarne.
Sʳ **James Haye**, Lord Yester.

Sʳ **John Lindsey.**
Sʳ **Richard Preston**, Earl of Desmond.
Sʳ **Oliver Cromwell** of Huntingdonshire.
Sʳ **Edward Stanley** of Lancashire.
Sʳ **William Herbert** of Montgomerie.
Sʳ **Fulke Grevile**, Lord Brooke.
Sʳ **Francis Fane**, after Earl of Westmoreland.
Sʳ **Robert Chichester** of Devonshire.
Sʳ **Robert Knowles** of Berkshire.
Sʳ **Jervase Clifton** of Nottinghamshire.
Sʳ **Francis Fortescue** of Buckinghamshire.
Sʳ **Richard Corbett** of Shropshire.
Sʳ **Edward Herbert**, Lord of Cherburye.
Sʳ **Thomas Langton** of Lancastershire.
Sʳ **William Pope** of Oxfordshire.
Sʳ **Arthur Hopton** of Somersettshire.
Sʳ **Charles Morrison** of Hartfordshire.
Sʳ **Francis Leigh** of Warwickshire.
Sʳ **Edward Montague** of Northamptonshire.
Sʳ **Edward Stanhope** of Yorkshire.
Sʳ **Peter Manwood** of Kent.
Sʳ **Robert Harley** of Herefordshire.
Sʳ **Thomas Strickland** of Yorkshire.
Sʳ **Christopher Hatton** of Northamptonshire.
Sʳ **Edward Griffin** of Northamptonshire.
Sʳ **Robert Bevile** of Huntingdonshire.

Sʳ **William Welby** of Lincolnshire.

Sʳ **John Mallett** of Somersettshire.

Sʳ **Walter Aston** of Staffordshire.

Sʳ **Henry Gawdye** of Essex.

Sʳ **Richard Musgrave** of Westmoreland.

Sʳ **John Stowell** of Somersettshire.

Sʳ **Richard Amcotes** of Lincolnshire.

Sʳ **Thomas Leedes** of Suffolke.

Sʳ **Thomas Jermin** of Norfolk.

Sʳ **Raphe Harre** of Hartford.

Sʳ **William Foster** of Barkshire.

Sʳ **George Speake** of Somersetshire.

Sʳ **George Hyde** of Berkshire.

Sʳ **Anthony Felton** of Suffolke.

Sʳ **William Browne** of Northamptonshire.

Sʳ **Thomas Wise** of Essex.

Sʳ **Robert Chamberlayne** of
Oxfordshire.

Sʳ **Anthony Palmer** of Suffolk
(Kent).

Sʳ **Edward Heron** of Lincolnshire.

Sʳ **Thomas Burton** of Surrey.

Sʳ **Robert Barker** of Suffolke.

Sʳ **William Norris** of Lancashire.

Sʳ **Edward Harwell** of Worcester-
shire.

Sʳ **Roger Bodenham** of Herefordshire.

At Whitehall, 26 of Julie :

Sʳ **Thomas Bennett.**	London.
Sʳ **Thomas Lowe.**	,,
Sʳ **Leonard Halliday.**	,,
Sʳ **John Watts.**	,,
Sʳ **Richard Goddard.**	,,
Sʳ **Henry Rowe.**	,,
Sʳ **Edward Holmden.**	,,
Sʳ **Robert Hampson.**	,,

Sʳ **Humphry Weld.**	London.
Sʳ **Thomas Cambell.**	,,
Sʳ **William Craven.**	,,
Sʳ **Henry Anderson.**	,,
Sʳ **William Glover.**	,,
Sʳ **James Pemberton.**	,,
Sʳ **John Swinerton.**	,,
Sʳ **William Romney.**	,,
Sʳ **Thomas Middleton.**	,,
Sʳ **Thomas Hayes.**	,,
Sʳ **William Cranley.**	,,

At Hampton Court, 5 August :

Sʳ **Thomas Beckingham.**	Essex.
Sʳ **James Murray.**	
Sʳ **John Ferou** (? Freame).	Lond.

At South Warnborough :

Sʳ **Richard White.**	Hants.

At Southampton :

Sʳ **John Geffrey.**	Worc.

At Winchester, — October :

Sʳ **James Ochterlony.**	
Sʳ **William Richardson.**	Worc.
Sʳ **James Lancaster.**	Hertf.

At Wilton, 8 of October :

Sʳ **James Lea.**	Devon.

At Wilton, — November :

Sʳ **Mounsier Doballe.**

At Woodstocke, 10 December :

Sʳ **Richard Cooke.**	Bucks.

At the Tower, the 14 of March :

Sʳ **Laurence Tanfeild.**	Oxon.
Sʳ **George Blount.**	
Sʳ **George Kempe.**	
Sʳ **Nicholas Browne.**	

Sᵣ Nicholas Tempest.	Kent.
Sᵣ William Browne.	Sussex.
Sᵣ Tym. Whittingham.	Bucks.
Sᵣ Anthony Browne.	Essex.
Sᵣ John Ashburnham.	Sussex.
Sᵣ Edward Bellingham.
Sᵣ George Yonge.
Sᵣ Hamond Strange.	Norf.
Sᵣ Gilbert Wakering.
Sᵣ Robert Dalington.
Sᵣ John Kerne.
Sᵣ Thomas Mullyns.
Sᵣ Alexander Temple.	Kent.
Sᵣ Thomas Worsman.	Linc.
Sᵣ William Bilsby.	„
Sᵣ John Boyse.	Kent.
Sᵣ John Williams.
Sᵣ Thomas Lewsey.
Sᵣ Justinian Lewen.	Kent.
Sᵣ Stephen Proctor.	York.
Sᵣ Christopher Martine.
Sᵣ John Collimore.	Kent.
Sᵣ John Conway.	Flint.

Sᵣ Edmond Ashfeild.	Bucks.
Sᵣ John Ackland.	Devon.
Sᵣ Thomas Stanley.	Derby.
Sᵣ William Webbe.	Wilts.
Sᵣ John Hampden.	Sussex.
Sᵣ Cavaliero Macott.	Kent.
Sᵣ Thomas Colepeper.	Sussex.
Sᵣ John Hall.	Hants.
Sᵣ Harbottell Grimston.	Suff.
Sᵣ Edward Mausfeild (? Mansell).
Sᵣ Richard Stroude.
Sᵣ Henrie St. Barbe.	Devon.
Sᵣ William Thorold.	Linc.
Sᵣ Clement Spillman.	Oxon.
Sᵣ Henry Constable.	York.
Sᵣ John Hedworth.	Durham.
Sᵣ John Webb.	Wilts.
Sᵣ Peter Garton.	Sussex.
Sᵣ Henry Jenkinson.
Sᵣ Francis Verney.
Sᵣ John Rodes.	Derby.
Sᵣ Francis Leake.	York.
Sᵣ Thomas Knevett.	Wilts.

1604.

At Royston, 1 of Aprill :

Sᵣ Richard Grobham.	Wilts.
Sᵣ George Gunter.	Sussex.
Sᵣ Richard Wide.	Cambr.
Sᵣ Charles Norwiche.	North'ton.
Sᵣ David Conningham.

At Whitehall, — Aprill :

Sᵣ Robert Brett.	Devon.
Sᵣ Thomas Neale.
Sᵣ George Coniers.	York.
Sᵣ Robert Dolman.	Berks.
Sᵣ Francis Fitch.
Sᵣ Thomas Bodley.
Sᵣ John Osborne.
Sᵣ Thomas Wiseman.	Essex.
Sᵣ Wilford Lawson.	Cambr.

Sᵣ Thomas Pigott.	Bucks.
Sᵣ Alexander Tutt.	Wilts.
Sᵣ Norton Knatchbull.	Kent.
Sᵣ Robert Yonge.	Somerset.
Sᵣ Michael Dormer.	Bucks.
Sᵣ Richard Greenway.	Sussex.
Sᵣ Thomas Dilkes.
Sᵣ George Throckmorton.	Glouc.
Sᵣ Richard Ingolsby.	Bucks.

†At S.W. Cornwall, 1 May :

†Sᵣ Bas. Brook (*but see* p. 140).

At Whitehall, 12 of Maie :

Sᵣ Francis Evers.	York.
Sᵣ Martine Colepeper.	Oxon.
Sᵣ Edward Boyes.	Kent.

Sᵣ Thomas Power. York.
Sᵣ Bartholomew Michell. Notts.
Sᵣ Mathew Bamfield. Devon.
Sᵣ Robert (*Roger*) Woodroffe.
Sᵣ Wolstan Dixie. Leic.
Sᵣ William Gratwicke.
Sᵣ Radulphus Carie.
Sᵣ John Bowyer. London.
Sᵣ Edward Crippes. Kent.
Sᵣ Edward Hext.
Sᵣ Nicholas Stalage. Sussex.

At Whitehall, 30 May :

Sᵣ Cuthbert Peper. Linc.
Sᵣ Robert Osborne. North'ton.
Sᵣ Gilbert Pryne. Wilts.
Sᵣ Waymond Carewe. Norf.
Sᵣ Roger Owen. Essex.
Sᵣ Gabriel Poyntz. London.
Sᵣ Richard Williamson. York.
Sᵣ John Jackson. „
Sᵣ William Gee. „
Sᵣ Hugh Bethell. „
Sᵣ Thomas Bland. „
Sᵣ Charles Egerton. Staff.
Sᵣ John Feron. York.
Sᵣ William Barwicke. Suff.

At Greenwich, 2 June :

Sᵣ John Speccott. Devon.

At Greenwich, 12 June :

Sᵣ Adam Sprakllnge. Kent.
Sᵣ George Smithe. Devon.
Sᵣ Thomas Honywood. Kent.
Sᵣ Richard Graves. Hertf.
Sᵣ Charles Hales. Kent.
Sᵣ John Whitbrooke. Salop.
Sᵣ John Clappoole.

At Layton, 16 June :

Sᵣ Richard Tracy (see p. 148).
Sᵣ William Stone. London.
Sᵣ David Wood.

At Whitehall, 29 June :

Sᵣ William Ford. Suff.

Sᵣ Robert Pitcham. Suff.
Sᵣ Henry Townsend. Salop.
Sᵣ Thomas Eden. Suff.

At Greenwich, 3 July :

Sᵣ William Hutton. Cumb.
Sᵣ William Hall. Kent.
Sᵣ Edm. Peckham (*Pelham*). Suss.

At Chatham, 4 July :

Sᵣ Francis Howard. Surrey.
Sᵣ Sackford Trevor. Flint.
Sᵣ Francis Cornewall. Salop.
Sᵣ George Curson.
Sᵣ Stephen Ridelsdon. York.
Sᵣ Roger Nevison. Kent.
Sᵣ Thomas Bludder. Essex.
Sᵣ John Lewis.
Sᵣ Walter Gore. Wilts.
Sᵣ William Lower. Cornw.
Sᵣ Peter Bucke. Kent.
Sᵣ Walter Chetwynd. Staff.
†Sᵣ Francis Cherry. London.
Sᵣ William Page. Kent.
†Sᵣ William Chetwynd. Staff.
Sᵣ William Horwood. „
Sᵣ Robert Jaudrell. Cambr.
Sᵣ John Scory.
Sᵣ William Pill. Kent.
Sᵣ Anthony Auger (Aucher). „
Sᵣ Jeremie Turner. Surrey.
Sᵣ Edward Bromley. Salop.
Sᵣ Edward Stoddert. Bucks.
Sᵣ John Rawlinson. Essex.
Sᵣ George Wright. Kent.

At Whitehall, 7 July :

Sᵣ Thomas Forster. Hertf.

At Whitehall, 8 July :

Sᵣ James Deane. London.
Sᵣ Roger Jones. „

At Whitehall, 10 July :

Sᵣ John Linwray. Som.
Sᵣ Edward Musgrave. Cumb.
Sᵣ Robert Johnson. Bucks.

x

At Otelands, 15 July :
   Sʳ **George Lynne.**
   Sʳ **Arthur Aston.**   • Staff.
   Sʳ **George Keere.**   Kaithnes.

At Whitehall, 21 July :
   Sʳ **Gilbert Hoghton.**   Lanc.
   Sʳ **Philip Howard.**   Hertf.
   Sʳ **Nathaniell Bacon.**   Norf.
   Sʳ **Martine Stutvill.**   Suff.
   Sʳ **James Bacon.**   „
   Sʳ **Henry Beningfeild.**   „

At Ware, in the King's Bedchamber,
   the 21 July :
   Sʳ **William Wiseman.**

At Theobald's :
   Sʳ **Michael Hicks.**   Essex.
   Sʳ **Stephen Powle.**   „
   Sʳ **Thomas Dacres.**   York.
   Sʳ **Christopher Pigott.**   Bucks.
   Sʳ **George Hayward.**   London.
   Sʳ **Arthur Dakins.**   York.
   Sʳ **Oliver Butler.**
   Sʳ **Edward Mansfeild.**

At Whitehall, 20 of August :
   Sʳ **Thomas Steward.**   Cambr.
   Sʳ **Thomas Thinne.**   Wilts.
   Sʳ **James Wingfeild.** North'ton.
   Sʳ **George Wauton.**   Hunts.
   Sʳ **Phillipp Cromwell.**   „
   Sʳ **Anthony Forrest.**   „

At Windsor, 21 September :
   Sʳ **Henry Savill.**   Bucks.

At Whitehall, 6 November :
   Sʳ **Richard Bulkleigh.**   Chesh.
   Sʳ **Humphry Orme.**   Linc.
   Sʳ **George Symons.**   Devon.
   Sʳ **Richard Hopton.**   Heref.
   Sʳ **William Hampden.**   Notts.
   Sʳ **John Drurie.**   Essex.

At Whitehall, 11 November :
   Sʳ **John Dawson** (? Dalston).

At Whitehall, 16 November :
   Sʳ **Francis Clare.**   Som.
   Sʳ **Clement Fisher.**   Warw.
   Sʳ **Walter Tichborne.**   Hants.

At Royston :
   Sʳ **Robert Jermine.**   Suff.

At Hinchinbroke, 24 November :
   Sʳ **Augustine Palgrave.**   Norf.

At Whitehall, 17 December :
   Sʳ **James Carnegye.**
   Sʳ **John Sharpe.**
   Sʳ **John Lermouth.**
   Sʳ **John Skinner.**
   Sʳ **Robert Lowreston.**

At Royston, 18 December :
   †Sʳ **Richard Hussey.**   Salop.
   †Sʳ **Isaac Jermy.**   Suff.

At Royston, 29 December :
   †Sʳ **Edward Bushell.**   Glouc.

At Royston, 17 January :
   Sʳ **John Rouse.**

At Royston, 18 January :
   Sʳ **John Fenwicke.**   North'l'd.

At Royston, 22 January :
   Sʳ **Thomas Muschampe.** Surrey.
   Sʳ **John Hewett.**   London.

At Hinchinbrooke, 30 January :
   Sʳ **Edward Ratcliffe.**   Cambr.

At Whitehall, 3 February :
   Sʳ **Thomas Snagge.**   Som.
   Sʳ **John Portman.**   „

At Whitehall, 14 February :
   Sʳ **Richard Welsh.**   Worc.

At Whitehall, 19 of February :
   Sʳ **Peter Yonge.**   Angus.
   Sʳ **Edward Dimmocke.**   Linc.

At Newmarket, 26 February :
   Sʳ **Richard Griffin.**   Warw.
   Sʳ **Francis Fulford.**   Devon,

At Newmarket, 27 February :
Sᵣ Thomas Fleming.   Hants.
Sᵣ Robert Crane.   Suff.
Sᵣ Thomas Huggon.   Norf.
Sᵣ Henry Colte.   Suff.

At Greenwich, 23 March :
Sᵣ Philip Cary.   Herts.
Sᵣ John Sheffeild.   York.
Sᵣ Henry Knolles.   Berks.
Sᵣ John Guevarra.   Linc.
Sᵣ John Eyre.   Wilts.
Sᵣ Thomas Rowe.   Glouc.

1605.

At Greenwich, 2 April :
Sᵣ William Herricke.   London.

At Greenwich, 9 April :
Sᵣ Thomas Cornwallis.   Norf.
Sᵣ John Seymore.   Som.
Sᵣ William Uvedale.   Hants.
Sᵣ George Aldridge.   Som.
Sᵣ Francis Calton.   Surrey.
Sᵣ George Ive.   Som.

At Greenwich, 14 April :
Sᵣ Clement Scudamore.   Lond.

At Greenwich, 22 April :
Sᵣ Christopher Clive.   Kent.
Sᵣ Thomas Glover.   London.

At Greenwich, 29 April :
Sᵣ Robert Banester.   Salop.

At Greenwich, 4 May :
Sᵣ John Selbie.   North'ton.
Sᵣ George Flower.   Devon.

At Richmond, 14 May :
Sᵣ Thomas Foliambe.   Derby.
Sᵣ Roger Dabill.   York.

At Richmond, 15 May :
Sᵣ Hugh Pollard.   Devon.
Sᵣ Hugh Montgomery.

At Richmond, 16 May :
Sᵣ Thomas Henley.   Kent.
Sᵣ John Bunkley.   Derby.

At Richmond, 17 May :
Sᵣ Robert Wright.   Surrey.

At Greenwich, 22 May :
Sᵣ John Meux.   Hants.
Sᵣ William Kirkham.   Devon.
Sᵣ John Fitz Williams.   Bedf.
Sᵣ Robert Payne.   Hunts.
Sᵣ Hugh Platt.   Midd.
Sᵣ Edward Cope.   North'ton.
Sᵣ Henry Mallory.   Cambr.
Sᵣ Rich. Hall (? Halsewell). Devon.
Sᵣ Anselm Wildegos.   Sussex.
Sᵣ John Lee (Leigh).   Surrey.
Sᵣ William Cobham.   Devon.
Sᵣ Ambrose Button.   Wilts.
Sᵣ Robert Albanie.   Surrey.

At Dartford, 25 May :
Sᵣ John Spilman.   London.

At Greenwich, 26 May :
Sᵣ David Murray.

At Greenwich, 29 May :
Sᵣ George Chaworth.   Derb.
Sᵣ Gilbert Knifton.   Notts.

At Whitehall, 5 July :
Sᵣ William Button.   Wilts.

At Eaton, 27 July :
Sᵣ George Periam.   Oxon.

At Oxford, 30 July :
Sᵣ William Sidley.   Kent.
Sᵣ George Rivers.   „

Upon the way, the same day :
Sᵣ George Tipping.   Oxon.

At Windesore :
Sᵣ Thomas Hoskins.   Surrey.
Sᵣ Peter Saltonstall.   London.

At Huntingdon :
Sᵣ Charles de Cambray.   France.

At Royston:
  Sᵣ **John Smith.**   Essex.
At Hinchinbrooke :
  Sᵣ **Thomas Hayward.**   Norf.
At Whitehall, 16 December:
  Sᵣ **Richard White.**   Hants.
  Sᵣ **Philip Stanhop.**   Leic.
  Sᵣ **Ambrose Grey.**   ,,
  Sᵣ **Francis Kettlebie.**

Knights of the Bathe made at the crea-
c'on of Charles, Duke of Yorke
(Twelfth Day 1605) :

Charles, Duke of Yorke.
Sᵣ **Rob. Bertie,** Lord Willoughbye.
Sᵣ **Will. Compton,** Lord Compton.
Sᵣ **Grey Bridges,** Lord Chandos.
Sᵣ **Francis Norris,** Lord Norris of
  Ricott.
Sᵣ **William Cecill,** after Earle of
  Salisburie.
Sᵣ **Allan Percye,** brother of the
  Earle of Northumberland.
Sᵣ **Francis Manners,** after Earle
  of Rutland.
Sᵣ **Henry Clifford,** sonne to the
  Earle of Cumberland.
Sᵣ **Thomas Somersett,** after Vi-
  cont Somerset of Cassell.
Sᵣ **Thomas Howard,** Earle of
  Barkshire.
Sᵣ **John Harrington,** of Exton.

At Whitehall, 23 January :
  Sᵣ **Nicholas de Mollin,** *Venetian
    Ambassador.*
At Whitehall, 2 February :
  Sᵣ **William Tate.**   North'ton.
  Sᵣ **Robert Purcell.**   Salop.

At Whitehall, 16 Februarie :
  Sᵣ **Timothy Hutton.**   York.
  Sᵣ **John Throgmorton.**   Linc.
At Whitehall, 18 March :
  Sᵣ **Henry Moody.**   Wilts.

1606.

At Whitehall, 14 May :
  Sᵣ **John Wynne.**   Carnarv.
  Sᵣ **John Digby.**   Warw.
At Theobald's :
  Sᵣ **Thomas Brooke.**   North'ton.
At Royston :
  Sᵣ **Henry Payton.**   Suff.
At Whitehall :
  Sᵣ **William Lisley.**   Hants.
At Greenwich, 23 May :
  Sᵣ **George Marbury.**   Linc.
  Sᵣ **Roger Moston.**   Flint.
At Greenwich, 25 May :
  Sᵣ **Henry Middleton.**   Chesh.
At Richmond, 19 June :
  Sᵣ **Thomas Dale.**   Surrey.
At Greenwich :
  Sᵣ **John Burlacy.**
At Greenwich, 13 July :
  Sᵣ **Thomas Wingfeild.**
At Otelands, 15 July :
  Sᵣ **Henric Baker.**   Kent.
  Sᵣ **Arthur Harris.**   Essex.
At Greenwich, 23 July :
  Sᵣ **John Jolles.**   Lond.
At Hampton Court, 17 August :
  Sᵣ **Thomas Glover,** Ambass.
  Sᵣ **Reignold Argall.**   Essex.
At Windsor :
  Sᵣ **Thomas Jordaine.**
At Farneham Castle :
  Sᵣ **George Erskine.**

At Beaulieu, 30 August :
Sr John Leigh. Hants.

At Hampton Court :
Sr William Oglander. Hants.
Sr George Philpot. „

At Newmarket, 17 October :
Sr William Hewett. London.

At Newmarket, 18 October :
Sr Nicholas Hayes. Hants.

At Newmarket, 19 October :
Sr Thomas Playter. Suff.
Sr Edward Lewkenor. „

At Royston :
Sr Henry Cheney. Cambr.
Sr John Leigh.

At Whitehall, 1 November :
Sr Edward Tarbocke. Lanc.

At Whitehall, 3 November :
Sr John Grey.
Sr William Wright. Suff.

At Richmond, 13 November :
Sr Nicholas Prideaux. Cornwall.

At Whitehall, 22 November :
Sr Robert Lovett. Bucks.

At Enfield, 5 December :
Sr John Fleming. Derb.

At Enfield, 6 December :
Sr Isaake Sidley. Kent.

At Whitehall, 11 December :
Sr George Fullwood. Derb.
Sr Anthony Hungerford. Glouc.

At Whitehall, 15 December :
Sr William Button. London.

At Whitehall, 23 December :
Sr Thomas Palmer. Kent.

At Whitehall, 3 January :
Sr George Fitz Williams. Linc.

At Royston, 20 January :
Sr John Milliscent. Cambr.

At Whitehall, 8 February :
Sr John Rives. Dorset.

At Whitehall, 15 February :
Sr James Altham. London.
Sr John (William) **Poole.** Devon.

At Whitehall, 17 February :
Sr Henry Oxendon. Kent.
Sr Augustine (*John*) **Nicholls.**

At Whitehall, 1 March :
Sr Thomas Bowles. Lanc.

At Whitehall, 2 March :
Sr Thomas Panton. Denbigh.

At Whitehall, 4 March :
Sr Thomas Crofton (? *Crompton*).
Sr William Feilding.

At Royston :
Sr (*Thomas*) **Tyrell.**

At Royston :
Sr Roger Millescent.
Sr George Fitzgeffery.

1607.

At Whitehall, 30 March :
Sr Francis Russell.
Sr Robert Butler.

At Newmarket, 13 April :
Sr Edward Vere.
Sr John Vere.

At Royston, 16 April :
Sr John Gibson.

At Whitehall, 29 April :
Sr George Wencage. Linc.
Sr Dudley Digges. Kent.
Sr George Wandesford. York.
Sr Thomas Chichley. Cambr.

At Whitehall, 3 May :
Sr Edward Gostwicke. Bedf.

At Whitehall, 14 May :
†**Sr Charles Egerton.**

At Whitehall, 24 May :
  S͏ʳ **John Bowyer.**

At Whitehall, 27 May :
  S͏ʳ **John Reyes.** York.
  S͏ʳ **Richard Conquest.** Bedf.

At Whitehall, 28 May :
  S͏ʳ **William Dillon.** Devon.
  S͏ʳ **Charles Wren.** York.

At Whitehall, 30 May :
  S͏ʳ **Henrie Leigh.** Midd.

At Whitehall, 4 June :
  S͏ʳ **John Stanhop.** Derb.

At Whitehall, 7 June :
  S͏ʳ **Christopher Harris.** Devon.

At Whitehall, 11 June :
  S͏ʳ **George Sayer.** Essex.

At Whitehall, 19 June :
  S͏ʳ **Henry Mildmay.** Essex.

At Whitehall, 29 June :
  S͏ʳ **Will'm Mewes** (Meux). Hants.
  S͏ʳ **George Dalton.** Westm'l'd.

At Richmond :
  S͏ʳ **Francis Freeman.** North'ton.
  †S͏ʳ **Ralph Wynwood,** *Sec. of State.*
  S͏ʳ **John Pethouse.** Norw.

At Whitehall, 5 July :
  S͏ʳ **John Doderidge.** London.
  S͏ʳ **Christopher Pickering.** York.
  S͏ʳ **Henry Frankland.**
  S͏ʳ **John Wilde.**
  S͏ʳ **George Paule.** Surrey.

At Greenwich, — July :
  S͏ʳ **John Rouse.** Worc.
  S͏ʳ **George Douglasse.** Scotus.
  S͏ʳ **John Butler.** Bedf.

At Greenwich, 10 July :
  S͏ʳ **Gervaise Price.** Wales.
  S͏ʳ **Vincent Corbett.** Salop.

At Greenwich, 19 July :
  S͏ʳ **Edward Walgrave.** Norf.

At Otelands, 20 July :
  S͏ʳ **Thomas Norton.** Kent.
  S͏ʳ **Edward Dennis.** Hants.

At Salisbury, 20 August :
  S͏ʳ **Edward Duke.** Kent.
  S͏ʳ **Thomas Jervis.** Hants.
  S͏ʳ **Bowyer Worsley.** ,,

At Salisbury, 26 August :
  †S͏ʳ **Edmond Udedall.** Wilts.

At Salisbury, 29 August :
  S͏ʳ **Edward Estcourt.** Salisb.
  S͏ʳ **Gabriell Pile.** Wilts.

At Windsor, 8 September :
  S͏ʳ **Edward Tyrell.**

At Theobald's, 23 September :
  S͏ʳ **Thomas Darrell.**

At Royston, — October :
  S͏ʳ **Henrie Lovell.** Essex.

At Royston, 5 October :
  S͏ʳ **Fabian Levens.**

At Royston, 7 October :
  S͏ʳ **Henry Clovall.**
  S͏ʳ **John Constable.** York.

At Whitehall, 8 November :
  S͏ʳ **Thomas Estcourt.** Glouc.

At Hampton Court, 17 November :
  S͏ʳ **William Danvers.** Wilts.

At Whitehall, 20 November :
  S͏ʳ **James Oxenden.** Kent.
  S͏ʳ **Thomas Wilford.** ,,

At Theobald's, 30 November :
  S͏ʳ **James** (*John*) **Colvile.** Norf.
  S͏ʳ **Raphe Shelton.** ,,

At Whitehall, 20 December :
  S͏ʳ **William Hamond.** Kent.
  S͏ʳ **Robert Cooke.** Lond.

At Hampton Court, 23 December :
  S͏ʳ **John Thompson.** Kent.
  S͏ʳ **Charles Bray.** Oxon.
  S͏ʳ **Robert Carre.** Scotus.

At Whitehall, 7 January: .
   Sʳ **William Powell.**   Wales.

At Theobald's, 15 January:
   Sʳ **Francis Clearke.**   Surrey.
   Sʳ **Edward Fisher.**   Berks.

At Whitehall, 25 January:
   Sʳ **Robert Lewknor.**   Suff.

At Whitehall, 1 February:
   Sʳ **Raphe Delaball.**   North'l'd.

At Whitehall, 11 February:
   Sʳ **John Davies.**   Lond.
   Sʳ **Molton Lambard.**   Kent.

At Whitehall, 15 February:
   Sʳ **Anthony Hungerford.**   Wilts.
   Sʳ **Henry Guntherope** (*Gontheraut*), *Teutonicus.*
   Sʳ **William Aclam.**   Essex.

At Newmarket, 5 March:
   Sʳ **Edward Lewkenor.**   Suff.
   Sʳ **Robert Quarles.**
   Sʳ **Thomas Seckford.**   Bedf.

1608.

At Newmarket, 25 March:
   Sʳ **John Crompton.**
   Sʳ **Stephen Leisures** (? Lescher).

At Whitehall, 26 March:
   Sʳ **William Fitche.**   Essex.
   Sʳ **John Isham.**   North'ton.

At Whitehall, 29 March:
   Sʳ **Edward Hussey.**

At Whitehall, 30 March:
   Sʳ **Anthony Barker.**
   Sʳ **Mervine Tuchett** (*alias Audley*).
   Sʳ **James Altham.**

At Newmarket, 8 April:
   Sʳ **Francis Harris.**

At Newmarket, 17 April:
   Sʳ **Edward Barrett.**   Essex.

At Whitehall, 26 April:
   Sʳ **Edward Lewis.**   Wales.

At Whitehall, 29 April:
   Sʳ **William Yonge.**   Berks.

At Whitehall, 30 April:
   Sʳ **Thomas Herne** (see 3 July 1603).   Norf.

At Whitehall, 2 May:
   Sʳ **Thomas Wotton.**   Kent.

At Whitehall, 7 May:
   Sʳ **William Harvey.**   Suff.

At Whitehall, 8 May:
   Sʳ **William Cutt.**   Cambr.
   Sʳ **Francis Swan.**   Kent.

At Whitehall, 13 May:
   †Sʳ **(Oliver) Pytt.**   Surrey.

At Whitehall, 15 May:
   Sʳ **John Stradling.**   Salop.
   Sʳ **Samuel Payton.**   Kent.

At Greenwich, 24 May:
   Sʳ **Thomas Holland.**   Norf.
   Sʳ **Rotheram Willoughby.**
   Sʳ **Anthony Pell.**

At Greenwich, 27 May:
   Sʳ **Everard Whitney.**   Heref.

At Greenwich, 29 May:
   Sʳ **George Goring.**   Sussex.

At Greenwich, 5 June:
   Sʳ **Thomas Hawkins.**   Kent.

At Greenwich, 7 June:
   Sʳ **John Browne.**   Essex.

At Greenwich, 13 June:
   Sʳ **Warham St. Leger.**   Kent.
   Sʳ **Richard Buller.**   Cornw.
   Sʳ **Alexander Hayes.**   *Scotus.*

At Greenwich, 19 June:
   Sʳ **Thomas Overburie.**   Glouc.

At Lamore in Bedf. (co. Hertf.):
   Sʳ **Henry Goodyeere.**

At Grafton (co. Northampton):
- Sr Charles Morden.
- Sr Richard Catchmay.
- Sr Thomas Rotheram. Bedf.

At Bletsoe, July:
- Sr Thomas Tresham. North'ton.
- Sr Alexander St. John. Bedf.
- Sr Anthony St. John. „

At Grafton:
- Sr William Sanders. North'ton.
- Sr Thomas Haselrigge. Leic.
- Sr Thomas Cheney. Bucks.

At Alderton, at Sr Thomas Haselrigg's, 4 August:
- Sr Henry Anderson. London.

At Holmby, 6 August:
- Sr Richard Harpur. Derb.

At Grafton, 19 August:
- Sr Richard Marwood. York.
- Sr Seymour Knightley. North'ton.
- Sr Edward Griffen. „
- Sr Lewis Watson. „
- Sr Thomas Butler.

At Windsor:
- Sr Edmund Lenthall.
- Sr Robert Lee.
- Sr Thomas Lee.

At Hampton Court:
- Sr William Bodenham.

At Hampton Court, 1 October:
- Sr Phillip Fairfax. York.

At Whitehall:
- Sr Justine Clarke.

At Whitehall, 1 November:
- Sr George Justinianus, *Venetian.*

At Royston:
- Sr Francis Heale. Som.
- Sr George Chaworth. York.
- Sr John Peyton. Suff.

At Whitehall, 7 November:
- Sr Charles Vaughan. Heref.

At Whitehall, 10 November:
- Sr John Molineux. Notts.

At Whitehall, 13 November:
- Sr Rowland Cotton. Salop.
- Sr William Swann. Kent.

At Whitehall, 2 January:
- Sr Francis Neale. Hants.

At Whitehall, 8 January:
- Sr Thomas Finch. Kent.

At Whitehall, 9 January:
- Sr Robert Brooke. London.

At Theobald's, 1 February:
- Sr Richard Burnaby. North'ton.
- Sr John Andrewes. Glouc.

At Whitehall, 2 February:
- Sr John St. John.
- Sr Peter Pettesworth.

At Whitehall, 7 February:
- Sr Henry Whettenhall. Kent.
- Sr William Webbe.
- Sr George Hunte. Suff.
- Sr Robert Dowglas. Scotl.

At Whitehall, 5 March:
- Sr John Davers. Glouc.

At Whitehall, 7 March:
- Sr William Cavendish. Derb.
- Sr Edmund Paston. Norf.
- Sr Humphry Baskerville. Heref.
- Sr William Maynard. Essex.
- Sr Leventhorpe Franke. „
- Sr Thomas Edolfe. Kent.
- Sr Henry Samborne. Oxon.
- Sr Thomas Aubrey. Heref.
- Sr James Bogg. Linc.

At Whitehall, 22 March:
- Sr George Beston. Lond.

1609.

At Whitehall, 30 March :

S^r 𝕳enry 𝕹evill.   Berks.

At Whitehall, 18 April :

S^r 𝕿heodore 𝕹ewton.   Som.

S^r 𝕵ohn 𝕮rooke.   Oxon.

At Whitehall, 27 April :

S^r 𝕿homas 𝕲ainsford.   Surrey.

S^r 𝖂illiam 𝕰rskine.   *Scotus.*

At Whitehall, 8 May :

S^r 𝕳enry 𝕭artlett.   Som.

At Greenwich, 23 May :

S^r 𝕬nthony 𝕮awdie.   Norf.

At Greenwich, 28 May :

S^r 𝕵ohn 𝕯enham.   Berks.

S^r 𝕱rancis 𝕬ungier.   Surrey.

At Whitehall, 2 June :

S^r 𝕵ohn 𝕭ourchier.   York.

At Greenwich, 24 June :

S^r 𝕵ohn 𝕮age.   Cambr.

S^r 𝕰dward 𝕾outhcott.

S^r 𝕬drian 𝕸anmaker. Middleb'g.

At Greenwich, 25 June :

S^r 𝕮ornelius 𝕳offeman. Antwerp.

At Whitehall, 26 June :

S^r 𝕽obert 𝕱isher.   Warw.

At Greenwich, 2 July :

S^r 𝕲eorge 𝕳ollis.

S^r 𝕿homas 𝕮ottele.   *Teutonicus.*

At Greenwich, 3 July :

S^r 𝕿homas 𝕳erne (see 30 April
1608).   Norf.

At Richmond, 5 July :

S^r 𝕰dward 𝕭ullocke.

At Whitehall, 7 July :

S^r 𝕵ohn 𝕽ing.   Ireland.

At Whitehall, 9 July :

S^r 𝕭rian 𝕮ave.   Leic.

At Whitehall, 10 July :

S^r 𝕿homas 𝕯elves.   Chesh.

At Whitehall, 19 July :

S^r 𝕳enry 𝕾kipwith.   Linc.

At Windsor, 23 July :

S^r 𝕳enry 𝕸inne.   Rutl.

S^r 𝕵ohn 𝕳ayward.   Salop.

At Salisbury :

S^r 𝕿homas 𝕿racie.

At Basing :

S^r 𝕬nthony 𝕸ayney.   Kent.

At Theobald's, 20 September :

S^r 𝖂illiam 𝕷ovelace.   Kent.

At Hampton Court, 3 October :

S^r 𝕳enry 𝕲ostry.

S^r 𝕵ohn 𝕷idcott.   Oxon.

S^r 𝕵ohn 𝕽idermister.

At Royston, 15 October :

S^r 𝕵ohn 𝕭lenerhassett.   Norf.

At Whitehall, 11 November :

S^r 𝕬nthony 𝕿errell.

At Royston :

S^r 𝕵ames 𝕳amilton.   *Scotus.*

At Theobald's, 27 November :

S^r 𝕳enry 𝕭owyer.

At Whitehall, 6 January :

S^r 𝖂illiam 𝕾t. 𝕮lere.

At Whitehall, 7 January :

S^r 𝕮harles 𝕵ones.

At Whitehall, 9 January :

S^r 𝖂illiam 𝕷ygon.   Worc.

S^r 𝕵ames 𝕬ltham.   Essex.

S^r 𝕳enry 𝕯abyes.

S^r 𝕵ohn 𝕳orton.   Chesh.

At Theobald's, 10 January :

S^r 𝕵ohn 𝕷unsford.   Sussex.

S^r 𝕲eorge 𝕱arewell.   Som.

At Royston, 16 January :

S^r 𝕳enry 𝕿ancred.   York.

S^r 𝕵ohn 𝕷aurence.   London.

At Whitehall, 25 February :

S^r 𝕰dmund 𝕯owse.   Hants.

Y

, 1610.

At Whitehall, 25 March :
Sr Edward Bromley.   Salop.

At Whitehall, 14 May :
Sr John Berke.
Sr Albert de Veer.
Sr Helias Oldenbarnebeld.
Sr Albert Joachimi.
(Ambassadors.)

Knights of the Bath at the creation of Henry, Prince of Wales, 4 June 1610.

Henry Vere, Earl of Oxenford.
George, Lord Gordon, of Scotland.
Henry, Lord Clifford.
Henry Radcliffe, son to the Earl of Sussex.
Edward Bourchier, after Earl of Bathe.
James, Lord Haye, Earl of Carlile.
James, Lord Erskinne, son to the Earl of Mar.
Thomas Windsore, after Lord Windsore.
Thomas, Lord Wentworth, after Earl of Cleveland.
Sr Charles Somersett, sonne to the Earle of Worcester.
Sr Edward Somersett, his brother.
Sr Francis Steward (Stuart), sonne to the Earle of Murray.
†Sr Thomas Ratcliff, son to the Earl of Surrey.
Sr Ferdinando Sutton, sonne to the Lord Dudley.
Sr Henry Carye, after Earle of Dover.
Sr Oliver St. John, Lord St. John.
Sr Gilbert Gerard, after Lord Gerard.

Sr Charles Stanhope, Lord Stanhope.
Sr William Stuart.
Sr Edward Bruce, Lord Kinlosse.
Sr Robert (William) Sidney, after Earle of Leycester.
Sr Mervin Touchett, after Lord Audley.
Sr Peregrine Bertie, Colonell.
Sr Henry Riche, after Earle of Holland.
Sr Edward Sheffield, Lord Sheffield.
Sr William Cavendish, after Viscount Mansfield.

At Whitehall, 25 June :
Sr Thomas Cesar.

At Windsor :
Sr Dudley Carleton.   Surrey.
S^r .... Murray.

At Whitehall, 7 January :
Sr Peter Osborne.
Sr Edward Verney.   Bucks.

At Whitehall, 8 January :
Sr William Sidney.   Kent.
Sr John Leedes.   Surrey.
Sr Richard Lea.   Salop.

At Hampton Court, 10 January :
Sr Richard Norton.   Hants.
Sr Thomas Brereton.   Chesh.

At Theobald's, 15 January :
Sr Francis Wortley.

At Whitehall, 22 January :
Sr Henry Croftes.

At Whitehall, 8 February :
Sr Richard Worsley.

At Whitehall, 10 February :
Sr Thomas Mewtas.
Sr Thomas Erskine.

Sᵣ Bernard Dewhurst (*Dias*).
Sᵣ Henry Ringsmill.

At Theobald's, 12 February:
Sᵣ Francis Prince. Salop.
Sᵣ William Spring. Suff.

At Newmarket, 16 February:
Sᵣ Henry Pallavicini. Cambr.
Sᵣ Charles Howard.

At Newmarket, 3 March:
Sᵣ Henry Vane. Kent.

1611.

At Newmarket, — March:
Sᵣ Robert Bell.

At Whitehall, 28 March:
Sᵣ Edward Peyto.

At Royston, 13 April:
Sᵣ John Steward.

At Whitehall, 24 April:
The Earl of Arundell, at which
time he was elected of the Garter.

At Whitehall, 25 April:
Sᵣ Thomas Wharton.

At Greenwich, 5 May:
The Venetian Ambassador.

At Otelands:
Sᵣ Richard Bingley.

At Bagshot, 1 September:
Sᵣ Lawrence Stoughton. Surrey.

At Whitehall, 1 November:
Sᵣ John Hobart. Norf.

At Whitehall, 10 November:
Sᵣ Gilbert Pickering. North'ton.
Sᵣ Edward Whorwood. Staff.
Sᵣ John Hunt. Leic.

At Royston, 6 December:
Sᵣ Thomas Wentworth. York.
Sᵣ Augustine Pethouse. Norf.

At Theobald's, 20 December:
Sᵣ Ferdinando Hebborne.
Sᵣ James Leveson. Kent.
Sᵣ Henry Lee.

At Whitehall, 16 March:
Sᵣ William (*Thomas*) Methold,
Chief Justice (*Baron*) of Ireland.

1612.

At Whitehall, 9 April:
Sᵣ Thomas Brudnell (created
Bart. 29 June 1611). North'ton.
Sᵣ Lewis Tresham (created Bart.
29 June 1611). North'ton.
Sᵣ John Shelley (created Bart.
22 May 1611). Sussex.

At Whitehall, 24 May:
Sᵣ Lyonell Talmache (created
Bart. 22 May 1611).
Sᵣ Thomas Spencer (created Bart.
29 June 1611).

At Whitehall, 3 June:
Sᵣ John Molineux (created Bart.
29 June 1611).
Sᵣ George Greisley (created Bart.
29 June 1611).
Sᵣ Thomas Puckering.

At Eltham, 5 June:
Sᵣ John Hackett.

At Whitehall, 7 June:
Sᵣ John Wray (created Bart.
13 August 1617).

In the progresse, 21 July:
Sᵣ Robert Sandie *alias* Napper
(created Bart. 25 Nov. 1612).

At Leicester, 19 August:
Sᵣ Edward Devereux (created
Bart. 25 Nov. 1612). Warw.

At Rycott (co. Oxford), 30 August:
Sᵣ Robert Eaton.

At Royston, 11 October :
  Sr **Charles Howard** (see p. 163).

At Whitehall, 15 November :
  Sr **Lionell Tallmache.**

At Theobald's, 10 January :
  Sr **Robert Knolles.**

At Newmarket, January :
  Sr **Humphry May.**   Sussex.
  Sr **Francis Leigh.**   Warw.
  Sr **Robert Wingfeild.**
  Sr **Edmund Wilde.**
  Sr **Edward Ayscough.**
  Sr **Joseph Killegrewe.**
  Sr **Edward Underhill.**   Warw.
  Sr **Nevill Poole.**

At Whitehall, 5 February :
  Sr **William Pordage.**   Kent.

At Royston, 21 March :
  Sr **Edward Altham.**
  Sr **William Tresham.** North'ton.
  Sr **John Woodward.**
  Sr **John Temple.**
  Sr **Roger James.**
  Sr **Edward Cockett.**   Norf.

At Theobald's, 22 March :
  Sr **Thomas Corney.**   London.

1613.

At Whitehall, 27 March :
  Sr **Richard Molineux.**

At Whitehall, 19 May :
  Sr **John Wynne.**   Carnarvon.
  Sr **Robert Houghton,** *the Judge.*

At Greenwich, 27 June :
  Sr **Henry Apleton** (created Bart.
    16 Jan. 1614).   Essex.

At Otelands, 4 July :
  Sr **Lyonell Cranfeild.**   London.

At Theobald's, 9 July :
  Sr **Arthur Ingram.**   London.

At Theobald's, 6 October :
  Sr **Charles Cæsar.**

At Royston, 23 October :
  Sr **Francis Seymor.**
  Sr **Henry Wardlaw.**   Scotus.
  Sr **Edward Baynton.**   Wilts.

At Royston, 25 October :
  Sr **Gerrard Herbert.**
  Sr **Thomas Billson.**

At Royston, 29 October :
  Sr **Humphry Lyne.**   Surrey.
  Sr **Robert Clarke.**

At Whitehall, 8 November :
  Sr **Henrie Yelverton.**   London.

At Theobald's, 12 November :
  Sr **Thomas Wrothe.**

At Royston, 13 November :
  Sr **William StewarD.**   Scotus.

At Royston, 19 November :
  Sr **William Uvedall.**

At Royston, — November :
  Sr **William Selbie.**   North'l'd.
  Sr **Thomas Brook.**   Leic.
  Sr **Robert Bell.**   Norf.
  Sr **Charles Gawdie.**   ,,
  Sr **Thomas Walsingham.** Kent.
  Sr **John Gill.**

At Theobald's, 14 December :
  Sr **Thomas TrencharD.**   Dorset.

At Theobald's, 15 December :
  Sr **Thomas Hewett.**   London.

At Royston, 18 January :
  Sr **Humphry Tufton.**   Kent.
  Sr **John Clavering.**

At Royston, 9 February :
  Sr **Michaell Everard.**

At Theobald's, 4 March :
  Sr **John Steede.**   Kent.
  Sr **William Clopton.**   Norf.

1614.

At Theobald's, 1 April :
Sᵣ Robert Darrell.   Kent.
Sᵣ Henry Robinson.

At Theobald's, 3 May :
Sᵣ Tymothy Thornhill.   Kent.

At Somerset House, 29 May :
Sᵣ Edward Rodney.

At Whitehall, 8 June :
Sᵣ Randall Crewe.

At Greenwich, 13 June :
Sᵣ John Merricke.
Sᵣ William Crofte (*Crosse*).

At Windsor, 7 July :
Sᵣ John Horner.   Som.

At the Rye in Hatfield B. Oak, 18 July :
Sᵣ James Scordicke.   *Belg.*

At Awdley Ende, 19 July :
Sᵣ Paule Bayning, Bar't (created 10 James I.).   London.

At Woodstock, 18 August :
Sᵣ Hen. Lee, Bar't (25 June 1611).

At Theobald's, 2 October :
Sᵣ John Franklin.   Midd.

At Whitehall, 7 November :
Sᵣ Lawrence Hyde, *the Queene's Attorney.*

At Newmarket, 20 November :
Sᵣ William Some.
Sᵣ John Reppington.   Warw.

At Whitehall, 31 December :
Sᵣ Edward Moseley.

At Newmarket, 19 January :
Sᵣ Dudley Norton.

At Newmarket, 30 January :
Sᵣ John Savage.

At Newmarket, 3 February :
Sᵣ Robert Anstrother.

At Theobald's, 15 February :
Sᵣ Robert Dillon.

At Whitehall, 26 February :
Sᵣ John Blagrave.
Sᵣ John Garrard.

At Theobald's, 2 March :
Sᵣ Edmund Wheeler.
Sᵣ Charles Noell.

At Newmarket, 17 March :
Sᵣ William Lampton.

At Newmarket, 19 March :
Sᵣ Nich. Claudius Foster.

At Royston, 21 March :
Sᵣ Thomas Gerrard.

At Theobald's, 23 March :
Sᵣ Thomas White.

1615.

At Oking, 30 March :
Sᵣ Robert Vernon, *the Avener.*

At Whitehall, 13 April :
Sᵣ Fulke Greville.
Sᵣ Edward Banister.
Sᵣ David Bafford.

At Somerset House, 24 April :
Sᵣ George Villers.   Leic.

At Theobald's, 25 April :
Sᵣ Thomas Lamplough.
Sᵣ John Offley.

At Newmarket :
Sᵣ Samuel Tryan.   London.

At Greenwich, 26 May :
Sᵣ Richard Carrell.

At Theobald's, 2 June :
Sᵣ Roger Manners.
Sᵣ Richard Newport.

At Theobald's, 3 June :
Sᵣ John Ashfeild.

At Greenwich, 10 June :
Sʳ Thomas Blakston.

At Greenwich, 13 June :   •
Sʳ Thomas Cave.   North'ton.

At Greenwich, 18 June :
Sʳ Henry Cowley.

At Greenwich, 22 June :
Sʳ William Elways.

At Wanstead, 22 June :
Sʳ Thomas Winne.
Sʳ William Zouche.

At Greenwich, 26 June :
Sʳ Thomas Elliott.

At Otelands, 2 July :
Sʳ William Lister.

At Havering, 13 July :
Sʳ Godfrey Rodes.

At Theobald's, 16 July :
Sʳ William Garway.

At Theobald's, 19 July :
Sʳ Henry Southwell.

At Whitehall, 21 July :
Sʳ Thomas Southwell.
Sʳ Thomas Smith.   Chesh.
Sʳ Barnaby Bryan.   Ireland.

At Bagshot, 22 July :
Sʳ Thomas Belley (? Bellew).

At Salisbury, 5 August :
Sʳ John Lambill.

At Lullworth, 15 August :
Sʳ John Fitz James.

At Broadlands, 27 August :
Sʳ John Richards.

At Tichborne, 29 August :
Sʳ Henry Clarke.
Sʳ John MacDowgall.   Scotus.

At Farnham, 31 August :
Sʳ John Dingley.

At Windsor, 7 September :
Sʳ Robert Naunton.

At Theobald's, 21 September :
Sʳ Francis Thorney.

At Royston, 6 October :
Sʳ George Marshall.

At Royston, 9 October :
Sʳ Patricke Murray.

At Royston, 14 October :
Sʳ William Harington.
Sʳ Edward Hinde.

At Theobald's, 31 October :
Sʳ Henry Crooke.

At Whitehall, 6 November :
Sʳ George Hastings.

At Newmarket, 4 December :
Sʳ William Brounker.
Sʳ Thomas (John) Leighton.

At Newmarket, 15 December :
Sʳ Alexander Moncrieff.

At Royston, 22 December :
Sʳ John Oglander.   Hants.

At Theobald's, 23 December :
Sʳ Robert Brooke.

At Theobald's, 22 January :
Sʳ Thomas Perient.
Sʳ Robert Leigh.
Sʳ Robert Offley.
Sʳ John Leigh.
Sʳ John Suckling.

At Newmarket, 27 February :
Sʳ Thomas Bland.

At Theobald's, 16 March :
Sʳ Giles Waterfleete.   } Belg.
Sʳ Cornelius Waterfleete. }

At Whitehall, 21 March :
Sʳ John Finett.

1616.

At Theobald's, 4 April :
S͏ʳ 𝔉rancis 𝔥enderson.   *Scotus.*

At Whitehall, 24 April :
S͏ʳ 𝔄nthony 𝔐arbury.

At Theobald's, 25 April :
S͏ʳ 𝔗homas 𝔯ydell.
S͏ʳ 𝔚alter 𝔖mithe.

At Thetford, 4 May :
S͏ʳ 𝔚alter 𝔈arle.

At Thetford, 8 May :
S͏ʳ 𝔥enry 𝔇oyley.

At Thetford, 9 May :
S͏ʳ 𝔈dmund 𝔊awsell.

At Newmarket, 14 May :
S͏ʳ 𝔖tephen 𝔅utler.

At Greenwich, 18 May :
S͏ʳ 𝔗homas 𝔠hamberlaine.

At Greenwich, 3 June :
S͏ʳ 𝔍ohn 𝔇ackombe.

At Theobald's, 6 June :
S͏ʳ 𝔈dward 𝔅ashe.
S͏ʳ 𝔗homas 𝔅rapthwaite.

At Alderm. Cockaine's House, 8 June:
S͏ʳ 𝔚illiam 𝔠ockaine.

At Theobald's, 15 June :
S͏ʳ 𝔊errard 𝔖ames.   London.
S͏ʳ 𝔍ohn 𝔅ennett.

At Greenwich, 16 June :
S͏ʳ 𝔗homas 𝔗ildesley.   Lanc.
S͏ʳ 𝔯ichard 𝔚ynne.   Carnarv.

At Whitehall, 20 June :
S͏ʳ 𝔥enry 𝔉inche.   Kent.
S͏ʳ 𝔠onor 𝔐acgwire.   Ireland.

At Greenwich, 26 June :
S͏ʳ 𝔯obert 𝔚iseman.   London.
S͏ʳ 𝔥enry 𝔉ox.

At Greenwich, 27 June :
S͏ʳ 𝔗heobald 𝔊orges.   Wilts.

At Greenwich, 28 June :
S͏ʳ 𝔓atricke 𝔉ox.   Ireland.

At Otelands, 30 June :
S͏ʳ 𝔍ohn 𝔙illers.   Leic.
S͏ʳ 𝔯obert 𝔊orges.

At Otelands, 2 July :
S͏ʳ 𝔍ohn 𝔖idley.   Kent.
S͏ʳ 𝔗homas 𝔚iseman.   Norf.

At Otelands, 3 July :
S͏ʳ 𝔊eorge 𝔖toughton.

At Otelands, 4 July :
S͏ʳ 𝔗homas 𝔐ildmay.

At Whitehall, 10 July :
†**S͏ʳ 𝔥umphrey 𝔐ildmay.**   Essex.

At Theobald's, 15 July :
S͏ʳ 𝔊eorge 𝔖mithe.   Heref.

At Theobald's, 16 July :
S͏ʳ 𝔥enry 𝔩eveston.   *Scotus.*
S͏ʳ 𝔠harles 𝔖nell.

At Theobald's, 17 July :
S͏ʳ 𝔖ebastian 𝔥arvey.   Lond.
S͏ʳ 𝔓eirce 𝔠rosbie.   Ireland.

At Theobald's, 18 July :
S͏ʳ 𝔈dward 𝔠hichester.
S͏ʳ 𝔉rancis 𝔄nnesley.
S͏ʳ 𝔄rthur 𝔅assett.
S͏ʳ 𝔈dw. 𝔠arington (*Dorrington*).
S͏ʳ 𝔚illiam 𝔉enton (*Henton*).

At Theobald's, 19 July :
S͏ʳ 𝔯ichard 𝔩umley.   Sussex.
S͏ʳ 𝔯obert 𝔩loyd.

At Royston, 28 July :
S͏ʳ 𝔄rchibald 𝔑apper.   *Scotus.*
S͏ʳ 𝔉rancis 𝔠ragge.
S͏ʳ 𝔖idney 𝔐ontague.   North'ton.

At Bletsoe, 26 July :
S͏ʳ 𝔗homas 𝔓atton.   Cambr.

At Burley, 6 August :
S͏ʳ 𝔉rancis 𝔅odenham.

At Dingley, 17 August :
  Sʳ **Thomas Cave.**   Leic.

At Holmeby, 18 August :   •
  Sʳ **James Ware.**   Som.

At Woodstocke, 28 August :
  Sʳ **John Burke.**   Ireland.
  Sʳ **Francis Rogers.**   Som.
  Sʳ **William Pope.**   Oxon.
  Sʳ **Richard Cecill.**   North'ton.

At Rycott, 29 August :
  Sʳ **John Denham.**

At Bysham, 30 August :
  Sʳ **Andrew Grey.**   *Scotus.*

At Windsor, 7 September :
  Sʳ **Edward Fillers.**   Leic.
  Sʳ **Henry Butler.**   Hertf.
  Sʳ **John Drake.**   Devon.

At Theobald's, 17 September :
  Sʳ **Giles Bridges.**   Glouc.

At Enfield, 23 September :
  Sʳ **Francis Coningsby.**   Hertf.
  Sʳ **William Plomer.**   Surrey.

At Hampton Court, 28 September :
  Sʳ **Richard St. George,** *Norroy.*

At Theobald's, 2 October :
  Sʳ **Robert Tracy.**   Glouc.

At Royston, 11 October :
  Sʳ **George Sexton.**

At Hinchinbrooke, 12 October :
  Sʳ **George Hamilton.**   *Scotus.*

—

Knights of the Bathe at the creac'on
of Charles, Prince of Wales, 3 Nov. :

James, Lord Maltravers.
Algernon, Lord Percy.
James, Lord Wriothesley.
Theophilus, Lord Clinton.
Edward Seymour, Lord Beau=
champ.
George, Lord Barkley.

John, Lord Mordant.
John, Lord Erskine.
Thomas, Viscount Fenton.
Sʳ **Henry Howard.**
Sʳ **Robert Howard.**
Sʳ **William Howard.**
Sʳ **Edward Howard.**
Sʳ **Edward Sackvile.**
Sʳ **William Seymour.**
Sʳ **Montague Bertie.**
Sʳ **William Stourton.**
Sʳ **William Parker.**
Sʳ **Dudley North.**
Sʳ **Spencer Compton.**
Sʳ **William Spencer.**
Sʳ **Rowland St. John.**
Sʳ **John Cavendish.**
Sʳ **Thomas Nevile.**
Sʳ **John Roper.**
Sʳ **John North.**
Sʳ **Henry Carye.**

At Whitehall, 5 November :
  Sʳ **William Segar,** *Garter.*
  Sʳ **Richard Roberts.**   Cornw.

At Theobald's, 12 November :
  Sʳ **George Newman.**   Kent.
  Sʳ **Charles Bowles.**

At Royston, 14 November :
  Sʳ **John Lenthall.**

At Newmarket, 18 November :
  Sʳ **Giles Mompeson.**   Wilts.

At Newmarket, 20 November :
  Sʳ **William Pelham.**

At Newmarket, 25 November :
  Sʳ **Moses Hill.**

At Newmarket, 28 November :
  Sʳ **Huntington Colbie.**   Suff.
  Sʳ **Ferd. Knightley.**   North'ton.

At Newmarket, 29 November :
  Sʳ **Robert Oxenbridge.**   Hants.

At Newmarket, 6 December :
Sr **Charles Grosse.**
Sr **Henry Radley.**
Sr **Samuel Somester.**
Sr **Richard Sandford.**

At Newmarket, 12 December :
Sr **Richard Waldron.**

At Newmarket, 14 December :
Sr **Patricke Monypenie.**

At Newmarket, 16 December :
Sr **George Lamplough.**
Sr **Thomas Wentworth.**

At Theobald's, 21 December :
Sr **Thomas Leigh.**

At Hampton Court, 16 January :
Sr **John Herbert.**
Sr **Henry Martin.**

At Theobald's, 31 January :
Sr **William Martin.**

At Theobald's, 1 February :
Sr **John Gresham.**

At Hampton Court, 8 February :
Sr **Owen Smith.**

At Whitehall, 10 February :
Sr **Thomas Middleton.**

At Whitehall, 16 February :
Sr **Francis Howard.**

At Theobald's, 19 February :
Sr .... **Neetens,** *a Dutchman.*

At Theobald's, 22 February :
Sr **Thomas Dacres.**
Sr **Thomas Norcliffe.**   York.

At Whitehall, 23 February :
Sr **Philip Cartwright.**

At Whitehall, 28 February :
Sr **John Smithe.**

At Theobald's, 1 March :
Sr **John Rowland.**
Sr **William Acclom.**

At Whitehall, 6 March :
Sr **Thomas Sabile.**

At Whitehall, 9 March :
Sr **John Leman,** *Lo. Maior.*

At Whitehall, 10 March :
Sr **George Blundell.**

At Whitehall, 12 March :
Sr **Robert Hatton.**
Sr **Thomas Fisher.**
Sr **John Wolstonholme.**
Sr **Francis Jones.**
Sr **Nicholas Salter.**
Sr **William Jones.**

At Whitehall, 14 March :
Sr **Rowland Egerton.**

At Theobald's, 16 March :
Sr **Thomas Coventrie.**
Sr **Philip Deckham** (?Dackombe).

At Theobald's, 17 March :
Sr **Francis Moore.**
Sr **James Poynes** (*Poyntz*).

These Knights following were made by his Majesty in his iourney into Scotland and backe againe, beginning at Royston 18 March 1616.

At Royston, 18 March :
Sr **Edward Fynes.**
Sr **Francis Swift.**

At Hinchinbrooke, 21 March :
Sr **Thomas Hutchinson.**   Notts.
Sr **William Byrd.**

1617.

At Burley-on-the-Hill, 26 March :
Sr **James Ebington.**   London.
Sr **Richard Conny.**   Rutl.

At Lincoln, 4 April :
Sr **Thomas Willoughbie.**
Sr **John Bucke.**   Linc.
Sr **Henry Britton.**   Surrey.
Sr **Will'm Willmer.**   North'ton.

z

At Newmarket, 7 April :
Sr George Peckham.   Derb.
Sr Henry Herbert, *a Captain.*

At York, 11 April :
Sr William Ellis.   Linc.
Sr William Ingram.
Sr William Sheffield.   York.
Sr William Hungate.   „
Sr Peter Middleton.   „
Sr John Hotham.   „
Sr Richard Darley.   „
Sr Walter Bethell.   „

At York, 12 April :
Sr Edwin Sandes.
Sr Ferdinando Leigh.

At York, 13 April :
Sr Rob. Askwith, *Lo. M. of York.*
Sr Richard Hutton, *Recorder.*

At York, 14 April :
Sr Richard Harper.   Derby.
Sr John Hippesley.
Sr William Bellasis.   Durham.

At York, 15 April :
Sr William Chater.   York.
Sr Thomas Ellis (*of Grantham*).
        Linc.
Sr George Reresby.   York.

At Ripon, 16 April :
Sr John Vavasor.   York.
Sr Michaell Warton.

At Auckland in Durham, 18 March
   (*April*) :
Sr John Stanhop.   York.
Sr Tho. Merrie, *Clerk Compt'ler.*

At Auckland, 19 April :
Sr Arthur Grey.   North'l'd.
Sr Marmaduke Wivell.   York.

At (*the Bishoprick*, 23), 24 April :
Sr George Tonge.   B'prick.
Sr William Blackston.   „
Sr Talbot Bowes.   „

Sr Raphe Coniers.   B'prick.
Sr Mathew Forster.   „
Sr John Calverley.   „
Sr William Wray.   „

At Newcastle, the same day :
Sr William Kennett.   Newcastle.

At Hexham, 1 May :
Sr Henry Babington.

At Newcastle, 4 May :
Sr Peter Riddell.   Newcastle.
Sr John Delavall.   „

At Chillingham, 9 May :
Sr Edmund Gray.

At Berwick, 11 May :
Sr Anthony Weldon, Clearke of
   the Kitchine.   Kent.

At Berwick, 12 of May :
S^r Wm. Muschamp.   North'l'd.

At Berwick, 13 May :
Sr Robert Jackson.   North'l'd.

At Lanark in Scotland, 29 May :
Sr William Fenwick.   North'l'd.

At Edinburgh, 8 June :
Sr Thomas Lake.   Midd.

At Edinburgh, 2 July :
Sr Roger Grey.   North'l'd.
Sr Thomas Savage.   Chesh.
Sr John Cæsar.

At   in Scotland, 17 July.
These following were Pentioners that
did attend the King's Maj'tie into
Scotland in that journey :
Sr Arthur Tirringham.
Sr Edward Goring.
Sr Raphe Sidenham.
Sr John Brand.
Sr Sanders Duncombe.
Sr Richard Greene (*Clark of their
Band*).
Sr Edward Fowler.
Sr Arnold Herbert,

Sᵣ **Henry Reene** (*Reve*).
Sᵣ **Thomas Eveline.**
Sᵣ **John Hales.**
Sᵣ **Wm. Fryer.**
Sᵣ **Edward Burnell.**
Sᵣ **Edward Gilborne.**
Sᵣ **John Farewell** (*Farmer*). Kent.

At Carlisle, 6 August : -

Sᵣ **Richard Fletcher.**   Cumb.
Sᵣ **Henry Blenco.**   „
Sᵣ **Wm. Musgrave.**   „

At Brome (Brougham) Castle, 8 Aug.:

Sᵣ **Francis Brandlyn.**   North'l'd.
Sᵣ **Henry Trotter.**   Ebor.
Sᵣ **William Thorold.**   „
Sᵣ **Thomas Hutton.**   „
Sᵣ **Chris. Dalston.**   Westm'l'd.
Sᵣ **Philip Mountney.**   York.
Sᵣ **George Bowes.**   B'prick.
Sᵣ .... **Dromond.**   *Scotus.*

At Kendall, 9 August :

Sᵣ **Henry Mildmay,** ⎱ Sewers to
Sᵣ **George Spencer,** ⎰ the King.
Sᵣ **Francis Knightley,** Cupbearer.

In the Parke, neere the E. of Cumberland's, the same day :
Sᵣ .... a Scotchman.

At Ashton, 11 August :

Sᵣ **Charles Garrett.**   Midd.
Sᵣ **Thomas Walmesley.**   Lanc.

At Houghton Tower, 18 August :

†Sᵣ **Arthur Lake.**   Midd.
†Sᵣ **Cecil Trafford.**   Lanc.

At Lathom, 20 August :

Sᵣ **William Massie.**   Lanc.
Sᵣ **Rob. Binlosse** (*Bendloes*).   „
Sᵣ (*Gilbert*) **Clifton.**   „
Sᵣ **John Talbot.**   „
Sᵣ **Gilbert Ireland.**   „
Sᵣ **Edward Osbaldeston.**   „

At Busey (Bewsey), 21 August :

Sᵣ **Thomas Ireland.**
Sᵣ **Lewis Pemberton.**   Hertf.

At Leigh, 23 August :

Sᵣ **George Calverly.**

At Vale Royal, 24 August :

Sᵣ **Henry Ley.**
Sᵣ **Richard Grosvenor.**   Chesh.

At Sᵣ John Done's house, 25 August :

Sᵣ **John Done.**
Sᵣ **Andrew Corbett.**   Salop.

At Nantwich, 26 August :

Sᵣ **Hugh Wrotesley.**   Chesh.
Sᵣ **William Owen** of Condover.
Sᵣ **John Davenport.**   Chesh.

At Gerards Bromley (co. Stafford), 28 August :

Sᵣ **Roger Puleston.**   Flint.
Sᵣ **Thomas Wolseley.**   Staff.
Sᵣ **Richard Lydall.**   Berks.

At the last bounds of the Shire :

Sᵣ **Henry Agard,** Sheriff of Derb.

At Ashby de la Zouche, 2 September :

Sᵣ **Walter Devereux** (*base brother to the Earl of Essex*).
Sᵣ **Mathew Sanders.**   Leic.
Sᵣ **John Ball.**   „
Sᵣ **William Hartop.**   „
Sᵣ **Francis Ashbie.**   Midd.
Sᵣ **Thomas Trentham.**   Staff.

At Coventry, 4 September :

Sᵣ **William Bowyer.**
Sᵣ **Henry Snelgrove.**
Sᵣ **Wm. Cade,** *Pensioner.* Hertf.
Sᵣ **John Bodley.**   Surrey.
Sᵣ **Fran. Crane,** *Sec. to the Prince.*

At Warwick, 5 September :

Sᵣ **William Burlacie.**   Berks.
Sᵣ **Humph. Ferrers.**   Warw.

At Compton, 6 September :

Sᵣ **William Marey.**   Warw.

Sʳ **Richard Samuell.** North'ton.
Sʳ **Henry Gibbes.** Warw.
Sʳ **William Somerville.** · „
Sʳ **Hercules Underhill.** „

At Woodstock, 10 September :
  Sʳ **Thomas Glemham.** Suff.
  Sʳ **Henry Rowe.** Midd.
  Sʳ **Thomas Waynman.** Oxon.

At Rycott, 11 September :
  Sʳ **Arthur Vincent.**
  Sʳ **Robert Dormer.** Oxon.
  Sʳ **John Colepeper.** Sussex.

At Windsor, 15 September :
  Sʳ **Raphe Freeman.** London.

At Hyde Park, the same day :
  Sʳ **Anth. Benn,** Recorder of Lond.

At Whitehall, 16 September :
  Sʳ **Alexander Denton.**

At Enfield, 23 September :
  Sʳ **Arthur Capell.** Hertf.

At Hampton Court, 29 September :
  Sʳ **Clement Edmonds.** North'ton.
  Sʳ **George Calvert.** York.
  Sʳ **Albert Morton.** Kent.
  (Clerks of the Counsell.)

At Whitehall, 1 October:
  Sʳ **Grevill Verney.**

At Theobald's, 3 October :
  Sʳ **Nicholas Rempe.** London.

At Hinchinbrooke, 22 October :
  Sʳ **Richard Ingolsbie.**

At Royston, 28 October :
  Sʳ **George Aylofe.** Essex.

At Whitehall, 8 November :
  Sʳ **John Killegrewe.**

At Hatton House, the same day :
  Sʳ **William Wythipole.**
  Sʳ **Nathaniel Riche.** London.

Sʳ **Francis Needham.**
Sʳ **Peter Chapman.**

At Theobald's, 11 November :
  Sʳ **John Wild.** Kent.

At Theobald's, 12 November :
  Sʳ **Edward Gresham.** Surrey.
  Sʳ **Thomas Porter** (*Parker*).
  Sʳ **Christopher Buckle.** Essex.
  Sʳ **Gabriel Dowse.** Hants.

At Newmarket, 17 November :
  Sʳ **Robert Digbie.**

At Newmarket, 27 November :
  Sʳ **William Fishe.**

At Newmarket, 3 December :
  Sʳ **Charles Hussey.**

At Newmarket, 6 December :
  Sʳ **Richard Saltingstall** (see 12 November 1618).

At Newmarket, 14 December :
  Sʳ **.... Skept,** Ambassador.

At Whitehall, 7 January :
  Sʳ **Richard Yonge.** London.

At Whitehall, 8 January:
  Sʳ **Richard Lucie.** Warw.

At Theobald's, 10 January :
  Sʳ **Edward Fleetwood.**
  Sʳ **Rowland Vaughan.**
  Sʳ **John Bingley.**

At Newmarket, 30 January :
  Sʳ **Francis Blundell.** Ireland.

At Newmarket, 3 February :
  Sʳ **Simon Norwich.**

At Newmarket, 7 February :
  Sʳ **Michael Longvile.**

At Newmarket, 8 February :
  Sʳ **Jasper Herbert.**

At Whitehall, 23 February :
  Sʳ **Henry Yelverton.**

At Theobald's, 25 February :
Sr **James Hales.**   Kent.

At Theobald's, 26 February :
Sr **Walter Scott.**

At Whitehall, 16 March :
Sr **Hugh Clotworthie.**   Devon.

At Hampton Court, 18 March :
Sr **Edward Broughton.**

At Okeing (Woking), 20 March :
Sr **Henry Manwaring.**   Surrey.

At Whitehall, 23 March :
Sr **Gabriel Lowe.**

1618.

At Whitehall, 25 March :
Sr **Edward Conway.**

At Theobald's, 28 March :
Sr **Henry Palmer.**   Kent.

At Whitehall, 30 March :
Sr **Benjamin Rudiard.**

At Whitehall, 3 April :
Sr **John Manwood.**

At Whitehall, 6 April :
Sr **Raphe Birkenshawe.** Ireland.

At Theobald's, 10 April :
Sr **Thomas Stepney.**
Sr **Thomas Garton.**

At Whitehall, 22 April :
Sr **Thomas Bludder.**
Sr **John Tracie.**

At Whitehall, 25 April :
Sr **William St. Leger.**

At Theobald's, 28 April :
Sr **James Reynolds.**

At Theobald's, 29 April :
Sr **William Russell.**

At Theobald's, 30 April :
Sr **Robert Jenkinson.**

At Whitehall, 4 May :
Sr **Thomas Hawkins.**   Kent.

At Whitehall, 6 May :
Sr **William Andrewes.**

At Whitehall, 9 May :
Sr **Mathew Boynton.**

At Whitehall, 10 May :
Sr **John Elliott.**

At Whitehall, 14 May :
Sr **Francis Beamont.**

At Theobald's, 20 May.
Sr **Henry Bosbile.**   Kent.

At Greenwich, 26 May :
Sr **Andrew Hume.**

At Greenwich, 31 May :
Sr **Geo. Bowles,** Lo. M. of Lond.

At Greenwich, 8 June :
Sr **Francis Weynman.**

At Theobald's, 16 June :
Sr **William Houghton** (*Halton*).
Sr **Roger North.**

At Greenwich, 22 June :
Sr **Francis Metcalfe.**

At Greenwich, 23 June :
Sr **William Ford.**

At Halsted, 25 June :
Sr **Thomas Watson.**   Kent.

At Greenwich, 26 June :
Sr **William Campion.**

At Greenwich, 29 June :
Sr **William Barnes.**

At Otelands, 30 June :
Sr **John Stepney.**

At Otelands, 4 July :
Sr **Edmund Scorie.**

At Windsor, 5 July :
Sr **Francis Ashley.**

At Windsor, 6 July :
  Sr **James Kirton.**
  Sr **Edward Morley.**

At Windsor, 7 July :
  Sr **Francis Wyatt.**

At Windsor, 8 July :
  Sr **Charles North.**

At Theobald's, 15 July :
  Sr **William Wendy.**
  Sr **John Price.**

At Whitehall, 20 July :
  Sr **Thomas Willson.**
  Sr **Edward Wardour.**
  Sr **Henry Spiller.**

At Woking (*Halsted*), 21 July :
  Sr **Charles Pleydell.**

At Bromham, 1 August :
  Sr **Rawlyn Bussey.**

At Salisbury, 10 August :
  Sr **George Wroughton.**
  Sr **Anthony Bugg.**

At Cranborne, 14 August :
  Sr **Hercules Pawlett.**

At Tichborne, 29 August :
  Sr **Thomas Timperley.**
  Sr **Benjamin Tichborne.**
  Sr **John Chapman.**

At Aldershot, 2 September :
  Sr **Richard Uvedale.**

At Whitehall, 22 September :
  Sr **John Smith.**

At Hampton Court, 30 September :
  Sr **William Drurie.**

At Whitehall, 1 October :
  Sr **Gregory Fenner.**

At Royston, 8 October :
  Sr **Thomas Clarke.**

At Theobald's, 31 October :
  Sr **Edward Stafford.**

At Whitehall, 3 November :
  Sr **Thomas Littleton.**

At Wycombe, 9 November :
  Sr **Edward Sulyard.**

At Theobald's, 11 November :
  Sr **Shilston Calmadie.**

At Theobald's, 12 November :
  Sr **Richard Saltingstall** (see
    3 Dec. 1617).
  Sr **George Ellis.**
  Sr **Robert Kempe.**

At Newmarket, 23 November :
  Sr **Benjamin Thornborough.**

At Newmarket, 24 November :
  Sr **George** (*Edward*) **Yardley.**
  Sr **Nathaniel Napper.**

At Newmarket, 30 November :
  Sr **Thomas Derham.**

At Newmarket, 1 December :
  Sr **John Hare.**

At Newmarket, 4 December :
  Sr **Philip Bedingfield.**

At Newmarket, 5 December :
  Sr **Robert Willoughbie.**

At Newmarket, 11 December :
  Sr **Francis Leigh.**

At Newmarket, 12 December :
  Sr **John Brewse.**

At Newmarket, 15 December :
  Sr **Nathaniel Barnardiston.**
  Sr **Stephen Soame.**

At Theobald's, 21 December :
  Sr **Francis Kynaston.**

At Whitehall, 1 January :
  Sr **Walter Hebeningham.**

At Whitehall, 2 January :
  Sr **Robert Mordaunt.**

At Theobald's, 8 January :
  Sr **Robert Baynard.**   Norf.

At Theobald's, 9 January:
Sᵣ **Francis Vibyan.**
Sᵣ **John Lane.**

At Newmarket, 21 January:
Sᵣ **Robert Lacie.**
Sᵣ **John Miller.**

At Newmarket, 22 January:
Sᵣ **Edward Dering.** Kent.

At Newmarket, 24 January:
Sᵣ **Robert Filmer.** Kent.

At Theobald's, 1 February:
Sᵣ **Thom. Polley** (*Polhill*). Kent.

At Whitehall, 2 February:
Sᵣ **Nicholas Fortescue.**
Sᵣ **John Osborne.**
Sᵣ **Francis Gofton.**
Sᵣ **Richard Sutton.**
Sᵣ **William Pitt.**

At Whitehall, 10 February:
Sᵣ **George Etherington.**
Sᵣ **George Morsey.**
Sᵣ **Robert Seymour.**
Sᵣ **Richard Wiseman.**

At Theobald's, 17 February:
Sᵣ **Thomas Musgrave.**
Sᵣ **Henry Roswell.**

At Newmarket, 26 February:
Sᵣ **Thomas Fleetwood.**

1619.

At Royston, 9 April:
Sᵣ **Isaake Wake.**

At Royston, 19 April:
Sᵣ **Henry Mervin.**
Sᵣ **John Jackson.**

At Royston, 20 April:
Sᵣ **Henry Hungate.**

At Theobald's, 24 April:
Sᵣ **Charles Rich.** Lond.

At Theobald's, 26 April:
Sᵣ **Robert Knolles.**

At Theobald's, 27 April:
Sᵣ **Peter Wrothe.** Kent.

At Theobald's, 10 May:
Sᵣ **John Wingfeild.**

At Greenwich, 18 May:
Sᵣ **Charles Chibborne.** Essex.
Sᵣ **John Walter.**
Sᵣ **John** (*Thomas*) **Trevor.** Lond.

At Greenwich, 21 May:
Sᵣ **Chris.** (*Charles*) **Parfleete.**
Kent.

At Greenwich, 24 May:
Sᵣ **Alexander Muncrife.** Scotus.

At Whitehall, 1 June:
Sᵣ **Nicholas Lower.**

At Whitehall, 8 June:
Sᵣ **Miles Sandes.**

At Greenwich, 9 June:
Sᵣ **John White.**

At Greenwich, 10 June:
Sᵣ **Joseph Mayes.**

At Greenwich, 11 June:
Sᵣ **Robert Bennett.**

At Greenwich, 13 June:
Sᵣ **Robert Gorges.**
Sᵣ **Sampson Darrell.**

At Wansted, 18 June:
Sᵣ **John Monywood.** Kent.

At Wansted, 22 June:
Sᵣ **Nicholas Fuller.**

At Greenwich, 24 June:
Sᵣ **Thomas Ridley.**

At Greenwich, 28 June:
Sᵣ **Charles Smith.**

At Wimbledon, 28 June:
Sᵣ **Samuel Rolles.**

At Greenwich, 29 June:
Sʳ James Wolveridge.
Sʳ Richard Moore.
Sʳ Eubule Thelwall.
Sʳ Robert Rich.

At Otelands, 1 July:
Sʳ Thomas Pinton.
Sʳ Baptist Jones.

At Windsor, 7 July:
Sʳ Thomas Trevor.
Sʳ Alexander Hume.
Sʳ John Powell.

At Windsor, 8 July:
Sʳ Robert Vaughan.

At Wanstead, 9 July:
Sʳ Edward Widnall.   Surrey.

At Theobald's, 13 July:
Sʳ John Cochre (Coker).
Sʳ Edmund Vanderduffin.
Sʳ Joachim Lynes.
Sʳ John Tunstall.   Surrey.

At Theobald's, 15 July:
Sʳ John Clarke.
Sʳ Edward Engham.   Kent.

At Theobald's, 19 July:
Sʳ Nicholas Trott.
Sʳ James Chisseline.
Sʳ George Crapford.
Sʳ William Parkhurst.   Kent.
Sʳ James St. Low.

At Royston, 21 July:
Sʳ Thomas Reade.

At Bletsoe, 24 July:
Sʳ Henry St. John.
Sʳ Beauchamp St. John.

At Ashby, 25 July:
Sʳ Cornelius Vancheline.

At Ashby, 27 July:
Sʳ Francis Browne.

At Rockingham Park, 28 July:
Sʳ Edward Watson.

At Kirkby, 29 July:
Sʳ William Beecher.
Sʳ Robert Charnocke.

At Beaver Castle, 3 August:
Sʳ Wm. Roberts, *Sheriff of Leic.*

At Beaver, 6 August:
Sʳ James Buchanan.   *Scotus.*

At Welbeck, 10 August:
Sʳ Sutton Conny.   Linc.
Sʳ Charles Cavendish.
Sʳ Edward Richardson.
Sʳ William Carnabie.

At Nottingham, 12 August:
Sʳ Raphe Hansbie.   Linc.
Sʳ John Ramsden.   Derby.

At Nottingham, 13 August:
Sʳ William Balfour.   *Scotus.*
Sʳ Thomas Barton.

At Tutbury, 17 August:
Sʳ Francis Cooke.
Sʳ William Powell.

In the fields in Staffordshire:
Sʳ Thomas Scrimshire, *Sheriff.*

At Tamworth, 12 August:
Sʳ Philip Eaton.

At Warwick, 21 August:
Sʳ Bartholomew Hales.   Warw.
Sʳ Richard Browne.

At Woodstock, 25 August:
Sʳ Hector Pawlett.

At Rycott, 27 August, in the fields:
Sʳ William Guise.
Sʳ Edward Fenner, *Sher. of Oxon.*
Sʳ Francis Duncombe. North'ton.
Sʳ John Catcher.   Lond.

At Windsor, 5 September:
Sʳ Anthony Thomas.   Lond.

At Theobald's, 19 September:
Sʳ Francis Nethersole.   Kent.

At Theobald's, 23 September :
Sr John Fowle. Kent.
Sr Thomas Colepeper. „

At Alderman Jaye's house, 23 Sept. :
Sr Thomas Moord. Salop.

At Whitehall, 23 September :
Sr Samuel Thwaites.

At Royston, — October :
Sr William Steward.

At Royston, 13 October :
Sr Edmund Skerne. Linc.

At Royston, 14 October :
Sr William Lewis.

At Hinchinbrook, 19 October :
Sr Henry Grimston. Kent.
Sr John Pickering.

At Whitehall, 3 November :
Sr George Hastings.

At Whitehall, 4 November :
Sr George (*Thomas*) Hughes.

At Whitehall, — November :
Sr John Bruen.
Sr Edward Lawrence.

At Greenwich, 8 November :
Sr Edward Vowell.
Sr Rich. (*John*) Carnshaw. Linc.

At Whitehall, 9 November :
Sr John Amy.
Sr James Hussey.
Sr John Hayward. Salop.
Sr John Michell. Surrey.
Sr Edward Lawley. Hertf.

At Theobald's, 10 November :
Sr William Reeves.
Sr John Thornhill. Kent.

At Theobald's, 11 November :
Sr John Bourchier.
Sr Richard Roberts.

At Whitehall, 2 March :
Sr George Sherley, Ch. J. Ireland.

1620.

At Theobald's, 1 April :
Sr Archibald Atcheson. *Scotus.*

At Hampton Court, 11 April :
Sr George (*Gra.*) Abercromie.

At Hampton Court, 15 April :
Sr Archibald Beton. *Scotus.*

At Whitehall, 19 April :
Sr Lewis Dive.

At Greenwich, 1 May :
Sr Allan Zouch. Greenwich.

At Greenwich, 13 May :
S^r . . . . Ramsey.

At Theobald's, 31 May :
Sr Henry Bellingham.

At Greenwich, 1 June :
Sr Roger Twisden.

At Theobald's, 18 June :
Sr Clipsbie Crewe.

At Otelands, 4 July :
Sr Daniell de Ligne.
Sr Anthony Hinton.

In the Progresse since the 5 July.
At . . . ., — August.
Sr Samuell Awbrey. Heref.

At . . . ., — September :
Sr Stafford Willmott. Heref.
Sr Andrew Boyd.
Sr Paule Pindar.
S^r (*John*) Heydon.

At . . . ., — October :
Sr Thomas Lambert.
Sr James Whitlocke.

At Theobald's, 5 November :
Sr Henry Stradling.
Sr William (*Henry*) Pelverton.
Sr David Watkins.

At Newmarket, — December :
Sr Francis Michell, since degraded
(*June* 1621).

A A

At Theobald's, — December :
(Sʳ 𝔄lex. 𝔑orton, Harl. MS. 6062.)
Sʳ 𝔊ilbert 𝔠ornwall.

At Whitehall in Christmas, 26 Dec. :
Sʳ 𝔠lem. 𝔠otterell, *Groome Porter.*
Sʳ 𝔓enry 𝔠arvell.

At Theobald's, 23 January :
Sʳ 𝔊ervaise 𝔓ollis.

At Whitehall, 28 January :
Sʳ 𝔕obert 𝔓eathe.

At Whitehall, 1 February :
Sʳ 𝔚illiam 𝔈lliott.

At Whitehall, 13 February :
Sʳ 𝔕ichard 𝔅rooke.

1621.

At Whitehall, 25 March :
Sʳ 𝔗homas 𝔕ichardson, *Speaker.*

At Whitehall, 2 April :
Sʳ 𝔓eter 𝔖cott.

At Whitehall, 8 April, the States of
the Low Countries sente to the
King as Ambassadors :
Sʳ 𝔍acob 𝔡e 𝔚ingerden.
Sʳ 𝔍o. 𝔠amerling.
Sʳ 𝔄lbertus 𝔖uche.
Sʳ 𝔄lbertus 𝔅ruyning.
Sʳ 𝔍acob 𝔡e 𝔖chott.
Sʳ 𝔉rederike 𝔡e 𝔉erber.
All sine feodo.

At Theobald's, 10 April :
Sʳ 𝔠harles 𝔚illiams.

At Whitehall, 24 April :
Sʳ 𝔏eonard 𝔅osvile.

At Theobald's, 11 May :
Sʳ 𝔚m. 𝔓all, Capt. in Ireland.

At Greenwich, 13 May :
Sʳ 𝔍ames 𝔅aylie.

At Greenwich, 16 May :
Sʳ 𝔉rancis 𝔊lanvile.

At Greenwich, 18 May :
Sʳ 𝔄lexander 𝔠haulke.
Sʳ 𝔕obert 𝔍oselyne.

At Greenwich, 23 May :
Sʳ 𝔄nthony 𝔓aselwood. X

At Theobald's, 31 May :
Sʳ 𝔚illiam 𝔑uce.

At Theobald's, 2 June :
Sʳ 𝔓eter 𝔓aye.
Sʳ 𝔓atrick 𝔓aye.

At Theobald's, 18 June :
Sʳ 𝔑icholas 𝔗empest.

At Wanstead, 22 June :
Sʳ 𝔗homas 𝔖pringett.

At Greenwich, 24 June :
Sʳ 𝔚illiam 𝔚hitmore.

At Windsor, 9 July :
Sʳ 𝔓enry 𝔠ampion.   Kent.

At Theobald's, 13 July :
Sʳ 𝔕obert 𝔓ye.

At Theobald's, 16 July :
Sʳ 𝔄rthur 𝔌ngram.
Sʳ 𝔗homas 𝔏evison.
Sʳ 𝔗homas 𝔈versfield.

At Royston, 19 July :
Sʳ 𝔍ohn 𝔉enner.
Sʳ 𝔕ichard 𝔕ogers.

At Ampthill, 21 July :
Sʳ 𝔚illiam 𝔠rawford.
Sʳ 𝔕obert 𝔠ooke.
Sʳ 𝔈dward 𝔖alter.

At Bletsoe, 24 July :
Sʳ 𝔉rancis 𝔖tanton.

At Castle Ashby, 26 July :
Sʳ 𝔍ohn 𝔏ambe.

At Burley-on-the-Hill, 4 August :
Sʳ 𝔄nthony 𝔠olly.

At Belvoir Castle, 6 August :
Sʳ 𝔈dward 𝔚ortley.
Sʳ 𝔗homas 𝔖avage.

At Tutbury, 19 August :
 Sr **Robert King.**

At Willenhall, 20 August :
 Sr **Henry Merry.**

At Tamworth, 21 August :
 Sr **Edmond Windesore.**

At Warwick, 22 August :
 Sr **Nicholas Overbury.**
 Sr **Edward Littleton.**

At Woodstock, 28 August :
 S^r (Richard) **Hawkesworth.**

At Esthamsted, 31 August :
 Sr **Richard Harrison.**

At Windsor, 9 September :
 Sr **Edward Leach.**

At Whitehall, 11 September :
 Sr **Maurice Berkley.**

At Theobald's, 18 September :
 Sr **Arthur Gorges.**

At Whitehall, 5 November :
 Sr **Peter Vanlore.**

At Theobald's, 9 November :
 Sr **Henry Bourchier.**

At Newmarket, 19 November :
 Sr **Alexander Colepeper.**

At Newmarket, 8 December :
 Sr **Thomas Liddell** (*Lydall*).

At Theobald's, 22 December :
 Sr **Thomas Farnfield.** Sussex.

At Whitehall, 31 December :
 Sr **Francis Godolphin.**

At Whitehall, 5 January :
 Sr **Thomas Stanley.**
 Sr **John Botiler.**

At Theobald's, 11 January :
 Sr **Tracy Smart.**

At Theobald's, 14 January :
 Sr **John Colepeper.** Kent.

At Theobald's, 17 January :
 Sr **William Washington.**

At Newmarket, 12 February :
 Sr **George Hayes.**

At Newmarket, 21 February :
 Sr **Thomas Barker.** Suff.

1622.

At Hampton Court, 6 April :
 Sr **Mathew Brand.**

At Whitehall, 7 April :
 Sr **Marmaduke Lloyd.**

At Theobald's, 13 April :
 Sr **Robert Sharpeigh.** Kent.

At Whitehall, 18 April :
 Sr **Thomas Gee.** Suff.

At Whitehall, 1 May :
 Sr **Henry Holcroft.**

At Whitehall, 14 May :
 Sr **Paule Bowle,** *a Dutchman.*

Knights made since his Mat^s direction to the Earle of Arundell, Earle Marshall, for recording theire names by Privie seale dated the 15 of May 1622, whereof all such are written with this Paragraph ¶ uppon them have brought certificates into the Office of the certaine tyme of theire Knighting, the rest have not :

At Whitehall, 22 May :
 ¶ Sr **Tho. Sherley** of Betlebrig.

At Greenwich, 31 May :
 Sr **William Courteen.**

At Whitehall, 5 June :
 Sr **Peter Moton.**

At Greenwich, 11 June :
 ¶ Sr **Jeromino** (*Sercomius*) **Lando,** the Venetian Ambassador.

At Whitehall, 12 June:
¶ Sr **Tho. Sackvile**, Gent. Usher.

At Greenwich, 16 June :
¶ Sr **Edw. Barkham**, *Lo. Maior.*

At Wanstead, 18 June :
¶ Sr **Francis Lower.** Cornw.

At Wanstead, 20 June :
¶ Sr **William Waller.** Kent.

At Rochester, 26 June :
¶ Sr **Samuel Argall.** Essex.

At Otelands, 3 July :
¶ Sr **William Sherrard.**

At Windsor, 10 July :
Sr **John Cowper.**

At Wanstead, 13 July :
Sr **John Prescott.**
Sr **Francis Ireland.**

At Wanstead, 14 July :
Sr **William Hobby.**

At Woodford-row, 14 July :
¶ Sr **Humphry Hanford,** Sheriff of London.

At Theobald's, 23 July :
¶ Sr **Richard Reynell.**

At Whitehall, 25 July:
¶ Sr **Thomas Holland.**

At Guildford, 27 July :
¶ Sr **Richard Weston.**
¶ Sr **Robert Spiller.**

At Windsor, 6 August :
Sr **John Meldrum.** Scotus.

At Eschampsted, 10 August :
Sr **Francis Englefeild.**

At Farnham, 11 August :
Sr **Humphry Style.** Kent.

At Holte, 12 August :
Sr **John Compton.**
Sr **Thomas Holmeden.**

At Windsor, 5 September :
¶ Sr **Thomas Greeve.**

At Windsor, 6 September :
Sr **Francis Byondy.** *Italicus.*

At Theobald's, 17 September :
¶ Sr **Thomas Villersdon.** Bedf.

At Royston, 21 October :
Sr **Charles Herbert.**

At Theobald's, 7 November :
Sr **Percy Herbert.**

At Royston, 8 November :
S^r .... **Ballantine.** *Scotus.*

At Newmarket, 16 November :
Sr **William Beecher,** *Clerke of the Counsell.*

At Newmarket, 3 December :
Sr **Giles Estcourte.**
Sr **William Master.**

At Newmarket, 9 December :
Sr **John Madeson.**

At Newmarket, 11 December :
Sr **Thomas Wauton.**

At Newmarket, 13 December :
Sr **Peter Beelen.**

At Theobald's, 18 December :
Sr **Walter Waller.**

At Theobald's, 1 February :
Sr **Henry Batten** (Batty).

At Theobald's, 12 February :
Sr **John Proude.** Kent.
Sr **William Monson.**

At Newmarket, 21 February :
Sr **John Washington.**

At Newmarket, 2 March :
Sr **John Meade.**

At Newmarket, 12 March :
Sr **Thomas Sanders.**

1623.

At Newmarket, 25 March:
Sr **John** (*Thomas*) **Simons.**

At Hampton Court, 27 April:
Sr **Richard Higham.**
Sr **William Dorrington.**

At Hampton Court, 29 April:
Sr **Charles Howard**, son to the Earl of Notts. Also 2 April 1624.

At Whitehall, 30 April:
Sr **Robert Napper.**

At Greenwich, 4 May:
Sr **John Burgh.**

At Greenwich, 6 May:
Sr **Christopher Pelverton.**

At Theobald's, 9 May:
Sr **Henry Audley.**

At Theobald's, 28 May:
S^r .... **Spott.**

At Greenwich, 2 June:
Sr **Paule Fleetwood.**

At Greenwich, 8 June:
Sr **Peter Proby**, *Lo. Maior.*

At Greenwich, 15 June:
Sr **Erasmus de la Fountain.**

At Greenwich, 22 June:
Sr **Heneage Finch.**   Kent.

At Greenwich, 29 June:
Sr **George Crooke.**

At Greenwich, 30 June:
Sr **Edward Barkham.**
Sr **Thomas Cannon.**

At Wanstead, 12 July:
Sr **Richard Lechford.**

At Theobald's, 18 July:
Sr **Thomas Cecill.**

At Whitehall, 21 July:
Sr **Randall Cranfeld.**

At Wilton, 7 August:
Sr **Henry Herbert**, *Master of the Revells.*

Sr **Thomas Morgan**, *Steward to the Lo. Chamb.*

At Salisbury, 8 August:
Sr **John Eveline.**
Sr **Thomas Sadler.**
Sr **Miles Hobart.**
Sr **Augustine Sotherton.**
Sr **William Browne.**

At Cranborne, 19 August:
Sr **John Bath.**

At Bewley, 26 August:
Sr **Charles Barkley.**

At Tichborne, 29 August:
Sr **Henry Tichborne.**

At Easthamsted, 3 September:
Sr **Bevis Thelwall.**

At Windsor, 7 September:
Sr **Richard Kingsmill.**

At Wansted, 12 September:
Sr **William Playter.**

At Hampton Court, 29 September:
Sr **Christopher Darcy.**

At Theobald's, 3 October:
Sr **Simon Harvie.**

At Theobald's, 4 October:
Sr **James Hillersdon.**
Sr **John Cotton**, *Serg.-at-Arms.*

At Royston, 20 October:
Sr **Thoby Mathew.**

At Hinchinbrooke, 28 October:
Sr **Kenelme Digby.**

At Theobald's, 12 November:
Sr **Christopher Wray.**   Kent.
Sr **Jasper Fowler.**   Dover.

At Whitehall, 17 November :
Sr Thom. Crewe, S. L. North'ton.
Sr Thomas (Hetley *vulgo*) Hadley,
S. L.   Hants.

At Theobald's, 22 November :
Sr Thomas Moston.   Flint.

At Theobald's, 1 December :
Sr Giles Overburie.   Glouc.
Sr John Stroude.   Dorset.

At Theobald's, 2 December :
Sr William Smithe.   Essex.

At Theobald's, 3 December :
Sr Thomas Longvile.   Berks.

At Whitehall, 7 December :
Sr John Bridgman.   Glou.

At Whitehall, 8 December :
Sr William Howard.

At Whitehall, 11 January :
Sr John Lloyde.   Merioneth.

At Theobald's, 15 January :
Sr Egremont Thinne.   Hertf.

At Whitehall, 12 February :
Sr Walter Covert.   Kent.

At Whitehall, 22 February :
Sr Peter Courteen.   Lond.

At Whitehall, 25 February :
Sr William Ingram.   York.

At Hampton Court, 26 February :
Sr Arthur Smith.   Glouc.

At Theobald's, 4 March :
Sr Thomas Croke.   Ireland.

At Woking, 11 March :
Sr Raphe Cantrell.   Suff.

At Whitehall, 23 March :
Sr William Dove.   North'ton.

1624.

At Theobald's, 9 April :
Sr Cornelius Baltis, of Tregose in
Zealand.

At Theobald's, 19 April :
Sr John Sanders.   Bedf.

At Greenwich, 7 May :
Sr Walter Roberts.   Kent.

At Greenwich, 18 May :
Sr William Roberts.   Midd.

At Greenwich, 19 May :
Sr John Brereton.   Chesh.

At Greenwich, 23 May :
Sr Martin Lumley, Lo. Maior of
Lond.

At Theobald's, 1 June :
Sr John Danvers.   North'ton.

At Theobald's, 2 June :
Sr Anthony Irebie.   Linc.
Sr Richard Onslowe.   Surrey.

At Greenwich, 10 June :
Sr Lucas Dillon.   Ireland.
Sr Thomas Conny.   Rutland.

At Greenwich, 13 June :
Sr Peter Gleene.   Norf.

At Theobald's, 15 June :
Sr John Huyon.   Zealand.
Sr William Cobbe.   Oxon.

At Greenwich, 17 June :
Sr Hum. Davenport, S.L. Chesh.

At Wanstead, 19 June :
Sr William Theckston.

At Wanstead, 23 June :
Sr Edward Hawley.   Som.

At Otelands, 2 July :
Sr George Winter.   Glouc.

At Windsor, 4 July :
Sr Robert Craford.   Kent.

At Windsor, 7 July :
Sr Raphe Done.   Chesh.

At Kensington, 9 July :
Sr Francis Bindlosse (*Benloss*).
                            Lanc.

At Wanstead, 10 July :
Sͬ 𝕿homas 𝖂thorwood.   Staff.
Sͬ 𝖂illiam 𝕷ee.   Glouc.

At Theobald's, 14 July :
Sͬ (*Theodore*) 𝕸ayherne, *the K.'s*
Phisitcon.
Sͬ 𝕿homas 𝕮onway, Sen.
Sͬ 𝕿homas 𝕮onway, Jun.

At Theobald's, 17 July :
Sͬ 𝕵ohn 𝕭orrough, *Norroy.*
Sͬ 𝕵ohn 𝕮oniers.   Worc.
Sͬ 𝕵acob 𝕬stley.   Norf.

At Royston, 18 July :
Sͬ 𝕻eter 𝕷e 𝕸aire.   London.

In the waie betweene Royston and
Houghton Lodge, 19 July :
Sͬ 𝕮lement 𝕾cudamore, *Sheriff of*
Hereford.

At Houghton Lodge, 20 July :
Sͬ 𝖂illiam 𝕱leetwood.
Sͬ 𝕾amuel 𝕷uke.   Bedf.

In the way betweene Bletsoc and Castle
Ashby, 23 July :
Sͬ 𝕱rancis 𝕮lerke, *Sheriff of Bedf.*

At Castle Ashby, 23 July :
Sͬ 𝖂ill'm 𝕷ytton.   Hertf.

At Burley, 3 August :
Sͬ 𝕲eorge 𝕼uarles.

At Belvoir, 4 August :
Sͬ 𝕵ohn 𝕭ale, *Sheriff of Leic.*

At Belvoir, 5 August :
Six Frenchmen K'ted.

At Belvoir, 7 August :
Sͬ 𝕵ohn 𝕾avage.
Sͬ 𝕵ohn 𝖂inter.
Sͬ 𝕵ohn 𝕿himbleby.   Linc.
Sͬ 𝕵ohn 𝕸edlicott.

At Newmarket, — August :
Sͬ 𝕿homas 𝕳artop.   Leic.

At Welbeck, 10 August :
Sͬ 𝕵ohn 𝕱itzherbert.   Norbury.
Sͬ 𝕵ohn 𝕱itzherbert.   Tissington.

At Nottingham, 14 August :
Sͬ 𝕸athew 𝕻almer, *Sher. of Notts.*

At Derby, 16 August :
Sͬ 𝕽oger 𝕮ooper.   Notts.

At Tutbury, 17 August :
Sͬ 𝕳enry 𝕽ainsford.   Glouc.

At Tutbury, 18 August :
Sͬ 𝕰dward 𝖁ernon.   Derby.
Sͬ 𝕲ervaise 𝕮utler.   York.

At Tamworth, 19 August :
Sͬ 𝕵ohn 𝕾keffington.   Leic.

At Bastwell Hall, 24 August :
Sͬ 𝕽ichard 𝕾keffington.   Staff.

At Warwick, 27 August :
Sͬ 𝕾imon 𝕬rcher.   Warw.

At Woodstock, — August :
Sͬ 𝕵ohn 𝕽epington.   Warw.
Sͬ 𝕽alph 𝕯utton.   Glouc.

At Sͬ Timothy Tirrell's Lodge in Ox-
fordshire, 29 August :
Sͬ 𝕿imothy 𝕿irrell.   Oxon.
Sͬ 𝕵ohn 𝕱ermer.   „

At Whitehall, 9 September :
Sͬ 𝕵ohn 𝕮ooke, Mͬ *of the requests.*
Hertf.

At Theobald's, 19 September :
Sͬ 𝕿homas 𝕱anshawe.   Essex.
𝕿he 𝖁enetian 𝕬mbassador.

At Enfield, 23 September :
Sͬ 𝖂illiam 𝕿erry.   London.

At Hampton Court, 26 September :
Sͬ 𝕬nthony 𝕭rowne.   Surrey.
Sͬ . . . .   *Scotus.*

At Theobald's, 3 October :
Sͬ 𝕰dward 𝕮arr, Sen.   Surrey.
Sͬ 𝕰dward 𝕮arr, Jun., Pencioner.

At Theobald's, 5 October :
Sᵣ Henry Gibb.

At Royston, 29 October :
Sᵣ William Gourdon.   *Scotus.*

At Chesterford Park, 6 November :
Sᵣ William Mason.   Bering.

At Newmarket, 19 November :
Sᵣ Phillipp Parker.   Suff.

At Newmarket, 2 December :
Sᵣ Alexander Brett.

At Royston, 19 December :
Sᵣ Robert Rokewood.   Suff.

At Whitehall, 25 December :
†Two Scotch Captains.

At Whitehall, 27 December :
Sᵣ Archibald Douglas.

At Whitehall, 29 December :
†Four Frenchmen.
Sᵣ . . . . Hudson.

At Whitehall, 30 December :
Sᵣ Robert Dallington.
Sᵣ James St. Clerc.

At Whitehall, 3 January :
Sᵣ . . . . Drummond, *a Scotchman.*

At Whitehall, 4 January :
Sᵣ . . . . Boswell, *a Scotchman.*
Sᵣ . . . . St. Cleer, *a Scotchman.*

At Whitehall, 29 January :
Sᵣ James Rey, *a Scotchman.*

At Newmarket, 8 February :
Sᵣ Thom. Swinborne.   North'l'd.

At Newmarket, 15 February :
Sᵣ Nicholas Martin.   Devon.

At Newmarket, 20 February :
Sᵣ Thomas Culpeper.   Kent.

At Chesterford Park, 24 February :
Sᵣ Roger Thornton.   Cambr.
Sᵣ Edmund Sawyer.   London.

At Royston, 28 February :
Sᵣ Richard Bettenson.   Essex.

Knightes made by our Most Gratious Soberaigne Lord

Kinge Charles

after his happie comeinge to the Croune, being proclaimed at London on the 27 of March 1625.

(Harl. MS. 6062 to the year 1636, compared with, and from that time continued from, Walkley's Catalogue, 1652, the differences in the latter being given in italics. A few additions are also made from 'Symonds's Diary.')

1625.

At Whitehall, 12 April :
Sᵣ Morris Abbott, Ald. of Lond.

At Whitehall, 22 April :
Sᵣ Abraham Williams.

At Whitehall, 25 April :
Sᵣ John Lisley.   *Scotus.*

At Whitehall, 30 April :
Sᵣ Paul Harris.   Salop.

At Whitehall, 6 May :
Sᵣ John Miller.   Dorset.
Sᵣ Charles Glemham.   Suff.

At Whitehall, 15 May :
Sᵣ Edward Clerk.   Berks.

At Whitehall, 20 May :
Sr **Edward Griffin.** North'ton.

At Whitehall, 24 May :
Sr **John Wales.**

At Whitehall, 26 May :
Sr **Walter Long.** Wilts.
Sr **Thurston Smith.** Suff.

At Canterbury, 15 June :
Sr **Christopher Man.** Kent.
Sr **John Finch.** „
Sr **Robert Ponywood.** „

At Whitehall, 18 June :
Sr **Thomas Power.** Newcastle.

At Whitehall, 20 June :
Sr **Hugh Stewkley.** Hants.

At Whitehall, 27 June :
Sr **Roger Martin.** Suff.

At Whitehall, 4 July :
Sr **William Gourdon.** Scotus.

At Hampton Court, 9 July :
Sr **Martin Lister.** London.

At Hampton Court, 10 July :
Sr **Maurice Drummond.** Scotus.

At Windsor, 16 July :
Sr **Nicholas Rowe.** Midd.

At Windsor, 17 July :
Sr **Richard Hutton.** York.

At Woking, 19 July :
Sr **Morgan Randall.** Surrey.

At Woodstock, 3 August :
Sr **Thomas Pope.** Oxon.

At Woodstock, 7 August :
Sr **Thomas Morton.** Kent.
Sr **Thomas York.** North'ton.

At Woodstock, 8 August :
Sr **Thomas Baker.**

At Woodstock, 15 August :
Sr **Henry Killigrew.**

At Holbury (Albury), 31 August :
Sr **William Sanderson.** Linc.
Sr **Thomas Brodrick.** Wilts.

At Tichfield, 4 September :
Sr **William Morley.**

At Tichfield, 12 September :
Sr **John Ashburnham.** Surrey.

At Burton, 13 September :
Sr **Edward Barkley.** Som.

At Ford, 15 September :
Sr **Richard Reynell.** Devon.
Sr **Thomas Reynell,** his brother.
Sr **John Younge.** Devon.

At Plymouth, 16 September :
Sr **John Chichester.** Devon.

At Plymouth, 17 September :
Sr **John Carew.** Devon.

At Saltcombe, 19 September :
Sr **James Bagg.** Devon.

At Plymouth, 23 September :
Sr **Thomas Thornix.**
Sr **William Courtney.**
Sr **Henry Sprye.**
Sr **Thomas** (*James*) **Scott.**
Sr **John** (*Sheffield*) **Clapham.**
Sr **John Gibson.**
Sr **Henry Willoughby.**
Sr **Thomas Loue** (*Love*).
Sr **Michael Gere.**
Sr **John Watts.**
Sr **John Chidley.**
(Sea-captains.)

At Ford, 26 September :
Sr **Simon Leech.** Devon.

At Hinton St. George, 27 September :
Sr **Francis Doddington.** Som.
Sr **Ampas** (*Thomas*) **Paulet.** „

At Wilton, 3 October :
Sr **Thomas Jay.** Wilts.

B B

At Salisbury, 18 October :
Sᵣ Robert Cock, Cl. of the Cheque.

At Hampton Court, 31 October : *
Sᵣ Richard Shelton (*Shelden*).

At Nonsuch, 3 November :
Sᵣ Edward Bathurst.   Kent.

At Hampton Court, 18 December :
Sᵣ Edward Bishop.   Sussex.

At Hampton Court, 27 December :
Sᵣ Edward Spencer.   Midd.

At Hampton Court, 29 December :
Sᵣ Peter Killigrew.

Knights of the Bath made at the Coronation of King Charles, 2 Feb. 1625 (Lansd. MS. 866) :

George Feilding, Visc. Callon.
James Stanley, Lord Strange.
Charles Cecil, Lo. Cranbourne.
Charles, Lo. Herbert, of Shurland.
Robert, Lord Riche.
James, Lord Maye.
Basill, Lord Feilding.
Oliver, Lord St. John.
Mildmay, Lord Fane.
Henry, Lord Pawlett.
Sᵣ Edward Montague.
Sᵣ John Carye.
Sᵣ Charles Howard.
Sᵣ William Howard.
Sᵣ Robert Stanley.
Sᵣ Pawlett St. John.
Sᵣ Francis Fane.
Sᵣ James Howard.
Sᵣ William Cavendish.
Sᵣ Thomas Wentworth.
Sᵣ William Pagett.
Sᵣ William Russell.
Sᵣ Henry Stanhope.
Sᵣ Richard Vaughan.
Sᵣ Christopher Nevill.
Sᵣ Roger Bertie.

Sᵣ Thomas Wharton.
Sᵣ St. John Blunt.
Sᵣ Rafe St. Clare.
Sᵣ John Maynard.
Sᵣ Francis Carew.
Sᵣ John Byron.
Sᵣ Roger Palmer.
Sᵣ Henry Edwards.
Sᵣ Rafe Hopton.
Sᵣ William Brooke.
Sᵣ Alexander Radcliffe.
Sᵣ Edward Scott.
Sᵣ Christopher Hatton.
Sᵣ Thomas Sackbile.
Sᵣ John Monson.
Sᵣ Peter Wentworth.
Sᵣ John Butler.
Sᵣ Edward Hungerford.
Sᵣ Richard Leveson.
Sᵣ Nathaniel Bacon.
Sᵣ Robert Poyntz.
Sᵣ Robert Bevile.
Sᵣ George Sands.
Sᵣ Thomas Smith.
Sᵣ Thomas Fanshawe.
Sᵣ Miles Hobart.
Sᵣ Henry Hart.
Sᵣ Francis Carew *alias* Throgmorton.
Sᵣ John Backhouse.
Sᵣ Mathew Mynnes.
Sᵣ John Stowell.
Sᵣ John Jennings.
Sᵣ Steven Harbye.

1626.

At Whitehall, 12 April :
Sᵣ Dodmer Cotton.

At Whitehall, 12 May :
Sᵣ William Killigrew.

At Whitehall, 29 May :
Sᵣ Hugh Cholmley.   York.

At Whitehall, 4 June:
Sʳ **John Gore,** late Lo. Maior.
Sʳ **Allen Cotton,** then Lo. Maior.

At Whitehall, 6 June:
Sʳ **John Lowther.**   Westm'l'd.

At Whitehall, 2 July:
Sʳ **Francis Harvey.**   North'ton.

At Otelands, 22 July:
Sʳ **John Underhill.**

At Hampton Court, 7 September:
Sʳ **William Gardner.**   Peckham.

At Whitehall, 27 November:
Sʳ **George Knevett,** a Captain.

At Whitehall, 30 November:
Sʳ **Thomas Punches,** Lieut.-Col.

At Whitehall, 2 December:
Sʳ **Thomas Richardson.**   Norf.

At Whitehall, 3 December:
Sʳ **Walter Leech.**   Devon.

At Whitehall, 6 December:
Sʳ **Symond D'Ewes.**   Suff.

At Whitehall, 9 December:
Sʳ **Miles Sandes.**   Cambr.

At Whitehall, 11 December:
Sʳ **Richard Minshull.**   Chesh.
Sʳ **Robert Sandes,** bro. of Sʳ M.

At Whitehall, 16 December:
Sʳ **Peter Wiche.**

At Whitehall, 28 January:
Sʳ **Nicholas Pyne.**   Wilts.

At Whitehall, 8 February:
Sʳ **Francis Clarke.**   Bucks.

At Whitehall, 4 February:
Sʳ **George Kempe.**   Essex.

At Newmarket, 4 March:
Sʳ **William Craven.**   Berks.

At Newmarket, 6 March:
Sʳ **William Carr.**

At Whitehall, 22 March:
Sʳ **William Alexander.**

1627.

At Whitehall, 9 April:
Sʳ **Christopher Trentham.**   Staff.

At Whitehall, 10 April:
Sʳ **Edward Sebright.**   Worc.

At Whitehall, 14 April:
Sʳ **Robert Berkeley.**   Worc.

At Whitehall, 19 April:
Sʳ **Thomas Rellion.**   *Scotus.*

At Whitehall, 21 April:
Sʳ **Toby Cage.**   Woodford Br.

At Whitehall, 29 April:
Sʳ **John Manbury.**   North'ton.
Sʳ **William Bryers.**   Bedf.

At Whitehall, 20 May:
Sʳ **Cuthbert Hacket,** Lo. Maior.

At Whitehall, 23 May:
Sʳ **Martin Snouckaert.**   Flanders.

At Portsmouth, 20 June:
Sʳ **Richard Grenvile.**
Sʳ **Thomas Fryer.**
Sʳ **William Cunningham.**
Sʳ **John Colcarne.**
(Captaynes going the voyage with the Duke of Buckingham.)

At Southwick, at Sʳ Daniel Norton's house, 22 June:
Sʳ **John Savill.**   York.

At Whitehall, 26 June:
Sʳ **Symon Harcourt,** *Captain.*

At Otelands, 7 July:
Sʳ **Robert Honywood,** servant to the Queen of Bohemia.

At Theobald's, 17 July :
Sᵣ **Drew Deane.**   Essex.

At Ampthill, 22 July :   •
Sᵣ **John** (George) **Russell.** Bedf.

At Ampthill, 23 July :
Sᵣ **Henry Austrey.**   Bedf.

At Alderton, 29 July :
Sᵣ **Lawrance Washington.**

At Birham, 7 August :
Sᵣ **Edward Clarke.**   Berks.

At Windsor, 22 July :
Sᵣ **Cope Dopley.**   Bucks.

These six Knights following were knighted by the King of Sweden at Darsen in Prussia in the midst of his whole Armie in the King's tent with great honor and triumph, the King himself at the same time receiving the Order of the Garter, being upon Sunday, 23 Sept. :

Sᵣ **Peter Yonge,** a Gent. Usher and dayly wayter to K. Charles.

Sᵣ **Henry St. George,** Richmond Herald.

    Being both sent with the Order of the Garter as Ambassadors from the King to the King of Sweden, who likewise gave to each of them as a perpetual badge of Honor the Arms of the Kingdom of Sweden to be joyned with their own Arms for ever.

Sᵣ **Palmer Ruthin.**   *Scotus.*
Sᵣ **Alexander Lesley.**   ,,
Sᵣ **Thomas Muschamp.**   ,,
Sᵣ **John Weborn,** Lief.-Colonel.

At Whitehall, 8 October :
Sᵣ **Henry Morison.**   Leic.

At Whitehall, 13 October :
Sᵣ **William Blake.**   Midd.
Sᵣ **Garret Rainsford.**

At Whitehall, 31 October :
Sᵣ **William Denny.**   Norw.

At Whitehall, 5 December :
Sᵣ **John Tufton,** son and heir to the Lord Tufton.

At Whitehall, 23 December :
Sᵣ **George Vernon.**   Chesh.

At Whitehall, 20 January :
Sᵣ **Francis Radcliffe.** Northumb.

At Whitehall, 27 January :
Sᵣ **John Tirrell.**   Essex.

At Whitehall, 1 February :
Sᵣ **Philip Oldfield.**   Chesh.

At Whitehall, 5 February :
Sᵣ **Marmaduke Langdale.** York.

At Whitehall, 15 February :
Sᵣ **White Beconshaw.**   Hants.

At Whitehall, 18 February :
Sᵣ **Basill Dixwell.**   Kent.

At Whitehall, 21 March (*Newmarket,* 21 March 1626) :
Sᵣ **William Peshall.**   Cannell.

1628.

At Whitehall, 1 April :
Sᵣ **Timothy Fetherstonhalgh.**
           Northumberland.

At Whitehall, 14 April :
Sᵣ **Thomas Lucas.**   Essex.

At Whitehall, 16 April :
Sᵣ **John Sackvile.**   Sussex.

At Whitehall, 29 April :
Sᵣ **Thomas Lewis.**   Glam.

At Whitehall, 12 May :
Sᵣ **Charles Crofts.**   Suff.

At Whitehall, 20 May :
Sᵣ **Edward Richards.**   Hants.

At Whitehall, 23 May:
Sr **John Lister.** York.

At Whitehall, 25 May:
Sr **Hugh Bethell.** York.

At Whitehall, 3 June:
Sr **Robert Morton.** Kent.

At Whitehall, 4 June:
Sr **Thomas Hope.** *Scotus.*

At Whitehall, 8 June:
Sr **Hugh Hammersley,** Lo. Maior.

At Whitehall, 29 June:
Sr **Thom. Garret** (*Gerrard*). Leic.
Sr **John Trelawny.** Cornw.
Sr **Walter Langdon.** „

At Whitehall, 11 July:
Sr **John Fotherby.** Kent.
Sr **John Rowth.** Derby.

At Whitehall, 12 July:
Sr **William Hopkins.** Warw.

At Beverley, 5 August:
Sr **John Mills.** Kent.

At Southwick, 16 August:
Sr **Thomas Esmond** (*Ismond*).
Sr **John Crosby.**
Sr **Robert Grise.**
Sr **John Harbye.**
Sr **John Langworth.**
(Captains.)

At Southwick, 1 September:
Sr **John Leigh.** Hants.

At Farnham, 8 September:
Sr **Cheney Culpeper.** Sussex.

At Windsor, 13 September:
Sr **John** (*George*) **Willmott.** Berks.

At Windsor, 24 September:
Sr **Lodovick ab Alteren.** Dutch.

At Windsor, 25 September:
Sr **Cornelius Fairmedow.** Midd.

At Whitehall, 29 October:
Sr **Edward Dodsworth.** York.

At Whitehall, 2 November:
Sr **William Salter.** Bucks.

At Whitehall, 8 November:
Sr **Gervaise Nevill.** Linc.

At Whitehall, 6 December:
Sr **William Catchmay.** Glouc.

At Whitehall, 10 December:
Sr **William Quadring.** Linc.
Sr **Thomas Culpeper.**

At Theobald's, 19 December:
Sr **William Ashton.** Bedf.
Sr **George Grymes.** Surrey.

At Whitehall, 23 December:
Sr **James Harrington.** Oxon.

At Whitehall, 1 January:
Sr **John Bracken.** Bedf.

At Whitehall, 6 January:
Sr **Cornelius Vermuyden.** York.

At Whitehall, 7 January:
Sr **John Haydon.** Norf.

At Whitehall, 9 January:
Sr **Richard Graham** (*Grimes*).

At Whitehall, 22 January:
Sr **William Rowe.** Essex.

At Whitehall, 27 January:
Sr **Richard Manley,** one of the Grene Cloth.

1629.

At Whitehall, 25 March:
Sr **Lewis Morgan,** son of Sr Tho.

At Whitehall, 26 April:
Sr **Gervais Elwes.** London.

At Whitehall, 28 April:
Sr **William Dalton.** York City.

At Greenwich, 3 May:
Sr **Robert Vere,** E. of Oxford.

At Greenwich, 31 May :
Sʳ **Richard Deane,** Lo. Mayor.
Sʳ **William Acton,** Sher. of Lond.

At Greenwich, 11 June :
Sʳ **William Calley.**   Wilts.
Sʳ .... **Balthezar.**   Dutch.

At Greenwich, 21 June :
Sʳ **Cranmer Harris.**   Essex.

At Greenwich, 28 June :
Sʳ **John Lee.**   Suff.

At Nonsuch, 6 July :
Sʳ **Hardres Waller.**   Kent.

At Greenwich, 19 July :
Sʳ **Anthony Mansel.**   Glam.

At Otelands, 11 August :
Sʳ **Popham Southcote.**   Devon.

At Bagshot, 14 August :
Sʳ **Henry Cason.**   Peyton, Suff.

At Barton, 18 August :
Sʳ **Charles Wiseman.**   Berks.

At Barton, 19 August :
Sʳ **John Pate.**   Berks.

At Woodstock, 23 August :
Sʳ **Nathaniel Brent,**
      LL.D. Merton Coll.

At Oxford, 27 August :
Sʳ **William Spencer.**   Oxon.

At Abingdon, 28 August :
Sʳ **William (*John*) Stonehouse.**
      Berks.

At Hampton Court, 24 September :
Sʳ **Thomas Worteley.**

At Hampton Court, 4 October :
Sʳ **Thomas Warner,** *Capt. Ship*
   Sᵗ *Christopher.*

At   , 16 October :
Sʳ **Christopher Abdy.**   Kent.

At Whitehall, 9 December :
Sʳ **Lennard Ferby.**   Kent.

Sʳ **Edmond Mondeford.**   Norf.
Sʳ **Thomas Gawdy.**   „

At   , 6 February :
Sʳ **Ferdinando Cary.**

At Whitehall, 11 February :
Sʳ **Thomas Thornborow.**   Worc.

At Whitehall, 12 February :
Sʳ **Nicholas Biron.**   Notts.

At Whitehall, 15 February :
Sʳ **Edmund Scott.**   Surrey.

At Whitehall, 21 February :
Sʳ **Ralph Blackstone.**   Durham.
Sʳ **Peter Paul Rubens.**

At Newmarket, 1 March :
Sʳ **Dudley Carleton.**   Oxon.

At Whitehall, 21 March :
Sʳ **George Herbert.**   Ireland.

1630.

At Somerset House, 17 April :
Sʳ **Lawrence de la Chambre.**
      Sussex.

At Whitehall, 25 April :
Sʳ **George Wentworth.**   York.

At Whitehall, 1 May :
Sʳ **John Morley.**   Sussex.

At Somerset House, 3 May :
Sʳ **Oliver Nicholas.**   Wilts.

At Whitehall, 23 May :
Sʳ **James Cambell,** Lo. Mayor.

At Whitehall, 25 May :
Sʳ **Philip Stapleton.**   York.

At Whitehall, 1 June :
Sʳ **William Fairfax.**   York.

At St. James's, 4 June :
Sʳ **Robert Needham.**

At Whitehall :
Sʳ **Philip Langton.**   Leic.

At St. James's, 7 June :
 Sʳ 𝕰𝖉𝖜𝖆𝖗𝖉 𝕸𝖆𝖘𝖙𝖊𝖗𝖘. Kent.

At Whitehall, 24 June :
 Sʳ 𝕿𝖍𝖔𝖒𝖆𝖘 𝕲𝖔𝖜𝖊𝖗. York.
 Sʳ 𝖂𝖎𝖑𝖑𝖎𝖆𝖒 𝕾𝖙𝖗𝖎𝖈𝖐𝖑𝖆𝖓𝖉. „

At Whitehall, 27 June :
 Sʳ 𝕮𝖊𝖗𝖛𝖆𝖘𝖊 𝕾𝖈𝖗𝖔𝖔𝖕𝖊. Linc.

At St. James's, 28 June :
 Sʳ 𝕰𝖉𝖜𝖆𝖗𝖉 𝕷𝖑𝖔𝖎𝖉. Montgomery.

At Whitehall, 29 June :
 Sʳ 𝖂𝖆𝖑𝖙𝖊𝖗 𝕻𝖞𝖊. Heref.

At St. James's, 29 June :
 𝕵𝖆𝖒𝖊𝖘 𝕾𝖙𝖚𝖆𝖗𝖙, 𝕯𝖚𝖐𝖊 𝖔𝖋 𝕷𝖊𝖓𝖓𝖔𝖝.

At Whitehall, 4 July :
 Sʳ 𝕾𝖙𝖊𝖕𝖍𝖊𝖓 𝕾𝖈𝖔𝖙𝖙. Kent.
 Sʳ 𝕵𝖔𝖍𝖓 𝕳𝖆𝖗𝖕𝖊𝖗. Derb.

At Whitehall, 7 July :
 Sʳ 𝕵𝖆𝖒𝖊𝖘 𝕸𝖔𝖓𝖙𝖌𝖔𝖒𝖊𝖗𝖞. *Scotus.*

At Theobald's, 9 July :
 Sʳ 𝕽𝖎𝖈𝖍𝖆𝖗𝖉 𝕻𝖎𝖌𝖔𝖙𝖙. Bucks.

At Nonsuch, 19 July :
 Sʳ 𝕿𝖍𝖔𝖒𝖆𝖘 𝕭𝖔𝖜𝖊𝖘. Essex.

At Moore Park, 14 September :
 Sʳ 𝕵𝖔𝖍𝖓 𝕿𝖍𝖔𝖗𝖔𝖜𝖌𝖔𝖔𝖉.

At Theobald's, 19 September :
 Sʳ 𝕵𝖔𝖍𝖓 𝕾𝖚𝖈𝖐𝖑𝖎𝖓𝖌, Witton (in
 Twickenham), co. Midd.

At Hampton Court, 27 September :
 Sʳ 𝕻𝖊𝖓𝖗𝖞 𝕯𝖆𝖜𝖙𝖗𝖊𝖞. Sussex.

At Windsor, 5 October :
 𝕵𝖆𝖒𝖊𝖘, 𝕸𝖆𝖗𝖖𝖚𝖊𝖘𝖘 𝕳𝖆𝖒𝖎𝖑𝖙𝖔𝖓.

At Hampton Court, 16 October :
 Sʳ 𝕿𝖍𝖔𝖒𝖆𝖘 𝕮𝖆𝖗𝖑𝖙𝖔𝖓. Cumb.
 Sʳ 𝕱𝖗𝖊𝖉𝖊𝖗𝖎𝖈𝖐 𝕮𝖔𝖗𝖓𝖜𝖆𝖑𝖑𝖎𝖘. Suff.
 Sʳ 𝖂𝖆𝖑𝖙𝖊𝖗 𝕬𝖑𝖊𝖝𝖆𝖓𝖉𝖊𝖗. Sᵗ James's.

At Whitehall, 27 September :
 Sʳ 𝕻𝖊𝖓𝖗𝖞 𝕬𝖙𝖐𝖎𝖓𝖘. London.

At Theobald's, 13 January :
 Sʳ 𝕿𝖍𝖔𝖒𝖆𝖘 𝕾𝖜𝖆𝖓. Kent.

At Whitehall, 15 February :
 Sʳ 𝕬𝖗𝖙𝖍𝖚𝖗 𝕽𝖔𝖇𝖎𝖓𝖘𝖔𝖓. York.

1631.

At Whitehall, 25 April :
 Sʳ 𝕸𝖆𝖗𝖙𝖎𝖓 𝕭𝖆𝖗𝖓𝖍𝖆𝖒. Kent.

At Greenwich, 21 May :
 Sʳ 𝕵𝖆𝖒𝖊𝖘 𝖂𝖊𝖘𝖙𝖔𝖓. Cambr.

At Greenwich, 5 June :
 Sʳ 𝕽𝖔𝖇𝖊𝖗𝖙 𝕯𝖚𝖈𝖞, 𝕭𝖆𝖗𝖙., Lo. Mayor.

At St. James's, 12 June :
 Sʳ 𝕵𝖔𝖍𝖓 𝕭𝖆𝖓𝖐𝖘. Gray's Inn.
 Sʳ 𝕽𝖔𝖇𝖊𝖗𝖙 𝕻𝖊𝖑𝖛𝖊𝖗𝖙𝖔𝖓.

At Hampton Court, 13 October :
 Sʳ 𝖂𝖎𝖑𝖑𝖎𝖆𝖒 𝕻𝖔𝖑𝖊𝖞. Suff.

At St. James's, 30 October :
 Sʳ 𝕵𝖔𝖍𝖓 𝕮𝖆𝖘𝖜𝖊𝖑𝖑, a Captain with
 the King of Sweden.

At St. James's, 21 November :
 Sʳ 𝕰𝖉𝖜𝖆𝖗𝖉 𝕻𝖔𝖜𝖊𝖑𝖑, 𝕭𝖆𝖗𝖙.

At , 27 November :
 Sʳ 𝕿𝖍𝖔𝖒𝖆𝖘 𝖂𝖎𝖓𝖉𝖍𝖆𝖒. Som.

At St. James's, 6 February :
 𝕿𝖍𝖊 𝖁𝖊𝖓𝖊𝖙𝖎𝖆𝖓 𝕬𝖒𝖇𝖆𝖘𝖘𝖆𝖉𝖔𝖗.

At Newmarket, 18 March :
 Sʳ 𝖂𝖎𝖑𝖑𝖎𝖆𝖒 𝖂𝖎𝖉𝖉𝖗𝖎𝖓𝖌𝖙𝖔𝖓.
  Northumberland.

At Theobald's, 22 March :
 Sʳ 𝕲𝖊𝖔𝖗𝖌𝖊 𝕯𝖊𝖛𝖊𝖗𝖊𝖚𝖝. Warw.

1632.

At Whitehall, 30 April :
 Sʳ 𝕱𝖗𝖆𝖓𝖈𝖎𝖘 𝕬𝖘𝖙𝖑𝖊𝖞. Warw.

At Whitehall, 6 May :
 Sʳ 𝕵𝖔𝖍𝖓 𝕾𝖔𝖒𝖊𝖗𝖘𝖊𝖙. Glouc.

At Greenwich, 23 May :
Sᵣ **Richard Prince.**   Salop.

At Greenwich, 27 May :   •
Sᵣ **George Whitmore,** Lo. Mayor.

At Greenwich, 3 June :
Sᵣ **George Fleetwood,** Col. to the King of Sweden.

At Greenwich, 6 June :
Sᵣ **George Carnegie.**   Scotus.

At Greenwich, 18 June :
Sᵣ **Francis Windebank.**

At Theobald's, 22 June :
Sᵣ **Francis Rainsford.**

At Otelands, 2 July :
Sᵣ **James Carmichael.**   Scotus.

At Greenwich, 3 July :
Sᵣ **George Carp,** son of Sᵣ Edw.

At St. James's, 5 July :
Sᵣ **Anthony Vandyke.**

At Otelands, 29 July :
Sᵣ **John Hall.**

At Bagshot Hill, 4 August :
Sᵣ **Robert Pain.**   Hants.

At Nonsuch, 24 August :
Sᵣ **Nicholas Slanning.**   Devon.

At Wanstead, 11 September :
Sᵣ **John Melton.**   York.

At Whitehall, 4 November :
Sᵣ **Francis Crawley.**   Bedf.

At Hampton Court, 22 November :
Sᵣ **Thomas Honywood.**   Essex.

At Whitehall, 8 December :
Sᵣ **Edward Alford.**   Sussex.

At Whitehall, 18 February :
Sᵣ **William Brockman.**   Kent.

At Whitehall, 24 February :
Sᵣ **Arnold Waring.**   Bucks.

At Whitehall, 4 March :
Sᵣ **John Colt.**   Hertf.

1633.

At Whitehall, 21 April :
Sᵣ **Henry Knolles.**
Sᵣ **John Ramsey.**

At Whitehall, 2 May :
Sᵣ **Alexander Hall.**

At Whitehall, 5 May :
Sᵣ **Nicholas Rainton,** Lo. Mayor.

At Whitehall, 8 May :
Sᵣ **John Wolstenholme.**   Lond.
Sᵣ **Abraham Dawes.**   Putney.
Sᵣ **John Jacob.**   London.

At Worksop, — May :
Sᵣ **George Douglas.**   Scotus.

At York, 26 May :
Sᵣ **Wm. Allenson,** Lo. M. of York.
Sᵣ **William Belt,** Recorder   „

At Bishopsthorpe, 27 May :
Sᵣ **Paul Neile,** son to the Archb'p of York.   Derby.

At Newcastle, 4 June :
Sᵣ **Lyonell Maddison.**

In the Army of the States, at Buckstal near Balduck (Bois-le-Duc) in Brabant, 25 July :

Sᵣ **William Boswell,** Resident for the King of Great Britain with the States of the United Provinces, was made Knight by the Lord Vere of Tilbury and other Commissioners named in His Majesty's Letters Patent, the same day that the Prince Elector Palatine received the Order of the Garter ; which said Patent or Commission bare Teste in England 8 June.

At Edinburgh, 17 June :
Sᵣ **William Robinson.** ·

At Dunfermline, 4 July :

Sr **Edmund Bowyer.**   Surrey.

At Anderweek (Innerwick), 16 July :

Sr **Pelham Carp.**

Sr **John Coke**, son to Sr John Coke, Principal Sec. of State.

The names of such Gentlemen Pentioners as were knighted the 16 of July 1633 at Anderweek in Scotland in Master James Maxwel's House :

Sr **Patrick Abercromp.**
Sr **Thomas Hopton.**
Sr **Thomas Aston.**
Sr **William Eyre.**
Sr **James Aethmoti** (Achmuty).
Sr **Francis Sidenham.**
Sr **Robert Wood.**
Sr **Matthew Howland.**
Sr **George Theobalds.**
Sr **John Saltingston.**
Sr **George Windham.**
Sr **David Kirk.**
Sr **Thomas Cress.**
Sr **John Thorowgood.**
Sr **Nicholas Serbin.**
Sr **John Temple.**
Sr **Roger Higges.**

At Berwick, 17 July :

Sr **Tho. Dakers** (Dacre).   Cumb.

At Newcastle :

S^r **Wm. Riddell.**   Northumb'l'd.

At Greenwich, 5 August :

Sr **Richard Hobert.**

At Woodstock, 27 August :

Sr **Thomas Coghill.**   Oxon.
Sr **Selwin Parker**, Gent.-Pens'r.

At Abingdon, 27 August :

Sr **Francis Norris.**   Oxon.

At Whitehall, 4 February :

Sr **Thomas Darrell.**   Bucks.

1634.

Aboard the "Unicorn," 14 April :

Sr **Thomas** (John) **Pennington.**

At Whitehall, 23 April :

Sr **William Le Neve**, Norroy.

At Greenwich, 1 June :

Sr **Thomas Moulson**, Lo. Mayor.

At Wentridge (Hertf.), 17 July :

Sr **Anthony Cage.**   Cambr.

At Belvoir, 25 July :

Sr **Edward Hartopp.**   Leic.

At Whitehall, 24 November :

Sr **John Bramston.**   Essex.

1635.

At Whitehall, 8 April :

Sr **Jacob Skittee.**
Sr **John Rrus.**
Sr **Gustavus Banir.**
Sr **Gabriel Oxenstern.**

These four gentlemen came over with the Swedish Ambassador.

At Greenwich, 10 May :

Sr **John Skittee**, Junior.

At Greenwich, 24 May :

Sr **Robert Parkhurst**, Lo. Mayor.

At Whitehall, 6 June :

Sr **Edward Littleton.**

Aboard His Majestie's Royal Ship called the "Marie Honor" by the Earl of Lindsey, 23 September :

Sr **John, Lord Pawlet.**
Sr **John Pawlet**, his son.
Sr **James Douglas.**
Sr **John Digby.**
Sr **Charles Howard**, son and heir to Sr Francis.
Sr **Elias Hicks**, Gent.-Pens'r.

O C

At Hamptoñ Court, 4 October :
𝔖ʳ **Ralpḥ Whitfeild.**   Kent.

At Royston, 12 October :
𝔖ʳ **Thomas Corbett.**   Norf.

At Whitehall, 7 December :
𝔖ʳ **Richard Weston.**   Staff.

At St. James's, 8 January :
𝔖ʳ **John Dalton.**   Cambr.

At Whitehall, 1 March :
𝔖ʳ **Richard Vivian.**   Cornw.

At St. James's, 8 March :
𝔖ʳ **Henry Calthrop.**   Norf.

1636.

At St. James's, 28 March :
𝔖ʳ **William Shelley.**   Sussex.

At Hampton Court, 29 May :
𝔖ʳ **Chas. Herbert** of Moor. Hertf.

At Oxford, 30 August :
𝔖ʳ **Simon Baskervile,** M.D.

At Oatlands, 11 October :
𝔖ʳ **Matthew Lyster.**   London.

At Newmarket, 16 October :
𝔖ʳ **Thomas Ingram.**   York.

At Hampton Court, 15 January :
𝔖ʳ **Christ'r Clitheroe,** Lo. Mayor.

At Whitehall, 3 February :
𝔖ʳ **William Elverton.**   *Scotus.*

At Whitehall, 7 February :
𝔖ʳ **William Howard.**   York.

1637.

At Whitehall, 4 June :
𝔖ʳ **Edward Bromfield,** Lo. Mayor.

At Oatlands, 7 August :
𝔖ʳ **Charles Mordant.**   Norf.

At Whitehall, 4 December :
𝔖ʳ **Job Harvey.**   London.

At Whitehall, 2 February :
𝔖ʳ **Arthur Hopton.**   Som.

At Whitehall, 12 February :
𝔖ʳ **Rowland Wandesford.** York.

At Whitehall, 24 March :
𝔖ʳ **Thomas Milward.**   Derby.

1638.

At Whitehall, — May :
𝔖ʳ **John Barrington.**   Essex.

At Whitehall, 8 May :
𝔖ʳ **John Lucas.**   Essex.

At Windsor, 20 May :
Charles, Prince of Wales.

Knighted with the Prince's Highness at his Installation of Knights of the Garter :
Robert Devereux, E. of Essex.
Ulick de Burgh, E. of St. Albans.
Thomas Bruce, E. of Elgin.
William Villiers, V. Grandison.

At Whitehall, 27 May :
𝔖ʳ **Richard Fen,** Lo. Mayor.

At Greenwich, 23 June :
𝔖ʳ **Thomas Bedingfield.**   Midd.

At Hampton Court, 2 October :
𝔖ʳ **Balthazar Jarbire.**

At Whitehall, 8 January :
𝔖ʳ **Edmund Williams.**   London.

1639.

At Whitehall, 26 March :
𝔖ʳ **Arthur Jermy.**   Suff.
𝔖ʳ **Richard Allen.**
𝔖ʳ **Gillam Merrick.**

At York, 1 April :
𝔖ʳ **Roger Jaques,** Lo. M. of York.
𝔖ʳ **Tho. Widdrington,** Recorder.
𝔖ʳ **Alexander Davison.** Durham.
𝔖ʳ **Thomas Riddell.**   „

At Berwick, 23 June :

Sʳ **John Pele.** Devon.

Sʳ **James Thinne.** Wilts.

Sʳ **Bevil Grenvile.** Cornw.

Sʳ **Edward Sabage.** Westm'r.

Sʳ **William Darcy.** Durham.

At Berwick, 26 June :

Sʳ **William Bellasis.** Durham.

At Newcastle, 6 July :

Sʳ **Charles Cawdy.** Suff.

At Berwick, 26 July :

Sʳ **William Selby.** Durham.

At Berwick, 27 July :

Sʳ **Vivian Molineux.**

Sʳ **John Pawlett.**

Sʳ **Humphrey Sidenham.**

Sʳ **Peregrine Bertie.**

Sʳ **Charles Howard.**

Sʳ **Richard Bellors.**

Sʳ **John Morley.**

Sʳ **William Gun.** *Scotus.*

Sʳ **Charles Lucas.** Essex.

Sʳ **Michael Earnley.**

Sʳ **.... Douglas.**

Sʳ **John Barkley,**

Sʳ **William Barkley,**

Brothers to Sʳ Charles.

At Whitehall, 4 September :

Sʳ **Thomas Not.** Worc.

Sʳ **Jervis Eyre.** Notts.

Sʳ **William Craven.** Warw.

At Whitehall, 12 October :

Sʳ **Edmond Rebe.** Norf.

At Whitehall, 31 December :

Sʳ **Thomas Dawes.** Surrey.

At Whitehall, 1 January :

Sʳ **Nicholas Crispe.** London.

Sʳ **John Nulls.** „

Sʳ **Robert Forster.** Surrey.

At Whitehall, 21 March :

Sʳ **Henry Blunt.**

1640.

At Whitehall, 31 March :

Sʳ **Thomas Fotherly.** Hertf.

At Whitehall, 2 April :

Sʳ **George Sayer.** Essex.

At Whitehall, 12 May :

Sʳ **Nathaniel Finch.** Kent.

At Whitehall, 31 May :

Sʳ **Henry Garway,** Lo. Mayor.

At Whitehall, 23 June :

Sʳ **Henry Vane,** Junior.

At Whitehall, 30 June :

Sʳ **Thomas Ashton.** Lanc.

At York, — August :

Sʳ **Robert Belt,** Lo. Mayor.

Sʳ **Thomas Wrightington.** York.

At York, 11 October :

Sʳ **Thomas Harrison.** York.

At Whitehall, 22 November :

Sʳ **George Vane.**

At Whitehall, 24 December :

Sʳ **Heneage Proby.**

At Whitehall, 4 January :

Sʳ **John Harrison.** Hertf.

At Whitehall, 9 January :

Sʳ **Martin Lumley,** Bart. Essex.

At Whitehall, 25 January :

Sʳ **John Gore.** Hertf.

At Whitehall, 28 January :

Sʳ **Thomas Fairfax.** York.

Sʳ **Edward Herbert.**

At Whitehall, 1 February :

Sʳ **Robert Wildgoose.** Sussex.

At Whitehall, 11 February :

Sʳ **Simon Fanshaw.** Hertf.

Sʳ **Nicholas Cole,** Bart. Durham.

At Whitehall, 15 February :

Sʳ **Arthur Ashton.**

At Whitehall, 16 February :
Sᵣ **John Witterong.** Hertf.

At Whitehall, 25 February :
Sᵣ **Thomas Meautis.** Hertf.

At Whitehall, 26 February :
Sᵣ **Wilfrid Lawson,** Bart.
Northumberland.

At Whitehall, 8 March :
Sᵣ **Ralph Verney,** son of Sᵣ Edm.

At Whitehall, 21 March :
Sᵣ **Nicholas Miller.** Kent.

1641.

At Whitehall, 26 March :
Sᵣ **Richard Powel.**

At Whitehall, 18 April :
Sᵣ **William Palmer.**

At Whitehall, 19 April :
Sᵣ **William Pool.** Wilts.

At Whitehall, 27 April :
Sᵣ **Edmund Pye.** Bucks.

At Whitehall, 30 April :
Sᵣ **Peter Ricaut** of Aylesford in
Kent.

At Whitehall, 13 May :
Sᵣ **Samuel Oldfield.** Linc.

At Whitehall, 24 May :
Sᵣ **John Ray.** York.

At Whitehall, 29 May :
Sᵣ **William Butler.** Kent.

At Whitehall, 31 May :
Sᵣ **Nicholas Remis** of Keven
Mabley, co. Glam.

At Whitehall, 1 June :
Sᵣ **Robert Thorold.** Linc.

At Whitehall, 4 June :
Sᵣ **Simon Every.** Derby.
Sᵣ **John Worley.** Staff.
Sᵣ **George Winter.**

At Whitehall, 5 June :
Sᵣ **Roger Fielding.** Warw.

At Whitehall, 6 June :
Sᵣ **Peter Temple.** Bucks.

At Whitehall, 18 June :
Sᵣ **Herbert Whitfield.**

At Whitehall, 19 June :
Sᵣ **Thomas Dyke.** Sussex.

At Whitehall, 20 June :
Sᵣ **Edmund Wright,** Lo. Mayor.

At Whitehall, 23 June :
Sᵣ **George Courthope.** Sussex.
Sᵣ **Robert de Grey.** Norf.
Sᵣ **Christopher Athowe.** ,,

At Whitehall, 24 June :
Sᵣ **Thomas Cave.** North'ton.

At Whitehall, 25 June :
Sᵣ **John Evelyn.** Surrey.

At Whitehall, 26 June :
Sᵣ **John Cotton.**

At Whitehall, 28 June :
Sᵣ **Thomas Whitmore.** Salop.
Sᵣ **John Palgrave.** Norf.

At Whitehall, 29 June :
Sᵣ **Vincent Corbet.** Salop.
Sᵣ **John Mayney.** Kent.
Sᵣ **Gerrard Napper.** Dorset.

At Whitehall, 30 June :
Sᵣ **Rowland Barkley.** Worc.

At Whitehall, 2 July :
Sᵣ **Valentine Pell.** Norf.

At Whitehall, 4 July :
Sᵣ **William Butler.** Bedf.
Sᵣ **Anthony Aucher.** Kent.
Sᵣ **Richard Napper.** Bucks.
Sᵣ **Thomas Barnardeston.** Suff.

At Whitehall, 6 July :
Sᵣ **Thomas Mallet.**

At Whitehall, 8 July :
Sᵣ **Thomas Abdy.** Essex.
Sᵣ **Samuel Sleigh.** Derb.

At Whitehall, 9 July :

Sᵣ **William Doyle.** Norf.

Sᵣ **Thomas Guibon.** „

At Whitehall, 10 July :

Sᵣ **Thomas Hewit.** Hertf.

At Whitehall, 11 July :

Sᵣ **Edward Duke.** Suff.

At Whitehall, 13 July :

Sᵣ **Roger Smith.** Leic.

At Whitehall, 14 July :

Sᵣ **Robert Litton.** Warw.

Sᵣ **William Drake.** Bucks.

At Whitehall, 18 July :

Sᵣ **Roger Burgoyn.** Bedf.

At Whitehall, 19 July :

Sᵣ **John Norwich.** North'ton.

At Whitehall, 21 July :

Sᵣ **Thomas Godfrey.** Kent.

Sᵣ **Peter Godfrey.** „

At Whitehall, 22 July :

Sᵣ **Thomas Woolridge.** Salop.

At Whitehall, 23 July :

Sᵣ **Thomas Eversfield.** Sussex.

At Whitehall, 26 July :

Sᵣ **Henry Pratt,** Bart. Berks.

At Whitehall, 27 July :

Sᵣ **John Henden.** Kent.

Sᵣ **John Gore.** Hertf.

At Whitehall, 29 July :

Sᵣ **John Wilde.** Salop.

Sᵣ **Thomas Bridges.** Som.

At Whitehall, 30 July :

Sᵣ **Norton Knatchbull.** Kent.

Sᵣ **George Stroud.** „

At Whitehall, 31 July :

Sᵣ **Wm. Dalston,** Bart. Cumb.

Sᵣ **Edward Partridge.** Kent.

At Whitehall, 5 August :

Sᵣ **John Curson.** Derb.

Sᵣ **Robert Barkham.** Midd.

At Whitehall, 7 August :

Sᵣ **Robert Kemp.** Essex.

Sᵣ **Sampson Eure.**

Sᵣ **Henry Heyman.** Kent.

Sᵣ **John Glanvile.** Wilts.

At Whitehall, 8 August :

Sᵣ **Thomas Hamersly.**

At Whitehall, 9 August :

Sᵣ **John Rolt.** Bedf.

Sᵣ **Francis Rhodes.** Derb.

Sᵣ **Robert Crook.** Oxon.

Sᵣ **John Potts.** Norf.

Sᵣ **Thomas Bishop.** Linc.

Sᵣ **George Ascough.**

Sᵣ **Francis Williamson.**

Sᵣ **Robert Fen,** Clerk Comptrouller.

Sᵣ **Michael Hutchinson.**

Sᵣ **Isaac Sidley.** Kent.

At Whitehall, 10 August :

Sᵣ **Hugh Owen.** Pembr.

Sᵣ **Hugh Windham.** Dorset.

At Kingsland, 25 November :

Sᵣ **Richard Gurney,** Lo. Mayor.

Sᵣ **Thomas Gardner,** Recorder.

At Guildhall, 25 November :

Sᵣ **John Pettus.** Norf.

At Whitehall, 30 November :

Sᵣ **Edward Nicholas.**

At Hampton Court, 3 December :

Sᵣ **John Cordell.**

Sᵣ **Thomas Soame.**

Sᵣ **John Gayer.**

Sᵣ **Jacob Gerrard.**

Sᵣ **John Wollaston.**

Sᵣ **George Garret.**

(The last five Aldermen.)

Sᵣ **George Clark,** Sheriff of Lond.

At Whitehall, 5 December :

Sᵣ **Edward Astley,** bro. to Sᵣ Isaac.

At Whitehall, 8 December :

Sᵣ **Anthony Percival.** Kent.

At Whitehall, 12 December :
Sᵣ **Thomas Treuer.** Midd.

At Whitehall, 18 December :
Sᵣ **John Spelman.** Norf.

At Whitehall, 20 December :
Sᵣ **John Roberts.** Kent.

At Whitehall, 21 December :
Sᵣ **John Tufton.** Kent.

At Whitehall, 23 December :
Sᵣ **John Mallory.** York.

At Whitehall, 27 December :
Sᵣ **Henry Cholmley.**

At Whitehall, 28 December :
Sᵣ **Thomas Lunsford.** Sussex.

At Whitehall, 5 January :
Sᵣ **Thomas Martin.** Cambr.
Sᵣ **Richard Walford.** Leic.

At Windsor, 12 January :
Sᵣ **John Dorrell.** Kent.

At Whitehall, 21 January :
Sᵣ **Isaac Astley,** son to Sᵣ Jacob,
the famous general.
Sᵣ **John Rayney.** Kent.

At Hampton Court, 10 February :
Sᵣ **William Springate.** Kent.
Sᵣ **John Jermy.** Suff.

In His Majesty's journey towards
Dover, 14 February :
Sᵣ **Henry Palmer.** Kent.

At Canterbury, 15 February :
Sᵣ **Edward Filmer.** Kent.

At Dover, — February :
Sᵣ **Henry Stradling.** Glam.
Sᵣ **John Menys,** Vice-Admiral.
Sᵣ **William Man.** Kent.
Sᵣ **Martin Van Tromp,** Admiral
of Holland.

At Theobald's, 1 March :
Sᵣ **William Cooper.** Kent.

At Theobald's, 2 March :
Sᵣ **William Cawley.**

At Newmarket, 12 March :
Sᵣ **John Read,** 2 son to Sᵣ Thomas.
Sᵣ **Robert Crompton.** Midd.

At Newmarket, 13 March :
Sᵣ **John Fortescue.** Suff.

At Huntingdon, 14 March :
Sᵣ **Richard Stone.** Hunts.

At York, 20 March :
Sᵣ **Edmund Cooper,** Lord Maior
of York.

1642.

At York, 18 April :
James, Duke of York.
Robert, Earl of Carnarvon.
(George) Stuart, Lo. D'Aubigny.
Lord John Stuart.
Lord Barnard Stuart.

At   , 21 April :
Sᵣ **Brian Palmes.** Rutland.

At Durham, 23 April :
Sᵣ **Thomas Norcliff.** York.

At York, 24 April :
Sᵣ **Thomas Pennyman.** York.

At York, 1 May :
Sᵣ **Francis Butler.** Hertf.

At York, 2 May :
Sᵣ **Tho. Boswell** (? Bosvile). Kent.
Sᵣ **Jordan Metham.** York.

At York, 21 May :
Sᵣ **Richard Tankard.** York.

At York, 6 June :
Sᵣ **John Girlington.** York.

At York, 7 June :
Sᵣ **Thomas Williamson.** York.

At York, 25 June :
Sᵣ **Ingram Hopton.** York.
Sᵣ **Francis Monkton.** „

At York, 26 June :
Sr **George Middleton.** Lanc.

At York, 27 June:
Sr **Edmond Duncomb.** York.

At York, 28 June :
Sr **Peter Courtney.** Cornw.

At Newark, 12 July :
Sr **John Digby.** Notts.

At Lincoln, 14 July :
Sr **Charles Dallison.** Linc.
Sr **William Conny.** ,,
Sr **Robert Tredway.** ,,
Sr **Richard Wingfield.** ,,
Sr **John Burrell.** ,,
Sr **Jordan Crosland.** York.

At Leicester, 26 July :
Sr **Euseby Pelsant.** Leic.

At Beverley, 28 July :
Sr **George Binnion.** Lond.
Sr **Anthony Sellenger.** Kent.

At Beverley, 30 July :
Sr **Francis Cob.** York.

At York, June or July :
Sr **Patrick Drummond.** *Scotus.*

At York, 8 August :
Sr **William Clark.** Kent.

At York, 9 August :
Sr **Edmond Fortescue.** Devon.
Sr **Edward Garret,** Colonel.

At Leicester, 19 August :
Sr **George Theam.**

At Stoneleigh Abbey, 21 August :
Sr **Robert Leigh.** Warw.

At Stoneleigh Abbey, 22 August :
Sr **Thomas Leigh.** Staff.

At Nottingham, 24 August :
Sr **John Middleton.** York.

At Nottingham, 7 September :
Sr **Henry Jones.** Carm.

At Nottingham, 13 September :
Sr **Robert Stapleton.** York.

At Wellington, 19 September :
Sr **John Wilde.** Salop.

At Shrewsbury, 21 September :
Sr **Francis Otley.** Salop.

At Shrewsbury, 22 September :
Sr **John Wilde,** Junior. Salop.
Sr **Walter Wrottesley.** Staff.

At Chester, 25 September :
Sr **Hugh Calveley.** Chesh.

At Chester, 26 September :
Sr **Richard Crane.**

At Shrewsbury, 27 September :
Sr **Thomas Biron.**

At Shrewsbury, 29 September :
Sr **Arnold de Lille.** *French.*

In the field at the head of his Company, at Shrewsbury, 29 Sept. :
Sr **Thomas Scriven.** Salop.

At Shrewsbury, 1 October :
Sr **Richard Willis,** brother to Sr Thomas.
Sr **Thomas Lister.**
Sr **Richard Biron.**

At Wrexham, 7 October :
Sr **Richard Lloyd.** Denbigh.

At Shrewsbury, 9 October :
Sr **Garret Eaton.** Derby.

At Shrewsbury, 11 October :
Sr **Thomas Eaton.** Salop.

At Southam, 21 October :
Sr **Anthony Morgan.** North'ton.

At Edgecot, 22 October :
Sr **Richard Shukborough.** Warw.

At Edgehill, 24 October :
Sr **John Smyth,** bro. to Sr Chas. He recovered the King's great banner which the rebels had taken in battle the day before.
Sr **Robert Walsh.**

At Oxford, 2 November:
　Sʳ **William Palmer.**

At Reading, 7 November:　·
　Sʳ **Wingfield Bodenham.** Rutl'd.

At Reading, 9 November:
　Sʳ **Edward Sidenham.**　Essex.

At Maidenhead, 10 November:
　Sʳ **Henry Bene.**　Berks.

At Coalbrook, 12 November:
　Sʳ **John Tirringham.**　Bucks.

At Reading, 29 November:
　Sʳ **Thomas Manwaring.**　Berks.

At Oxford, 27 December:
　Sʳ **Thomas Blackwell.**　Notts.

At Oxford, 1 January:
　Sʳ **Henry Muncks.**

At Oxford, 9 January:
　Sʳ **Edward Chester.**　Hertf.

At Oxford, 10 January:
　Sʳ **Robert Murray.**　*Scotus.*

At Oxford, 14 January:
　Sʳ **Henry Vaughan,** Lieut.-Col.

At Oxford, 1 February:
　Sʳ **William Mallory,** Captain.

At Oxford, 3 February:
　Sʳ **William Neal,** Scout Master,
　upon bringing the news to the
　King of the taking of Cicester.

At Oxford, 6 February:
　Sʳ **George Vaughan.**　Wilts.

At Oxford, 22 February:
　Sʳ **Edward Hide.**

At Oxford, 23 February:
　Sʳ **Isaac Astley,** son to Sʳ Jacob.

At Oxford, 24 February:
　Sʳ **John Penruddock.**　Wilts.

At Oxford, 26 February:
　Sʳ **John Winford.**　Worc.

At Oxford, 2 March:
　Sʳ **Henry Hunlock.**　Derby.

At Oxford, 5 March:
　Sʳ **Thomas Bad.**　Hants.
　Sʳ **John Penruddock** (*see* 24 Feb.).

At Oxford, 22 March:
　Sʳ **John Scudamore.**　Heref.

At Oxford, 24 March:
　Sʳ **Walter Lloyd.**　Card.
　Sʳ **Francis Lloyd.**　Carm.

1643.

At Oxford, 12 April:
　Sʳ **William Blackstone.** Durham.

At Oxford, 23 April:
　Sʳ **Lewis Kirk.**　Salop.

At Oxford, 17 May:
　Sʳ **Edward Laurence.**　Dorset.

At Oxford, 1 June:
　Sʳ **James Murray.**　*Scotus.*

At Oxford, 13 June:
　Sʳ **Charles Kemish.**　Glam.
　Sʳ **Edward Stradling.**　,,
　Sʳ **John Urrey.**　*Scotus.*

At Oxford, 24 June:
　Sʳ **Humble Ward.**　Staff.

At Oxford, 15 July:
　Sʳ .... **Butler.**　*Irish.*

At Bristol, 3 August:
　Sʳ **Charles Mohun.**　Cornw.
　Sʳ **John Greenvile,** son to Sʳ
　Bevil.
　Sʳ **Samuel Cosworth.**　Cornw.
　Sʳ **Christopher Wray.**　,,

In the Army, by Sudley, 15 August:
　Sʳ **Richard Chomley.**

At Sudley Castle, 8 September:
　Sʳ **William Merton.**　Oxon.

At Sudley Castle, 9 September :
S͏ʳ 𝔚illiam 𝔥aꜹward.   Surrey.

At Gloucester, — September :
S͏ʳ 𝔚m. 𝔇avenant, Poet Laur.

At Newbury, 22 September :
S͏ʳ 𝔐ichael 𝔚oodhouse.

At Oxford, 24 September :
S͏ʳ 𝔗imothꜹ 𝔗irrel.   Oxon.

At Oxford, 28 September :
S͏ʳ 𝔊eorge ap 𝔯oberts.   Monm.

At Oxford, 30 September :
S͏ʳ 𝔈dward 𝔄lstone.   Oxon.

At Oxford, 4 October :
S͏ʳ 𝔈dward 𝔣ord.   Sussex.

At Oxford, 7 October :
S͏ʳ 𝔭eter 𝔅all.   Devon.

At Oxford, 20 October :
S͏ʳ 𝔣rancis 𝔠hoke.   Berks.

At Oxford, 9 November :
S͏ʳ 𝔄rthur 𝔅lanꜹ.   Montgom.

At Oxford, 10 November :
S͏ʳ .... 𝔒tleꜹ.

At Oxford, 11 November :
S͏ʳ 𝔍oseph 𝔩eamore.   Devon.

At Oxford, 17 November :
S͏ʳ 𝔒rlando 𝔅ridgman.   Lanc.

At Oxford, 22 November :
S͏ʳ 𝔥enrꜹ 𝔅ard, Colonel.

At Oxford, 24 November :
S͏ʳ 𝔈dward 𝔙aughan.   Cornw.

At Oxford, 6 December :
S͏ʳ 𝔯obert 𝔅reertwood.   Chesh.

At Oxford, 9 December :
S͏ʳ 𝔈dmund 𝔙erneꜹ.

At Oxford, 12 December :
S͏ʳ 𝔠harles 𝔠ompton.
S͏ʳ 𝔚illiam 𝔠ompton.
S͏ʳ 𝔖pencer 𝔠ompton.
(Brothers to the Earl of Northampton.)

At Oxford, 28 December :
S͏ʳ 𝔐armaduke 𝔯awdon.   Hertf.

At Oxford, — December :
S͏ʳ 𝔗homas 𝔭ert, Colonel.

At Oxford, 4 January :
S͏ʳ 𝔯ichard 𝔩ane.

At Oxford, 9 January :
S͏ʳ 𝔚illiam 𝔐anwaring.   Chesh.

At Oxford, 19 January :
S͏ʳ 𝔯obert 𝔥olborn.

At Oxford, 5 February :
S͏ʳ 𝔍ohn 𝔯eed.   *Scotus.*

1644.

At Oxford, 25 March :
S͏ʳ 𝔗homas 𝔊ardner, who was knighted by his Majesty whilst he sat at dinner upon the delivery of the news of Prince Rupert's success against the Rebels that had besieged Newark.

At Oxford, 2 April :
S͏ʳ 𝔥ugh 𝔠artwright.   Notts.

At Oxford, 9 April :
S͏ʳ 𝔚illiam 𝔠ourtneꜹ.

At Oxford, 16 April :
S͏ʳ 𝔥enrꜹ 𝔚ood.

At Oxford, 19 April :
S͏ʳ 𝔗homas 𝔠hedle.

At Oxford, 24 April :
S͏ʳ 𝔊eorge 𝔙illiers.

At Oxford, 25 April :
S͏ʳ 𝔣rancis 𝔊amull.

At Oxford, 6 May :
S͏ʳ 𝔚illiam 𝔊odolphin.   Cornw.

At Oxford, 12 May :
S͏ʳ 𝔯obert 𝔅iron.
S͏ʳ 𝔊eorge 𝔭arreꜹ.

At Burford, 18 June:
Sᵣ 𝕭ernarð 𝕬stleᵽ.

At Worcester, 18 June:
Sᵣ 𝕸artin 𝕾anðes.
Sᵣ 𝕯aniel 𝕿ᵽas, Mayor.

At Evesham, — June:
Sᵣ 𝕵ohn 𝕶notsforð.   Warw.

At Cropredy Bridge, 29 June:
Sᵣ 𝕽obert 𝕳oᵹarð, a younger son
to the Earl of Berks, for taking
Wemes, the Scot, General of Sᵣ
William Waller's Artillery.

At Williamscot, 29 June:
Sᵣ 𝕿homas 𝕳ooᵽer.

At Exeter, 27 July:
Sᵣ 𝕳ugh 𝕮rocker, Mayor.

At Crediton, 30 July:
Sᵣ 𝕿homas 𝕭asset.
Sᵣ 𝕱rancis 𝕭asset.
Sᵣ 𝕵oseᵽh 𝕮𝕷agstaff.
†Sᵣ 𝕳enrᵽ 𝕮areᵽ.

At Boconnock, — August:
Sᵣ 𝕮harles 𝕿revanion.   Cornw.
Sᵣ 𝕵ohn 𝕬runðel.   „
Sᵣ 𝕵ames 𝕮obb.

At Liskeard, 3 August:
Sᵣ 𝕵ohn 𝕲rills, Sheriff.

In the field, at the pursuit of Essex's
Army, 1 September:
Sᵣ 𝕰ðᵹarð 𝕭rett, Colonel.
Sᵣ 𝕿homas 𝕻restᵹich.
Sᵣ 𝕾ackvil 𝕲lemham, son of Sᵣ
Thomas.
Sᵣ 𝕨illiam 𝕽atcliff.

Upon Redheath, 22 October:
Sᵣ 𝕵ohn 𝕭oᵽs.

Near Newport Pagnell, — October:
Sᵣ 𝕵ohn 𝕮ampsfielð.

At Oxford, 1 November:
Sᵣ 𝕳enrᵽ 𝕲age, Governor.
Sᵣ 𝕮harles 𝕷loᵽð.   Card.

At Oxford, 2 November:
Sᵣ 𝕻eter 𝕭roᵹn.   Oxon.

At Oxford, 3 November:
†Sᵣ 𝕬nthonᵽ 𝕲reene.
†Sᵣ 𝕮harles 𝕨alðron, Captain.

At Oxford, 7 November:
Sᵣ 𝕨illiam 𝕮ampion.   Kent.

At Oxford, 17 December:
Sᵣ 𝕵ohn 𝕺ᵹen, Colonel.
†Sᵣ 𝕨illiam 𝕽ollock.   Scotus.

At Oxford, 18 December:
Sᵣ 𝕮hristoᵽher 𝕷eᵹkenor, Col.
†Sᵣ 𝕵ames 𝕮roft.

At Oxford, 14 January:
Sᵣ 𝕲ilbert 𝕿albot.

At Oxford, 17 January:
𝕿he 𝕷orð 𝕮aᵽel.
𝕿he 𝕷orð 𝕳enrᵽ 𝕾eᵽmore.

At Oxford, 23 January:
Sᵣ 𝕳enrᵽ 𝕮hichleᵽ.   Cambr.

At Oxford, 27 January:
Sᵣ 𝕽icharð 𝕳atton.   North'ton.

At Oxford, 30 January:
Sᵣ 𝕲eorge 𝕭unckly.   Greenwich.

At Oxford, 1 February:
Sᵣ 𝕿homas 𝕯'𝕬briðgecourt.

At Oxford, 2 February:
Sᵣ 𝕰ðᵹarð 𝕨alker, Garter.
Sᵣ 𝕾teᵽhen 𝕳aᵹkins, Colonel.

At Oxford, 20 March:
Sᵣ 𝕿homas 𝕽eeves, King's Advoc.

At Oxford, 21 March:
Sᵣ 𝕮harles 𝕮otterel.
Sᵣ 𝕽icharð 𝕭raham.

1645.

At Oxford, 28 March:
Sᵣ 𝕽icharð 𝕸aleverer.   York.
Sᵣ 𝕽obert 𝕻eake, Lieut.-Colonel.
†Sᵣ 𝕨illiam 𝕸ason.

At Oxford, 3 April:
Sr **John Ratcliff.**

At Oxford, 29 April:
Sr **Lodowick Wyer.** German.
Slain at Naseby Field.

At Oxford, 5 May:
Sr **Bartholomew La Roche.**
Gallus.

At Droitwich, 14 May:
Sr **Edward Barret.** Worc.

At the Countess of Devon's house near
Leicester, 2 June:
Sr **Richard Page,** Colonel.
Sr **William Bridges,** Mayor.
Sr **Matthew Appleyard,** Colonel.

At Leicester, 4 June:
Sr **Edward Hopton,** Colonel.

At Hereford, 25 June:
Sr **Dudley Wyat.**

At Hereford, 6 July:
Sr **Henry Lingen,** Colonel.

At Monmouth, 6 July:
Sr **Herbert Lunsford,** Governor.

At Ragland, 10 July:
Sr **Edmond Peirce.** Kent.

At Cardiff Castle, 31 July:
Sr **John Walpole.** Linc.

At Hereford, 5 September:
Sr **William Layton,** Colonel.
Sr **Barnaby Scudamore.**

At Chirk Castle, 15 September:
Sr **Henry Wroth,** Gent.-Pens'r.

At Chirk Castle, 23 September:
Sr **John Watts,** Gov. of the Castle.

At Newark, 27 October:
Sr **Theophilus Gilby,** Colonel.

At Oxford, 20 December:
Sr **Edward Cooper,** Gent.-Pens'r.

At Oxford, 21 December:
Sr **George Lisle,** Colonel.
Sr **Ferdinando Fisher.**

At Oxford, 25 December:
Sr **Charles Lee,** bro. to Sr Robert.

At Oxford, 2 February:
Sr **John Ogle.**

At Oxford, 4 February:
Sr **Anthony Willoughby.**

At Oxford, 16 February:
Sr **Allen Butler.** Bucks.

At Oxford, 17 February:
Sr **John Southcote.**

At Oxford, 25 February:
Sr **Thomas Shirley.** Sussex.
Sr **William Biron.**

1646.

At Oxford, 2 April:
Sr **George Aglionby,** Major.

At Oxford, 4 April:
Sr **Francis Rouse,** Scout M'r.-Gen.

At Oxford, 8 April:
Sr **James Bridgeman,** Colonel.

At Oxford, 11 April:
Sr **Edmund Poley.** Suff.

The King went from Oxford the 27 of
April 1646.

Knights made in this reign, but the
dates not known:
Sr **Thomas Longuebile.**
Sr **Edward Bathurst** of Lechlade.
Sr **Edward Bray.**
Sr **Edward Prideaux.**
Sr **Allen Zouch.**
Sr **William Morgan.**

Sᵣ **Edward Walgrabe.**
Sᵣ **John Norris.**   North'ton.
Sᵣ **Gamaliel Dudley.**   ·

In the Isle of Wight:

Sᵣ **John Duncomb** of Battlesden in the county of Bedford.

Knights made in 1649 by the Speaker of the House of Commons by re-commendation of the House :

Sᵣ **Thomas Andrews,** Lo. Mayor.
Sᵣ **Isaac Pennington,** Alderman.
Sᵣ **Thomas Atkins,** Alderman.

Knights made by

King Charles the Second

in Scotland, 1650-1.

(Sir James Balfour's Historical Works, vol. iv., pp. 81 and 256-7.)

1650.

At Falkland, 10 July :

Sᵣ **Thomas Nicolson,** his Majesty's Advocate.

1651.

At Scone, 2 January :

Sᵣ **Lawrence Oliphant.**   Gask.
Sᵣ **James Drummond.**   Machiny.
Sᵣ **George May,** Jun.   Meginche.
Sᵣ **John Ker.**   Lochetoure.

At Perth, 3 January :

Sᵣ **James Richardson.**   Synton.
Sᵣ **Alexander Blair.**   Balthayocke.

At Perth, 8 January :

Sᵣ **Archibald Douglas,** Jun., Sheriff of Teviotshire.   Cavers.

At the Earl of Wemyss's House, 14 February :

Sᵣ **David Achmuty.**
Sᵣ **Thomas Gourley.**   Kincraige.

At Largo Sands, the same day when the King ran at the glove :

Sᵣ **Walter Scott** of Whitsted, base son to Walter, First Earl of Balcleuche, Col. of a Regiment of Horse.

Sᵣ **Gilbert Ellet,** Jun., of Stobes, Col. to Whitsted.

Sᵣ **Alexander Seton,** 2 son to George, E. of Winton, created by His Majesty Viscount of Kingston and Lord Craigiehall, by Patent dated at Perth 4 January 1651.

At Dundee, 21 February :

Sᵣ **James Durham,** eldest son to the Laird of Pittcarrow.

At Dundee, 22 February :

Sᵣ **James Hay,** brother's son to the Earl of Tweedale.   Linplume.

At Aberdeen, — February :

Sᵣ **Patrick Lesley,** once Provost.
Sᵣ **Robert Farquhar,** present Provost.
Sᵣ . . . . **Mowat,** son to Mr. Peter Mowat of Baquhaley, Advocate.

At Dundee, — March :

Sᵣ **Thomas Mudie,** Provost.

𝕶nights made between 1653 and 1658.

(Memoirs of the House of Cromwell, by Mark Noble, 2 ed., vol. i., p. 442.)

By OLIVER CROMWELL, Protector.

Sr **Henry Cromwell**, his son.

Sr **Thomas Viner**, Lo. Mayor, 8 Feb. 1653.

Sr **William Boteler**, 1653 or 1654.

Sr **John Copleston**, 1 June 1655.

Sr **John Reynolds**, 11 June 1655.

Sr **Christopher Pack**, Lo. Mayor, 23 Sept. 1655.

Sr **Peter Julius Coyet**, 1655.

Sr **James Whitlock**, 6 Jan. 1655.

Sr **Thomas Pride**, 17 Jan. 1655.

Sr **John Barkstead**, 19 Jan. 1655.

Sr **Gustavus du Vale.**

Sr **George Fleetwood.**

Sr **William Lockhart.**

Sr **James Calthorp.**

Sr **Robert Titchborne.**

Sr **Lislebone Long**, 15 Dec. 1655.

Sr **Bulstrode Whitlock**, as least as early as 1655.

Sr **Richard Combe**, Aug. 1656.

Sr **John Dethick**, 15 Sept. 1656.

Sr **Tho. Dickinson**, 3 March 1656.

Sr **Richard Stainer**, 11 June 1657.

Sr **John Claypoole**, 16 July 1657.

S^r **Wm. Wheeler**, 26 Aug. 1657.

Sr **Edward Ward**, 2 Nov. 1657.

Sr **Thomas Foote**, 5 Dec. 1657.

Sr **John Hewson.**

Sr **James Drax**, 6 Jan. 1657.

Sr **Henry Pickering**, 1 Feb. 1657.

Sr **Philip Twistleton**, 1 Feb. 1657.

Sr **John Lenthall**, 9 March 1657.

Sr **John Ireton.**

Sr **Henry Jones**, 17 July 1658.

Sr **Heronymous Sankey.**

Sr **Anthony Morgan.**

Sr **Thomas Whitgrave.**

Sr **William Ellis.**

By RICHARD CROMWELL, Protector.

Sr **John Morgan**, 26 Nov. 1658.

Sr **Richard Beke**, 6 Dec. 1658.

Knights made in Ireland

between 1566 and 1698.

(From Add. MS. 4763; Carew MSS.; Lans. MS. 678; Harl. MS. 6063; and Sir Thomas Phillipps's book of Knights made in Ireland, to the end of 1631, and from that time from information kindly furnished by Sir Bernard Burke, Knight, Ulster King of Arms.)

By and in the time of Sr HENRY SIDNEY, Kt., Lo. Deputy.

1566.

Sr Thomas Butler, E. of Ormond.
Sr Owen MacCarty More, Earl of Clancarty.
Sr James Barry, Lord Barry.
Sr David Roche, Lord Roche.

At Limerick, — March :
Sr Thomas Gerald, Lord Fitzmaurice of Kerry.

At Drogheda :
Sr Christopher Nugent, Lord of Delvin.
Sr Robert Barnewell, Baron of Tremeleston.
Sr Thomas Plunket, Lo. of Lowth.
Sr Barnaby FitzPatrick, Lo. of Upper Ossory (see p. 116).
Sr Gerald Courcy.
Sr William Ockervill (O'Caroll), Baron of Elye.
Sr Derly McCarty, Lord of Muskerry.
Sr Robert de Lion of the New Town.
Sr Christopher Chivers of Massy Town.
Sr Oliver Plunket of Ramore.
Sr John Bedlo alias Bellew.
Sr Nicholas Bagnall.
Sr Edward Fitton.

Sr Peter Carew.
Sr James Fitz Gerald, bro. to the E. of Desmond at . . . .
Sr Christ'r Barnewell of Turvey.
Sr Patrick Barnewell of Fieldstown.
Sr Thomas Fitz William of Merion.
Sr William Sarsfeld of Lucan.

1567.

At Clonmell, 24 February :
Sr Theobald Butler.   Cahir.

At Limerick, 3 March :
Sr Donough MacCarty Reagh.
Sr John Desmond, bro. to Gerald, E. of Desmond.
Sr William Burke. Castle Eeny.

At Balliloughrea, 4 April :
Sr Hugh O'Donnel.
Sr Daniel O'Connor.   Sligo.

At Knockfergus, — September :
Sr Brian Phelim O'Neill.

1569.

At Drogheda, 9 February :
Sr Christopher St. Lawrence, Lo. of Howthe.

At Limerick, 2 September :
Sr Thomas Fitz Gerald alias O'Desmond.

At Drogheda, 1 January :
Sr Humphrey Gilbert (see p. 126).

By Sr WILLIAM FITZ WILLIAMS.

1572.
S^r 𝕮𝖔𝖓𝖓𝖔𝖚𝖌𝖍 𝕸𝖈𝕿𝖊𝖌𝖊.

1573.
S^r 𝕵𝖆𝖒𝖊𝖘 𝕱𝖎𝖙𝖟 𝕲𝖊𝖗𝖆𝖑𝖉, of the House of Dromaney, 26 April.

1576.
At Drogheda :
S^r 𝕷𝖚𝖈𝖆𝖘 𝕯𝖊 𝕷𝖔𝖓𝖊 *alias* 𝕯𝖊 𝕷𝖎𝖔𝖓.
At Dublin, 23 April :
S^r 𝕳𝖊𝖓𝖗𝖞 𝕮𝖔𝖚𝖑𝖐𝖊.

1578.
At Athlone, 7 October :
S^r 𝕹𝖎𝖈𝖍𝖔𝖑𝖆𝖘 𝕸𝖆𝖑𝖇𝖊𝖞.
S^r 𝕳𝖊𝖓𝖗𝖞 𝕳𝖆𝖗𝖗𝖎𝖓𝖌𝖙𝖔𝖓.
S^r 𝕳𝖊𝖓𝖗𝖞 𝕭𝖆𝖌𝖓𝖆𝖑𝖑.
S^r 𝕭𝖗𝖎𝖆𝖓 𝕺'𝕽𝖔𝖗𝖐𝖊.

By Sr WILLIAM DRURY, Lo. Deputy.

1578–1579.
S^r 𝖂𝖎𝖑𝖑𝖎𝖆𝖒 𝕻𝖊𝖑𝖍𝖆𝖒.
S^r 𝖂𝖎𝖑𝖑𝖎𝖆𝖒 𝕲𝖊𝖗𝖆𝖑𝖉, Lo. Chanc.
S^r 𝖂𝖎𝖑𝖑𝖎𝖆𝖒 𝕲𝖔𝖗𝖌𝖊.
S^r 𝖂𝖎𝖑𝖑𝖎𝖆𝖒 𝕾𝖙𝖆𝖓𝖑𝖊𝖞.
S^r 𝕰𝖉𝖜𝖆𝖗𝖉 𝕸𝖔𝖔𝖗𝖊. Melivant.
S^r 𝕲𝖊𝖔𝖗𝖌𝖊 𝕭𝖔𝖚𝖗𝖈𝖍𝖎𝖊𝖗.
S^r 𝕰𝖉𝖜𝖆𝖗𝖉 𝕱𝖎𝖙𝖙𝖔𝖓. ⎫ See previous
S^r 𝕻𝖊𝖙𝖊𝖗 𝕮𝖆𝖗𝖊𝖜. ⎭   page.
S^r 𝕿𝖍𝖔𝖒𝖆𝖘 𝕻𝖊𝖗𝖗𝖔𝖙𝖙.
S^r 𝕻𝖆𝖙𝖗𝖎𝖈𝖐 𝖂𝖆𝖑𝖘𝖍.

By ARTHUR, LORD GREY of Wilton, Lo. Deputy.

1580.
S^r 𝖂𝖎𝖑𝖑𝖎𝖆𝖒 𝕽𝖚𝖘𝖘𝖊𝖑𝖑, 11 Sept.
S^r 𝖂𝖎𝖑𝖑𝖎𝖆𝖒 𝕭𝖚𝖗𝖐𝖊, 16 Sept.
S^r 𝕽𝖔𝖇𝖊𝖗𝖙 𝕯𝖎𝖑𝖑𝖔𝖓 of Riverstone, Ch. J. Com. Pleas, 11 November.

By ADAM LOFTUS, Archb'p of Dublin, and Sr HENRY WALLOP, Kt., Lords Justices.

1582.
S^r 𝕬𝖓𝖙𝖍𝖔𝖓𝖞 𝕮𝖔𝖑𝖈𝖑𝖔𝖚𝖌𝖍, Tinterne, 7 September.

1583. 6 May.
S^r 𝕵𝖔𝖍𝖓 𝕭𝖚𝖗𝖐𝖊, Baron of Leitrim.
S^r 𝕿𝖍𝖔𝖒𝖆𝖘 𝕱𝖑𝖊𝖒𝖎𝖓𝖌, Baron of Slane.
S^r 𝕻𝖆𝖙𝖗𝖎𝖈𝖐 𝕭𝖆𝖗𝖓𝖊𝖜𝖊𝖑𝖑, Baron of Trimleston.

By Sr JOHN PERROTT, Kt., Lo. Deputy.

1584.
S^r 𝕵𝖆𝖒𝖊𝖘 𝕯𝖔𝖜𝖉𝖆𝖑𝖑, Ch. Justice K.B., 12 June.
S^r 𝕰𝖉𝖜𝖆𝖗𝖉 𝖂𝖆𝖙𝖊𝖗𝖍𝖔𝖚𝖘𝖊.
S^r 𝕽𝖎𝖈𝖍𝖆𝖗𝖉 𝕭𝖎𝖓𝖌𝖍𝖆𝖒.
S^r 𝕹𝖎𝖈𝖍. 𝖂𝖍𝖎𝖙𝖊, M^r of the Rolls.
S^r 𝕿𝖍𝖔𝖒𝖆𝖘 𝕷𝖊 𝕾𝖙𝖗𝖆𝖓𝖌𝖊.
S^r 𝖂𝖎𝖑𝖑𝖎𝖆𝖒 𝕮𝖔𝖑𝖑𝖞𝖊𝖗.
S^r 𝕿𝖍𝖔𝖒𝖆𝖘 𝕵𝖔𝖓𝖊𝖘.
S^r 𝕬𝖗𝖙𝖍𝖚𝖗 𝕹𝖊𝖆𝖑𝖊.
S^r 𝕮𝖍𝖆𝖗𝖑𝖊𝖘 𝕺'𝕮𝖆𝖗𝖗𝖔𝖑𝖑.
S^r 𝕸𝖔𝖗𝖔𝖌𝖍 𝕹𝖊𝖉𝖔 𝕺'𝕱𝖑𝖆𝖗𝖍𝖆𝖗𝖙𝖊.

1585.
S^r 𝕽𝖔𝖇. 𝕭𝖔𝖚𝖗𝖐𝖊 *alias* 𝕸𝖈𝕯𝖆𝖛𝖎𝖊𝖘, 16 May.
S^r 𝕸𝖔𝖗𝖗𝖎𝖈𝖊 𝕱𝖎𝖙𝖟 𝕵𝖆𝖒𝖊𝖘.
S^r 𝕲𝖊𝖔𝖗𝖌𝖊 𝕮𝖆𝖗𝖊𝖜.
S^r 𝕮𝖔𝖓𝖓𝖔𝖌𝖍 𝕸𝖆𝖈𝕲𝖚𝖞𝖗𝖊.
S^r 𝕵𝖔𝖍𝖓 𝕯𝖔𝖌𝖍𝖊𝖗𝖙𝖞.
In Christchurch, 24 February :
S^r 𝕵𝖔𝖍𝖓 𝕿𝖎𝖗𝖗𝖊𝖑𝖑 of the Pace.

1588.
In Christchurch :
S^r 𝕿𝖍𝖔. 𝕱𝖎𝖙𝖟 𝖂𝖎𝖑𝖑𝖎𝖆𝖒𝖘, 14 April.
S^r 𝕹𝖎𝖈𝖍𝖔𝖑𝖆𝖘 𝕾𝖙. 𝕷𝖆𝖜𝖗𝖊𝖓𝖈𝖊, son and heir to the Lo. Howth, 1 May.

Sᵣ William Brereton.   Chesh.
Sᵣ Patrick Barnewell of Gracedew,
    28 February.   .
Sᵣ John Owgan.   Beleston.
Sᵣ Edward Barkley, 14 May.

By Sᵣ WILLIAM FITZ WILLIAMS, Kt.,
    Lo. Deputy.
Sᵣ George Clive, 4 July.
Sᵣ Thomas Norris, Vicegerent of
    Munster.
Sᵣ George Bingham.   Sligo.
Sᵣ Thomas Masterson.
Sᵣ Henry Duke.
Sᵣ Tirlough Lynagh O'Neill.
Sᵣ Geoffery Fenton.
Sᵣ Nicholas Le Strange.

1589.
Sᵣ Richard Shee, 12 Aug.   Kilk.
Sᵣ Edward Denny, 26 Oct. Essex.
Sᵣ Thomas Shirley.
Sᵣ Walter Longe.   Wilts.
Sᵣ Hugh Magwier, 24 January.

1591.
Sᵣ George Delops (? Delvers).
Sᵣ Nicholas Devereux.   Wexf.
Sᵣ Thomas Colclough, 24 Oct.

1592.
Sᵣ Michael Molyns, — Feb.

1593.
Sᵣ Tho' Moore, 28 May. King's Co.
Sᵣ Edward Rynaston, 17 Jan.
    Salop.
Sᵣ Anthony Maney.   Kent.
Sᵣ George Villiers.
Sᵣ Edward Fitz Gerald.
Sᵣ John Hollis.   Notts.
Sᵣ Robert Salisburie.
Sᵣ Raphe Lane.
Sᵣ George Colley.   King's Co.
Sᵣ Dudley Loftus.

Sᵣ Edward Herbert.   King's Co.
Sᵣ John Dowdall.
Sᵣ Thomas Posthumous Hoby.
Sᵣ Stephen Thornehurst.

By Sᵣ WILLIAM RUSSELL, Kt.,
    Lo. Deputy.
1594.
Sᵣ William Clarke, upon a hill
    near to Enishkillinge, which was
    then distressed, 1 Sept.
Sᵣ Robert Needham, — Sept.

1595.
Sᵣ Edward Monins, at Mone,
    20 April.
Sᵣ Edward Brabazon.   Leic.
In Christchurch :
Sᵣ Wil. Waldegrabe, 24 Aug.
Sᵣ Richard Wingfield, 9 Nov.
    North'ton.
Sᵣ Henry Warren, 4 Jan.

1596.
In Christchurch :
Sᵣ John North, 11 April.
In the Glynes, where that Traytor
    Feagh Mac Hugh sometymes re-
    mayned, 4 March :
Sᵣ John Chichester.   Devon.

1597.
In St. Patrick's Church, 27 March :
Sᵣ William Lane.   North'ton.
In the Glynes, 8 May :
Sᵣ Richard Trevor.   Denbigh.
Sᵣ Calisthenes Broke.   Kent.
Sᵣ Thomas Maria Wingfield.

By Lo. THOMAS BURGH, Baron Gains-
    borowe, Lo. Deputy.
At the Fort of the Blackwater, 19 July :
Sᵣ Thomas Waller.   Kent.

At his Manor House, Dunsaghly:
Sr Christopher Plunkett.

At Drogheda, 24 September:
Sr Henry Brounker. Essex.

By Sr THOMAS NORRIS, Kt., Lord Justice.
Sr Nicholas Walsh.
Sr Warham St. Leger.

By ADAM LOFTUS, Archb'p of Dublin, and Sr ROBERT GARDINER, Kt., Joint Lords Justices.

In St. Patrick's Church, 22 January:
Sr Walter Butler, son and heir to John Butler third brother to the Earl of Ormond.
Sr James Butler. Lismalyne.

1598.

In Christchurch:
Sr Garrett Aylmer, 8 June.
Sr Richard Pearse, 24 Sept.
Sr Robert Ashfield, 24 Sept.

1599.

In Christchurch:
Sr John Egerton, 8 April.

By ROBERT, EARL OF ESSEX AND EWE, Lo. Lieut. and Governor-General of Ireland.
At Dublin, 9 May:
Sr Thomas Mustian.
Sr Thomas Tasborough. Bucks.

At the Fort of Lease, Maryborough:
Sr Francis Rushe, 17 May.

At Kiltanan in Munster:
Sr Terence O'Dempsy, 22 March.

At Cahir Castle, 30 May:
Sr Roger Manners, E. of Rutland.

At Asheton:
Sr Francis Barkley, 12 June.

At Killmallock:
Sr George Thornton, 19 June.

At Sr John Colley's House:
Sr James Devereux.

At his own house at Fernes:
Sr Richard Masterson.

At Dublin, 12 July:
The Lord Grey of Wilton.
The Lord Mounteagle.
Sr Thomas West.
Sr Robert Vernon.
Sr Henry Cary.
Sr Arthur Champernoun.
Sr William Constable.
Sr John Davies.
Sr John Pooley.
Sr Carew Reynell.
Sr George Manners.
The Lord Cromwell.

At Dublin:
Sr William Godolphin, 13 July.
Sr William Courtney, 13 July.
Sr Francis Lacon, 13 July.
Sr Robert Bassett, 15 July.
Sr Robert Constable, 22 July.
Sr Edward Warren, 22 July.
Sr Cuthbert Halsall, 22 July.

At Meath, 24 July:
Sr Hewet Osborne.

In the Camp, 24 July, at the meeting with Sr Conyers Clifford, who fought well the day before:
Sr Hugh O'Connor.
Sr John McCoghlan.
Sr Mullmore MacSwine.
Sr Theobald Dillon.

At the rising of the Camp after the fight at Ophaley, 30 July:
Sr Jocelin Percy.
Sr Thomas Burke.
Sr William Warren.
Sr Henry Linley.
Sr Theophilus Finch.
Sr John Vaughan.

Sʳ William Lovelace.
Sʳ John Harrington.
Sʳ William Gascoigne. •

At Dublin, 4 August :
Sʳ Robert Digby.
Sʳ Edward Blunt.

At Dublin, 5 August, in the forenoon :
Sʳ Henry Goodyer.
Sʳ Edward Essex.
Sʳ William Cornwallis.
Sʳ Richard Lovelace.
Sʳ Edward Read, in the afternoon.
Sʳ Edward Morgan.
Sʳ Henry Carew.
Sʳ Richard Morison.
Sʳ Charles Willmot.
Sʳ Edw. Michelborne, the same day.
Sʳ John Haydon.
Sʳ Francis Merrick.

At Dublin, 6 August :
Sʳ John Croftes.
Sʳ George Leicester.

At Dublin :
Sʳ Henry Wallopp.
Sʳ John Sames.
Sʳ Henry Fookes.
Sʳ William Boustred.

At Dublin, 6 September :
Sʳ John Chamberlaine.
Sʳ Robert Paxley.
Sʳ Gerratt Moore.
Sʳ John Talbott.

At Dublin, 10 September :
Sʳ Jonathan Petto.
Sʳ Robert Brooke.

At Sʳ Robert Gardiner's house in Dublin, 24 September :
Sʳ Robert Osborne.
Sʳ John Pooley.

On the Sands, same day :
Sʳ John Ratliff.
Sʳ Edward Baynham.

Sʳ Thomas Loftus.
Sʳ Edward Loftus.

By Adam Loftus, Archb'p of Dublin, and Sʳ George Cary, Kt., Joint Lords Justices :
Sʳ Edmund Sandes.

By Sʳ Charles Blunt, Baron Mountjoy, Lord Deputy.

In Christchurch, 28 February :
Sʳ Oliver St. John.

1600.

In Christchurch, 6 April :
Sʳ Francis Shane.

At Dublin, 1 May :
Sʳ James Fitz Pierse.

At Drogheda, 17 November :
Sʳ William Fortescue.
Sʳ John Rotherham.
Sʳ James Dillon.

At Dublin :
Sʳ Benjamin Berry, 19 November.
Sʳ Richard Creame, 10 March.

1601.

Sʳ Thomas Savage, 31 October.

At Tyrone's overthrow at Kinsale, 24 December :
Sʳ Richard Bourke, Earl of Clanrickard.
Sʳ John Fitz Edward Fitz Gerrald of Clone, 11 March.

At   14 March :
Sʳ Tegue Tirlough O'Brian, uncle to the Earl of Thomond.

At Waterford, 18 March :
Sʳ John Fitz Gerald.
Sʳ Edward Gough.

1602.

At Dublin :
Sʳ Henry Slingsby, 19 April.
Sʳ Miles Fleetwood, 29 April.

In the Castle, 13 May :
  Sr **Richard Ailward.**
  Sr **Edward Noell.**
  Sr **Neale Garry O'Donnell.**
  Sr **Cahir O'Doghertie.**
  Sr **Randolph McDonell.**
  Sr **Randal MacSorley Boy.**
  Sr **Theobald Bourke** *alias* **Mac=
  Long,** 4 January.

At Trim :
  Sr **Randolfe Mannering,** 5 Dec.

1603.

In his Majesty's Castle at Dublin :
  Sr **Henry Leigh,** 19 April.
  Sr **Jarman Poole,** 19 April.
  Sr **Edward Blaney,** 29 May.

By Sr GEORGE CAREY, Lo. Deputy.

At Christchurch, 25 July :
  Sr **Ralph Bingley.**
  Sr **Thomas Williams.**
  Sr **Edmond Fetteplace.**
  Sr **Toby Caulfeild.**
  Sr **John Tirrell,** Mayor of Dublin.

At Dublin Castle, same day :
  Sr **Thomas Coach.**
  Sr **Ferdinando Freckleton.**
  Sr **George Greame.**
  Sr **Mulrony O'Carroll.**
  Sr **Thomas Ash.**
  Sr **William Usher.**
  Sr **Richard Boyle.**
  Sr **Laurence Esmond,** after supper.

At Christchurch, 4 September :
  Sr **Richard Wilbraham.**

At Christchurch, 16 September :
  Sr **Thomas Roper.**

At Christchurch, 18 September :
  Sr **William Windsor.**

At Dublin Castle, 29 September :
  Sr **Roderick O'Donnell,** Earl of
  Tirconell.
  Sr **Francis Rooe.**
  Sr **Henry Crofte.**
  Sr **Rafe Constable.**
  Sr **Richard Nugent,** Lo. of Delvin.
  Sr **Ralphe Sydly.**
  Sr **James Gough.**
  Sr **John Macnamara,** Thomond.

At St. Mary's Abbey, 2 October :
  Sr **William Harpole.**
  Sr **Edward Fisher.**

At Dublin Castle, 18 October :
  Sr **John Jephson.**
  Sr **John Davies.**

At Reban Castle, 22 February :
  Sr **William Brabazon.**
  Sr **Francis Kingsmill,** 9 March.
  Sr **Elias Jones.**

1604.

At Reban Castle, 25 March :
  Sr **Josias Bodley.**
  Sr **John Owesley.**
  Sr **William Taafe.**

At Reban Castle, 17 April :
  Sr **Teige O'Rourke.**
  Sr **Donnoghe O'Connor.** Sligo.
  Sr **Terloghe McHenry O'Neale.**

At Lexlipp :
  Sr **Lyonell Guest,** 5 May.
  Sr **Parr Lane,** 8 May.
  Sr **George Beverley,** 8 May.
  Sr **Richard Grymes.** 1 July.
  Sr **Daniel O'Brian,** 1 July.
  Sr **Nicholas Mordante,** 1 July.
  Sr **Ambrose Foord,** 2 August.
  Sr **John Sydney,** 15 August.
  Sr **Bryan McHugh Oge Mc=
  Mahowne,** 27 August.
  Sr **Patrick McCarty Moyle,**
  28 August.

Sʳ Penry Oge O'Neale, 12 Oct.
Sʳ Richard Hansard, 12 Oct.
Sʳ Arthur Magennis, 1 Nov.
Sʳ Gawen Harvey, 7 November.
Sʳ Christopher Nugent.

At Christchurch :
Sʳ Adam Loftus, 25 December.

By Sʳ ARTHUR CHICHESTER, Kt.,
Lord Deputy.

At Dublin Castle, 10 February :
Sʳ Thomas Rotheram.
Sʳ John Everard.
Sʳ Dominick Sarsfeild.
Sʳ Charles Calthorpe.

1605.

Sʳ Charles Butler, 12 April.
Sʳ Henry Mildmay, 25 May.
Sʳ Francis Slingsbie, 5 June.
Sʳ Allen Apslye, 5 June.
Sʳ Robert Newcomen, 9 June.
Sʳ John Bingham, 19 June.
Sʳ Edmond Wayneman, 18 July.
Sʳ Cormack McBaron O'Neale
of Merion.
Sʳ Thomas FitzWilliams.
Sʳ Christ'r Bellew or Bedlowe,
20 September.
Sʳ Thomas Burton, 5 October.
Sʳ Hugh Owen, 13 October.
Sʳ Thomas Muncke, 24 Nov.
Sʳ Robert Nugent, 14 January.

1606.

At Christchurch, 1 June :
Sʳ Edmond Walsh.

At Dublin Castle, 7 June :
Sʳ William Glynn.
Sʳ William Synnott, 22 June.
Sʳ George Sherlock, 28 Nov.

At Drogheda :
Sʳ Edmond FitzGerald, 1 Dec.
Sʳ Roger Jones, 24 March.

Sʳ Thomas Phillips, 24 March.
Sʳ Jo. More of Croaghan, 24 Mar.

1607.

At Slane :
Sʳ George Pawlett, 26 June.
Sʳ Donnell O'Cahan, 28 June.
Sʳ Thomas Chichester, 10 Aug.

At Christchurch, 5 November :
Sʳ Robert Jacob.

At Dublin Castle :
Sʳ Thomas Browne, 29 Nov.
Sʳ William St. John, 21 Dec.

1608.

Near Dundalk, 6 July :
Sʳ Robert Ridgeway.

At Christchurch :
Sʳ George Chute, 14 October.
Sʳ Barnard Grenvile, 5 November.

At Dublin Castle :
Sʳ Robert Oglethorpe, 6 January.
Sʳ John Elliott, 14 February.

1609.

Sʳ Nicholas White, 30 Sept.
Sʳ James Carroll, 30 September.
Sʳ Robert Pigott, 30 September.
Sʳ William Power, 24 March.

1610.

Sʳ Francis Willoughbie, 30 Oct.
Sʳ Adam Loftus, 22 January.
Sʳ John Bourchier, 24 March.

1611.

Sʳ Francis Cooke, 6 October.
Sʳ Mathew Carew, 6 October.
Sʳ Thomas Stafford, 6 October.

1613.

Sʳ Richard Aldworth, 22 April.
Sʳ Edward Moore, 20 July.
Sʳ Gamaliel Capell, 1 August.

By Thomas, Lo. Archbishop of Dublin, and Sʳ Richard Wingfield, Kt., Lords Justices.

1614.

Sʳ John Smyth, 5 Nov.   Warw.
Sʳ Rowland Ridgley, 5 Nov.
Sʳ Oliver Shortales, 12 February.
Sʳ Christopher Dillon, 21 Feb.

1615.

Sʳ Pierce Butler, 30 April.
Sʳ .... Porter, 11 July.
Sʳ William Cooly of Edendery, 23 July.
Sʳ Henry Belyng, 19 July.
Sʳ John Beare, the King's Serjᵗ.

By Sʳ Oliver St. John, Lord Deputy.

1616.

Sʳ Thomas Button, 30 August.
Sʳ Charles Coote, 5 November.
Sʳ Basil Brooke, 2 February.
Sʳ John Vaughan, 2 February.
Sʳ Roger O'Shaghnes, 14 Feb.
Sʳ Beverley Newcomen, 24 Mar.

1617.

Sʳ John FitzGerrald, 27 April.
Sʳ John Ringsmill, 29 June.
Sʳ George Trevellian, 29 July.
Sʳ Edward Trevor, 5 November.
Sʳ William Cole, 5 November.
Sʳ Thomas Moore, 24 November.
Sʳ William Sarsfeild, 30 Nov.
Sʳ John Dowdall, 24 March.

1618.

Sʳ Christopher Sibthorpe, 3 May.
Sʳ Garret Lowther, 3 May.
Sʳ Henry Lee, 19 May.
Sʳ William Caulfield, 8 June.
Sʳ Charles Blunt, 4 July.
Sʳ Richard Bolton, 4 July.
Sʳ Richard Calveley, 19 July.

Sʳ Thomas Tibbotts, 5 Nov.
Sʳ Edward Davies, 21 February.
Sʳ James Blunt, 24 March.

1619.

Sʳ Robert Loftus, 5 November.
Sʳ John Bellew, 5 November.
Sʳ Edward Butler, 5 November.
Sʳ Edmund Tuite, 5 November.
Sʳ William Hill, 5 November.
Sʳ Maurice Griffith, 5 November.
Sʳ William Sparke, 21 Nov.
Sʳ Charles McCarty, 24 March.

1620.

Sʳ William Parsons, 7 June.
Sʳ Robert Tuite, 4 July.
Sʳ John Dillon, 5 November.
Sʳ Laurence Parsons, 26 Nov.

1621.

Sʳ Thomas Walrond, 12 August.
Sʳ Hercules Langford, 19 Aug.
Sʳ Robert Cressie, 17 December.
Sʳ Thomas Nugent, 11 January.
Sʳ John Meade, 28 January.
Sʳ Daniel Leigh, Bart., 2 Feb.

1622.

Sʳ James Barrett, 7 February.
Sʳ John Parsons, 31 March.
Sʳ Randall Cleyton, 28 April.
Sʳ William Temple, 4 May.
Sʳ Roger Hope, 4 May.

By Sʳ Adam Loftus and Sʳ Richard Wingfield, Kt., Visc. Powerscourt, Lords Justices.

Sʳ Thomas Allen, Bart., 8 June.
Sʳ Charles O'Connor, Bart.

By Adam, Viscount Loftus, and Richard, Earl of Cork, Lords Justices.

1629.

Sʳ Edward Povey, 15 November.

Sᵣ Percy Smith, 17 January.
Sᵣ Dudley Loftus, 28 February.
Sᵣ James Ware, 28 February.
Sᵣ John Browne, 12 March.

1630.

Sᵣ Christ'r Forrester, 15 July.
Sᵣ James Moore, 15 July.
Sᵣ Walsingham Coke, 15 July.
Sᵣ Robert Eton, — August.
Sᵣ Roger Langford, 14 December.
Sᵣ Vincent Gookins. 13 February.

1631.

Sᵣ Samuel Mayart, 5 November.
Sᵣ Gerrard Lowther, 9 Nov.
Sᵣ John Philpot, — November.
Sᵣ Lancelot Lowther, 4 Dec.
Sᵣ John Sherlock, 11 December.
Sᵣ William Piers, 2 February.

By Lo. WENTWORTH, Lo. Deputy.

1633.

At Dublin Castle, 25 July :
Sᵣ George Wentworth, 5 bro. to
the Lo. Dep.
Sᵣ Thomas Danby.   York.
Sᵣ Thomas Remington.   „

At Dublin Castle :
Sᵣ Richard Plomley.

At Dublin Castle, 1 November :
Sᵣ George Radcliffe.   York.

1634.

At Dublin Castle :
Sᵣ Lorenzo Cary, 27 March.
Sᵣ Arthur Loftus, 27 April.
Sᵣ Philip Mainwaring, 13 July.

At the Mayor's House, 22 September :
Sᵣ Robert Dixon, Ma. of Dublin.
Sᵣ Robert Farrer, 5 November.

1635.

Sᵣ Nathaniel Catlyne, 18 April.

Sᵣ William Wentworth, eldest
son to the Lo. Deputy, 28 June.
Sᵣ Edward Rhodes, bro. to the
Lady Wentworth, 28 June.
Sᵣ Richard Scott, 30 June.

At Galway, 11 August :
Sᵣ Dominick Browne, Mayor.

At Dublin :
Sᵣ Robert Meredyth, 6 September.
Sᵣ Richard Dyett, 13 September.
Sᵣ John Sherlock, 13 January.
Sᵣ John Cyfford, 16 January.
Sᵣ Edward Bolton, 2 February.
Sᵣ Leo. Blenerhassett, 6 March.

1636.

Sᵣ John Gibson, 3 April.   York.
Sᵣ William Usher, 26 May.
Sᵣ Paul Davies, 2 June.
Sᵣ Philip Percival, 2 June.
Sᵣ John South, 27 November.
Sᵣ Henry Frankland, 27 Novemb.

1637.

Sᵣ Richard Osbaldeston, 9 April.
Sᵣ Wʼm Wentworth, 23 July.
Sᵣ Dominick White, 28 August.

1638.

Sᵣ Morrice Williams, 22 April.
Sᵣ Robert Parkhurst, 29 April.
Sᵣ Randall MacDonell, Earl of
Antrim, 17 March.
Sᵣ Phelim O'Neale, 17 March.

1639.

Sᵣ Andrew Barrett, 7 July.
Sᵣ William Sambrick, — Sept.

1640.

Sᵣ James Barry, — August.
Sᵣ Thomas Tempest, 30 Dec.

1641.

Sᵣ John Paye, 23 October.
Sᵣ John Borlase, 1 November.
Sᵣ William Courtenay, 1 Nov.

By Henry Cromwell, Lord Deputy-General of Ireland.

1657.

In the Council Chamber:

Sᵣ Mathew Thomlinson, 24 Nov.

1658.

Sᵣ Robert Goodwin, 3 May.

At Cork House, 7 June, forenoon:

Sᵣ Maurice Fenton.

In the Council Chamber, 7 June, afternoon:

Sᵣ John Ring.

At Dublin Castle:

Sᵣ William Berry, 21 July.
Sᵣ John Percivall, 22 July.
Sᵣ Anthony Morgan, 26 July.
Sᵣ Thomas Herbert, 26 July.
Sᵣ Pierome Sankp, 16 November.
Sᵣ Daniel Abbott, 16 November.
Sᵣ Henry Piers, 30 November.
Sᵣ William Pen, 30 December.
Sᵣ Thomas Stanley, 24 January.
Sᵣ Oliver St. George, 23 Feb.

By Sᵣ Maurice Eustace, Lord Chancellor, Roger, Earl of Orrery, and Charles, Earl of Mountrath, Lords Justices.

1660.

Sᵣ William Bury, 26 January.
Sᵣ Arthur Denny, 16 February.
Sᵣ Boyle Maynard, 16 February.
Sᵣ Herb. Adrian Verbere, 21 Feb.
Sᵣ Richard Lane, 22 February.
Sᵣ John Rowley, 13 March.
Sᵣ Nicholas Purdon, 14 March.
Sᵣ Peter Courthop, 15 March.
Sᵣ William Ring, 16 March.
Sᵣ Ralph Wilson, 18 March.
Sᵣ Francis Foulke, 19 March.
Sᵣ St. John Broderic, 20 March.

1661.

Sᵣ James Donnalan, 23 April.
Sᵣ William Titchborne, 23 April.
Sᵣ William Dixon, 23 April.
Sᵣ Francis Gore, 8 May.
Sᵣ Richard Rearles, 19 May.
Sᵣ George St. George, 29 May.

By James, Duke of Ormonde, Lord Lieut.

1662.

Sᵣ James Weymes, 3 August.
Sᵣ William Davies, 3 August.
Sᵣ George Carr, 3 August.
Sᵣ Nicholas Loftus, 24 August.
Sᵣ Toby Poynty, 7 September.
Sᵣ George Gilbert, 30 Sept.
Sᵣ Daniel Bellingham, 30 Sept.
Sᵣ Henry Waddington, 16 Nov.

1663.

Sᵣ Peter Pett, 30 March.
Sᵣ John Temple, 15 August.
Sᵣ Thomas Fortescue.

By Thomas, Earl of Ossory, Lord Deputy.

1664.

Sᵣ Thomas Parman, 5 June.
Sᵣ Henry Brookes, 5 June.
Sᵣ Francis Peasley, 7 August.
Sᵣ Thomas Worssop, 4 Sept.
Sᵣ Tristram Beresford.
Sᵣ George Ingoldsby.
Sᵣ Albert Cunningham.
Sᵣ Charles Meredith.
Sᵣ Thomas Newcomen.
Sᵣ John Davys.
Sᵣ John Edgeworth.
Sᵣ Michael Cole.
Sᵣ John Totty, 7 April, 1672.
Sᵣ Charles Fielding.
Sᵣ Richard Aldworth.

' 1674.

Sr **Joshua Allen,** 29 May.
Sr **Arthur Jones.**
Sr **John Champanti,** 13 Dec.
Sr **Robert Colvile.**
Sr **John Parker.**
Sr **John Topham.**

By JAMES, DUKE OF ORMOND, Lord-
Lieut.

1677.

Sr **John Dillon.**
Sr **Thomas Crosley.**
Sr **Henry Wemys.**
Sr **John Meade.**
Sr **Richard Hull.**
Sr **Samuel Foxen.**   Limerick.
(The last three made in the progress.)

1678.

Sr **Robert Gore,** 23 February.
Sr **Thomas Osborne,** 5 November.
Sr **Henry Ponsonby.**

1680.

Sr **John Magill,** 5 November.
Sr **Mathew Deane,** 3 December.
Sr **Philip Coote,** 21 December.

1681.

Sr **Richard Reves,** 1 May.
Sr **Pumphrey Jervis,** 5 Nov.

By RICHARD, EARL OF ARRAN, Lord
Deputy.

1682.

Sr **Thomas Atkins,** 29 January.

1683.

Sr **James Leigh,** 21 April.
Sr **Richard Dixon,** 24 February.

1684.

Sr **Richard Carney,** King of
Arms, 6 April.
Sr **Elias Best,** Lo. Mayor, 23 April.

By JAMES, DUKE OF ORMOND, Lo. Lieut.

Sr **Abell Ram,** Lo. Mayor, 13 Nov.
Sr **William Dombille,** 7 Jan.

1685.

By HENRY, EARL OF CLARENDON,
Lo. Lieut.

Sr **John Fleming,** 6 February.
Sr **John Knox,** Lo. Mayor, 6 Feb.

1686.

Sr **Michael Creagh,** 23 April.
Sr **John Coghill,** 5 June.
Sr **John Castleton,** 1 January.

By RICHARD, EARL OF TYRCONNEL,
Lo. Deputy.

Sr **Richard Nagle,** 20 February.

1687.

Sr **Stephen Rice,** 21 August.
Sr **Thomas Hackett,** Lo. Mayor,
31 October.
Sr **John Barnewall,** Recorder,
1 November.
Sr **Anthony Mullaly,** 13 March.

1688.

Sr **Mathew Bridges,** who brought
news of the Prince's birth.

By his Majesty King JAMES II., who
landed at Kinsale, 12 March.

Sr **Theodore Butler.**

1690.

Sr **Terence McDermot,** Lord
Mayor, 14 May.
Sr **Teigue O'Regan,** 12 May.

By HENRY, VISCOUNT SYDNEY,
Lord Lieut.

1692.

Sr **Michael Mitchell,** Lo. Mayor,
5 September.
Sr **Rich. Levinge,** 28 September.

In the Presence Chamber, 5 Nov. :

Sr Richard Pyne, Lo. Ch. J. Com. Pleas.

Sr John Hely, Lo. Ch. Baron.

Sr Richard Cox, Judge Com. Pleas.

Sr John Jeffreyson, Judge Com. Pleas.

Sr John Lyndon, Judge Q. Bench.

Sr Henry Echlin, Judge Q. Bench.

1693.

Sr Thomas Packenham, 12 May.

Sr John Rogerson, Lo. Mayor Elect, 12 June.

By LORD CAPEL, SIR CYRIL WYCH, and WILLIAM DUNCOMBE, Lords Justices.

1694.

Sr Henry Titchbourne, 28 March.

By CHARLES, EARL OF MOUNTRATH, and HENRY, EARL OF DOUGLAS, Lords Justices.

1696.

Sr Patrick Dunn, 29 January.

By the MARQUIS OF WINCHESTER, the EARL OF GALWAY, and the LORD VILLIERS.

1697.

Sr William Billington, Lo. Mayor, 17 June.

1698.

Sr John Mason, 20 July.

APPENDIX.

KNIGHTS NOT INCLUDED IN THE PRECEDING PAGES.

1449.

Knights of the Bath made at Christmas at Greenwich (Sir N. H. Nicolas's Orders of Knighthood):

Sʳ Edmund Tudor.
Sʳ Jasper Tudor.
Sʳ Thomas Neville.
Sʳ John Neville.
Sʳ William Herbert.
Sʳ Roger Lewknor.   Sussex.
Sʳ William Catesby.

1464.

Knights of the Bath made at the Coronation of Elizabeth, Queen of Edward IV., 20 May (*Ibid.*):

Sʳ Hen. Stafford, 2 Duke of Bucks.
Sʳ . . . . Stafford, his brother.
Sʳ John de Vere, 13 E. of Oxford.
Sʳ Thomas Talbot, 2 Visc. Lisle.
Sʳ John Fitzalan, Lord Maltravers, son and heir of John Fitzalan, 2 Earl of Arundel.
Sʳ George Grey, son and heir of Edmund, 1 Earl of Kent.
Sʳ Richard Widvile.
Sʳ John Widvile.
Sʳ Ralph Josselyne.
Sʳ Richard Bingham, Justice of the Common Pleas.
Sʳ Robert Danvers, Justice of the King's Bench.

Sʳ John Needham, Justice of the Common Pleas.
Sʳ Richard Choke, Justice of the King's Bench.
Sʳ Walter Moyle, Justice of the King's Bench.
Sʳ Richard Illingworth, Chief Baron of the Exchequer.
Sʳ . . . . Hingham.
Sʳ John Arundell.
Sʳ William Calthorp.
Sʳ Thomas Brewce.
Sʳ George Daville.
Sʳ Richard Harcourt.
Sʳ Walter Mantell.
Sʳ Edmund Rede.
Sʳ William Hawte.
Sʳ John Clifford.
Sʳ John Say.
Sʳ John Cheyney of Canterbury.
Sʳ Robert Darcy.
Sʳ Thomas Uvedale.
Sʳ John Durward.
Sʳ John Heningham.
Sʳ John Savage.
Sʳ Roger Corbet of Murton.
Sʳ (Nicholas ?) Culpeper.
Sʳ Thomas Cooke.
Sʳ John Plomer.
Sʳ Henry Wafyr.
Sʳ Mathew Philip.
Lord Duras, a Gascon.
Sʳ Bartelot de Robert, a Bayonne Gascon.

1522.

Knights made by the Lord Admiral after the taking of Morlaix, 1 July, 15 Hen. VIII., "for ther hardines and noble courage" (Hall's Chronicle):

Sr FRANCIS BRYAN.
Sr ANTHONY BROWNE.
Sr RICHARD CROMWELL.
Sr HENRY MORE.
Sr GILES HUSSEY.
Sr JOHN RUSSELL.
Sr JOHN RAYNSFORD.
Sr GEORGE COBHAM.
Sr JOHN CORNWALLIS.
Sr EDWARD RIGLEY, and divers others.

1553.

Knights made at the Coronac'on of Queen Mary, not included in Cotton MS., Claudius, c. iii. (1., 7, Coll. Armor.; Harl. MS. 6063):

Sr HENRY GASTON (Gascon, Harl. 6063).
Sr RICHARD MORGAN, Chief Justice.
Sr THOMAS WHITE, M^r of the requests.
Sr RICHARD LAWSON.
Sr HENRY CRIPPS.
Sr THOMAS ANDREWS.
Sr JOHN CROFTS.
Sr EDWARD, LORD DUDLEY (but see p. 107).
Sr ROWLAND STANLEY.
Sr RICHARD BRAYE.
S^r EDW. PYLSON (1.,7, Coll. Armor.; Edmond Pinson, Harl. 6063).
Sr WILLIAM LAWSON.
Sr JOHN BREWSE.
Sr RICHARD CHUDLEY.

Knights not included in Cotton MS., Claudius, c. iii., taken from "a Catalogue of all the Knights dubbed in the tyme of Queene Elizabeth, drawne into Alphabet," Harl. MS. 6063, compared with and corrected from Lans. MS. 678:

Sr EDWARD BUTLER, brother to the Earl of Ormond. 1559.
Sr EDWARD STANLEY, brother to the Earl of Derby. 1559.
Sr JOHN ALLOTT, Lo. Mayor. 1591.
Sr EDMOND BUTLER, Ireland. 1567.
Sr EDMOND BUTLER, Ireland. 1583.
Sr RICHARD BOURK. 1583.
Sr GEORGE BARNE, Lo. Mayor. 1586.
Sr BARTHOLOMEW BAFFORD. 1586.
Sr GEORGE BOND, Lo. Mayor. 1587.
Sr PAUL BACKES. 1588.
Sr THOMAS BASKERVILE. 1588.
Sr WILLIAM BEVILL. 1589.
Sr MICHAEL BLOUNT. 1590.
Sr GEORGE BROWNE. 1591.
Sr WILLIAM BRIDGES. 1592.
Sr WILLIAM BRINKERD. 1592.
Sr HENRY BROMLEY. 1592.
Sr HENRY BILLINGSLEY, Lo. Mayor. 1596.
Sr GEORGE BOOTH. 1599.
Sr EDWARD BROOKE. 1599.
Sr CUTHBERT COLLINGBOURNE. 1570.
Sr HENRY COWLEY. 1576.
Sr ROWLAND CLARKE. 1578.
Sr ROBERT CLARKE, Baron of the Exchequer. 1578.
Sr WILLIAM CLARKE. 1578.
Sr THOMAS CUSACK. 1583.
Sr HENRY CONSTABLE. 1586.
Sr MARTIN CALTHORPE, Lo. Mayor. 1588.
Sr GEORGE E. of Cumberland. 1588.
Sr ROBERT CECILL. 1591.
Sr WALTER COVERT. 1591.
Sr JOHN CARRELL. 1591.
Sr CONYERS CLIFFORD. 1591.

Sr ANTHONY COPE.	1591.		Sr EDWARD LAYTON.	1591.
Sr ARTHUR CHICHESTER.	1596.		Sr THOMAS LUCY, Junior.	1592.
Sr THOMAS DESMOND.	1583.		Sr RICH. LEVER, a stranger.	1596.
Sr LEWIS DYVE.	1587.		Sr PETER LEE, Ireland.	1599.
Sr ROBERT DORMER.	1591.		Sr JOHN LYNE.	1599.
Sr FRANCIS DARCY.	1591.		Sr RICHARD LEE.	1599.
Sr EDWARD DYER.	1596.		Sr RICHARD LEWKENOR.	1600.
Sr ROBERT DUDLEY.	1596.		Sr RICHARD LEE (see above).	1600.
Sr OCHEMACH DRINIR.	1596.		Sr PETER MANNERINGE.	1565.
Sr WILLIAM EYRE.	1592.		Sr JOHN McCOSTLYN.	1584.
Sr CHRISTOPHER EDMONDS.	1592.		S^r .... McNEALE (Neale, Lans.	
Sr THOMAS FITZ WILLIAM.	1565.		678).	1584.
Sr THOMAS FITZ MORRIS.	1567.		Sr RICHARD MALORY.	1586.
Sr FRANCIS FLEMING.	1583.		Sr JOHN MANNERS.	1587.
Sr PIERCE FITZJAMES.	1585.		Sr THOMAS MORGAN.	1587.
Sr EDWARD FERRERS.	1590.		Sr ANTHONY MANEY (but see p. 208).	
Sr HUMPHRY FOSTER.	1592.			1588.
Sr RICHARD FYNES.	1592.		Sr RICH. MARTIN, Lo. Mayor.	1589.
Sr JOHN FORTESCUE.	1592.		Sr GEORGE MANNERING.	1595.
Sr RICHARD FETIPLACE.	1599.		S^r .... MOLINES, Junr (Lans. 678).	
Sr THOMAS GORGES.	1586.			1596.
Sr HENRY GREY.	1587.		Sr BARRENTINO MOLINES (Harl.	
Sr ROBERT GARDINER.	1591.		6063).	1596.
Sr HENRY GLEMHAM.	1591.		Sr HENRY NORTH.	1586.
Sr HENRY GORING.	1591.		Sr HENRY NEWTON.	1592.
Sr HENRY GUILFORD.	1591.		Sr THOMAS NAPPER.	1593.
S^r .... GUILFORD.	1596.		S^r ONY OBASTRICH (Oshastrich,	
Sr BASSINGBOURNE GAWDY.	1597.		Lans. 678).	1567.
Sr ARTHUR GORGES.	1597.		Sr FRANCIS ODRISCOLL.	1583.
Sr NICHOLAS HERON.	1565.		Sr DONOUGH OLIVER.	1583.
Sr THOMAS HUMFREY.	1581.		Sr JOHN ODONERLEY.	1585.
Sr JOHN HART, Lo. Maior.	1590.		Sr JOHN PERROTT.	1561.
Sr RALPH HORSEY.	1590.		Sr BRYAN PHILLYN.	1567.
Sr JOHN HUNGERFORD.	1590.		Sr HORATIO PALAVICHINI.	1587.
Sr WALTER HARCOURT.	1591.		Sr JOHN PACKINGTON.	1587.
Sr CLEMENT HIGHAM.	1591.		Sr RICHARD PAWLETT.	1591.
Sr JOHN HICKFORD.	1591.		Sr JOHN PUCKERINGE.	1592.
Sr FRANCIS HASTINGS.	1592.		Sr JOHN POPHAM.	1592.
Sr HUGH JAMES.	1597.		Sr WILLIAM PERIAM.	1592.
Sr HENRY KILLEGREW.	1591.		Sr JOHN PEYTON.	1596.
Sr HENRY LEA.	1561.		Sr JOHN ROPER.	1587.
Sr EVAN LLOYDE.	1586.		Sr THOMAS READ.	1592.
Sr WALTER LEVESON.	1587.		Sr WILLIAM ROWE.	1593.
Sr WILLIAM LEIGH.	1589.		Sr WILLIAM READ.	1595.
Sr JOHN LEVESON.	1589.		Sr THOMAS RIDGWAY.	1600.
Sr THOMAS LLOYDE alias FLUDD.			Sr ANTHONIE STANDEN.	1559.
	1589.		Sr GEORGE STANLEY.	1565.

Sᵣ Warhám St. Leger.   1565.
Sᵣ Warham St. Leger.   1583.
Sᵣ Connogh McSkrine.   1585.
Sᵣ Martin Skinke.   1586.
Sᵣ Alexander Steward.   1586.
Sᵣ John Spencer.   1588.
Sᵣ William Sackvill.   1589.
Sᵣ Walter Sandes.   1591.
Sᵣ John Seymour.   1591.
Sᵣ Anthony Shelley.   1591.
Sᵣ William Spencer.   1592.
Sᵣ Anthony St. Leger.   1593.
Sᵣ John Spencer, Lo. Mayor.   1595.
Sᵣ John Stanhop.   1596.
Sᵣ Richard Saltingstall, Lord
   Mayor.   1597.
Sᵣ Francis Stafford.   1599.
Sᵣ John Savage.   1599.
Sᵣ Thomas Throckmorton.   1587.
Sᵣ George Trenchard.   1588.
Sᵣ James Whitney.   1578.
Sᵣ Thomas West.   1587.
Sᵣ Richard Welche.   1590.
Sᵣ Thomas West (but see above).
                                1591.
Sᵣ Wm. Webb, Lo. Maior.   1592.
Sᵣ Edward Wotton.   1592.
Sᵣ Henry Winston.   1592.
Sᵣ John Woolley.   1592.
Sᵣ William Weston.   1593.
Sᵣ Edward Winter.   1595.
Sᵣ William Wray.   1596.
Sᵣ Anthony Wingfield.   1597.
Sᵣ William Zouch.   1579.

Knights made during the reign of
James I., not included in Cotton
MS., Claudius, c. iii. (MS., Coll.
Armor., and Lans. MS. 678):

1603.

At Newcastle, 9 April:
Sᵣ Nicholas Scriven (struck out
   of Lans. MS. 678).
Sᵣ Robert Dudley.

At the Charterhouse, 4 May:
Sᵣ John Hevesingham.   Norfolk.

At Sir John Fortescue's, — June:
Sᵣ Edmond Herrick (perhaps same
   as Sᵣ Edward Horrell at p. 144).

At Hanworth, 23 July:
Sᵣ Robert Kelligrew.

At Whitehall, 23 July:
Sᵣ Thomas Verney (probably the
   same as Richard at p. 146, there
   being a Richard at p. 141).
Sᵣ Thomas Phillips.
Sᵣ Charles Pershall.
Sᵣ Thomas Crowe.

At the Tower, 14 March:
Sᵣ Nicholas Blunt.
Sᵣ Robert Donalt.
Sᵣ Thomas Montford.
Sᵣ Robert Verney (probably same
   as Francis p. 152).

1604.

At Newmarket, 20 February:
Sᵣ Edw. Francis (but see p. 142).

1607.

At Whitehall, 21 January:
Sᵣ Henry Lille or Lillie.

At Theobald's, 30 January:
Sᵣ Ferdinando Fairfax.

1610.

Sᵣ James Vanden Eynden (Rot.
Tractat., 8 Jac. I., m. 1).

1612.

Sᵣ William Van der Rit (Rot.
Tractat., 10 Jac. I., m. 12).
(Both quoted in Rymer's 'Fœdera,'
with arms and crest granted to
the first.)

Lord Mayors Knighted, not included
in Cotton MS., Claudius, c. iii.
(Stow's 'Survey of London'):
Sᵣ John Rainewell.   1426.
Sᵣ John Gedney.   1427.
Sᵣ Henry Barton.   1428.

Sʳ WILLIAM EASTFIELD,	1429.
made Knight of the Bath.	1437.
Sʳ JOHN DE WELLES.	1431.
Sʳ JOHN PARVEIS.	1432.
Sʳ JOHN BROCKLEY.	1433.
Sʳ ROGER OTLEY.	1434.
Sʳ HENRY FROWICKE.	1435.
Sʳ JOHN MICHELL.	1436.
Sʳ STEPHEN BROWN.	1438.
Sʳ JOHN PADDESLEY.	1440.
Sʳ SIMON EYRE.	1445.
Sʳ THOMAS CHALTON.	1449.
Sʳ WILLIAM GREGORY.	1451.
Sʳ GEFFREY FIELDING.	1452.
Sʳ JOHN NORMAN.	1453.
Sʳ STEPHEN FOSTER.	1455.
Sʳ WILLIAM MARROW.	1455.
Sʳ THOMAS CANNING.	1456.
Sʳ GODFREY BULLEN.	1457.
Sʳ THOMAS SCOT.	1458.
Sʳ WILLIAM HULIN.	1459.
Sʳ RICHARD LEE.	1460.
Sʳ HUGH WICHE.	1461.
Sʳ THOMAS COOKE (see p. 219).	
	1462.
Sʳ MATHEW PHILIP (see p. 219).	
	1463.
Sʳ RALPH JOCELIN (see p. 219).	
	1464.
Sʳ THOMAS OWLGRAVE.	1467.
Sʳ WILLIAM EDWARDS.	1471.
Sʳ JOHN TATE.	1473.
Sʳ ROBERT DROPE.	1474.
Sʳ ROBERT BASSET.	1475.
Sʳ HUMFREY HEYFORD.	1477.
Sʳ JOHN BROWNE.	1480.
Sʳ WILLIAM HERIOT.	1481.

Sʳ EDMOND SHAA.	1482.
Sʳ THOMAS HILL.	1484.
Sʳ ROBERT TATE.	1488.
Sʳ WILLIAM WHITE.	1489.
Sʳ HUGH CLOPTON.	1491.
Sʳ WILLIAM MARTIN.	1492.
Sʳ RICHARD CHAWRY.	1494.
Sʳ JOHN PERCIVAL.	1498.
Sʳ NICHOLAS ALDWINE.	1499.
Sʳ WILLIAM REMINGTON.	1500.
Sʳ JOHN SHAA.	1501.
Sʳ BARTHOLOMEW REDE.	1502.
Sʳ WILLIAM CAPELL.	1503.
Sʳ JOHN WINGER.	1504.
Sʳ THOMAS KNESWORTH.	1505.
Sʳ STEPHEN JENNINGS.	1508.
Sʳ HENRY KEBLE.	1510.
Sʳ ROGER ATCHERLEY.	1511.
Sʳ WILLIAM COPINGER.	1512.
Sʳ WILLIAM BROWNE.	1513.
Sʳ GEORGE MONOX.	1514.
Sʳ JOHN REST.	1516.
Sʳ THOMAS MERFINE.	1518.
Sʳ JOHN BRUGES.	1520.
Sʳ JOHN MILBORNE.	1521.
Sʳ THOMAS SEYMER.	1526.
Sʳ NICHOLAS LAMBERT.	1531.
Sʳ CHRISTOPHER ASKEW.	1532.
Sʳ JOHN CHAMPNEIS.	1533.
Sʳ WILLIAM ROCHE.	1540.
Sʳ WILLIAM BOWYER.	1543.
Sʳ RICHARD DOBBES.	1551.
Sʳ GEORGE BARNE.	1552.
Sʳ CUTHBERT BUCKLE.	1593.
Sʳ RICHARD MARTIN.	1593.
Sʳ JOHN GERRARD.	1601.
Sʳ THOMAS BENNET.	1603.

NOTES AND CORRECTIONS.

Page 4, *dele* Sir Richard Charleton, it is clearly a double entry (see page 5). Sir ... Pilkington is called *John* in Sir N. H. Nicolas's " Orders of Knighthood."

„ 7, Sir William should probably be Sir *Richard* Wentworth (see page 5).

„ 11, line 24, *for* bars *read pales.*

„ 15, line 7 from bottom, *read* saltire *engrailed.*

„ 16, last line, *for* orant *read Or and.*

„ 18, line 4, *for* eight *read six ;* line 6, *for* leaves *read feathers ;* line 8 from bottom, *read* saltire *engrailed.*

„ 20, lines 2 and 4, *for* Or *read Argent ;* line 7, *read* invected *Gules.*

„ 22, line 6, *for* logenzy *read lozengy ;* line 12, *for* field *read second ;* line 26, *dele* engrailed.

„ 24, line 1, *read* a chevron *Gules between three cranes proper ;* line 11, *for* Or *read Argent.*

„ 25, line 10, *for* rampant *read passant.*

„ 26, line 21, *read* indented *Azure.*

„ 27, line 7 from bottom, *for* 22 *read 23.*

„ 28, after Sir John Rodney *add* 𝔖r 𝔍oḥn 𝔐ontgomerp, Quarterly, 1 and 4, Or, an eagle displayed Azure ; 2 and 3, Ermine, on a bordure gules eight horse-shoes Or.

„ 30, line 6 from bottom, *read Sable, between four Cornish choughs proper ;* lines 3 and 4 from bottom, *read, on a fess Gules between three annulets Sable.*

„ 31. I am indebted to Mr. William Brown of Arncliff Hall, for the insertion of the following very interesting document, discharging William Maleverer, Esq., from taking knighthood of the Bath on the marriage of Prince Arthur. The original is in the possession of Douglas Brown, Esq., Q.C., of Arncliff Hall :
" This bill indentyd made at Westm' the xxij^{th} day of May the xxviij^{th} yere of the Reigne of oure Souerayne lord Kyng Henr^y the vij^{th} (1503) wittinessith that Mr John Walles clerc hathe receyued in the name and for thuse and behove of our said Souereigne lord Kyng off William Maleuerer of Wedersom (in Bardsey) in the Com^r of York Esquier in redy money sevyn poundes and ten shelinges of lawfull money of England in full contentacon of xv li. for the fine of the said William made and geven to the Kynges grace for his pardon to be relissid frome thordre of Knyghthod of the Bath at the mariage of my lord Arthur late Prince. In wyttinesse hereof th'ether pertie enterchangeabully hathe sette ther seales and subscribed ther names the day and yere above said, per me
" Joh'em Walles."

., 32, Sr Richard Fowler *add* Crest, a wolf's head erased Gules.

,. 33, line 9, *read* saltire *engrailed.*

„ 34, line 5, *read* bend *engrailed ;* line 6 from bottom, *for* Or *read Azure.*

„ 36. line 2, *for* of the second *read Azure ;* line 21, *read* crusily *Or.*

., 37, line 10, *for* sejant *read couchant ;* line 18 from bottom, *read* Gules *crusily fitchée.*

„ 38, line 3 from bottom, *read* lion *passant.*

., 39, line 20, *read* bend *engrailed ;* line 20 from bottom, *read a bordure gobony of the third and first.*

,. 42, line 19, *dele* fitchée ; line 14 from bottom, *for* Or *read Argent.*

., 44, line 9 from bottom, *for* bars *read pales.*

., 45, line 5 from bottom, *for* bend *read fess.*

,: 47, Tourraine means *Tervueren,* 6 miles E.S.E. from Brussels.

„ 48, line 18 from bottom, *for* Azure *read Gules.*

„ 49, line 14, *add* Crest, out of a ducal coronet Or, a plume of feathers Argent, a mullet for difference.

„ 50, line 16, *for* Ermine *read pied ;* last line but 2, *read* patée fitchée.

„ 51, line 2, *for* leopard *read wolf.*

„ 52, line 13 from bottom, *for* Or *read Azure.*

„ 54, line 1, *for* sergeant Or *read* segreant *Argent ;* line 17 from bottom, *read on a saltire Argent a pellet,* but probably it should be an annulet sable for difference ; line 12 from bottom, *for* bend *read chevron.*

„ 55, line 2, *for* and *read as in ;* line 15, this coat really is Vair Argent guttée de poix and Gules ; line 16, *for* Azure *read Argent.*

Page 56, line 17 from bottom, *for* Or *read* *reall Argent.*

„ 57, line 11, *for* a crescent *read but no crescent.*

„ 60, line 17 from bottom, *for* Or *read of the second;* in the next line, *for* fourth *read fifth.*

„ 61, line 12, the pallisadoes are in fact *spears.* Sir *Thomas* Pargeter was Mayor of London 1530.

„ 62, line 19 from bottom, *for* bend *read fess.*

„ 63, line 7, *read* 1 and 4 as 1, and 2 and 3 as 2 ; line 7 from bottom, *read* per pale indented *Or and Gules,* in the first and fourth quarters five lozenges in cross *of the second.*

„ 67, line 8 from bottom, *read* Arms *of Evers;* line 12 from bottom, *read* three bows *paleways in fess.*

„ 68, line 22, *read* in chief *Or;* and in the next line, *read* in base *Argent.*

„ 69, Sir Nicholas Forman is probably the same as Sir *William* mentioned by Stow as Lord Mayor in 1538 ; line 21, *add* his CREST, a demi-wyvern segreant Or, scaled Vert ; line 31, *for* second *read third;* line 8 from bottom, *for* Argent *read Or;* and line 9 from bottom, *read* three bows *paleways in fess.*

„ 70, line 23, *for* pale *read fess.*

„ 71, line 23, *add* CREST, a boar's head erect Argent, eared Or.

„ 73, line 10 from bottom, *for* fourth *read fifth.*

„ 74, line 1, *for* Azure *read Sable;* and next line, *for* Sable *read of the field.*

„ 75, line 18, *read* erased Or.

„ 78, lines 21 and 22, *read* Quartering, 1, *Argent, three turnpikes Sable, and* 2, *Argent, on a chevron Gules between three goats' heads Azure as many billets Or;* line 11 from bottom, *read* ARMS—Quarterly, 1 and 4 as at p. 74 ; 2, Gules, three water-bougets Argent— quartering, 1, Gules, three wheels Argent ; 2, Azure, a Catherine-wheel Or ; 3, Gules, an eagle displayed Argent ; 4, Argent, two chevrons Gules ; 5, Argent, a fess between two bars- gemelles Gules ; 3, quarterly, 1, 2, and 4, as at p. 74 ; 3, Chequy Argent and Gules.

„ 79, line 5, *for* Argent *read Or;* line 12, *after* as at p. 27 *add* but 2 and 3 are *Vair three bends Gules;* line 18 from bottom, *for* fess *read chevron;* line 5 from bottom, *for* spears *read spurs.*

„ 80, line 7 from bottom, *add, over the crest a bendlet sinister.*

„ 81, line 9, *for* fleurs-de-lis *read water-bougets;* and next line, *after* Vert *read over all a bend Gules.*

„ 83, line 9 from bottom, *read* heads *erased.*

„ 85, line 4, *for* chevron *read saltire* charged with a martlet Or and four bezants ; and line 6, *for* Or *read of the third.*

„ 86, line 6, *for* chevron *read saltire.*

„ 87, line 10, for 45 *read 44;* line 19 from bottom, *after* as at p. 32 *read, but no saltire on the bend.*

„ 88, line 16 from bottom, *for* of the first *read second.*

„ 90, line 12, *read* ARMS—Quarterly, 1, Tyrell as at p. 17 ; 2, *Paly of six Argent and Sable* (Burgatt) ; 3, *Gules,* on a chevron Argent *three dolphins embowed Vert* (Flambert) ; 4, Coggeshall as at p. 48 ; Crest as at p. 47, without the difference. Line 11 from bottom, *for* 52 *read* 47.

„ 91, line 17, *dele* and crest ; and *after* p. 22 *add* CREST, a wolf salient Argent, collared and lined Or.

„ 92, line 20 from bottom, *dele* in pale ; line 8 from bottom, *for* chequy *read counter-compony.*

„ 93, line 11 from bottom, *read* Or, attired Argent; last line, *read* Arms *within a bordure engrailed of the second.*

„ 94, line 2 from bottom, *for* Ermine *read Argent;* line 12 from bottom, *for* gorged *read crowned.*

„ 95, line 8, *for* gobony *read counter-compony;* line 12 from bottom, *dele* 2, 3, 4, 5, 6.

„ 96, line 6, *for* erased *read maned.*

„ 97, line 15, *for* second *read third;* line 17, *add* CREST, a wyvern's head erased Gules, gorged with two bars Or ; line 19 from bottom, *for* eight *read seven.*

„ 99, line 6, *read* Or, a chevron *between* three escallops Gules.

„ 100, line 23 from bottom, *read* but the tinctures are reversed.

„ 102, line 16, *for* Or *read Argent;* line 23, *add* but the Crest is Gules ; line 20 from bottom, *for* chevron *read saltire;* line 6 from bottom, *for* lion *read tiger.*

„ 103, line 18 from bottom, *for* bend *read chevron.*

„ 105, line 18, *after* Argent *read within a bordure gobony Or and of the second, on every first division a torteau.*

G G

Page 106, line 20, *for* boar *read* bear; next line but two, *after* p. 67 *add* but on the chief a demi-lion rampant issuant Sable.

,, 107, line 1, *for* eight *read* seven; line 15 from bottom, *for* bend *read fess.*

,, 108, line 4, *read* fess *engrailed*; line 11 from bottom, *for* barry *read paly.*

,, 109, line 21 from bottom, *for* Gules *read Azure*; and last line but one, *for* 76 *read 39.*

,, 110, last line, *after* Or *read a bendlet Sable.*

,, 111, line 20, *for* lion's gambs *read eagle's legs.*

,, 112, line 6 from bottom, *add* but the cross is Or; last line, *add* CREST, an arm erect vested Gules between two wings Sable, in the hand proper a falcon Azure belled and jessed Or.

,, 113. In Harl. MS. 6064 𝔖𝔦𝔯 𝔍𝔬𝔥𝔫 𝔚𝔥𝔦𝔡𝔡𝔬𝔫, the Judge, is given instead of 𝔖𝔦𝔯 𝔍𝔬𝔥𝔫 𝔚𝔶𝔫𝔡𝔬𝔲𝔱 as knighted 27 January 1554; he certainly was a judge at that time, and probably Wyndout is given in Cotton, Claudius, c. iii., in error for Sir John Whiddon; the arms here given are those of Wyndout.

,, 115, line 6, *after* difference *add* 5, Argent, a fess between six leaves Gules.

,, 116, line 3 from bottom, *for* mullet *read label.*

,, 118, line 15, *read* Arms—1, 2, and 4 *as* 1, 2, and 4 at p. 9; 3, Or, three piles conjoined in base Azure; and the same crest. Line 12 from bottom, *for* barry *read paly.*

,, 120. line 8 from bottom, *for* potent *read moline.*

,, 121, line 11 from bottom, *after* p. 19 *read* but omitting the coat barry of ten.

,, 123, line 5. *read 1 and 4 as at p. 44;* line 9, *for* 88 *read 44.*

,, 124, line 6 from bottom, *for* paly *read barry.*

,, 126, line 19, *for* eagles' heads *read griffins' heads.*

,, 127, line 8 from bottom, *for* Or *read Argent.*

,, 128, line 21 from bottom. *for* chevron *read saltire.*

,, 130, line 8 from bottom, *for* potent *read moline*; line 4 from bottom, *for* barry *read paly.*

,, 131, line 2, *for* fleur-de-lis *read trefoil slipped.*

,, 132, line 22 from bottom. *for* bars *read poles.*

,, 135, line 14 from bottom, *for* eagles' heads *read griffins' heads.*

,, 136, *dele* line 17 from bottom.

,, 137, *dele* line 14.

,, 142, col. 2, *dele* Sir John Shirley entered in col. 1; col. 2, *for* 𝔖𝔦𝔯 𝔈𝔡𝔴𝔞𝔯𝔡 𝔚𝔞𝔱𝔰𝔬𝔫 *read* 𝔖𝔦𝔯 𝔈𝔡𝔴𝔞𝔯𝔡 𝔏𝔶𝔤𝔬𝔫.

,, 144, *after* At Sir John Fortescue's *add* .... June. Sir Thomas Preston is here probably a double entry, see p. 142; also Sir John Langton, see p. 143. Sir Edmund Horrell is given as HERRICK in Lans. MS. 678, see Appendix, p. 222; *dele* the second Sir Henry Billingsley, evidently a double entry.

,, 146, col. 2, Sir Richard Etherington is called *Elderton* in Lans. MS. 678.

,, 147, Sir Gideon Awnsham is called *Julian Hanson* in the same MS.

,, 148, Sir Roger Horton is called *Robert* Horton in the same MS.

,, 149, Sir William Howson is called *Wilford* Howson in the same MS.

,, 155, Sir Nicholas Hall is called *Halse* in the same MS.

,, 158, col. 1, *read* Sir George Dalston.

,, 176, *for* Edmund Vanderduffin *read* Ewold Van der Dussen (Rymer's " Fœdera ").

,, 184, *for* 𝔖𝔦𝔯 𝔚𝔦𝔩𝔩𝔦𝔞𝔪 𝔐𝔞𝔰𝔬𝔫 𝔬𝔣 𝔅𝔢𝔯𝔦𝔫𝔤 *read* 𝔖𝔦𝔯 𝔚𝔦𝔩𝔩𝔦𝔞𝔪 𝔐𝔞𝔧𝔬𝔲 𝔡𝔢 𝔅𝔢𝔯𝔦𝔫𝔤, a Dutchman.

INDEX.

H H

London : Mitchell and Hughes, Printers, 140 Wardour Street, W.